MOUNT FUJI

MOUNT

STUDIES IN COMPARATIVE RELIGION • FREDERICK M. DENNY, SERIES EDITOR

FUJI

Icon

of

Japan

H. BYRON EARHART

The University of South Carolina Press

© 2011 University of South Carolina

Published by the University of South Carolina Press
Columbia, South Carolina 29208

www.sc.edu/uscpress

Manufactured in the United States of America

20 19 18 17 16 15 14 13 12 11   10 9 8 7 6 5 4 3 2 1

LIBRARY OF CONGRESS CATALOGING-IN-PUBLICATION DATA

Earhart, H. Byron.
    Mount Fuji : icon of Japan / H. Byron Earhart.
        p. cm.— (Studies in comparative religion)
    Includes bibliographical references.
        Summary: "A survey of the symbolism—religious, aesthetic,
    and cultural—of Japan's Mount Fuji."—Publisher's description.
    ISBN 978-1-61117-000-9 (cloth : alk. paper)
        1. Fuji, Mount (Japan) 2. Mountain worship—Japan—Fuji, Mount.
    I. Title. II. Series: Studies in comparative religion (Columbia, S.C.)
    BL2211.M6E23 2011
    299.5'61350952166—DC22   2011012498

This book was printed on Glatfelter Natures, a recycled paper
with 30 percent postconsumer waste content.

This book is dedicated
to the majestic form of Fuji
and to the spirit of all who have climbed it
or who have admired it from afar.

CONTENTS

ILLUSTRATIONS

SERIES EDITOR'S PREFACE

H. Byron Earhart, the author of this comprehensive study of Mount Fuji as a national sacred symbol, is a distinguished scholar of comparative religion with a focus on Japanese religion. The book is based on his deep knowledge of many textual and artistic sources as well as extensive field study on and around the great volcanic peak itself. The central focus in this study is Fuji's role as a "symbol of religious belief and practice." He goes on to remark, in his preface, that "some literary, artistic, social, and even political and economic factors must be drawn upon to contextualize this picture of Fuji as a religious symbol; indeed this overview of Fuji through time could hardly be considered without some such delimitation."

This series has published many excellent books over its twenty-six-year history. All of them have been scholarly works that have made significant contributions to their specialized fields within the broad borders of comparative religion. Some have also appealed to a wider reading public beyond academe. I expect that this book will be eagerly read and assigned by scholars in the humanities, arts, and social sciences. But I am confident that it will also appeal to a wide range of readers in Japan as well as globally because of Mount Fuji's great symbolic power and beauty as both a national and world treasure.

FREDERICK M. DENNY

ACKNOWLEDGMENTS

Those who make ascents of the loftiest peaks, such as Everest, give credit to the guides and others without whose assistance they could not have achieved their goals. My trips up Mount Fuji, less than half the altitude of the Himalayan heights, required no mountaineering experts and special equipment. Even so, traversing the territory of this mountain's conceptual imagery was quite complex, made possible only by people and institutions whose help is gladly acknowledged here.

Western Michigan University granted me a sabbatical for the 1988–89 year, providing the time to travel to Japan and carry out the research for this study. This work was supported in part by grants from Western Michigan University's Faculty Research Fund. George Dennison, then provost at Western Michigan University, kindly provided a provost's research grant to support the conversion of raw video footage into the documentary *Fuji: Sacred Mountain of Japan*. The library resources and staff at Western Michigan University, Keio University, and the University of California at San Diego helped in the background research for this study. A Japan Foundation grant for 1988–89 gave financial support during this time. Risshō Kōseikai kindly offered an apartment in Tokyo, enabling my wife and me to live close to universities and within easy reach of Fuji.

Professor Miyake Hitoshi sponsored my affiliation with Keio University, which afforded access to an office and a library. Professor Miyake also discussed the project with me and helped plan the research. He accompanied me on one trip to the mountain with his graduate students; on another occasion his wife drove us to the mountain. Miyata Noboru, Hirano Eiji, and Murakami Shigeyoshi were the major scholars in Japan who gave freely of their knowledge, advice, and contacts to carry out the fieldwork and research.

The leaders and members of three religious groups—Miyamotokō, Maruyamakyō, and Jūshichiyakō—extended considerable hospitality in allowing me to accompany them on pilgrimages to Fuji and observe them in meetings. They also allowed the distribution of a questionnaire and answered many requests for information and explanations.

So many people aided in this research that it is not possible to mention all of them here; some are credited within the text. One blanket thanks offered here is to all the scholars who in their research monographs and articles have provided the bits and pieces enabling the creation of the mosaic of Fuji's imagery that is the purpose of this book; brief mentions in notes hardly account for their valuable contributions.

A fringe benefit of other publishing projects is the help provided by Mike Sirota. I wish to thank him for that assistance.

Special thanks also go to Frederick M. Denny, the series editor, and to Jim Denton and Karen Beidel of the University of South Carolina Press for their invaluable assistance in the publication of this work. Brandi Lariscy Avant was responsible for the design of the book. Careful copyediting was provided by Pat Coate. Readers who noted mistakes and gave freely of advice to improve the manuscript include Andrew Bernstein and anonymous reviewers. Harry H. Vanderstappen read an early draft of the book and suggested the rubric of "icon" for Fuji. My son David C. Earhart not only read various versions of the manuscript but also offered a number of suggestions and images, especially for the latter chapters of the work. David and my wife, Virginia, helped secure and prepare the illustrations. For any missteps in this excursion through the ever-changing imagery of Fuji, the author alone is responsible.

PERMISSIONS FOR REPRINTING

Thanks are gratefully acknowledged here for permission to reprint material from the following publications:

Manyoshu: The Nippon Gakujutsu Shinkokai Translation of One Thousand Poems, by Nippon Gakujutsu Shinkokai, Copyright c 1965 Columbia University Press. Reprinted with permission of the publisher.

Traditional Japanese Poetry: An Anthology, translated, with an introduction, by Steven D. Carter, Copyright © 1991 by the Board of Trustees of the Leland Stanford Jr. University. All rights reserved. Used with the permission of Stanford University Press, www.sup.org.

Tales of Yamato, translated by Mildred Tahara, © 1980 University of Hawaii Press. Reprinted with permission of the publisher.

Mirror of the Moon, translated by William LaFleur, New Directions Press, 1978. Reprinted with permission of Mariko LaFleur.

Mt Fuji: Selected Poems 1943–1986, by Kusano Shinpei, translated by Leith Morton, Katydid Books, 1991. Reprinted with permission of the translator.

H. Byron Earhart, "Fuji and Shugendō," *Japanese Journal of Religious Studies* 16, nos. 2–3 (June–September 1989): 205–26. Reprinted with permission of the publisher.

Invitation to Fuji

The gracefully sloping, symmetrical silhouette of Mount Fuji is immediately recognizable throughout the world as an icon for the land and nation of Japan. For Japanese and non-Japanese alike, Fuji is so closely associated with the very idea of Japan that the two are nearly inseparable. My first glimpse of the image of Fuji is blended imperceptibly with my earliest memories of Japan—the cheap folding fans and book illustrations of the snow-capped peak that were in vogue during my childhood and can still be seen today.

Conversations with Japanese people provide sharper memories. A well-known painter remembers distinctly when a primary-school teacher had the students in his class draw Fuji: without looking at Fuji or a picture of the mountain, he portrayed it in the classic fashion with three small peaks and steep slope. Elderly Japanese recollect singing in school the familiar children's song praising Mount Fuji; while humming the tune, they recall the words about this incomparable peak.

A number of man-made monuments—the pyramids, the Eiffel Tower, the Statue of Liberty—have taken on the role of national icon. Much rarer is the case of a natural object becoming universally accepted, both domestically and internationally, as the hallmark of a country. This book is an exploration of Fuji as a symbol of Japan and the Japanese. Like any tale worth its salt, this story insists that there is much more to Fuji than meets the eye. Three of the less obvious aspects of Fuji may be previewed here, as preparation for approaching the peak.

In the first place, Fuji's significance within Japan is only partly due to its being a natural formation (actually a dormant volcano). Throughout history Fuji has been celebrated more as a religious or sacred site and as a cultural and aesthetic ideal than as a physical mountain. Second, Fuji's preeminence as Japan's premier mountain and most important landmark is a relatively recent affair, a phenomenon of the past two centuries. Third, the history of Fuji within Japanese culture displays a remarkably diverse repertoire of images.

The versatility of Fuji is truly remarkable. For more than twelve hundred years the mountain has stimulated the imagination and has been adapted to the situations and tastes of different ages, inspiring an incredible variety of literary, artistic, and religious expressions: a host of images tend to overlap and coexist rather than replace one another. These permutations might be compared to the ever changing configurations of a kaleidoscope.

The claim of this book, to trace the symbolism of Fuji from earliest times to the present, may appear too ambitious. An old Japanese saying about Fuji intones: "He who does not climb once is a fool; he who climbs twice is a fool." The author is a fool of the latter variety, who has climbed twice and then some. This admission of foolhardiness, I hope, will be accepted by Japanese readers and by scholars of Japanese culture as an apology for attempting so much in so little space.

Admittedly this book takes a particular view of Fuji, mainly from the vantage point of its role as a symbol of religious belief and practice. Some literary, artistic, social, and even political and economic factors must be drawn upon to contextualize this picture of Fuji as a religious symbol; indeed this overview of Fuji through time could hardly be considered without some such delimitation. Because "religion" in Japan cannot be compartmentalized into institutional partitions and because Fuji's career-as-symbol cannot be contained by religion—however it is understood—this book will follow the course of Fuji through some of its secular scenes as well as in its spiritual episodes.

In 1969 I had my first chance to climb Fuji, fortunately by invitation of the new religion Fusōkyō, whose origins are rooted in devotion to Fuji. In that initial experience the mountain was beautiful, the shrines and rituals fascinating, and the pilgrims intriguing. That maiden ascent created such a vivid impression—not just viewing the mountain but also witnessing firsthand the peak's spiritual significance for the people who through the centuries have worshiped it from afar and climbed it—that I vowed to undertake a more thorough study of the subject someday.

Two decades passed before I was able to return to this theme. Spending some sixteen months of 1988–89 in Japan for the sole purpose of studying Fuji, I made three ascents of the mountain during the summer of 1988. I also visited the surrounding area many times, read Japanese publications about Fuji, and discussed various aspects of the religious significance of the mountain with Japanese scholars. Some of the most enjoyable experiences occurred while I was accompanying three religious groups on their respective pilgrimages to Fuji (each of which in modern times means taking a tour bus halfway up the mountain and then hiking to the summit).

Quite appropriately during those sixteen months I happened to be living in the Fujimichō neighborhood of Nakano Ward in Tokyo. "Fujimichō" is literally "Fuji-view district," one of the many place names around Tokyo that refer to Fuji. Every time I traveled around Tokyo, I got on the subway system at the Nakano Fujimichō Station, passed by the Fujimi Pachinko[1] Parlor, and crossed over the Fujimi Bridge.

A number of other stores and businesses within a minute or two of my Tokyo apartment borrowed the Fuji name: the Fuji Film Company (whose fame has been carried aloft in America by the Fuji blimp), the Fuji coffee shop, the Fuji dress store; and I banked at the Fuji Bank (now defunct). Like my Tokyo neighbors, in no time I was voicing "Fuji," "Fujimi," and "Fujimichō" as part of my everyday vocabulary with no conscious thought of Fuji the mountain.

Whenever the weather was clear in Tokyo, early in the morning and sometimes at sunset, Fuji could be seen from the tenth-floor balcony of my apartment building. Fuji was always a welcome sight, whether bare in summer or in snow-clad beauty the rest of the year. When reading through materials on Fuji became tedious, I would go down the hall to see the mountain and gain fresh inspiration. Even when Fuji was hidden behind mist or clouds, its image was present in a number of pictures gracing our apartment: traditional Japanese woodblock prints, a modern Japanese oil, a reproduction of van Gogh's portrait of Père Tanguy.

This book is a vicarious pilgrimage through the scenery of Fuji in three modes. First, it is a geographical trip to the actual mountain; second, it is a chronological journey back in time to various epochs of Fuji through the ages; and third, it is a conceptual exploration of Fuji as both physical and symbolic, viewed through the panorama of images that have characterized the mountain and its significance through successive eras and transformations. While my primary interest has been to view Fuji as a sacred mountain, the complex character of Fuji's imagery has led me from religious beliefs and rites to poetry and painting and even to commercial logos and patriotic mantras.

The mountain is visited across successive ages and through quite disparate and sometimes conflicting images. Each of these tours portrays a particular dimension of this unfolding drama; each chapter focuses on a distinctive episode in Fuji's varied career. The journey begins by considering the conception or "place" of Fuji in the natural, cultural, and spiritual history of Japan, starting in prehistoric times and recovering the earliest traces of the sacred mountain. The "classic" image of Fuji is located in the earliest writings and first graphic representations in Japan, notions and depictions that resonate down to the present day. The medieval period saw the development and flowering of Fuji religiosity. Politics and economics have dominated Japan from early modern times when Fuji morphed into a more prominent national symbol and commercial commodity. Europeans and Americans have come to share a similar view of Fuji as a badge of identity for the land, people, and country of Japan, especially as they encountered the picturesque woodblock prints of the peak. In more recent times Fuji emerges from its sacred and aesthetic wrappings in a rewrapped (or repackaged) guise, as a highly secularized, occasionally parodied, and crassly exploited name and form. And yet, remarkably, Fuji appears at the summit of the zeitgeist of each of these ages: Fuji is the enduring, adaptable, and diversified icon of Japan.

One of the results of my fieldwork is a twenty-eight-minute video, *Fuji: Sacred Mountain of Japan.* While collecting materials and especially during the three pilgrimages to Fuji in the company of three religious groups, I used a video camera to document the trip for the benefit of those who may wish to make their own audiovisual journey to Fuji. You are invited to join me on reading through this textual sojourn to Fuji and then continue the trip by viewing the colorful sights and distinctive sounds of Fuji in the video.[2]

A NOTE ON JAPANESE NAMES
AND TERMS AND ON CITATIONS

Japanese names and terms present particular problems for consistency. Long vowels for o and u are indicated by macrons (ō and ū), and division of syllables is signaled by an apostrophe, as in *Man'yōshū*. However, when quoting works not using these indicators, the same word appears in the text or notes as *Manyoshu*.

The majority of Japanese names appearing in this book are cited family name first, in accordance with Japanese convention. However, those authors who have been published in English are cited with their given names preceding their surnames, in accordance with Western convention. Some famous people are customarily referred to either by their professional name, which is often distinctive or even unique, or by their given name. The short form of the painter Andō Hiroshige's name, for example, is Hiroshige (rather than Andō).

Simple citations to a single work usually appear as in-text citations. Longer citations and explanations are located in the notes at the back of the book.

Part 1

THE POWER AND BEAUTY
OF A MOUNTAIN

In the land of Yamato [Japan],
It is our treasure, our tutelary god.
It never tires our eyes to look up
To the lofty peak of Fuji.

Manyoshu 1940, 215

1

The Power of the Volcano

Fire and Water

From prehistoric times to the present, Fuji has been revered as a majestic sacred peak. Behind the multitude of aesthetic and religious symbolic associations with this landmark is the actual geographical entity, whose bare description can hardly do justice to its long cultural pedigree. Located on the main Japanese island of Honshu, between the 35th and 36th latitudes and the 138th and 139th longitudes, it is situated about one hundred kilometers (sixty-two miles) southwest of present-day Tokyo on the border of Yamanashi and Shizuoka prefectures. Viewed from a distance, the peak presents its familiar triangular shape. Experienced firsthand by trudging up the zigzag paths of its slopes, what the observant climber notices, and is constantly reminded of by the crunching sound made by one's boots, is that Fuji, for all its spiritual glory and aesthetic splendor, is really a heap of volcanic ash, solidified lava, and rock.

Known as a mountain, Fuji is actually a volcano, the highest of many such geological formations in Japan.[1] The technical term for Fuji's perfect shape is "stratovolcano"—a composite volcano, tall and conical, formed by a number of layers (strata) of hardened lava and ash—a kind of volcanic inverted cone found throughout the world. The Japanese terrain features a large number of these symmetrical mountains (called *fujigata*, literally "Fuji-shaped"); people living near one of these triangular peaks claim it as their "local-Fuji" by coupling a regional name with "-Fuji."[2] In recent history this practice of "Fujifying" has even extended to the United States, where Japanese Americans living in Washington State renamed the perfectly shaped stratovolcano Mount Rainier, borrowing its Indian name of Tacoma and calling it "Tacoma-Fuji."

Seen over the long span of prehistory, Fuji is three volcanoes in one: two earlier volcanoes hidden under the mass of the third and latest volcano. This third volcano was formed about ten thousand years ago, giving Fuji the distinctive appearance it has retained to the present. Subsequent activity and eruptions have altered Fuji's appearance somewhat, but not to the extent of the three prehistoric events. In early recorded history Fuji erupted nine times between 781 and 1083, with a major eruption in 864. The last eruption, in 1707 (in the Hōei era of the Edo period), formed a crater on the southeastern slope of Fuji, called Mount Hōei. Because Fuji has been inactive for three centuries, neither giving off steam nor releasing lava, it is usually considered a benign mountain rather than a dangerous volcano, but like any "dormant" volcano, it is "sleeping" only until it awakes and could erupt at any time.

In a land with abundant volcanoes and mountains, two physical characteristics of Fuji qualify it as "naturally" outstanding. First, its height at 3,776 meters, or 12,385 feet, marks the highest point in Japan. Second, its shape and location, an almost perfect cone with gradual slopes rising up from a surrounding plain with no nearby mountains, accentuate its visual appearance, emphasizing its towering stature and perfectly shaped form. Perception of the peak is heightened by the daily and seasonal change of colors on the mountain. During summer the bare rock above the tree line, actually solidified lava, takes on hues from sunlight and sky in shades ranging from warm red to blue or purple or almost black. When the mountain is snow covered, the light conditions and sky color may present a dazzling white triangle contrasting with a dark blue background or an off-white mass blending more subtly with a light sky.[3]

Fuji has become so thoroughly overlaid with more than a millennium of Japanese and centuries of Western cultural perceptions that it is almost impossible to observe or describe this volcanic mountain in its naked, unadorned state. It is understandable that the appreciation for its grandeur has led to rather romantic notions of its dramatic symbolism—idealizing the process whereby Fuji became the premier Japanese mountain, was worshipped as a sacred site, and assumed its status as the badge of the country. These sentiments and notions have even led to claims about the genesis of the Japanese "love of nature." D. T. Suzuki, the renowned popularizer of Zen in the West, wrote that the "Japanese love of Nature, I often think, owes much to the presence of Mount Fuji in the middle part of the main island of Japan" (D. T. Suzuki 1988, 331). Another Japanese argument attributes the particulars of this island country's climate as having fostered the Japanese people's idiosyncratic affinity for nature (Watsuji 1988). Such seemingly innocent or naive claims have at times served dubious purposes, even supporting arguments for the uniqueness and superiority of the Japanese people and culture and justifying imperialism and aggression during World War II (Asquith and Kalland 1997, 26). The nationalistic or patriotic "mantra" of Fuji will be encountered during the modern epoch, when Fuji too was pressed into service to shore up essentialist views of Japanese "naturism" and ultra-nationalism.

A host of stereotypes about the Japanese view of, love of, appreciation of, and harmony with nature have been advanced by both Japanese and non-Japanese writers. However, "the Japanese understandings of nature are as varied as those found in the West" (Asquith and Kalland 1997, 8). Therefore it would be a mistake to adopt the stereotype of Japanese harmony with nature as contrasted with Western antipathy toward nature. Similarly we would miss the mark by trying to identify a single "natural" origin or explanation behind the religious veneration and aesthetic appreciation of the peak. Indeed geographers remind us that the very notion of "mountain" is a cultural creation (Price 1981, 2). This means that any Japanese (or Western) statement about "nature" is not just a description of the raw, naked physical setting but also already an acquired perception of the geographical surroundings. Actually the *idea* of Fuji, or an idealized nature, often was valued more highly than the empirical phenomenon since in Japan "representations of nature may become more important than real nature."[4] In fact in recorded history the portrayed reality of Fuji is much weightier than its physical actuality is: many poets wrote poems about Fuji and many artists created pictures of Fuji without ever seeing the mountain with their own eyes.

As we peruse the panorama of images associated with Fuji, we will discover that there is almost no limit to the conceptions used to portray and even exploit the mountain. The present book is a discussion of the interrelationship between the mountain and its cultural perceptions—the sentimental and the patriotic, the exotic as well as the erotic—without privileging one particular image or notion, focusing primarily on religious and aesthetic symbolism. All of these images and conceptions of Fuji are closely interrelated, but for ease of discussion they will be taken up separately. The emergence of religious beliefs will be treated in this chapter, and the early aesthetic views of Fuji are discussed in the next chapter. Subsequent chapters take up other aspects and episodes of Fuji's conceptualization and visualization.

FROM VOLCANO TO SACRED MOUNTAIN

The date and circumstances of Fuji's transition from nature to culture, from a fiery volcano to a holy peak, are not known. Archaeological evidence documents people living around the foot of Mount Fuji in prehistoric times, and yet there is no clear connection between them and the religious beliefs and practices associated with Fuji in early historic times. Some think that the "rough" or "wild" *kami* (deities) in the mythological accounts of the *Kojiki* (*Record of Ancient Matters,* eighth century) and the *Nihon shoki* (*Chronicle of Japan,* eighth century) may represent violent or destructive forces of nature such as volcanoes (Aramaki 1983, 194). Historical documents suggest that in ancient times faith in Fuji was closely associated with its eruption and its character as a powerful "fire deity." Fuji faith may have emerged out of the fear and awe resulting from volcanic eruptions, especially at Fuji and Mount Asama, in relationship to the rise of Sengen belief. (The same two Sino-Japanese characters can be pronounced either *asama* or *sengen*.[5] The name Asama probably means "volcano"; Mount Asama (Asama yama) is a volcano on the border of present-day Nagano and Gunma prefectures. Asama or Sengen is the name of shrines (Sengen Jinja) that came to be associated closely with Fuji.[6]

In the ninth century, especially after the major eruption of Fuji in 864, the government ordered offerings of "pacification-thanks" and had Buddhist sutras read to avoid catastrophes, and in 865 they installed ritualists and priests in the area close to Fuji. The name Asama was linked with Fuji, and the government viewed the Asama *kami* (deity) as a means of pacifying "rough spirits."[7] The *Engishiki*, a tenth-century government record, mentions three shrines in the vicinity of Fuji, including Asama (Sengen) Shrine and Fuchi (Fuji) Shrine (Bock 1972, 134). The Fuchi Shrine of the *Engishiki* was probably a shrine in relationship to the Asama Shrine, possibly a sub-shrine. Eventually Fuji and Asama became inseparable, even though later the shrines were known only by the variant pronunciation Sengen.

Japanese volcanoes, often explosive and causing widespread destruction (especially through heavy deposits of ash), inspired views of a malevolent deity that had to be pacified (Aramaki 1983, 194). However, for both volcanoes and mountains, the matter is more complicated than just their "benevolence" or "malevolence": geographers remind us of the duality or polarity of all mountains.[8] The fame of holy mountains is as universal as it is legendary, and Fuji is but one local example of the worldwide phenomenon of sacralized peaks (Bernbaum 1990).

At Fuji, as is true within all of Japanese religion, power—even destructive force—may be venerated as well as feared, worshipped at the same time as it is pacified. An interesting example is the Japanese folklore surrounding catfish, seen as the dreaded cause of earthquakes and also revered as a source of divine protection (Ouwehand 1964). Throughout Japanese religion the order of the world is based on "a ritual transformation of chaos to cosmos." The eighteenth-century writer Motoori Norinaga held the view that the "wild, primordial and natural aspect [of] . . . disorder and chaos" and "a calm, peaceful, benevolent aspect, reflecting the human order imposed upon chaos. . . . as applied to deities and man, are potential manifestations of the same personalities" and must be seen holistically.[9]

This wider understanding of the duality or polarity within Japanese religiosity helps us appreciate the interrelationship between nature and culture in Japan: "the Japanese have . . . an ambivalent attitude toward nature," and "nature oscillates between two poles: nature in the wild (often abhorred by Japanese) and domesticated aesthetic nature which is identical with culture (usually loved)" (Asquith and Kalland 1997, 29–30). Simply stated, Fuji was worshipped as having power.[10] This power was sometimes destructive, as seen in the fire of explosions and eruptions; records of the 864 eruption tell of loss of lives and houses, vegetation and trees, and even the animal life in ponds (which were heated to the boiling point). Another side of Fuji's potentiality, however, was in the water that actually quelled the flow of lava. The largest and most important of the Sengen shrines, at present-day Fujinomiya City in Shizuoka Prefecture to the south of Fuji, was built at the very spot where the lava flow stopped, which is also where a large cold water spring gushes forth. Early inhabitants of the region believed this spring flowed directly underground from Fuji and saw it as sacred in its own right, being a source of fertility. Traditionally it has been used as purifying water by pilgrims on their way to Fuji.

Readers who have become acquainted with Fuji through Hokusai's woodblock prints may wonder why this sketch of Fuji and its early origins of faith has not mentioned Konohana Sakuya hime, the "enshrined deity" associated with Mount Fuji today. Indeed this female deity was immortalized in a monochrome woodblock print as the first plate of Hokusai's *One Hundred Views of Mt. Fuji* during late Edo (1600–1868) times when she had come to be seen as the goddess of Fuji.[11]

In the mythological account found in the *Kojiki*, the heavenly grandson of the sun goddess Amaterasu, Ninigi no mikoto, meets and marries the beautiful Konohana Sakuya. After cohabiting with her only one night she becomes pregnant, raising his suspicions about the real father of the child. Konohana Sakuya is angered and vows to demonstrate her virtue by giving birth in a parturition hut to which she sets fire; mother and three offspring emerge unscathed.[12] Mountains in Japan and mountain *kami* have been seen as female, and Konohana Sakuya may have become paired with Fuji because of the associations in Japanese folklore: she is the daughter of the ruler of mountains (Ōyamatsumi), and as a beautiful princess she was fitting to be the goddess of the mountain. Her emergence unscathed from the burning parturition hut shows that, like the volcano Fuji, she is not destroyed by fire. Indeed both create through fire: the mountain supplies water (for growing rice); the deity delivers offspring.

The sacrosanct nature of Fuji was established in prehistoric times, but its specific expression varied from time to time in a number of divine figures preceding Konohana. For many centuries, especially under Buddhist influence, the specific character of Fuji's object of worship—Shinto *kami* or Buddhist *bosatsu* (bodhisattva), male or female (or neither or both)—was not fixed.[13] The ambiguity and shifting identity of Fuji's divinity is more the rule than the exception in Japanese religion. Not only shrines and temples but mountains as well record a long history of various objects of worship, beliefs, and practices—which were supplemented or replaced not only after a change in spiritual commitment but also to accommodate political and economic conditions.[14]

Fuji as a religious symbol in ancient Japan, though elusive, is connected with the power of fire (volcanoes) and water (fertility and purification). This is the "power of fire and water," the ancient foundation for the elaboration of Fuji's religious symbolism in later ages.

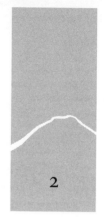

2

The Beauty of the Ideal Mountain

Early Poetry and Painting

FUJI IN EARLY WRITING

The earliest poetry and writing, and also some of the first graphic representations in Japan, feature Fuji as the nascent icon of Japan, anchoring its image in a poetic and artistic tradition that has continued to be appreciated by and serve as an inspiration for all later generations. Although the mountain never dominated either the literary or the art world, this symbol was prominent in a wide variety of genres. A look at some major examples of early Fuji imagery highlights its "classic" forms.

The divinity of Fuji, celebrated within shrines, is also lauded in poetry—a seamless transition from the holiness and power of the sacred mountain to its beauty in verse. The intimate interrelationship within the triad of nature, religion, and art in Japan was perhaps first put into words by Ki no Tsurayuki in his introduction to the early tenth-century collection of court poetry *Kokinshū:* "Poetry it is which without effort moves heaven and stirs to pity the invisible demons and gods; which makes sweet the ties between men and women; and which comforts the hearts of fierce warriors" (Keene 1955, 23). Lyricism, which has been widely cited as a key to classical or traditional Japanese poetry, "employed a few privileged topics, chief among them the beauties of the natural world and the obsessions of the human heart."[1]

The lyrical treatment of Fuji is found in the earliest Japanese poetic anthology, the eighth-century *Man'yōshū*. This collection of poetry has been highly valued for its fresh and unaffected tone; its extolling of nature (including mountains) set an important precedent for Japanese poets in later ages. The *Man'yōshū* poems about

Fuji simultaneously present the mountain as landscape, as an object of religious veneration, and as a subject for aesthetic appreciation. Such *Man'yōshū* poems praise the soaring peak, proclaiming its divinity while describing the awesome sight to behold (and to visualize imaginatively):

> Since that ancient time
>   when heaven and earth were sundered,
> like a god soaring
>   in high towering majesty
>   over Suruga
>   has stood Fuji's lofty peak.
>
> . . . .
>
> At Tago Bay
>   I came out, and looked afar–
>   to see the pure white
>   of Mount Fuji's lofty peak,
>   amidst a flurry of snow.[2]

In this and the previous quotation from the *Man'yōshū*, the divinity of Fuji is mentioned, and yet the focus is on the aesthetic grandeur of this "natural" wonder: nature accedes to this marvel. Even though these poems were written in an age when Fuji was still an active volcano, they do not manifest the fear of a fire *kami* who must be pacified. Poetic depiction of the mountain—probably indirectly visionary rather than directly visual—is pleasant: respectful but also breathing an air of friendship from having been refreshed and fulfilled by the mental image. This predilection for the beauty and pleasure of appreciating nature, and the silence about natural calamities and formal worship, may be owing to the distance of the Japanese court (and the courtly poets) from Fuji at the time of the *Man'yōshū*'s compilation. In ensuing poetic anthologies this tendency may be an expression of a rather restrained poetic tradition, which preferred the delights of scenery and seasons and love (Sakamoto 1991, 25, 24). Explicitly religious poetry appears later, especially under the influence of Buddhism.

Mountains in the *Man'yōshū* are viewed from a number of widely varying perspectives and offer widely varying illustrations of the notion of mountain. Mount Fuji and Mount Tsukuba present interesting contrasts in this anthology, for the "lofty" Fuji is usually viewed from below or afar, while the more easily accessible Tsukuba (at 876 meters or 2,873 feet) was climbed and became the vantage point for viewing the surrounding landscape (*Manyoshu* 1940, 93, 220). Tsukuba also was famous for its spring and fall festivals, when people gathered for nights of dancing and singing (*Manyoshu* 1940, lx, 22). In the eighth-century *Hitachi Fudoki*,[3] the praise of Tsukuba at the expense of Fuji is a historical reminder of the heated competition among regional cultural powers in early times. The ancestral god Mioya-no-mikoto, having been denied a place to stay the night at Fuji because of ongoing ceremonies, cursed the mountain and wished that the mountain would be cold and snow covered in both winter and summer, preventing future offerings there. By contrast, when this god went to Tsukuba, also celebrating the harvest ceremonies, and was nevertheless welcomed, the deity said that thereafter, "Generation upon generation without end, / People will congregate here with abundant offerings of food and drink / Day by day for thousands and ten thousands of autumns, your prosperity will continue" (Akashi et al. 1976, 31–32). This work reflects the regional pride of Hitachi, valuing its own sacred mountain Tsukuba over Fuji, but also highlights different physical characteristics: Fuji is snow covered and inaccessible most of the year, and although it is not difficult to climb during the summer, the ascent does take a great deal more time and energy than does an ascent of Tsukuba, which is less than one-fourth the height of Fuji.[4]

Not only at Tsukuba but also at other mountains appearing in the *Man'yōshū*, the *Kojiki*, and the *Nihon shoki*, the emperor or local officials climbed for the purpose of "land viewing," *kuni-mi*, which combined ritual as well as political intent in this act of ascent and visual inspection. The verb *miru* or *mi* can be seen as a ritual activity: "As used in *Manyoshu* poetry, *mi* refers not only to gazing at something strange or beautiful but beholding something that, symbolically powerful and meaningful for humanity, is appropriated for periodic renewal purposes" (Plutschow 1990, 106). *Mi* can be ritual or magical or divinatory, even including flower viewing and moon viewing. The political motive of *kuni-mi* was simultaneously pacifying and controlling the land.[5] No explicit mention of *kuni-mi* related to Fuji is found in the *Man'yōshū* or other ancient documents, but "gazing upon Mt. Fuji may have been a means to renew the order of the occupied land, by contrasting it to something as powerful, stable and permanent as Mt. Fuji. Gazing up at mountains was a ritual act and the poetry a ritual language or expression of this act" (Plutschow 1990, 115).

The *Man'yōshū* portrayal of Fuji, already emphasizing the mountain's perennial features, provides important clues to the abundantly rich variations of the Fuji images that appear later. "In early poetry, as seen most conspicuously in Akahito's paean to the mountain . . . Fuji was often treated as a symbol of steadfastness specifically associated with the gods—a place always snow-capped and thus beyond the reach of time. This treatment continued into the Edo period but was supplemented with poems focusing on the smoke that occasionally rose from the peak . . . as symbolic of the fickleness and uncertainty of human passion" (Carter 1991, 480–81).

The contrast and interplay between the *power* of Fuji—sacred for its volcanic destruction and beneficial water—and the *beauty* of Fuji—aesthetically prized for its majestic grandeur and as a mystery of nature—pose interesting questions about the development of such divergent attitudes. The tension between these two notions probably arises out of the varied contexts in which Fuji is perceived. At least four major contextual factors influencing the imagery of Fuji can be identified: 1) the point in time and prevailing ideas when it is observed; 2) the location or distance from which Fuji is seen or considered; 3) the social class of the people creating or appreciating the imagery; and 4) the cultural dimension of the images (religious and/ or artistic) and the particular religious mode or artistic genre.

These four factors distinguish the power of Fuji and the beauty of Fuji in the earliest historical records. The first factor, time and prevailing ideas, is generally the same for the images of both the power and the beauty of Fuji: the time in both cases was about the eighth and ninth centuries; then-current attitudes toward nature and mountains have already been mentioned. However, the other three factors are dissimilar.

The second factor, location, varies greatly. The power of Fuji was observed directly from the foot of the volcano and the surrounding area, as indicated in the gruesome reports of destruction sent to the capital (Nara); this power was acknowledged secondhand at the capital, through the reports, and as a threat not to the immediate surroundings but to the stability of the country at large. However, the beauty of Fuji, as the heading of one *Man'yōshū* poem indicates, was predicated "*On a distant view of Mount Fuji.*" The effect of location here is measured not simply by physical distance but by the assumed, indeed affected, isolation of the capital and the court, which espoused beauty and refinement in all things deemed worthy of notice, from more "mundane" matters. The perception of the mountain from this exclusive vantage point embraced its aesthetic appeal while eschewing its imminent threat or ominous power. In later times too the prevailing view of Fuji differed radically depending on the location from which it was observed.

The third factor, social class, again is remarkable for the sharp division between the people on the scene who witnessed with awe the power of Fuji and those who from afar who imagined with praise the beauty of Fuji (often without having ever viewed it). The eruption of Fuji and the ash fallout affected such a wide area that many people were at risk from Fuji's destructive power and also were the recipients of its beneficial power. Obviously, though, those most tangibly affected were the ones directly in touch with the mountains—the farmers and local officials of relatively lower social status. The people who compiled the poems of the *Man'yōshū* were from the court, and apparently their poetic tastes precluded mention of Fuji's eruption; or the poets of the time chose not to write about it.

The fourth factor, the cultural dimension, also presents heterogeneity. In general the power of Fuji was grasped through the overtly religious dimension, with an elaborate set of conceptions and institutions: these notions emphasized the ambivalent power of nature, which had to be pacified and celebrated through rituals and offerings in order to avoid destruction and to invoke blessings; their organization and implementation involved establishing and supporting shrines and priests. But the beauty of Fuji (although related to Fuji as a deity) was appropriated mainly through the poetic dimension of praise, appreciating and expressing through language and emotion the enjoyment of Fuji and nature. Poetry shared the notions and sentiments of religion, but without the priestly and institutional trappings. The early Shinto priests and shrines used ritual to invoke the benevolent power of Fuji and, to fight fire with fire, to ward off malevolent power, while poets of the court found in Fuji another foil for expounding on the virtues apparent in the natural world.

When *kuni-mi* is understood as "ritual gazing," the power and beauty of Fuji can be seen as interrelated aspects of the same symbolic complex. These four factors too must be seen as interconnected forces in a larger process. The interplay between and among these four factors, a constantly changing pattern, leads to Fuji being perceived and conceived in many different ways. Truly remarkable in this scenario is Fuji's central position in cultural creativity through such a long time span. One of the hallmarks of poetry established in the *Man'yōshū* was "the use of so-called 'pillow-words.' These *makura kotoba* were fixed imagistic epithets," and Fuji has been type-cast as a symbol (pillow word) of steadfastness and divinity, its snow-capped peak placing it "beyond the reach of time" (Carter 1991, 4, 480–81). This is rather aston-ishing in light of Fuji's volatile eruptions of the eighth and ninth centuries. Yet the *Man'yōshū* poets' selection of Fuji as a symbol worthy of poetic appreciation persists in subsequent poetry to the present.

The period after the *Man'yōshū* saw dramatic shifts in the imperial capital and also in poetry, which "took an inward turn. . . . And no longer was its inspiration the Japanese state or Mount Fuji" (Carter 1991, 5). The long poem form that was used to extol Fuji "was a dying genre even before the end of the Ancient Age (fifth century–794)" (Carter 1991, 4); Chinese models of poetry and Buddhist ideals of spir-ituality came to the fore.[6]

"After the *Man'yōshū*, poets become more subjective" (Miner Odagiri, and Mor-rell 1985, 5). In the tenth-century poetic anthology *Kokinshū* (or *Kokin Wakashū*, lit-erally "Collection of Poems Old and New"), the fame of Fuji continues, mainly as a symbol for love. Fuji is seen not so much as a sacred mountain or as an example of natural beauty but as a reminder of human affection.

> I will look upon
> Mount Fuji in Suruga
> as another self,
> for deep within each of us
> hidden fires forever burn. (McCullough 1985, 122)

This poem by an unknown author contains no hint of fear or veneration of the fire *kami* of Fuji; nor does it praise the cloud-piercing sight of Fuji. Rather it likens the mountain to a self and indirectly compares the imagery of Fuji's volcanic fire to ardent flames within two lovers. In another poem, by Fujiwara Tadayuki, the heat of passion is stated even more forcefully:

> As the deathless fire
> smolders inside Mount Fuji,
> so burns my passion,
> unaltered by occasions
> of seeing and not seeing. (McCullough 1985, 151)

In the new setting of Kyoto a more elaborate courtly culture developed, with much greater emphasis on the codification of aesthetic sensibilities and amorous adventures.[7] In Japanese the word "Fuji" can be written with different characters, or the sound itself can be a play on "unparalleled" or "undying" or "unextinguished";[8] poets made full use of these and other nuances. Even when written with the more commonly used characters, the term *fuji* could be linked, through its homophones, to "not dying" or "eternal," and the mountain was remembered especially for its fire (passion) or (unextinguished) smoke: in this manner just to mention "Fuji" in post-*Man'yōshū* classical poetry was to invoke the imagery and mood of burning passion, unquenched desire.[9]

In a tenth-century work, *The Kagero Diary* by Fujiwara Michitsuna no Haha, the author borrows Fuji's physical features to express her emotional turmoil over her unhappy marriage and wayward husband, the mountain's smoke emerging from her own fire of jealousy. Men also used Fuji to express the affairs of the heart. In an exchange between two happy lovers in a tenth-century collection of tales, the man tells his sweetheart:

> My love for you,
> Like the smoke that rises
> From Mount Fuji,
> Is eternal.... (Tahara 1980, 125)

Fuji poems of the thirteenth-century imperial poetic anthology *Shinkokinshū* (literally New *Kokinshū*) again transform the imagery of Fuji's smoke. By this time Buddhism's influence had become stronger, persuading some Japanese to appropriate mountains as places of ascetic practice where individuals could work toward enlightenment. Thus mountains came to represent both the separation from the world and the isolation within nature necessary for asceticism and meditation. In addition "the somber contemplative qualities of many poems in *Shinkokinshū* derive partly from the profound impact on Japanese courtiers of the poets of the Tang Dynasty," leaving behind "the lightheartedness of *Kokinshū* days" (Carter 1991, 9, 8). Saigyō, a leading poet of the twelfth century and considered by some to be one of Japan's greatest poets, gave up his commission at the court to leave the "world" and become a monk. He devoted much of his life to pilgrimage and meditation in mountain settings. For Saigyō, mountains were necessary places of solitude apart from the ordinary world:

> What a wretched world
> This would be if this despised,
> Quickly passing world
> Had no place to hide away—
> That is, no mountains in it. (LaFleur 1978, 46)

Saigyō's favorite mountain retreat was Yoshino; he also spent time at Mount Kōya as well as other pilgrimage sites. His contact with Fuji was brief but quite fruitful, as seen in this text:

> While undertaking religious exercises in the eastern region, I wrote the following in view of Mount Fuji:
>
>> The wisps of smoke from Fuji
>> Yield to the wind and lose themselves
>> In sky, in emptiness—
>> Which takes as well the aimless passions
>> That through my life burned deep inside. (LaFleur 1978, 88)

Saigyō "draws a parallel between Fuji and himself," referring "to the passions that had been so much a part of his own life" (LaFleur 2003, 59). The poetic encounter of Saigyō with Fuji was echoed in later poetry, literature, and graphic arts and also was portrayed in many genres of the decorative arts, from sword hilts to netsuke and inro.[10]

Here, as in other poems of the *Shinkokinshū,* Fuji represents not so much the bounty and beauty of nature as the impermanence of the world, and Fuji's smoke conjures up less the heat of love and emotion and more the evanescence of human life.[11] Such poems are difficult to interpret since their nuances are much more powerful than their summary in explicit prose. Can it be that Saigyō is turning on its head the courtly view of love (as found in the *Kokinshū*), taking the by-now-hackneyed metaphor of Fuji and stereotypical view of unextinguished (or unextinguishable) passion and seeing it as illusory? Saigyō certainly is exceptional in that he did journey to the mountain and actually eye it, which situates him in an on-the-spot position not enjoyed by the court-centered *Man'yōshū* and *Kokinshū* poets who idealized the famous place (*meisho*) without ever seeing it. Saigyō did more than observe a physical mountain; he "saw" Fuji. He envisioned it and "saw through" the illusory character of both the mountain and human passions. Saigyō's perception of the mountain permanently colored the way others have come to view it, both in literature and in art.

These glimpses of early written descriptions of Fuji amount to only a fraction of the genius of these figures and major collections. Yet they speak volumes about the variety of Fuji imagery: Fuji is an idealized mountain, but the ideal is transformed from one of natural beauty to burning passion to religious reflection/meditation.

Although the same Fuji, it is seen through different poetic lenses, and its image shifts dramatically. From the *Man'yōshū* through the *Kokinshū* and later poetry and writing—different forms with contrasting aesthetic ideals—all found Fuji a worthy subject matter for their creative work.

FUJI IN CLASSICAL PAINTING

The power of Fuji that was worshipped in shrines and its beauty that was lauded in poetry have also been featured in paintings, concrete visualizations enabling people other than the artists to vicariously view and thereby access this potency and majesty. Just as *kuni-mi* was a ritually empowering act, so too paintings of Fuji represent a lively interaction between the physical mountain and artistic creativity: "Fuji may be the enduring symbol of Japan, and one which has not changed shape radically since the last eruption in 1707, but artists have been indefatigable in trying to do something new with it" (Clark 2001, 8).[12] Indeed while the natural form of Fuji remained basically the same from earliest recorded times until the 1707 eruption, its aesthetic appreciation shifted dramatically. Even a brief sampling of a few major paintings, beginning with the earliest extant works, gives some indication of the range of possibilities tapped to graphically re-create—to envision (or re-vision)—the beauty of Fuji.

Fuji's fame certainly predates its praise in the eighth-century poetic anthology *Man'yōshū*, and some scholars have advanced the improbable notion that pictures of Fuji go back to at least as early as the poems of Fuji. Although it is conceivable that silk or paper representations of Fuji might have perished, the fact that no portrayals of the mountain appear on more durable materials—such as stone, pottery (the *haniwa*, clay cylinders decorating protohistoric tombs), or metal—make this unlikely. In China, by contrast, the concrete evidence for graphic representations of landscape in ancient times is quite clear: in Han China, "hills and trees were depicted in such other media as stone reliefs, inlaid bronzes, textiles, and molded pottery" (Sullivan 1962, 37–38).

In the earliest records from Japan, Nara and Heian graphic arts were so dominated by Buddhism that drawing a natural representation of Fuji was all but unthinkable. Art focused on Buddhism and religious subjects; landscapes were practically nonexistent, even in picture scrolls (Sawada Akira 1928, 4–5). Of course the assumption that places of natural beauty inevitably evoke artworks re-creating them is not self-evident.[13] In fact the opposite may be true. "As Sanari Kentarō wrote in his preface to the noh play *Fujisan*, 'The reason why there are curiously few fine poems in Japanese or Chinese [e.g., poems written by Japanese in Chinese style], or fine paintings about Fuji, is that the subject is too overpoweringly splendid'" (Tyler 1981, 140). In the earliest history of both Japan and in Western countries, the devotion of graphic arts to objects of worship may have precluded the painting of landscapes; in the earliest recorded times in both Japan and in Western countries,

religious thought was in control (Sawada Akira 1928, 4–5). On the Japanese side religion apparently was not opposed to the representation of nature (as often was the
case in the West; Nicolson 1963), but it did insist that artistic talent serve a higher
(religious) purpose. The late arrival of Fuji paintings can be seen from an evolution-
ary approach: "It is a given that literary descriptions of landscape precede pictorial
renditions in the parallel evolution of the two forms, and paintings of Fuji are no
exception to this rule. The earliest surviving reference to Fuji dates from the eighth
century; the earliest preserved painting, from the eleventh."[14]

The oldest extant image of Fuji is in Hata no Chitei's 1069 *Shōtoku Taishi eden*
(Pictorial Biography of Prince Shōtoku),[15] in which the prince flys over Mount Fuji.
In this picture, and also in later renderings of Fuji and Shōtoku, the emphasis is not
on the form and beauty of the mountain but rather on the prestige and glory of
the prince. One of the most revered figures of Japanese history, Prince Shōtoku[16] is
regarded as a great statesman (credited with the authorship of an early "constitution") as well as a patron and scholar of Buddhism. Written and illustrated accounts
of the prince recorded and disseminated the reputation of his life and achievements;
such pictures were painted on sliding doors or were hung in temples, and picture
scrolls were even used by wandering priests to educate the unlettered lower classes.
These priests, known as "picture explainers" (*etoki*), were important in the development of a national literature (Ruch 1977, 269).

The connection between Prince Shōtoku and Fuji is the story of how the prince
is seeking a good horse, which culminates in the choice of a black steed. One day the
prince mounted his horse and, followed by his servant, "flew" over the summit of
Fuji; he returned three days later. The graphic materials illustrating this story represent a highly abbreviated account of the tale. The 1069 *Shōtoku Taishi eden* is in poor
condition, but it does show Prince Shōtoku on his horse situated above Mount Fuji,
apparently flying over it.[17] Later examples feature a servant holding the black horse
as well as a scene of ascent to Fuji, which includes the accompanying servant alongside the prince and the horse above a diminutive Fuji. In these representations
clearly the prince and the horse are not on an ordinary ride, for the horse's feet are
not on the mountain: the horse and rider are transported over the mountain in
magical flight; the tales of the prince, of which the visual form is a graphic reminder,
state this explicitly. In short the prince possessed superhuman or divine powers enabling him to soar over Fuji; this scene was prominent in all the pictures of Fuji and
Shōtoku (Naruse 2005, 6).

The background traditions for this particular image of Fuji are open to several
possible interpretations. The prince's feat of magical flight has been seen as being
modeled on a similar story of the Buddha, "who is said to have scaled a snow-capped
mountain in a single night."[18] A Japanese parallel to the prince's celestial journey
is the account of En no Gyōja, the legendary mountain ascetic and founder of
Shugendō (mountain asceticism), who during his exile in Izu flew nightly to Fuji.[19]

The shape and features of the mountain in this and other paintings of Shōtoku are clues to identifying Chinese themes. The steep-sloped outline with multiple (sometimes three) layers of peaks and verdant (not snow-covered) vegetation reflects the influence of Chinese mythological mountains, especially Penglai (Hōrai or Hōraisan in Japanese)—which early Japanese Buddhists equated with Fuji (Takeya 2002, 21). Previously, Fuji had been seen as the realm of the immortals;[20] to this notion was added the homology of Fuji and Hōraisan (Takeya 2002, 21).[21] The prestige of the Chinese precedents is undeniable in the earliest surviving depictions of Fuji, which portray it as an ideal Chinese mountain, rather than the actual physical Japanese mountain.[22] The three layers or levels in the image of Fuji in some examples of *Shōtoku Taishi eden* have been attributed to the stylistic formalities of Chinese paintings of the mythical mountain K'un-lun (Konron in Japanese), which features three levels. Going beyond the three levels of K'un-lun, as a cosmic mountain, signifies the supernatural feat of transcending the world and attaining heaven.[23]

From the earliest graphic renderings of Fuji, even in the examples of the pictorial biographies of Shōtoku, and especially in subsequent artistic creations, an amazing array of depictions appeared. A Japanese art historian's fivefold typology of the visual forms of Fuji from ancient times to the present is a particularly useful guide to the comprehensive overview of the mountain's "iconology": (1) Heian era—steep mountain with three (or more) levels; (2) Kamakura era—steep mountain with three peaks; (3) Muromachi to Edo era—gently sloping mountain with three peaks (or with the appearance of three mountains, or three adjoining mountains); (4) mid-Edo era—three-peaked mountains becoming rare, replaced by idiosyncratic forms (and from Muromachi times Fuji confraternities developing distinctive three-peaked forms); and (5) recent and contemporary era—various mountain forms, including the new sawtooth style.[24]

In the creation of early Fuji imagery, Taoism and Taoist elements provide important ingredients, especially the notion of heavenly ascent: "For the Taoists, K'un-lun was a path leading to Heaven. It was made up of several stories representing the stages one had to ascend in order to be admitted into the spiritual hierarchy" (Baldrian 1987, 292). However, Taoist elements within the imagery of Fuji are mediated by Japanese perception of mythological ideals, not observation of Taoist mountains (in China) and their practices.[25] K'un-lun and Hu-ling have been viewed as examples of the symbolism of the "center of the world" (Eliade and Sullivan 1987, 167).

The primary theme of the tales and pictures about Prince Shōtoku is the portrayal of this great personality and his achievements. This theme is accentuated by the fact that Shōtoku "transcends" diminutive Fuji (Fuji does not tower over Shōtoku); the extraordinary ascent of Fuji is an event adding to his stature. While the concern in the present book is with the mountain rather than the man, the relationship between the two suggests mutual enhancement of the images of both. Prince Shōtoku's power and fame increase by virtue of being miraculously carried to and over this lofty mountain whose beauty and mystery were already legendary. In turn, Fuji's cachet as a sacred mountain is elevated through connection to one of the greatest figures of the imperial line. Formerly Fuji was a powerful volcano and sacred mountain of regional importance but recognized by the court; with this tradition Fuji's status moves from regional significance toward central importance as it is singled out to glorify, and be glorified by, Prince Shōtoku's ascent. The fivefold typology shows that the Heian depiction of Fuji as three layers (or levels) gave way to the Kamakura pattern of three peaks or mountains.[26]

By the time of the appearance of the tales and pictures of Prince Shōtoku's life, Fuji had become heavily overlaid with set notions not only about visual art and aesthetics in general but also about its spiritual dimensions as a sacred mountain and site of religious practice, which in turn made the very idea of a "naturalist" representation of the landscape inconceivable. "Pictures of famous places" (*meisho-e*) such as Fuji "had nothing to do with the place's 'empirical reality. . . . Rather, the image is intended to be read in conjunction with an extensive set of fixed historical, literary, and emotive associations that go far beyond simple sensory or visual appeal." At the time few poets and painters actually traveled to Fuji or other "famous places" in order to portray them. "Direct experience of the place played no role in the appreciation and understanding of early *meisho-e*, for poets and artists were provided with compilations informing them of the proper images associated with a given site." This tradition of Japanese painting (*yamato-e*) was determinative for the mode of depicting Fuji and "set the foundations for an approach to landscape that was above all associative and emotional rather than descriptive and literal. . . . There was no such thing as 'pure' landscape painting; specific sites were always depicted within a specific historical, narrative, religious, or literary context."[27]

If the painting of famous places has nothing—or next to nothing—to do with "empirical reality," that may well be because poets and painters need not travel to the mountain in order to journey there lyrically, aesthetically, and spiritually; perhaps they may even be said to imitate the extraterrestrial trip of Prince Shōtoku. *Yamato-e*, the Japanese style of painting, is a fresh, direct approach by early Japanese artists to the "world" they saw to be alive and full of energy, overflowing with detailed human figures and animals. Paintings of Fuji in the *yamato-e* style were among the earliest pictorial representations of the mountain and constituted one of the two major genres from the eleventh through the eighteenth centuries (Takeuchi 1984, 41). The influence of this three-domed or three-peaked configuration is evident even today: modern Japanese seeing this outline recognize not "a mountain" but "Fuji."

The third form of the fivefold typology witnesses the transition from the steep-sloped Kamakura Fuji to the gently sloped Muromachi Fuji; here the peaks appear as domes. Before Muromachi times Fuji was mostly in the background of pictures, but in this new age Fuji becomes the center of attention. The shift from steep to gradual slope in the representation of Fuji is attributed to the fact that a greater number of people saw the mountain as they passed by it in their travels to Kamakura, apparently creating the circumstances favorable for a more "actual" or "empirical" image of the peak. From the medieval era until more recent times, the main image of Fuji has been the snow-covered, three-domed peak (Naruse 2005, 21). Japanese landscapes, especially mountains, support complex symbolism and iconography; it is quite likely that Shugendō-mediated Buddhist notions of sacred sets of three played a role in the conceptualization and representation of triple peaks.

When the Fuji mandala (treated in the next chapter) appeared in the Muromachi period (1333–1568), the three-domed representation had become standardized; Buddhist influence expressed within and through Shugendō was deep seated and widespread. Many Shugendō mountain settings came to be conceived as "three mountains" (*sanzan*), such as Kumano Sanzan and Dewa Sanzan. Another model of the "three mountains" pattern may be Buddhist iconography, such as the configuration of a central Buddhist deity flanked by two consorts; "prevalent esoteric Buddhist ideas" present another precedent for "the three-peaked image."[28] Whatever its origins, the conception of Fuji as triple domed had lasting influence on its perception: even in premodern times João Rodrigues (1561?–1633) and also a Korean emissary who traveled by and actually saw Fuji described it as having three peaks (Takeya 2001, 25).

Yamato-e was soon joined by the *suiboku-ga* ("water and ink") or monochrome tradition patterned after Chinese (Sung) painting. *Suiboku-ga* emerged out of the Chinese tradition of sophisticated placement of a limited number of landscape features, with empty space or mist often occupying a major portion of a painting. This new painting tradition was not limited to the court, enjoying a closer association with the dominant warrior class from Kamakura times (1185–1333) and catering to the warrior concern for "true-to-life renderings of dramatic happenings."[29]

From the twelfth to the thirteenth and fourteenth centuries, art and literature shifted away from mere text or picture toward narrative performance, resulting in "Japan's first 'national literature.' . . . No longer court-oriented, the new narratives were conceived on battlefields and sacred mountains, in shrines and temples, and reflected, as had the media revolution, the energy born out of the wedding of newly risen Amidist sects and native Shinto cults" (Ruch 1977, 289–90). The rise of populist new religious movements in Kamakura times encouraged the development of artistic forms taking common people as their subject matter; because these new forms described actual social conditions, they necessarily incorporated natural landscape into the background (Sawada Akira 1928, 5).

The style of the painting in this scroll borrows both from the older *yamato-e* and the newer *suiboku-ga* form. Fuji appears in distinctive *yamato-e* style with its steep slope and snow-covered peak culminating in three domes, presenting a large-scale Fuji as a "famous place" (*meisho*). Also harking back to traditional Japanese painting are the bright colors and detailed human and animal figures. The painting also

This ink and paper scroll (*suiboku-ga*), *Mt. Fuji and Seiken Temple,* once attributed
to Sesshū Tōyō (1420–1506) but probably a copy of his work, incorporates Chinese
influences in a depiction of the triple-domed peak within a misty, mystical setting.
Reprinted with permission of Eisei Bunko Museum

includes the influence of the continental *suiboku-ga* tradition: much of the work is
devoted to space, clouds, and mist. Spaced strategically and rising out of the mist are
rooftops and tree-covered hills, in the same style as in Chinese painting.

In later paintings the contrast between the two styles becomes more obvious,
and yet the treatment of the landscape shows a similarity of approach. Unfortunately, "in the earliest surviving landmark of Fuji painting in the Suiboku tradition,
Miho no Matsubara, . . . attributed to Nō'ami . . . , Fuji can no longer be seen," but
the main images of this picture "clearly derive not from Chinese painting at all, but
from the pre-existing *meisho* tradition of Yamato-e" (Takeuchi 1984, 45–46).

The long and illustrious *suiboku-ga* tradition includes many painters who
completed a number of works on Fuji, most of which are characterized by this
combination of the older *yamato-e* style with the new continental style. The composition of one such painting, *Fuji and Seikenji,* attributed to the famous painter
Sesshū (1420–1506) or one of his successors,[30] owes much to Chinese models, with

jagged peaks rising out of water and mist, rendered with "rigid" brushwork. Nevertheless the native Japanese influence remains, for Fuji is shown in its classical three-domed form. The slopes of the mountain are not as steep as in the *yamato-e* pictures, but a photographic comparison of the same view shows that Sesshū's mountain is still much steeper than the gentle slope visible to the naked eye. According to traditional accounts, Sesshū did not see Fuji before he painted it, and he may have completed his painting while in China. This work is an interesting example of the perseverance of aspects of the *yamato-e* view of Fuji, although greatly modified (Takeuchi 1984, 47–48).

The sheer number of Fuji paintings in the *suiboku-ga* style makes characterizing all of them difficult; yet in general they do present a contrast to the atmosphere of the earlier *yamato-e* paintings. *Yamato-e* works are quite "busy" pictures, filled with people living out their lives in the midst of a rather naive or "primitive" freshness and innocence of the natural world. The *suiboku-ga* paintings are much more sophisticated and deliberate in design, emphasizing carefully placed elements within empty space—the human figure is conspicuous by its absence. In effect the personal component usually is outside the picture, gazing at and meditating on the mystery of nature. Indeed one of the famous *suiboku-ga* paintings of Fuji that does include a human figure depicts the poet Saigyō viewing Fuji, especially the *Fujimi Saigyō* (literally "Fuji-viewing Saigyō") by Kanō Tan'yū (1602–74);[31] in the vertical scroll the upper third is clouds, the middle third reveals a scant outline of Fuji emerging between clouds above and mist below, and the lower third shows Saigyō standing on a spit of land holding a staff and with his back toward the viewer. Saigyō is in the lower right corner, and his gaze is set on Fuji's peak, which is to the left of center in the middle third. The viewer is drawn by Saigyō's gaze into the picture toward Fuji in the moments before it vanishes. This painting seems to be a meditation on Fuji as a mystical mountain—in other words a visual aid to guide the viewer from this transient world to the otherworld of Fuji and possibly beyond. The exact religious content of such paintings cannot be definitely assigned, but obviously in the transition from *yamato-e* to *suiboku-ga* the symbol of Fuji has shifted from the location of magical flight to a mystical mountain in its own right. The diversity of the images of Fuji, in literary and aesthetic representations (across various genres) as well as in sacred conceptualizations (in contrasting forms of belief and practice), is a key feature of the cultural and religious history of the mountain.

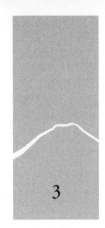

3

Asceticism

Opening the Mountain

FUJI PIONEERS: EN NO GYŌJA AND MATSUDAI SHŌNIN

Fuji asceticism has since early times conveyed its own spiritual themes, which freely commingle with and reinforce the power and beauty of the mountain. The distinctive feature of these themes is the perception of the mountain as more than either a natural foil for creating ideal aesthetic models or a distant destination for directing communal/seasonal religious ritual: Fuji asceticism opens the mountain as the actual site of individual spiritual discipline and, later, group ascetic practice.

The transformation of Fuji into a peak of ascetic practice reflects the trend of the times. At other mountains, and throughout Japan, "layers of myth, legendary bodies, symbols originating in native worship, Taoist practices, and Buddhist ritual" combined to express "Japanese views of territory" (Grapard 1986, 22), one example of which is sacred mountains. Just as many mountains were praised by *Man'yōshū* poets and were depicted in paintings, so too Fuji's career underwent dramatic changes as a result of the interaction of indigenous Japanese religious notions and imported religious traditions, combining prehistoric traditions with continental influence (H. B. Earhart 1970, 7–16).

A new ethos for Japanese sacred mountains evolved from the cumulative effect of a host of religious influences together with the formal introduction of Chinese culture in about the sixth century C.E. The dominant element of religious influences from China was Buddhism, but Taoist notions and Confucian ideas as well as many popular Chinese beliefs and practices also accompanied Chinese culture. During the Nara period most of the imported Chinese heritage was received and appreciated mainly at the court; many Buddhist beliefs and practices gradually found their way into the lives of the common people. The court sent Kūkai (Kōbō Daishi, 774–835) and Saichō (Dengyō Daishi, 767–822) to China in 804 to bring back "authentic" Buddhism. Each received different aspects of the Buddhist tradition, and each also established a mountain headquarters in Japan. Kōbō Daishi set up the esoteric tradition of Shingon on Mount Kōya, while Dengyō Daishi developed a more comprehensive Buddhist center on Mount Hiei (outside Kyoto).[1]

In each case these pioneers of "mountain Buddhism" consciously chose sites distant from the court and aristocracy, in concert with the local *kami* that were the guardian spirits of these remote areas. Kōbō Daishi clearly stated the rationale for locating his headquarters within the mountains: "According to the sutra, meditation should be practiced preferably on a flat area deep in the mountains," to be used "for the benefit of the nation and of those who desire to discipline themselves" (Hakeda 1972, 47, 48–52).

Kōbō Daishi's statement highlights several aspects of the transformation of Japanese sacred mountains. First, the mountain is valued not so much for its intrinsic power (in the case of Fuji, the power of fire and water) as for its suitability as a site for the practice of Buddhism (a place of retreat from society and the world). Second, the mountain was not worshipped from below (from afar, at the foot, or on the lower slopes) but was climbed as a religious practice, and buildings and rites were located on the mountainside or even on the summit. Third, the goal of such rites and practices placed less emphasis on seasonal and local community celebrations, instead stressing personal practice and national/cosmic realization. These later developments expressed the coexistence or mixture of a number of traditions. For example Kōbō Daishi invoked or pacified the local *kami* as the source of water on Mount Kōya and erected a shrine to honor it when establishing his Buddhist temple and site of esoteric Buddhist practices.

Mountains such as Kōya featured religious interaction of many elements—not only Shinto and Buddhist—and not only different strands of Buddhism, but also Chinese influences such as Onmyōdō (the way of yin and yang). A popular belief associated with Taoism, equally valid for Japanese sacred mountains, was that wizards or immortals (*hsien* in Chinese; *sen* or *sennin* in Japanese) lived in harmony with nature on sacred mountains, using magical elixirs and attaining immortality (H. B. Earhart 2003, 52–53, 56–62). Japanese embraced the notion that Japanese sacred mountains were the mysterious abodes of wizards who possessed special powers.

One early testament to the interaction of Chinese beliefs and Taoist elements with Japanese sacred mountains is the Heian-period *Taketori monogatari* (*The Tale of the Bamboo Cutter*). Because Fuji is not central to this story, appearing only at the conclusion, an overview of the plot is needed to place Fuji in perspective. The story begins with a bamboo cutter's discovery in a bamboo stem of a supernatural being, Kaguya hime, "Shining Princess." Through her magic he becomes rich; later her beauty attracts suitors throughout the land, even the emperor, but she sends each on an impossible quest to gain her hand, eventually refusing all of them when she is taken back to her true home, the Palace of the Moon. She leaves this "filthy" world by donning a robe of feathers, but she leaves the emperor a poem and an elixir of immortality. The emperor is so dismayed at losing the princess that he rejects the elixir, asking his ministers which mountain is closest to heaven; they tell him that it is a mountain in Suruga (Fuji). The final paragraph of the work focuses directly on Fuji: "He [the emperor] gave the poem and the jar containing the elixir to a messenger, whom he ordered to take these things to the summit of the mountain in Suruga. He instructed him to place the letter and the jar side by side, set them on fire, and let them be consumed in the flames. The man accepted the command and climbed the mountain with a great many other soldiers. They gave the name of Fuji to the mountain. Even now the smoke is said to be rising into the clouds" (Keene 1956, 355).

Here "the name of Fuji" is glossed as "example of a folk etymology. *Fuji*, meaning 'not die,' and referring to the elixir of immortality, is given as the origin of the mountain's name" (Keene 1956, 355). The importance of *The Tale of the Bamboo Cutter* was recognized from medieval times: "*Genji monogatari* refers to it as 'the archetype and parent of all romance'" (Mills 1983, 326). Fuji, which furnished "smoldering passion" to poetry and the "mystical mountain" to painting, supplies the all-important metaphor of the "not dying" smoking mountain to this early work of prose. The "natural" power and symbolism of Fuji as the highest mountain, closest to heaven, ties in with a universal theme of sacred mountains that point to, lead to, or participate in transcendence.[2] Here the physical form is enhanced by the pre-existing cultural reputation of Fuji and also by Chinese (or "Taoist") elements of immortality as well as Buddhist and Confucian elements, all of which were inseparably intertwined in the evolving drama of Fuji's ever changing imagery.

Nuances of the immortal wizard (*sen* or *hsien*) color even the name of Sengen shrines connected with Fuji; formerly "Sengen" was written with the character for *sen* that can be read *asama*, but later the *sen* of Sengen was written with the character for "immortal," and *sen* in the name of the deity of Fuji, Sengen[3] Daibosatsu, was also written with this character. The influence of the Chinese heritage was usually transmitted within calendrical and cosmological notions and as part of ritual practices, and it did not constitute a separate tradition. Confucianism, with its emphasis on filial piety and loyalty, was also part and parcel of this Chinese influence.

Such cultural interaction in Fuji imagery is also evident in the manner of idealizing the lives of great leaders. Prince Shōtoku, historically significant as an early leader and founding figure of the court-centered state, was the first to "ascend" the mountain, even though he did so on his airborne steed. The next person credited with visiting Fuji's summit also traveled there by a kind of magical flight, without the aid of a horse. En (or E) no Ozunu, later known as En no Gyōja (En the Ascetic), is the legendary founder of Shugendō, the way of mastering mysterious power on

sacred mountains.[4] His career highlights his flight to Fuji and his importance as a
precedent for establishing the asceticism of Fuji.

En no Ozunu is first mentioned in the *Shoku nihongi* of 699 as a practitioner of
magic at Mount Katsuragi who was banished on the charge of misusing magical
powers. The legendary setting of En no Ozunu would place him in primordial time,
preceding even Prince Shōtoku. The fact that En no Ozunu "often commanded spirits to draw water or gather firewood for him" (Snellen 1934, 178–79) probably reveals
the Buddhist influence of the *Lotus Sutra* (Murakami Toshio 1943, 48–49). By the
time of the ninth-century *Nihon ryōiki*, a full tradition had surrounded him as the
ideal mountain ascetic. In this tale En no Ozunu is treated as a miraculous figure
who exemplified the ideals of Buddhist asceticism and Taoistic mysticism. He with-
drew into a mountain cave and practiced the Buddhist magical formula of the Pea-
cock King (Kujaku Ō or Kujaku Myōō), thereby acquiring magical powers such as
flight through the air. This tale emphasizes his Buddhist ascetic powers by referring
to him as En no Ubasoku; *ubasoku* (*upasaka* in Sanskrit) refers to an unordained
Buddhist practitioner. However, he also exemplifies Taoist features: after his banishment following the slander of a jealous *kami*, he became a Taoist-style wizard
capable of magical flight. The story of his banishment tells how En no Ozunu flew
nightly to Fuji to practice austerities. As with Prince Shōtoku, the figure of En no
Ozunu glorifies and is glorified by magical flight to Fuji. En no Ozunu, the ascetic
par excellence, demonstrates that mere mortals cannot confine him: he exercises his
extraordinary powers of flight to Fuji, the highest mountain in the land. In turn the
fame of Fuji is enhanced by the presence of the great ascetic.

En no Ozunu was revered within Shugendō, whose practitioners referred to him
as En no Gyōja. The later traditions of the ascetic figure are "Shugendō-ized" versions of the *Nihon ryōiki* account, showing how he "opened" many sacred mountains for the practice of esoteric rituals and religious austerities. Eventually En no
Gyōja was seen as the originator of mountain asceticism, and his fame spread to
many sacred mountains. The later statues of En no Gyōja, as an aged, emaciated ascetic with long beard and pilgrim's robe and clutching a staff, resemble the mountain
hermits or immortals of China.[5]

A number of remarkable achievements are attributed to the figure of En no
Gyōja. He revered and linked a host of religious traditions, honoring age-old sacred
mountains and their *kami*, mastering Buddhist asceticism, and acquiring Taoist
powers, as well as expressing Confucian virtue: he is regarded as the founding figure
of Shugendō. His magical flight to Fuji is a significant precedent for its transformation into a mountain of asceticism and, later, of pilgrimage.

Especially during the Heian period many wandering practitioners entered sacred
mountains to undergo ascetic practices and to perform esoteric rituals in order to
gain extraordinary religious power. Rather than mere intellectual understanding,
the recitation of sutras and magical formulas was emphasized. These practitioners

maintained special diets and subjected their bodies to austerities such as standing under mountain waterfalls during their recitations. They adopted various popular titles;[6] some confined themselves atop the mountains, while others made pilgrimages from mountain to mountain (Hori 1958 [fasc. 2], 210). These wandering ascetics formed the core of later Shugendō groups at various sacred mountains. Usually a local mountain had its own founder who followed the precedent of the great En no Gyōja by pioneering the initial ascent (remembered as "opening the mountain"), recognizing a unity between indigenous *kami* and Buddhist divinities, developing religio-ascetic practices, and establishing shrines and temples at that mountain. Fuji too had a pre-Buddhist religious heritage that had been elaborated in early historic times through seasonal rituals at the foot but only later was "opened" for religious practice in the form of asceticism and ritual confinement on the mountain. The presence of religious practitioners on Fuji is indirectly attested by the late ninth-century *Fujisanki* (Record of Mount Fuji), which gives a somewhat flowery picture of the mountain and its crater. Japanese commentators find this picture incredible, not because of the unreliability of the author but because the author was depending on the accounts of others (Inobe 1928a, 174–75). The *Fujisanki* does show that "Fuji faith" and Fuji ascent customs existed already in mid-Heian times, although these beginnings of Fuji faith had no direct connection with ascent of the mountain by common people (Inobe 1928a, 175).

The twelfth-century figure Matsudai Shōnin, credited with opening Fuji, is reportedly the first "historical" person known to climb the mountain, although freelance religious practitioners must have climbed Fuji during Heian times, and Matsudai is the most illustrious example of those who chose Fuji as their "mountain-forest ascetic training site."[7] Matsudai Shōnin is also known as Fuji Shōnin (Saint Fuji) for his distinguished religious career at Fuji, especially his establishment of the Buddhist temple Dainichiji at the summit of Fuji in 1149.[8] He is remembered as an ascetic Buddhist priest who practiced among the mountain forests and, after climbing Mount Haku (Hakusan, on the border of present-day Ishikawa and Gifu prefectures), climbed Fuji several hundred times.

The record of several hundred ascents for Matsudai Shōnin is a generous number even for a devoted ascetic, but in contrast to Shōtoku Taishi and En no Gyōja, who used their magical powers to fly over Fuji, Matsudai Shōnin seems to have actually scaled the mountain with his feet on the ground. Matsudai hailed from Suruga; his Buddhist teacher was Chiin Shōnin, also known as Amida Shōnin, who had founded a Buddhist temple between 1145 and 1151. Amida Shōnin's name indicates that he surely was a devotee of Amida and spread the Pure Land faith associated with Amida. As his disciple Matsudai must have carried this Pure Land faith with him when he climbed Fuji. Amida Shōnin's temple was along the seacoast, but Matsudai apparently sought a more active practice among the mountains in establishing his own temple at the summit of Fuji. Matsudai also received Buddhist scriptures from the retired and cloistered Emperor Toba, which he buried on Mount Fuji as a religious offering; this practice is interpreted as a promise of this-worldly benefit in the here and now, and peace and tranquility in the Pure Land in the next life (Endō 1987, 27). The connection of the cloistered Emperor Toba to Matsudai is strengthened by the tradition that Matsudai's master, Amida Shōnin, was directed by Emperor Toba to found a temple and install Buddhist statues.

No trace remains of the Dainichiji (Dainichi temple) that Matsudai Shōnin built on Fuji. While the exact nature and significance of such a structure is not known, it was probably a small chapel (Inobe 1928a, 178) or a small hall for ascetic practices (Endō 1978, 34). Dainichi, the so-called Sun Buddha, is seen as the "embodiment of the reality of the universe" in Shingon Buddhism (Inagaki 1988, 33), and the summit of Fuji may be seen as Dainichi's paradise as well as the paradise of Amida. This imagery emerges later in several complex forms, overlaid with other symbolism. Matsudai was puzzled by the fact that Dainichi, a male form, was manifested at Fuji in the female form of Asama Daimyōjin.[9] Therefore he sat on a rock under a tree and fasted for one hundred days, at which time he received a revelation to walk 108 steps to a nearby spot and dig. He was rewarded with a quartz rock in the shape of Fuji.[10] This enabled him to see that *kami* and Buddha live in a world transcending male and female, which set his mind at ease so that he could preach to the masses in need of salvation. Matsudai discovered that Asama Ōkami equals Sengen Daibosatsu equals Dainichi Nyorai. Matsudai's revelatory experience of the unity of *kami* and Buddha in the mountain paradise of Fuji marks him as the major pioneer of Fuji spirituality.

The peak of Fuji is high enough to be covered with snow most of the year and usually is climbed only during two summer months. Matsudai Shōnin's choice to establish a permanent religious headquarters at Murayama on the lower slopes of the mountain is understandable. Ultimately he became the protective deity of the mountain; he was thought still to reside on the mountain when he assumed the form of a mummy and became a Buddha, and he was honored with the title Daitōryō Gongen. No extant records exist of Matsudai as a mummy, but the legend resonates with the Shingon tradition, embracing the notion of a future Buddha waiting to appear (as is the case of Kōbō Daishi at his Mount Kōya headquarters).

Matsudai's achievements define a more concrete contribution to the development of Fuji as a spiritual center than do the magical ascensions of Prince Shōtoku and En no Gyōja. Even after allowing for exaggeration in his record (the claim of "several hundred" ascents), his historical existence as the outstanding example of a number of people who climbed the mountain is irrefutable; and apparently later generations clothed him in the garb of founder and saint. He achieved the synthesis of the older sacred mountain with the newer Buddhist (and "Taoist") ascetic and mystical mountain.[11]

The highlight of Matsudai's career, and a landmark for Fuji faith, is the mountain's revealing itself to him as a miniature quartz Fuji. This precedent, including many details such as fasting and sitting in meditation on a rock, are important for later Fuji leaders. The Fujikō (Fuji pilgrimage associations) feature an altar whose centerpiece is a miniature stone Fuji. En no Gyōja is the saintly grand ancestor of all Shugendō; Matsudai Shōnin is the historical founder of Shugendō at Fuji.

SHUGENDŌ: FUJI AS AN ASCETIC OTHERWORLD

Subsequent generations followed Matsudai's precedent of mountain austerities to create the system of Fuji asceticism. They dedicated Buddhist statues (especially of Dainichi) and continued to bury scriptures on the mountain. "A cache of sūtras was unearthed from a sūtra mound on Fuji in 1930."[12] The scriptures (on silk and paper) are in poor condition, but some date from the Jōkyū era (1219–21) and indicate that a mere seventy years after Matsudai's founding of the Dainichi temple on Fuji's summit in 1149, he was referred to as a "holy man" and was worshipped. The earliest surviving statue of Dainichi placed on the mountain is dated at 1259 (Endō 1978, 36–37). Earlier statues may have disappeared during the persecution of Buddhism in the early years of Meiji (1868–1912), when many Buddhist materials on Fuji were destroyed, moved, or lost.

The most illustrious of Matsudai's followers was Raison, who like his mentor hailed from Suruga and proved capable of attracting large numbers of believers. An obscure figure, Raison is remembered as the "ancestor" of one of the three major temples of Murayama and is famous for having established the tradition of "Fuji asceticism." The exact dates of his life are unknown, but temple materials record his presence there circa 1320. This new tradition of Fuji asceticism is based on the notion that laypeople should not simply defer to the professional mountain ascetics (*yamabushi* or *shugenja*) to perform austerities for the individuals' benefit; rather they should participate in and perform ascetic practices themselves to acquire magical power and Buddhist merit (Endō 1978, 37).

From Heian times to Kamakura times Fuji belief gradually changed in several respects. In Heian times laypeople participated in Fuji belief indirectly and from a distance, copying sutras and then entrusting the scriptures to the mountain ascetics, who carried the scriptures to the summit and buried them; these laymen belonged to the upper class. During Kamakura times Fuji belief shifted to direct participation and asceticism on Fuji: lay believers (including lower-class people) climbed the mountain and performed actual austerities (rather than entrusting these activities to "professional" *yamabushi*). These laymen and priests constituted an interdependent system. The Shugendō priests were expected to carry out intense, severe asceticism on the mountain, especially during lengthy retreats. Their followers looked up to these priests and their practices as ideal models, performing less severe austerities for shorter periods. The *yamabushi* also shared their religious power directly with the people by providing religious rituals such as healing. Laypeople gave financial support to the *yamabushi*, especially for providing these rituals. From late Heian and

This recent photo of
gō no hakari, "weighing
of karma," shows a
Shugendō ascetic practice
whereby the individual
practitioner (*yamabushi*)
is suspended over a cliff,
prompting him to reflect
on his karma. Repro-
duced with permission
of Miyake Hitoshi and
Keiō University Press

Kamakura times an intensification of asceticism focused on this mountain otherworld came to include both lay and priestly groups, but the *yamabushi*'s austerities
were much more systematic and institutional. Meanwhile Shugendō developed as
a highly organized religious institution, and it became almost impossible for individuals to wander the mountain as freelance practitioners as they had done in Nara
times.

The organization of Shugendō at Fuji, as at many other mountains, involved
establishing a total complex consisting of buildings, ecclesiastical institutions (complete with internal hierarchical ranks and external institutional affiliation), doctrinal
and ritual systems, and reciprocal ties between priests and laypersons. Shugendō
groups vary considerably from mountain to mountain, but the ethos of this total
complex called "Shugendō" is centered in "mountain entry." In contrast to the pre-
Shugendō freelance practitioners who wandered the forests and mountains observing rituals, meditation, and practices of their own choice, "mountain entry" within
Shugendō was a highly defined group activity. Generally the purpose of mountain

entry is to leave the ordinary world, purify and transform oneself through contact with the sacred mountain, perform ascetic and devotional practices, and then return to the ordinary world in a renewed and empowered state. The distinctiveness of Shugendō was the combination of the setting of the sacred mountain, the ascetic and ritual practices of Buddhism, and the goal of personal transformation into a unified system.[13]

At Fuji the most important annual practice, mountain asceticism, purportedly founded by En no Gyōja, took place in midsummer, from the twenty-second day of the seventh month to the second day of the eighth month as determined by the lunar calendar (a month or so later than the present, solar calendar). During this time the *yamabushi*[14] confined themselves on Fuji, and laypeople were excluded. As at other Shugendō centers, "confinement" on the mountain was not static but rather a highly active round of pilgrimage, austerities, and devotions. *Yamabushi* left their headquarters at the foot of Fuji, received amulets, visited various sacred sites on the mountain, revered the *kami* and Buddhas there, recited portions of Buddhist scriptures, performed the *goma* fire ritual, drew sacred water, and after attaining the summit descended on the Suyama (eastern) side of the mountain. At night they stayed in the small "halls" on the mountain (Endō 1978, 41).

This practice of Fuji asceticism died out about 1930, but in 1967 one of the *yamabushi* who had actually participated in it gave his recollection of the performance. This record is particularly valuable for the light it throws on the practices of Fuji pilgrimage groups (*kō*) appearing later. The *goma* fire rite was performed before starting the mountain entry, as a prayer for safety during mountain entry. Nearby villagers viewed the fire rite and came into contact with the smoke of the fire in order to strengthen their health. Only the *yamabushi* climbed the mountain, honoring sacred sites along the way and visiting shrines, temples, and caves where *kami* and Buddhas were enshrined. They also underwent the practice of being held by the legs and dangled over a cliff. (This practice, followed by various Shugendō groups, was intended to frighten the participant with the fear of death and hell and to toughen his discipline; see the figure on page 29.) When they "confined" themselves in the "ascetic hut," their meal was a thin rice gruel of thirty-six grains of rice in a tea bowl. Reaching the summit, they circled the crater[15] and worshipped at the sites of "golden water" and "silver water." They confined themselves in a hut for ten days and listened to the teaching of their leader (*sendatsu*), which intensified their asceticism, and they went outside only for firewood and to relieve themselves. At the end of their austerities they cooked the celebratory "red rice" and descended the mountain on the eastern slope, where the villagers were eagerly awaiting them. After paying respects at various places, they arrived at a local Dainichi hall and performed a *goma* fire rite as a village festival. Twenty-six days after their departure from Murayama, this marked the closing of the Fuji "mountain asceticism," and the villagers joined in the festivities (Endō 1978, 41–44).

By the end of the Edo era (1600–1867) only three temples (*bō*) and thirteen priests remained at Murayama. In addition to its elaborate rite of "mountain entry" for its own professional *yamabushi*, Murayama established broader ties with people of the surrounding area in the Kansai (Kyoto-Osaka) region, supervising the so-called Fuji ascetics (Fuji *gyōnin*, also called *yamabushi* or *shugenja*) belonging to Honzan Shugendō (affiliated with Shōgoin) (H. B. Earhart 1970, 23–24). Murayama Shugen oversaw these Fuji ascetics and their leaders and bestowed rank and qualifications upon them. These leaders made annual summer trips to Murayama, where they stayed overnight and practiced under the leadership of the Murayama professionals, climbing the mountain and returning home.

The career of Murayama Shugen presents a picture of the ascetic otherworld of Fuji for both professional *yamabushi* and lay believers. However, the fortunes of Murayama Shugen were closely tied to social and political developments, especially within the turbulence of the Warring States period of the fifteenth and sixteenth centuries, when Murayama Shugen aligned itself with the feudal lord of Suruga, Imagawa Yoshitomo (1519–60). Imagawa's defeat and death at the hands of Oda Nobunaga in 1560 signaled the rapid decline of Murayama. Increasingly the political trends favored the large Sengen Shrine of Ōmiya, which was supported by warriors and later by the great shogun Tokugawa Ieyasu; after it burned, it was rebuilt by him on a grander scale. In a protracted legal suit from 1655 to 1679, Murayama Shugen was deprived of its land and authority, and its priests were reduced to being reciters of prayers and incantations (Suzuki Shōei 1978, 21).

Murayama Shugen, which actually constituted Fuji Shugendō, established the major pattern of practice for all the climbing routes of Fuji. Despite Murayama's missing the opportunity to organize the common people who eventually flocked to Fuji, and even losing out politically to Ōmiya Sengen Jinja (which in 1779 gained control of Fuji from the eighth station to the summit) (Bernstein 2008), its lasting importance is seen in having initiated the pattern of Shugendō still evident in the religious practices related to Fuji down to the present day. Shugendō established and spread the fame of Fuji as an ascetic mountain. This trend toward popularization of Fuji belief, Fuji asceticism, and Fuji pilgrimage was yet to reach its acme.

Part 2

THE DYNAMICS OF
A COSMIC MOUNTAIN

While Kakugyō was practicing austerities in a cave in northeastern Japan, En no Gyōja appeared to him and gave him advice on how to realize his vow of restoring peace to the realm and saving sentient beings: "The Deity Fuji Sengen Dainichi, whom you will find westward from here in the province of Suruga, is the pillar of the world after the parting of Heaven and Earth. This deity is the source of the Sun and Moon, of the Pure Lands, and of the human body. . . .

[This deity] is the pillar of our Realm and a sacred mountain without peer in the Three Lands. . . .

Now, to the west [of the Mountain] you will find a place to do your practice. It is called Hitoana. Go there and labor at your tasks. Never doubt that the Deity will help you."

From the *Gotaigyō no maki;*
Murakami and Yasumaru 1971a, 453–54
(from the translation of Tyler 1993, 286)

4

The Mountain Becomes the World

KAKUGYŌ: REBIRTH FROM FUJI

Murayama Shugen elaborated its organization of Fuji as an ascetic mountain, a regional Shugendō center, and a departure point for ascent; this pattern was imitated when four other climbing routes were opened.[1] Fuji's popular image was closely related to larger cultural, social, and political currents. From Kamakura times onward greater ease of travel and the shift of political power to Kamakura attracted people to eastern Honshu, where naturally they came more frequently within eyesight of Fuji. When Japanese-style mandalas came into vogue during this period (ten Grotenhuis 1999), Fuji mandalas were created, illustrating the trend of common people going on pilgrimages to the holy mountain.

Warriors and the increasingly powerful townsmen and common people were drawn to the dramas of salvation of Pure Land and faith in the *Lotus Sutra* and the miraculous tales of savior figures and sacred sites such as sacred mountains. The imperial family, the nobility, and eventually lower-class people took up the practice of making pilgrimages to holy sites such as sacred mountains.[2] For those who could not travel, "wandering religio-secular performers" carried illustrated scrolls, which they used as visual aids to retell miraculous tales as well as stories of suffering and salvation. The "religio-secular missionary jongleur" of the fourteenth and fifteenth centuries helped form and spread a "national ethic or national sentiment," creating "a body of myth that loomed larger than the central mythology of the *Kojiki* and *Nihongi* ever had or would" (Ruch 1977, 294).

Society and religion rapidly evolved in this time of political unrest during the Warring States period of the fifteenth and sixteenth centuries. The age called for a religious message and a religious leader capable of providing individuals with a solution to the political and social upheaval and promising them a personal way of salvation. The central message and key leader of Fuji religiosity came not from Murayama and its professional Shugendō priests but from the ranks of the common people—a wandering practitioner named Kakugyō (traditional dates, 1541–1646).

This figure, formally known as Kakugyō Tōbutsu Kū,[3] is credited with unifying the beliefs and practices related to Fuji as the basis for widespread pilgrimage customs.[4] Kakugyō has even been seen as establishing Japan's first "new religion"[5] and as the unifier and "founder" of "Fuji faith" (Fuji *shinkō*). In this book we consider Matsudai to be the founder of the basic system of beliefs and practices at Fuji and credit Kakugyō with promoting large-scale Fuji pilgrimage.

Few established historical facts document this important figure, who hailed from Nagasaki and whose family name was Hasegawa. After taking up ascetic practices early in life and traveling around the eastern part of Honshu and visiting various ascetic sites, Kakugyō settled at Fuji for his life work of providing a religious solution to the social unrest and personal suffering of the time. His sketchy life is remembered in vivid colors by the Fuji pilgrimage groups who honor him as a founding figure.[6]

Kakugyō's achievements are memorialized in the eighteenth-century *Gotaigyō no maki*, meaning literally "scroll of the great asceticism."[7] The significance of *The Great Asceticism* is that "Kakugyō sought to incarnate the power of the mountain, and his career inspired a legend that proclaims Mt. Fuji as the pillar and savior of Japan" (Tyler 1993, 252). This legendary account relates that Kakugyō's pious parents prayed for a son who could find a religious answer to the warfare and strife plaguing the country. Miraculous signs testified that the birth of this son was in fact a cosmic manifestation sent by the sun, moon, and stars to bring peace. When at age eighteen he set out for the eastern regions to undertake a life of asceticism and pilgrimage, he gave himself the name Kakugyō Tōbutsu Kū. In the district of Mutsu (present-day Aomori Prefecture) he entered a cave and underwent austerities, fasting for two periods of twenty-one days each. During the second period En no Gyōja appeared to him; in the exchange between the Shugendō patriarch and Kakugyō, En no Gyōja praised the latter's intent but told him to fulfill his vow by going to Fuji and seeking the help of Fuji Sengen Dainichi, who was practicing in the cave Hitoana on the lower slope of Fuji.

The Great Asceticism contains advice from En no Gyōja in the form of a florid description of Fuji Sengen Dainichi as the source of the entire universe (as quoted in the headnote to this part). This advice, and Kakugyō's later religious system, is a complex synthesis of many elements. When Kakugyō dutifully went to Hitoana (a compound of *hito* "man" and *ana* "hole") at Fuji to undergo asceticism, he was told by the local people that he should not enter because it was sacred and that those who had done so either did not leave the cave alive or suffered misfortune. However,

Kakugyō was advised by En no Gyōja to practice asceticism at the nearby Shiraito ("White Thread") Falls.[8] In answer to his prayers, a heavenly messenger appeared and guided him into the cave called Hitoana, where he had to affirm the seriousness of his vow to serve Sengen Dainichi. His instructions were to erect a square wooden post and stand tiptoe[9] on it as a form of ascetic practice. He was also to perform water ablutions and purify the six senses. After extensive ascetic practices, including not sleeping for a thousand days, he received a direct message from Sengen Dainichi to the effect that the reason for the discord on earth was the lack of harmony between heaven and earth. However, if Kakugyō performed his "great asceticism" and brought his heart into conformity with the harmony of heaven and earth, there would be peace. This traditional view of Kakugyō's experience in the cave is tempered by a modern observation: "Kakugyō's choice was significant, since by moving into the Hitoana he was able to ignore and bypass the established shugendō cult of Fuji" (Tyler 1984, 103).

Hitoana, a frightful mythical site, exists today both as a cave and as the name of the nearby village. Not a tourist attraction, the cave lacks illumination, and visitors must first bend low under the lip of the cave and then proceed (equipped with high rubber boots) through a pool of shallow water into a pitch-black cavern, using a flashlight to view the stone pillar upon which Kakugyō is said to have practiced. Even today Fuji is a complex collage of this-worldly and otherworldly scenes. Perceptions of this chthonic phenomenon inside the Hitoana vary widely: accounts of some Edo travelers voice their disappointment at the "mud, water, and bats." "Nonetheless, the Hitoana had a terrifying reputation," and *The Great Asceticism* "heavily stresses the Hitoana, rather than the heights of the mountain, as the central locus of Kakugyō's practice."[10]

The name Kakugyō Tōbutsu Kū is a play on several words. *Kaku*[11] is the word for "square" as in the square wooden post on which he stood; *gyō* means "practice" or "ascetic practice." *Tō* can also be read "fuji," a homophone for the name of the mountain Fuji, which is actually the character for "wisteria," also found in the name of the illustrious Fujiwara family, from which Kakugyō supposedly was descended. *Butsu* is the name of the Buddha, and *kū* is a term of honor. So Kakugyō Tōbutsu Kū means something like "Square-practice-fuji-Buddha-(honorable)."

Kakugyō was also given secret writings, diagrams (usually called *minuki*) in the shape of a mountain flanked by the sun and the moon and with a star above, as well as sets of characters referring to divinities and cosmic powers. The gist of such diagrams is the harmony of heaven and earth. Each diagram, the wooden post on which Kakugyō stood, and Kakugyō himself were all equated with the pillar of the world; Fuji too was called the pillar of the world. Such complex statements and convoluted restatements reiterate that Fuji the mountain is the key to cosmogony, the source of the universe and all life; at the same time Fuji is the clue to cosmology, the structure of the universe and its processes. Therefore, by practicing austerities within this mountain, Kakugyō brought himself in tune with the primordial and generic character of the universe, thus assuring peace to the country and empowering the people (by relieving their suffering). The revelation to Kakugyō concludes with a command: "Because of this blessing, and for the sake of peace in the realm, you shall climb the mountain."

Kakugyō continued his asceticism by climbing the mountain, confining himself within the "man-hole" (Hitoana), and performing ablutions or purifications at the eight sacred lakes around Fuji. Especially while he was fasting and performing purifications at these lakes he received means of blessing or curing (*fusegi*) people.[12] After three years of ascetic practices and water purifications, he visited his parents to tell of the fulfillment of his vow and his revelations from Sengen Dainichi, enabling them to die peacefully knowing that their prayers had been fulfilled. Kakugyō then performed lengthy rites for them and continued his asceticism.

Sengen Dainichi revealed to Kakugyō that the future shogun of the country, Tokugawa Ieyasu, would visit Hitoana where Kakugyō was again practicing. Kakugyō supposedly explained to Ieyasu the nature of his revelations and linked Fuji as the pillar of the world to the shogun (as the fountainhead of all things), in effect a cosmic legitimation of the future shogun. Unity with the Buddhas and *kami* also meant following Confucian notions of loyalty and social harmony. *The Great Asceticism* includes some criticism of previous rulers for being corrupt and not following the way of heaven, causing social disorder. The document is also mildly anticlerical, criticizing monks and priests for being more concerned with making money than cultivating faith. For this reason Kakugyō politely refused to accept anything from Ieyasu. He was performing his practice for the sake of the country and the people and wanted to keep his practice pure; this would assure that monks and priests later did not attempt to make money through the deity Sengen Dainichi. Kakugyō's message is the rule of Miroku granted by Sengen Dainichi and calls for pilgrimage to Fuji by the four social classes (warriors, farmers, artisans, and merchants).[13] Miroku (Maitreya in Sanskrit), the so-called future Buddha, comes to mean a kind of this-worldly paradise in popular Japanese religion (Miyata 1989).

Kakugyō and his two disciples went to Edo and healed many people during a great epidemic; as a result the authorities called these healers in for questioning, suspecting them of being Christian. As recorded in *The Great Asceticism*, when the government official asked, "'Devotees of Fuji, what deity do you honor?' We answered: 'Our honor goes to these and no other: we revere our Dual-spirit Parent [Sengen Dainichi as the original father and mother], and above our Parent the five grains. Morning and evening we faithfully worship Fuji Sengen Daibosatsu, and Namu Nitten [the sun] and Gatten [the moon]. We honor no other deity'" (Tyler 1993, 315, 328). With this response they were released. The fact that Kakugyō hailed from Nagasaki, a stronghold of Catholic Christianity during the "Christian century" (Boxer 1967), has led some contemporaries and later scholars to suspect that Kakugyō might have been influenced by Christianity,[14] but no solid evidence has been found to support such a claim (Inobe 1928b, 104–5). Kakugyō reportedly died at the age of 106. The account of Kakugyō's life was written down by his disciple Nichigan, who considered his master to be a manifestation or incarnation of Sengen Dainichi Bosatsu.

Analysis of Kakugyō's legendary life affords insight into the man, his accomplishments, the complex symbolism surrounding him, and the role of Fuji in his religious system. Kakugyō's origins and life present interesting contrasts with earlier Fuji figures. Matsudai, the founder of Fuji faith, and Raison, the organizer of Murayama Shugen, hailed from Suruga at the foot of Fuji. Matsudai carried out practice at other sacred mountains, such as the famous Hakusan, but did not travel extensively. Kakugyō is a more universal figure, hailing from Nagasaki in Kyushu and traveling throughout the eastern regions of Honshu, and performing ascetic practices at many places, especially ablutions and purifications (Iwashina 1983, 57).

Kakugyō's distinctive achievements were making contact with En no Gyōja and practicing within Hitoana, where he received a special message from Sengen Dainichi. This revelation was the unification of Fuji faith into a comprehensive cosmological and cosmogonic system that combined both ritual and ethical components assuring benefits for the individual and peace for the country. At the heart of this system was the emphasis on people of all classes climbing Fuji as an act of ritual pilgrimage and ethical self-cultivation. These achievements are also distinct from those of his predecessors. Kakugyō, without negating the foundation laid down by Matsudai and Raison, circumvented it by receiving the legitimation for his reconception of Fuji from the grand patriarch, En no Gyōja. Kakugyō's wide travels and rigorous asceticism qualified him for being granted his initial revelation from En no Gyōja, and subsequent extensive practices around and within Hitoana enabled him to obtain a definitive revelation from Sengen Dainichi about the true nature of Fuji.

An extremely complex set of beliefs and symbols is extrapolated from Kakugyō's revelatory experience in the "man-hole" cave. Fuji the mountain and Sengen Dainichi, its divinity, are in fact the source of the entire universe—including sun and moon, Pure Land, and the human body. The cosmic pillar is expressed in a number of forms: not only in Fuji and Sengen Dainichi but also in the pillar on which Kakugyō performed asceticism and even in Kakugyō himself and the secret diagrams he received. In short, Fuji is reconceived as a truly cosmic mountain—as the cosmos itself. Kakugyō, entering within a cosmic mountain where no human can survive, is reborn as a cosmic pillar. The abbreviated or condensed formula expressing Fuji as the cosmos is found in the secret texts revealed to Kakugyō within the Hitoana and during his ablution-purification in the lakes surrounding Fuji. These several pillars, which are in fact one, represent the unity of heaven and earth; and the observation and implementation of this principle, especially through Kakugyō's practices and in the climbing of Fuji, hold the power to transform the country.

This basic message is conveyed not in the abstract doctrine of a formal system but rather in overlapping images and tales. Fuji the sacred mountain of ancient times is still present, although its earlier form has been magnified and enhanced. The power of fire is subordinated to, or perhaps sublimated in, the form of Dainichi, the "great illumination" that in Shingon Buddhism is "the embodiment of the reality of the universe" (Inagaki 1988, 33) but within this scenario also signifies the sun. Similarly the power of water and fertility is appropriated and expanded in this notion of Fuji as the cosmic mountain giving birth to all life; at the same time the water around Fuji is seen as purifying the body in the sense of Buddhist asceticism (and healing).

Some Shinto elements have been absorbed or transformed, but other Shinto features come to the fore: by this time the *Kojiki* tales of Konohana Sakuya hime and her father, Ōyamatsumi no mikoto (the mountain *kami*), had become associated with Fuji, along with cosmological notions such as the parting of heaven and earth. Buddhist notions of the mountain as a place of asceticism enter in, along with the idea that the mountain is a Pure Land—linked both to Dainichi Nyorai and the this-worldly view of Miroku's paradise. The complex symbolism of sacred mountains is found throughout Japan: "One mountain could easily support more than one paradise. At the close of the Nō play *Fujisan*, ... (Kaguya-hime) ascends to the Naiin (the Inner Sanctum of the Tosotsu Heaven) of Miroku, for Fuji, like many other mountains, was associated with Miroku. Even so small a mountain as Kasuga-yama near Nara could support at once the paradises of Amida, Kannon, and Miroku" (Tyler 1984, 110).[15] The important Shugendō notion of Fuji as a site of ascetic practices becomes overshadowed by the new conception of Fuji as a cosmic mountain linking all four social classes in personal fulfillment and social harmony. The cosmic aspects of this message echo not only a reformulated mythic tale but also traces of Taoistic borrowings of the harmony of yin and yang and the five forces; the social aspects of Kakugyō's teaching bear the imprint of Confucian ethics. Some of the complexity and richness of this imagery are illustrated in the diagrams revealed to Kakugyō.

MINUKI: FUJI AS A MOUNTAIN MANDALA

The major expression of Fuji as a cosmic mountain is found in *minuki*, illustrated diagrams featuring the form of the mountain, cosmic forces—especially sun, moon,[16] and stars—and cryptic religious statements written with some unique Sino-Japanese characters devised by Kakugyō. He left many *minuki* but no explicit explanation of them. His disciples and later followers provided some interpretations (as well as developing their own *minuki* after the fashion of Kakugyō), but the full significance of these arcane formulas may never be reconstructed. They can be "vocalized"— that is, their Sino-Japanese characters can be pronounced or recited—but even the contemporary Fuji pilgrimage groups are not able to unravel all the mysteries of these diagrams (which they chant and worship rather than "read" for literal significance).

A Tokugawa-era *minuki,* a cosmic diagram (similar to a *mandala*) "extracted" from the "body" of Kakugyō (and also other Fuji practitioners). Note the stylized form of Mount Fuji, crowned by sun, stars, and moon, along with the created characters for the "original mother" and the "original father." Reproduced with the permission of Kokon Shoin

The following assessment of the diagrams must remain partial and tentative, but the crucial symbolism of Fuji therein is clear.

The *minuki* are best approached within the context of the religious practice of Kakugyō, who followed the precedent of mountain asceticism established by En no Gyōja. Kakugyō was acting on En no Gyōja's instructions when he entered the Hitoana cave and developed severe ascetic practices enabling him to become one with Sengen Daibosatsu, the major divinity of the mountain. In effect he was united with the sacred mountain, which is also expressed as realizing identity with—or being—the pillar of the world. Leaving the cave, he was reborn spiritually and Fuji was reconceived. Kakugyō entered the mountain to become one with it; the sacred mountain was internalized within his "body" (*mi*), which was "pulled out" or "extracted" (*nuki*[17]) in the form of mystic diagrams. In other words, the word *minuki* means "something taken out of the body," literally (something) "body-extracted." As an object of worship, the diagrams are usually referred to as *ominuki*, using the honorific prefix (*o-*). Through ascetic practice and unity with the sacred mountain and its divinity, the power and message of the mountain are incorporated within Kakugyō and become expressed in the *minuki*. Each *minuki* represents a kind of mountain mandala, a schematic depiction of the cosmos, drawing on the entire range of Buddhist and other religious traditions found in Japan.[18] These cosmic diagrams afford the devotees multiple benefits: mental and physical transportation to Fuji; transformation by being united with the axis mundi; and reintegration by orienting their daily lives around the structure of the cosmos.

Minuki are viewed by members of Fuji pilgrimage groups as objects of worship; usually their altars feature three scrolls hanging behind their miniature Fuji, the *minuki* being the middle scroll. Beholding and worshipping the *minuki*, and reciting its phrases, are ritual acts by which people follow the master Kakugyō's example and are united with both Kakugyō and the cosmic structure he revealed.[19] Viewing *minuki* as an act of worship makes it possible for laypeople to imitate Kakugyō's ideal of incorporating the cosmic mountain into their own bodies and lives, although of course only temporarily and at a lower level of intensity. Even so the *minuki* are powerful means of religious realization. A brief look at a *minuki* provides a glimpse into some of the secrets of Fuji's cosmic panorama and the kind of religious reality they portray.[20]

A *minuki* by Kakugyō, showing the form of the mountain, his unique Sino-Japanese characters, and his basic message, is reproduced on page 41. Although "writing" in the form of characters constitutes the bulk of the *minuki*, this cosmic diagram does not form a linear or consecutive statement but forms more of a total composite or configuration of many elements. Therefore it must be "scanned" or viewed in the same manner as a religious painting or sculpture, keeping in mind the illustrative features while moving from point to point among the written phrases, and integrating "picture" and "word" until the total import of the diagram is grasped and incorporated.

The dominant feature of the *minuki* is the outline of a mountain crowned by the three discs of the sun, stars, and moon, each cradled in a stylized cloud. These three heavenly bodies and the mountain represent a miniature universe, as indicated by the content of the writing. The outline of the mountain is traced by the two sloping lines, each of which folds back on itself just before the point where the two would intersect. These lines simultaneously represent the shape of Fuji and the stylized form of the character *myō*. This mountain/character *myō* is the first of a four-character phrase, the other three being the large characters directly below the "summit" and within the enclosure of the mountain. Beginning with the stylized character *myō*, the phrase is read *myō-tō-kai-san*. These characters are perceived as having double or even multiple significances through various connections, particularly by association with different characters with the same pronunciation and by different pronunciations of the same character.

The mountain/character *myō*, literally meaning "bright," also evokes the notion of another character, *myō*, meaning "wonderful," famous in the Nichiren tradition of praise of the *Lotus Sutra*, "namu myōhō rengekyō" (and still chanted today by Nichiren devotees and some new religions such as Sōka Gakkai). The second character, *tō*, may be associated with the character *tō* for "east," but this character can also be read "fuji" or "wisteria," here taken as indicating the mountain Fuji. The next two characters, *kai* and *san*, mean literally "open (the) mountain," in effect to open (or open up) the mountain; here it refers to the opening up of the land or country. However, the four characters *myō-tō-kai-san* are read and recited more as a phrase of praise or worship than as a literal statement (or set of associated meanings). This phrase, composed of the largest and centermost characters in the diagram, announces praise of Fuji as opening up the land (of Japan) in a cosmogonic/cosmological sense. Tyler (1993, 283) writes, "These characters read [MYŌ-] TŌ-KAI-ZAN, which mean in the language of the Fuji cult something like 'marvelous Fuji/[and Fujiwara?] mountain realization.'"

The two most significant characters of the *minuki* are the "invented" pair just below the summit of the mountain. The character on the right is *moto no chichi*, "original father"; the character on the left is *moto no haha*, "original mother." These two ideographs were, according to tradition, revealed to Kakugyō as expressing the "real" meaning of Fuji in its true (or secret or mystical or spiritual) significance. Both characters are preserved as his unique creations, new characters formed by combining other characters. This pair of terms, equated with yin and yang, not only establishes the foundation for the cosmology of the *minuki* but also identifies Fuji as identical with or containing the original father and original mother, the source of the entire universe. At the same time it represents the *honji suijaku* (original essence and manifestation) of the unity of *kami* and Buddha, as well as the harmony of yin and yang. In effect cosmogony and cosmology are linked: Fuji is the source or beginning of the cosmos, as well as the principle of the harmony or unity basic to the ongoing structure of the universe.

Below the pair of characters *moto no chichi* and *moto no haha* and *myō-tō-kai-san* are four columns of characters. The first three columns contain four characters each, and the last column contains six characters. This string of eighteen characters, known as *gojingo*, or "honorable divine words," is recited during the prayers of Fuji pilgrimage groups. The characters, some of which are unique or invented, have various readings that are difficult to decipher. Iwashina (1983, 61), in discussing the "sacred text" or *gomonku* of Kakugyō, which uses essentially the same phrase as in the *minuki*, treats the leading term of the "divine words," *kōkū*, as "human respiration" because Fuji pilgrims so explained it to the authorities investigating them in 1850. Tyler's comment on these divine words (or "formula") is that they are "an invocation containing Kakugyō's special characters for the in-breath and out-breath, and for *moto-no-chichihaha*, the 'primordial parents,'" which appears on *minuki* and *fusegi*.[21] This *gojingo* of Fuji pilgrimage groups is recited as an invocation of the power of Fuji—a practice similar to the "namu Amida Butsu" invoking the power of Amida or the "namu Myōhō Rengekyō" invoking the power of the *Lotus Sutra*.

This main phrase is flanked on the right and left by two other phrases, compact formulas or mantras that complement the cosmic/cosmogonic role of Fuji, combining the sacrality of Sengen Dainichi and the power of the sun and moon together with the orientation of the four directions and the unity of heaven and earth. Within Fuji spirituality humans should conform to this cosmic plan in order to prosper and foster benevolence. The other phrases balance the deity Sengen Dainichi, south and north, with the light of the sun, east and west, to provide cosmic unity.

At the very top of the diagram is the name of the *kami* Ama no minaka nushi, the "master of heaven." This *kami*, which originally appeared in the *Kojiki* and the *Nihon shoki*,[22] was important for the late medieval scholars who favored the way of the *kami* over the way of the Buddhas; it became a kind of creator divinity within Kokugaku (National Learning or Nativism).[23] Under Ama no minaka nushi are the three heavenly luminaries or lights: the moon on the left, the stars in the middle, and the sun on the right. Below these heavenly discs and to the side of the mountain are the names of Izanami no mikoto and Izanagi no mikoto, the parent *kami* (as described in the *Kojiki* and the *Nihon shoki*), whose union gives rise to the bulk of creation. On the right is Izanami no mikoto (the female parent), and on the left is Izanagi no mikoto (the male parent). These mythological figures link ancient formulations of male and female with Chinese ideas of yin and yang, invoking the power of sun, earth, and water.

On the right the three characters are "earth," the invented character "female wind," and "power"; on the left the three characters are "metal," the invented character "male wind," and "power." Under each set of three characters are dots, lines, and marks (apparently signifying the wind and/or rain). In general terms the pair of deities and pairs of cosmic forces on the sides of the mountain seem to indicate the balanced completeness of the mountain as containing or expressing both of the parent *kami* and the blessing of light and rain as well as the power of the winds. The seven columns of characters at the bottom of the diagram indicate the cosmic harmony that is the source of peace and prosperity for the country, families, and the realm.

The elements of the *minuki* on page 41 have been identified, and yet the significance of the total configuration is not exhausted by any particular sequence of analysis. The believer may "dwell" on one point or "travel" from point to point of this complex object of worship, or meditate on it as a sacred object and holy message. There are many "meanings" of such a diagram, but these *minuki* emphasize the mountain spirit as the source of the universe and all creation.[24] Although the details of the many *minuki* are obscure, the overall framework is consistent. Kakugyō's symbolic pattern of original parents, which occurs in a number of variations—such as *moto no chichi* and *moto no haha* (or as the compound term *moto no chichihaha*)— can be seen as a variation of Shugendō's distinctive yin-yang interpretation. These original parents appeared at the time the universe took shape; they brought forth land, sun, moon, stars, humans, and then all forms of animals, fishes, and plants. The original parents were creators linked to Izanagi and Izanami (Iwashina 1983, 64).

Not only the general pattern of the *minuki* but also the various components are clear. Like the Shugendō tradition from which it borrowed heavily, Kakugyō's numerous *minuki* and other creations took elements from many sources and wove them into a unified worldview. The pattern of *minuki* includes belief in *kami* (such as mountain *kami*) and elements of Shinto mythology (such as Izanagi and Izanami). It also incorporates the Buddhist divinity Dainichi and Buddhist ideals such as ascetic practices in the mountains, and Taoistic notions such as "wizards" (*sen* or *sennin*) in the mountains and the polarity or complementarity of cosmic forces were added to this. In addition the ethical aspect of this cosmic mountain is expressed in the Confucian ideal of harmonious family and social relations.

Kakugyō's *minuki* provide insight into his religious creativity but represent only one aspect of his many accomplishments. He also was responsible for a range of magical formulas and ethical teachings. While Kakugyō was practicing water austerities in the lakes around Fuji, he received sacred or magical phrases, or protective blessings (*fusegi*). About 150 of these survive, ranging from those for healing (colds and epilepsy) to various protective charms (including protection against plant diseases). Most of these protective charms are for changing bodily conditions (Iwashina

1983, 59). These "sacred phrases" praise the virtues of heaven and earth (nature), admiring the spiritual mystery of creation and praying to enjoy life in this world; the *fusegi* is a kind of amulet (Inobe 1928b, 101).[25] The general principle is the same as for the *minuki*: Kakugyō, by virtue of his ascetic practice and devotion, became one with Sengen, who revealed the sacred phrases to Kakugyō. These were distributed to believers; eventually they formed part of the regularly recited liturgy (*otsutae*) at the meeting of Fuji pilgrimage groups.

Fuji the cosmic mountain provided cosmogony and cosmology, magical charms, and even ethical teaching. Kakugyō taught that harmony with the mountain meant harmony in the family and peace in the realm.[26] Cosmic harmony is the basis for social and political harmony. The foundation of his ethical rules was to honor parents as well as the cosmic forces and Sengen and to follow the "pilgrim spirit." These ideals and platitudes were anything but vague. Kakugyō laid down specific rules including such "thou shall not's" as not hiring prostitutes.[27] With Kakugyō the ethical component linked to the cosmic mountain and its all-embracing pattern was secondary to the cosmological and magical aspects of Fuji, which were of primary importance. Kakugyō has even been called a magician; some of Kakugyō's successors, notably Jikigyō Miroku, made the ethical aspect a higher priority, but even Jikigyō carried on his person a *minuki* as a "body-protector" amulet (Iwashina 1983, 289). Fuji is overlaid with a bewildering array of beliefs, symbols, and practices, but they all contribute to the central theme of the cosmic mountain.

5

Touchstone of Ethical Life

JIKIGYŌ MIROKU: FROM OIL MERCHANT TO RELIGIOUS REFORMER

After Kakugyō's death a number of followers carried on his tradition, gradually establishing Fuji beliefs and practices in Edo and the surrounding Kantō Plain. As more disciples and believers gathered around his legend, Kakugyō's distinctive faith in Fuji spread, especially within Edo, and came to be represented by larger numbers who were more formally organized in local groups. Temple records indicate that especially from the third generation of leaders in Kakugyō's tradition, Fuji belief had put down roots in Edo. In the eighteenth century, in the fourth or fifth generation (depending on how the lineage is recorded), a major split developed around two powerful leaders, Murakami Kōsei and Jikigyō Miroku.

Murakami Kōsei (1682–1759) is noted for financing the rebuilding of the Kitaguchi Sengen Jinja between 1734 and 1749. Jikigyō Miroku (1671–1733), who had as many as four names, will be referred to by his full name to distinguish this historical figure from the Buddhist divinity Miroku. These two figures formed competing lines of Fuji practice, the Kōseiha (the Kōsei lineage) and the Mirokuha (the Miroku lineage), both of which were responsible for the rapid expansion of Fuji pilgrimage.[1] Although both traced their origins to the founder Kakugyō, the two lines were grounded in radically different lifestyles and personalities and were destined for divergent paths.

The Kōsei line was founded by Murakami Kōsei in the sixth generation of Kakugyō's lineage, claiming the official mantle of Kakugyō but never calling itself the "Kakugyō lineage" (Kakugyōha) (Iwashina 1983, 78). The Murakami line controlled the Hitoana and formally was the protector of this sacred tradition, including the practice of a twenty-one-day confinement at Fuji and Hitoana. The Murakami group also developed its own variation of Fuji customs, including its own *minuki*, featuring the main elements seen in Kakugyō's *minuki*: Fuji as the center of a cosmic diagram revered and utilized ritually for securing religious power.

The enduring fame of the Kōsei line is linked to Murakami Kōsei's personal wealth and his financing of the rebuilding of the Kitaguchi Sengen Jinja (in present-day Fujiyoshida, on the northern side of Fuji). This shrine, the main entry to Fuji from Edo and the Kantō Plain, remains an impressive monument to Fuji faith and pilgrimage, with its long entranceway flanked by towering trees and stone lanterns and leading to large shrine buildings. Less well known but equally impressive is the graveyard of Fuji pilgrimage leaders (*sendatsu*) in the Kōsei line, which is situated in a U-shaped enclosure outside the Hitoana. Graves of *sendatsu* of the Kōsei line form the nucleus around which more than three hundred graves of Fuji pilgrimage leaders are arranged. Some of these moss-encrusted gravestones are barely legible, but each represents the many annual ascents of Fuji (and confinement at Hitoana) by the head of a pilgrimage association, forming a mute but eloquent testimony to the depth of Fuji faith and pilgrimage. The cave is almost devoid of human traces, making it difficult to imagine what Kakugyō and others did therein. By contrast the silent and still formation of gravestones conjures up the image of hundreds of *sendatsu* instructing throngs of followers on their daily faith, leading worship services in local meetings, and guiding followers as they chanted and trudged their way up the sacred mountain.

From the eighteenth century to the early nineteenth century, when the Kōsei line and the Miroku line were competing for members and leadership in Fuji pilgrimage, the Kōsei line was wealthy and prosperous.[2] However, the material glory of the Kōsei line (whose pilgrimage groups all bore the name "Murakami") was soon surpassed by the spiritual vitality of the Miroku line. The reasons for the decline of the Kōsei line are not altogether clear, but several features of the Kōsei heritage may have helped hasten its demise. One was the emphasis on control over pilgrimage groups, not allowing them sufficient latitude for independence. Another factor was not recruiting dynamic *sendatsu* who were responsible for the grassroots activities of the pilgrimage groups (including the attraction and cultivation of members) (Inobe 1928b, 84). At present the Kōsei line is represented by a small religious group called Fuji Gohōke located near the Hitoana cave it still officially controls. This group is the repository of many documents of Kakugyō and the Miroku line, some of which have been cataloged but only a few published.

The secondary status of the Miroku line when it was competing with the Kōsei line is painfully apparent even today when visiting Hitoana and the nearby graveyard. The gravestones of the Kōsei line are within the U-shaped enclosure; the gravestones of *sendatsu* of the Miroku line pilgrimage groups are outside the enclosure "in the forest" (Iwashina 1983, 72). While the Miroku line did not have the direct pedigree of the Kōsei line, surely all Fuji ascetics, including those of the Miroku line, considered themselves to be linked to the founder Kakugyō (Iwashina 1983, 93) and must have been aware of continuing the ascetic tradition traced back to En no Gyōja. However, just as the Kōsei line did not carry the name of Kakugyō, so too the Miroku line kept its own name rather than handing down Kakugyō's name. In this sense the legacy of both Murakami Kōsei and Jikigyō Miroku can be considered as reorganizing or refounding Fuji pilgrimage. The higher degree of originality in Jikigyō Miroku's teaching and practice probably entitles him more than Murakami Kōsei to the rubric of a new founder. In fact Jikigyō's life and death were so remarkable that "some of the Fuji kō came to consider Jikigyō rather than Kakugyō as their ultimate founder" (Tyler 1984, 113–14).

More is known about Jikigyō Miroku's life than about his rival Murakami Kōsei's or about Kakugyō's, and he is set sharply apart from these two other figures. Jikigyō was as devout in his practice of Fuji pilgrimage as he was dedicated in his ethical teachings. He claimed to have climbed Fuji forty-five times and to have completed the mid-level circling of Fuji three times (at the level of the fifth station, the route called the *chūdō*) (Iwashina 1983, 142). However, Jikigyō's practice was not limited to acquiring a large number of ordinary experiences such as mountain ascents. Just as Kakugyō's asceticism was rewarded with Sengen's revelatory experience that enabled him to go beyond Shugendō, so Jikigyō's asceticism and devotion afforded him a transforming experience of unity with Sengen that compelled him to extend Fuji faith beyond Kakugyō's notions and to develop his own line of teaching.

Kakugyō's major contribution was cosmological and magical, with ethical overtones. Jikigyō Miroku accepted Kakugyō's cosmological system while deemphasizing the magical elements and focusing more on ethical teachings. Unlike Murakami Kōsei, Jikigyō Miroku was of humble origins. Hagiography claims that although Jikigyō eventually made considerable money, he gave it all away to promote inner purity over external worldly trappings. Jikigyō Miroku is certainly one of the most creative and vital leaders of Japanese popular religion, but he was not without his detractors. An unflattering quote from Itō Sangyō, an "important successor" of Jikigyō, notes: "They say he was a very difficult man. . . . Now everyone who has heard the least word about him is full of Miroku this, Miroku that. But if Miroku came back to life right now, they would find him a difficult man indeed, and quite unpleasant to be with; and they would have even less to do with him than before." Miroku had a reputation of being possessed or "crazy" and was hard to get along with.[3]

Jikigyō Miroku was born in Ise in the Kobayashi family in 1671. At age eight he went as an adopted son to a nearby family, and he traveled to Edo at age thirteen to be apprenticed to a merchant. He was both industrious and skillful in business, becoming a successful independent merchant. A number of people from Ise went to Edo and made their fortunes, often using "Ise" in their store names, and yet Jikigyō Miroku was not satisfied with commercial prosperity. At age seventeen he became a follower of the Fuji leader Getsugyō, of the fifth generation in the succession to Kakugyō.[4] In his early life Jikigyō cultivated devotion to Fuji while assiduously

50										THE DYNAMICS OF A COSMIC MOUNTAIN

working; toward the end of his life he gave up his occupation as oil merchant to devote his life entirely to this sacred mountain, and the teaching he developed centered on Fuji as a cosmic peak. Not enough is known about Jikigyō Miroku to reconstruct the development of his thought, which is too innovative to be reduced to one or more historical factors, but at least three important influences can be identified: the traditional customs and beliefs of his native Ise; his training in Fuji discipline under Getsugyō; and his life as a married merchant in Edo.

Jikigyō Miroku began his practice of Fuji devotion at age seventeen, only four years after arriving in Edo, so he must have been developing (or redeveloping) Fuji beliefs absorbed earlier in Ise, where Fuji piety was prevalent among the people. Faith in Sengen and Dainichi was widespread, as were local customs of undergoing purification before climbing mountains (including Mount Sengen) during summers to worship these deities (and also En no Gyōja). Fuji is visible from the Shima Peninsula where Ise is located, and Fuji pilgrimage flourished in this area, often by ship. Although no historical evidence links such customs and beliefs to Jikigyō Miroku, surely he was well acquainted with Fuji as a sacred mountain and object of pilgrimage when he went to Edo, and he must have retained this previous knowledge when he entered the Fuji practice led by Getsugyō. Japanese folk religions were transplanted to cities as rural peoples gravitated toward urban areas, a development also seen in the Fuji pilgrimage associations in and around Edo.

Getsugyō, fifth in the line of succession from Kakugyō, was born in Ise in 1643; he was forty-five years old in 1688 when the seventeen-year-old Jikigyō Miroku met him. At the time Jikigyō Miroku's name was Itō Iheibe; only after practicing under Getsugyō did he receive the name Jikigyō from his master (Iwashina 1983, 140–41). Fuji ascetics (*gyōja*) succeeding Kakugyō customarily received religious names of two characters, the second of which was *gyō* ("practice" or "ascetic practice"). The character *jiki* here probably is taken from the compound *danjiki*, meaning "to fast" (Inobe 1928b, 49). Getsugyō and his adept Jikigyō (Miroku) climbed Fuji together but also performed ascetic practices such as fasting as an expression of their reverence for rice and food. Jikigyō Miroku describes his devotions, including daily water ablutions and offerings to "parents" in the sense of parent deities (called simply *chichihaha sama*, "honorable father-mother"), the ruler, and Sengen Daibosatsu. He also attempted to repay the unrepayable debt of gratitude to "father-mother" (*chichihaha sama*), Sengen Daibosatsu, and (his) master[5] and strove to rid himself of his evil nature (Iwashina 1983, 141–42). Kakugyō and others had established Fuji as the cosmic parents and source of the universe; Jikigyō parlayed devotion to cosmic parents as a model for daily devotions and everyday ethics based on frugality and honesty. He was more interested in self-cultivation than worldly benefits as the result of religious practice. Self-cultivation, an important theme in Tokugawa times, still plays an important role in contemporary new religions. This-worldly rewards, or "practical benefits," are a contrasting but integral part of Japanese religious life (Tanabe and Reader 1998). "The name Miroku evokes a plenty to be enjoyed in average life by the average, but true and honest, man" (Tyler 1984, 111). Jikigyō's ethical teaching can be summed up in three basic principles:

1) If you do a good thing it is good, if you do an evil thing it is bad;
2) if you work hard, you will be rewarded (wealthy), you will not be sick, and will live a long life;
3) if you are lazy, you will be poor, sick, and live a short life. (Inobe 1928b, 107)

In short, Jikigyō's message is consistent with much of popular Japanese religion: renouncing luxurious life but basking in a prosperous life as a result of renunciation and hard work.

Another overview of Jikigyō's practical ethics states: "Jikigyō stressed particularly that the estate which one has received from one's parents is a 'borrowed thing' . . . temporarily entrusted to one by heaven; and that equally in the case of the wealth which one has amassed, it is the 'function of man' . . . to pass this estate on intact to his descendants. Moreover, he listed the true essentials of right action as follows: compassion . . . , kindness . . . , helpfulness . . . , and frugality. . . . Virtuous conduct guided by these principles will be rewarded by rebirth in a position of greater wealth and power" (Tyler 1984, 115).

Jikigyō Miroku's early belief in Fuji as a sacred mountain and awareness of purification must have been further refined by his ascetic practice under the master Getsugyō. Especially pilgrimage to Fuji and practices such as fasting intensified Jikigyō Miroku's religious faith. His life in Edo too must have colored his religious beliefs and practice. The ethic of hard work and frugality he taught was most appropriate for his career as a merchant and for the workers and merchants with whom he interacted. Such notions did not originate with Jikigyō Miroku: he built on the ethical teachings of Kakugyō and his line of successors. Surely he adopted features of the ethical teachings that flourished among the working people of Edo. Indeed, Iwashina calls Jikigyō Miroku's teaching "Shingaku-like," referring to the teachings of Ishida Baigan, founder of the popular movement Shingaku that emphasized Neo-Confucian principles.[6]

Whatever he assimilated from contemporary teachings, the content of Jikigyō Miroku's message was closely related to his life as a married merchant. Kakugyō emphasized that people should work hard, and for Jikigyō Miroku, hard work and frugality were the essence of religious life. His honesty was legendary. For Kakugyō and especially for Jikigyō Miroku, hard work was the way one acted out religion, but religion should not be a professional, moneymaking endeavor. Jikigyō was a Fuji ascetic, yet not a celibate; living with his wife and three daughters may have prompted his emphasis on improving the status and rights of women.[7] As Jikigyō Miroku's

religious practice was transformed from the custom of seasonal rites and purifications of his native Ise to the daily regimen of asceticism and devotions, he blossomed
into a creative religious leader with his own distinctive message.

Jikigyō Miroku's religious zeal forged the ethical dimensions of his Fuji predecessors (and possibly other influences) into a radical commitment of inner faith and
purity that rejected magical practice and external trappings. Indeed he called resorting to magic "heresy." Jikigyō Miroku was not educated, and his writings (in rather
unskilled Japanese) are not systematic, but their critique of religionists is biting and
their admonition of believers is relentless. He said that giving help to someone is
more valuable than erecting an entire Buddhist temple complex with all its seven
buildings or reading thousands or tens of thousands of Buddhist scriptures. He did
not utilize the magical practice of protective charms established by Kakugyō or the
prayers and rituals of esoteric incantations. He said that faith was between *kami* and
humans. Therefore worshipping pictures or wooden statues or metal Buddhas is a
"shadow request"—in other words, an inferior or inauthentic act. Believing in and
praying to *kami,* however, is a "direct request" and the proper mode of interacting
with divinity. Employing magic to intervene in human affairs is sorcery or witchcraft
and is only a means of obtaining money or valuable things (which has nothing to do
with religion). Authentic religious life is explaining the teaching of the *kami* and
buddhas and guiding people; it is not a moneymaking business. In this sense Jikigyō
Miroku was following Kakugyō's teaching that people should have their own occupation and practice their faith apart from any economic gain. Jikigyō Miroku continued some of Kakugyō's teachings, but his own message had evolved into such a
radical ethical commitment that he separated himself from Getsugyō. The line of
Getsugyō continued, and Jikigyō Miroku established his own tradition.

FASTING TO DEATH ON FUJI AND TRANSFORMATION OF SOCIETY

Jikigyō Miroku's exemplary career, combining a lifestyle of hard work, frugality, and
honesty with a spiritual record of intense devotion to Fuji and rigorous ascetic practice, would have been sufficient to earn him a place in the history of Fuji faith. However, Jikigyō is one of those extraordinary figures who becomes greater and larger in
death than in life, in his case because he planned and orchestrated the end of his
human existence in an unusually dramatic fashion. This exceptional life-and-death
story has caught the attention of Western scholars;[8] here his career is sketched within
the context of Fuji's spiritual heritage.

The outline of Jikigyō's demise is rather straightforward. First he concluded his
successful position as an oil merchant by giving away his personal fortune to his
workers. Then he took up a simpler life as an independent peddler, at the same time
intensifying his dedication to spreading his beloved Fuji faith. When his house
burned, he and his family moved to the home of a disciple. Jikigyō was receiving
visions from Sengen in the otherworld; when he looked at the world around him, he

"saw everywhere evidence of misrule and injustice," and he wrote down an account of "sharp criticism of the bakufu [feudal government]" (Tyler 1984, 112). Kakugyō had linked his cosmic vision of Fuji to the shogun; Jikigyō was critical of temporal powers but sought a nonconfrontational solution that sidestepped directly attacking the government. A series of visions from Sengen culminated in one directing Jikigyō "to achieve perfect union with Sengen by fasting to death on the summit of Mt. Fuji" (Tyler 1984, 112). He was carrying out his vow to spread devotion to Sengen and Fuji for eight years before his final fast, when, in "another intense encounter with Sengen Daibosatsu . . . , because of the famines and disasters of the age, he was urged to advance his death by five years, to 1733" (Collcutt 1988, 260).

In 1733 he announced his intention of traveling to Fuji with his own portable shrine and confining himself therein to fast until he expired, which he predicted would happen on the thirty-first day. His plan was to fast to death on the summit of Fuji, but the Sengen shrine in Fujinomiya that controlled the summit forbade him to do so (because of the fear of defilement by death). Therefore he set up his shrine at the site known as Eboshi-iwa above the seventh station on the north side of the mountain and "fulfilled his vow to 'stand in the Inner Sanctum of the Tosotsu Heaven, and to save all sentient beings.'" "Tosotsu" is the Japanese version of the Sanskrit (Buddhist) term "Tushita"; the inner sanctum or palace of Tosotsu or Tushita Heaven is where the Buddhist divinity Miroku resides. Saving all sentient beings is a Buddhist ideal, especially for a *bosatsu* (bodhisattva). (Both Sengen and Miroku are revered as "Bosatsu.") His followers believe that Jikigyō was possessed by Sengen during the time of his thirty-one-day fast; as he predicted, he passed away, and the disciple attending him covered the shrine with rocks.[9] "Jikigyo's thought . . . can be summarized as follows. To begin with, Jikigyo asserted the superiority of Japan over all the other countries, calling Japan the origin of the sun and moon, of the four directions and of the four seasons. Of course, it was Fuji which was the center of Japan. Thus Jikigyo called Fuji the 'pivot-stone of the Three Lands,' and the 'unitary Buddha . . . where appear the sun and moon.' Again, Fuji being the origin of all things, he said: 'In the Inner Sanctum of the Tosotsu Heaven of the countless worlds, there is a single jewel. . . . This true jewel . . . becomes form. Lord Miroku teaches that it is the origin of light in the east'" (Tyler 1984, 114).

Jikigyō was neither priest nor scholar, so his writings are not highly literate; nor are his theories couched in neat systems, but he incorporates and integrates a vast amount of folk piety and popular understandings of the elements of Japanese religion of the day. However, Jikigyō was selective in his utilization of folk tradition, presenting a sharp contrast with Kakugyō's much greater emphasis on worldly benefits through magical means, and in a message centered more around the authority of the shogun. Jikigyō shared his predecessor's devotion to Fuji but stressed the efficacy of ethical action rather than magical manipulation, and for him the world pivoted, quite literally, around Fuji. For Jikigyō the "system" of Fuji consists of a number of homologies. Jikigyō was devoted to two divinities (bodhisattvas) known as "Bosatsu": Sengen and Miroku. For Jikigyō, Fuji too was equated with Bosatsu. "He taught that it is above all rice (the essential food), which is both the product and the nature of Mt. Fuji. He therefore called rice 'the true Bosatsu' . . . , writing 'Bosatsu' with the character for 'rice.'" Because Sengen and Miroku are identified with food, "then by fasting into complete union with Sengen, Jikigyo Miroku died to feed the world" (Tyler 1984, 114).

In *The Great Asceticism*, attributed to Kakugyō, Fuji is seen as a heap of rice, and rice is equated with *bosatsu* (Tyler 1993, 259, 292). Rice is considered sacred throughout Japanese culture: "the symbolism of rice is bifurcated: on the one hand, 'rice as our food' and, on the other hand, 'rice paddies as *our* land,' each reinforcing the other" (Ohnuki-Tierney 1993, 4). Jikigyō's parsing of this phrase might go so far as to say that "those who eat rice are *our* people."[10]

Jikigyō was quite practical in the implementation of his worldview, which accepted and rejected different aspects of the status quo. He took quite literally the notion of rice as *bosatsu*, writing that people eat *bosatsu* every day; he saw the life force of the *bosatsu* as being responsible for the creation of a baby in the womb. In other words, life is a sacred gift of rice and Fuji and Miroku and Sengen. A human practicing filial piety (to one's mother and father) is following the way of heaven and also giving "full reverence to Sun-and-Moon Sengen Daibosatsu" (Tyler 1984, 115). In addition Jikigyō affirms the given of the four social classes of Tokugawa times—warriors, farmers, artisans, and merchants—but rejects their hierarchical ordering by teaching that these classes mutually support one another.

Jikigyō also stood apart from his contemporary situation on key points. His silence on the role of the shogun is a deviation from Kakugyō's shogun-centered rhetoric. "The ordering principle for Jikigyo's world was not an active, conquering leader but a mightily still mountain—Kakugyō without Ieyasu, as it were" (Tyler 1984, 114–15). Jikigyō might also be considered antiestablishment because he preferred a lay movement rather than clerical institutions. By the eighteenth century Shinto-Buddhist complexes of shrines and temples, and even Shugendō headquarters, had become highly institutionalized and formalistic, and a number of popular teachers and lay movements sought to provide messages and practices outside the established institutions (H. B. Earhart 2004, 143–57). Another deviation from the customary thinking of the day was Jikigyō's stress on the aspect of Fuji faith advocating a more equal role for women, particularly in religious matters. "The Fuji cult affirmed the full equality of women as participants in the cult. Jikigyo taught that menstruation does not render a woman impure" (Tyler 1984, 116). He also downplayed the role of purification for men and women. For a number of reasons—especially the unsystematic nature of Jikigyō's teaching but also the sometimes censorious and oppressive government, as well as the varied responses of the people to the government and criticism thereof—the nature of his message and the degree of its acceptance in his own day is hard to fathom. It is not surprising that scholars today have difficulty balancing his general support of the class system with his critique of personal and official ethics.

The life of Jikigyō was a model to emulate, even if it did not mean carrying out ritual starvation. Much more than the life of this figure, his awe-inspiring death was a great stimulus to the spread of Fuji faith.[11] For the eighteenth century, some of Jikigyō's views, such as greater equality for women, may be seen as progressive. However, his Fuji-centric notions are the basis for a Japan-centered world and anticipate nationalistic views of Fuji that became much more prominent later. (Jikigyō was not the first to develop Japan-centered religious notions, which are usually associated with the thirteenth-century Nichiren.) When Jikigyō called Fuji the "pivot-stone of the Three Lands," he was following up on Kakugyō's theme of "a holy mountain without peer in the Three Lands," placing Fuji and Japan above China and India. Fuji has a venerable tradition as the first among the three lands: "Most of the old writings on Fuji remind us that Fuji is *sangoku ichi no yama*, the most splendid mountain to be found in any of the Three Lands, namely, India, China, and Japan."[12] In short, Fuji marks Japan as the central and superior country in the entire world. This is a theme of Kokugaku (National Learning or Nativism), which comes to be of increasing importance in early modern and contemporary times.

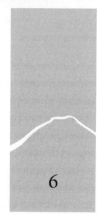

6

Cosmic Model and
World Renewal

FUJIDŌ: FUJI AS A COSMIC MOUNTAIN

Jikigyō Miroku's ritual fast to the death on the upper slopes of the mountain is a high point in Fuji religiosity; thereafter religious practices centering on and around Fuji expanded and developed rapidly, both in numbers and in complexity. This cluster of phenomena has been called "the cult of Fuji," but this general term—like any generic rubric for religion—includes a variety of religious possibilities. Those more familiar with the Western religions Judaism, Christianity, and Islam recognize that these conventional titles cover an amazing number of branches and denominations as well as a multitude of practices and themes. In Japanese religion, too, general rubrics such as "Shinto" and "Buddhism" cover a host of beliefs and activities. Shinto can refer to austere rituals or tumultuous festivals. Buddhism is known in the West for "cool" Zen meditation, but festivals, fortune telling, and healing are also found within Buddhist temples. Although it might seem that the religiosity of Fuji would be more limited and monolithic because it is centered around one mountain, the people who have climbed and worshipped Fuji and practiced there follow quite diverse, seemingly mutually exclusive paths.

No single term such as "the cult of Fuji" can do justice to such disparate, sometimes contradictory themes. To make sense of the panoply of beliefs and activities within the unity of what can be called "Fuji-centric spirituality," a threefold typology is offered: Fuji asceticism, Fuji faith, and Fuji piety. These three strands of Fuji spirituality are closely interrelated, separated here only for the sake of description and analysis.

Fuji asceticism,[1] appearing at an early stage of Fuji religious practice, embraces the ascetic practices derived from the Shugendō tradition pioneered at Fuji by the *yamabushi* of Murayama (as seen in chapter 3). The prestige of Fuji asceticism is upheld by its claim of carrying on the tradition of En no Gyōja, the founder of Shugendō and the source of much Fuji religiosity. However, Fuji asceticism remained on the sidelines and in the background of more activist and populist developments.[2]

Asceticism in various forms has been an enduring feature of Japanese religion. Blacker traces the role of "the archetypal figure of the 'religious traveller'" from the Nara period and Gyōgi Bosatsu down to recent times, with the conclusion that the "immense increase among ordinary lay people in journeys of pilgrimage" during the Edo period was largely owing to popular emulation of these "religious travellers" and their ability to escape the constraints of society and home to "another realm" (Blacker 1984, 593–94, 608). The increase in pilgrimage during Edo times, including pilgrimage to Fuji, was stimulated by such figures. The category of "ascetic traveller" is close to the notion of the Fuji ascetic: these figures tended to be the exceptional (or solitary) individuals who performed radical austerities, providing the inspiration for laypeople to undertake less rigorous ascetic practices (*gyō*). They are "less rigorous" since the followers of Jikigyō did not sacrifice their very lives for the sake of their faith.

Fuji faith is a rough translation of the term Fuji *shinkō*,[3] referring to the host of religious beliefs and practices associated with Fuji, some of which existed prior to Jikigyō and some of which came to flourish after his time in the rise of Fujikō, the Fuji confraternities. Fuji faith borrowed some of the notions and practices of Fuji asceticism but seldom was as strenuous as the regimen of Murayama Shugendō, and it did not emulate the ultimate extreme of Jikigyō's self-sacrifice. Fuji faith also accepted and advocated some of the ethical ideals of Fuji piety, but mainly those supporting social stability (and not directly questioning the status quo). Fuji faith defines the ethos of the majority of Fuji pilgrims, Fuji pilgrimage confraternities, and miniature Fujis.

Fuji piety is the elaboration and refinement of the ethical teachings of Kakugyō and Jikigyō, the result of Jikigyō's distancing himself from magical and ritual practices to focus more on self-cultivation for the individual and the reform of society. This rigorous ethical reflection reinforced the core values of the time while voicing criticism of the status quo of gender, social classes, and the government. The high standard of Jikigyō's strict ideals and his spiritual descendants' activist program form the nucleus of his teachings, but they were difficult to maintain during late Tokugawa times amid government suppression, and they were almost impossible to preserve during the early Meiji drive to unify and mobilize the country around the emperor and the nation-state. In this chapter the focus is on the development of Fuji piety that emerges from Jikigyō and his direct descendants, tracing this theme to the twentieth century and to a new religion that arose out of this heritage. After following the path of Fuji piety from Jikigyō to this new religion, we will return to a discussion of Fuji faith and the formative years of Fuji confraternities.

Jikigyō's dramatic message leaves a singular imprint on minds today; yet at the time of Jikigyō's death the possibilities for perceiving and implementing the teachings were manifold, and these different views led to a variety of religious developments. Following Jikigyō's demise, "his children and disciples formed several Fujikō groups and expanded the organization, so that through such activities as climbing Mt Fuji, faith-healing prayers, and the enshrining of models of Mt Fuji they were able to gain a large number of believers from among the common people in Edo and its surrounding regions. But the branch formed by Jikigyō's daughter Hana and then carried on by a silversmith named Sangyō Rokuō [or Rikuō] stressed the practice of Miroku's teachings and rejected the idea of gaining followers by means of prayers, etc." (Miyazaki 1990, 285).[4] Ambiguity is seen even among Jikigyō's children and disciples: some opting for the "Fuji faith" model of confraternities practicing a wide range of "faith-healing prayers" and rituals; others choosing the ethical path of self-cultivation, "Fuji piety."

The term Fuji *shinjin* (Inobe 1928b, 126) is translated here as Fuji "piety," to label the strict ethical teaching of Jikigyō and successors such as Sangyō and to distinguish it from the more popular and eclectic practices of Fuji *shinkō* (Fuji faith). Fujidō is the prime example of Fuji piety: a dividing line between the piety of Fujidō and the ritual and magical activities of "faith" in Fujikō is seen in the fact that Fujidō did not practice the *takiage* (fire rite), a hallmark of Fujikō (Miyazaki 1977, 108). The way of Fuji piety was opened by a daughter of Jikigyō and was elaborated and systematized by Sangyō Rokuō. Although there were many followers of Jikigyō in various Fujikō of Edo, Sangyō was critical of the other groups and set himself apart from them as the legitimate successor to Jikigyō. After troubles developed between him and Jikigyō's daughter, they separated, and he practiced rigorous asceticism alone. Rokugyō Sanshi was appointed Sangyō Rokuō's "successor and his followers called Jikigyō Miroku their founding father and organized religious groups that embraced his teachings" (Miyazaki 1976, 65).

Sangyō Rokuō retained and clarified the major teachings of Jikigyō Miroku on *furikawari* ("revolution," to be discussed later) and the age of Miroku, systematizing and supplementing this thought; after transmitting this message to Sanshi, he fasted to death at age sixty-four (Miyazaki 1976, 66). In his teaching Sangyō Rokuō advocated and emulated the Fuji piety of Jikigyō; in his ascetic practices and ritual death he exercised the rare and radical Fuji asceticism of Jikigyō's own ritual suicide. His life and death show how the major categories of Fuji spirituality could be mixed and matched according to individual predilections.

At the time the group was headed by Sanshi it had no formal designation; in 1838 the name Fujidō, literally "Fuji Way," was adopted (Miyazaki 1990, 285–86). Fujidō represents the coalescing of a religious group around Jikigyō as its founding figure, incorporating a wide range of elements and influences. Jikigyō's message was powerful and his personality dynamic; however, his teachings were fragmentary. These two successors systematized Jikigyō's teaching, in the process supplementing and refining it. "Sangyō's writings contain explanations which refer to the theories of yin-yang and the five elements, and Sanshi is said to have been influenced by the Shingaku scholar Nakazawa Dōni and others. . . . At least until the Meiji Restoration Fujidō doctrine was kept free of any great deviation from the teachings first expounded by Jikigyō Miroku" (Miyazaki 1990, 286). The heritage of Jikigyō Miroku and Fujidō can be treated as one continuous and coherent tradition.

Within the general setting of Japanese religion, Fujidō may be viewed in at least three contexts: first, as a folk religious phenomenon with features held in common within the contemporary religious milieu; second, as a new religious movement sharing general characteristics with other new religious movements appearing in late Tokugawa times; and third, as a distinctive and innovative teaching. On the first point, Jikigyō Miroku and Fujidō taught "diligence in the family occupation, matrimonial harmony, mutual support, and the practice of such ordinary virtues and services as the maintenance and repair of roads . . . , and other such public installations. To this extent, then, except for Fujidō's belief in one divine couple (the original father and mother), it did not go beyond the confines of the popular morality that Tokugawa authorities had taught to the general populace" (Miyazaki 1990, 287).[5]

On the second point, similarity of Fujidō to other new religious movements of late Tokugawa and early Meiji times, there are three common features: 1) the founder Jikigyō Miroku came from the class of commoners and based his movement on popular beliefs such as Miroku (Maitreya), the sacrality of rice, Shugendō, and Fujikō, and he also preached new doctrines; 2) it was an organization supported by common people transcending regional and social classes and occupations; 3) these groups emphasized "a goal of universal salvation of mankind and the reform of society" (Miyazaki 1990, 283).

The third context of Fujidō, its distinctive and innovative teachings, is a selective recombination of Jikigyō's (and Kakugyō's) teaching, his personal life and death, and his social teachings. Kakugyō's and Jikigyō's "theology," if it can be called that, is "Fuji-centric" in a radical sense: the tale of the original mother and original father (who gave birth to Fuji and rice and the whole world) presents an alternate account of creation. Fujidō's version is a refutation of the creation myth recorded in the *Kojiki* and the *Nihon shoki*, which Kokugaku (National Learning or Nativism) writers and the shapers of modern Shinto deemed authentic and sacrosanct, and which was further anointed as historical fact by the Meiji oligarchs who founded the modern nation-state. The creation (or emergence) of the world in the *Kojiki* and the *Nihon shoki*, compiled on the order of and for the benefit of the imperial line, reaches a climax when the sun goddess (Amaterasu Ōmikami) founds (and thereby legitimates) the imperial line. Within Kokugaku and in Shinto, especially after the separation of Shinto from Buddhism in the early Meiji era, the "age of the gods" as depicted in the *Kojiki* and the *Nihon shoki* has been seen as the sacred text of the divine founding of Japan as a sacred land, of the imperial household as a sacred lineage, and of the Japanese population as a sacred people.[6] Within Fujidō, however, this mythology was turned upside down, and the "age of the gods" was accorded a temporary span and a less highly valued position: "Jikigyō Miroku, Sangyō Rokuō, and Fujidō believers held a view of history according to which, for the first 6,000 years of human history, the world was governed by the original father and mother, the next 12,000 years were the 'age of the gods,' and the following 30,000 years would be the 'Age of Miroku,' and the period they were living in was a transition period from the 'age of the gods' to the 'Age of Miroku.' Of these three ages, they prized the first and the last as being ages when societies were and will be actualized, in which people did and would live uprightly in peace and abundance under the original father and mother, the creators and the overseers of heaven and earth" (Miyazaki 1990, 301–2).[7] In this context Amaterasu Ōmikami was given "the role of child of the sun and moon, the original father and mother," and Fujidō considered "the middle period as 'the age of the gods,' when the creators did not rule directly, human beings became self-seeking, and social harmony was in disarray, an inferior period" (Miyazaki 1990, 302).

This viewpoint is called "Fuji-centric" since within Fujidō (the "Fuji Way") Fuji has become transfigured as the center of the world, a cosmic model revealing both cosmogony—the beginning of the world *from Fuji*—and cosmology—the (proper) structure of the world *in Fuji*. In addition, "from Sanshi's time a consciousness of Japan's indigenous culture came to be frequently expressed within the Fujidō. Sanshi and others proclaimed that Fujidō was a 'pure Japanese' teaching, and attempted to sweep away all Buddhist elements" (Miyazaki 1990, 304–5). A Fujidō believer named Hisa Sen'emon commented on the proscription of Fujidō under the accusation of being a "new interpretation, heretical teaching": "The teaching of this way does not adhere to any of the three ways of Shinto, Confucianism, or Buddhism, but it is the teaching of the Great Way based on the most fundamental principle from the beginning of heaven and earth, that leads to the root origin of Japan, to the world of spiritual value." He admitted that "from the viewpoint of those who adhere to the three ways, who are aggressive, this teaching must be seen as a new interpretation and a heretical teaching" (cited in Miyazaki 1990, 306). In other words, the self-image of Fujidō in pre-Meiji times is "that Fujidō is a far older teaching than Shinto, Confucianism, or Buddhism, one that goes back to the creation of heaven and earth" (Miyazaki 1990, 307).

The nuances of the term "Fujidō" resonate more clearly in Japanese: the term "Fujidō" is written with three Sino-Japanese characters, the first two being the earlier form designating the mountain "Fuji" ("not-two" or "peerless"); the third character, *dō* or *michi* ("way"), is the same character as *tō* in Shinto (the "way of the *kami"*) and *dō* in Butsudō (the "way of the Buddha") and also the same character for *tao* or *dao* (also "way") found in the Chinese traditions of Taoism (Daoism) and Confucianism. The visual and conceptual interplay of the name Fujidō (in Japanese) borrows from the prestige of Shinto and Buddhism (and indirectly Taoism and Confucianism), while preempting them as the original and incomparable—"peerless"— way. This radical theology of Fuji as a cosmic model was the personal motivation and the divine justification for Fujidō leaders to make radical critiques of the status quo and even to present petitions to the authorities.

A crucial aspect of Jikigyō's and Fujidō's distinctive and innovative teaching is Jikigyō's supreme example of his own life and death. Jikigyō's lifestyle and insistence on frugality and industriousness were part and parcel of the core values of Tokugawa times, and his emphasis on the role of individual will in self-transformation and the reform of society was akin to the principles of Neo-Confucianism and Shingaku. However, his emphasis on "the reform of the world and the actualization of the ideal world [as] a responsibility of human beings, was clearly different from the concept of the age of Miroku in popular belief, according to which one had to wait in yearning for a dream world whose arrival could not be predicted" (Miyazaki 1990, 288).

Jikigyō was not merely satisfied with leading an exemplary life and preaching to others about how they could help transform the world. As revealed to him by Sengen Daibosatsu, Jikigyō's mission was to proclaim the age of Miroku and then to usher in this ideal age by fasting to death. The homology of Sengen Daibosatsu, rice, and Fuji—and the fulfillment of Sengen's revelation to Jikigyō—meant that he had become one with these divine forces. Convinced that the utopian era had begun, he urged others to welcome its beneficence and prosperity—the *bosatsu* that was both divine being (bodhisattva) and rice as the staff of life. His act of ritual starvation carried out the express wishes of the divinities identified with Fuji.

Not only the act of self-sacrifice but also its location are important. Deprived of using the summit, Jikigyō nevertheless achieved his goal of fulfilling the command of Sengen/Fuji *on Fuji,* thereby anchoring his life, death, and message to the mountain. The Shinto shrine's refusal to grant permission for his suicide on the summit it controlled is readily understood since throughout the world death is viewed as impurity and Japanese religion, Shinto in particular, has seen death as polluting. Therefore, Jikigyō's inversion of the impurity of death to the transforming power of death as sacrifice is all the more remarkable. Jikigyō's act and its location helped transform Fuji. Already established as a sacred mountain and (thanks to Kakugyō's pioneering revelations and asceticism *inside Fuji*) as the pillar of the world, Fuji was turned into a sacred mountain par excellence by Jikigyō's public announcement and actual implementation of his demise. Jikigyō's ritual death near the peak was the event crowning it as more than merely one among many sacred mountains; it signified Fuji as *the* cosmic mountain. Fujidō believers, fortified by the discovery in Fuji of the true, pure, original Japanese "way," were committed to the ultimate cosmogonic and cosmological truth, a veritable cosmic blueprint. This faith informed and emboldened their demands for personal and social transformation.

FURIKAWARI: THE "WAY OF FUJI" AS THE REVOLUTION OF SOCIETY

Central to Jikigyō's teaching and inspirational to his successors in Fujidō was the notion of *furikawari,* "the concept of a revolution of the whole of society" (Miyazaki 1990, 287). "This teaching of Jikigyō Miroku's, that men are able to bring about the ideal world through their own efforts, became the most important belief, the cornerstone, of the Fujidō doctrinal system" (Miyazaki 1990, 288), and it had great appeal to the common people. The relationship of religious commitment to social and political action was controversial in Tokugawa times, just as it is in modern Japan and throughout the world. When considering this "revolution of the whole society," at least three factors are relevant. First, in mid- and late-Tokugawa times there were populist supporters for "world-renewal" uprisings immediately preceding the Meiji Restoration, including some armed revolts, so the authorities felt that they had good cause to suspect and occasionally ban or prosecute such individuals and movements.[8] Second, important to the background of such developments were the impoverishment of peasants and urban workers, a sense of crisis in social and political affairs, and as time passed, a fear of foreign intrusion. Third, although Jikigyō and Fujidō were concerned with the state of affairs and actually tried to bring about a fundamental change, their actions, however bold and innovative, were peaceful rather than violent. They did not advocate or use force to overturn the status quo. Nevertheless, as early as the time of Kakugyō, these groups had their problems with the authorities.

Kakugyō, the spiritual forerunner of Jikigyō, was more oriented toward the established order, and yet even he and his followers were closely scrutinized by the government and accused of being Christian subversives. (In the seventeenth and eighteenth centuries the authorities also examined and persecuted a number of other movements.)[9] That Kakugyō and his disciples were under suspicion by the authorities is quite ironic because in the traditional accounts of Kakugyō, he taught that the shogun was responsible for establishing peace and prosperity. "Kakugyo's affirmation of Fuji as the central pillar of the world coincides here with an affirmation of the centrality of Ieyasu's role" (Tyler 1984, 107).

Jikigyō shares with his predecessor Kakugyō a passion for an otherworldly paradise combined with a yearning for this-worldly prosperity, an ambiguity of having his cake and eating it too—although perhaps more appropriate is a negative metaphor with rice. His denying himself food and rice made possible society's enjoying prosperity and plenty of rice: "by fasting into complete union with Sengen, Jikigyo Miroku died to feed the world" (Tyler 1984, 114). The more problematic ambiguity or ambivalence in Jikigyō's teaching is his support of the core values of Tokugawa society (and the government) while expressing "sharp criticism of the bakufu" (Tyler

1984, 112). "What particularly concerned Jikigyo, therefore, was maintenance of stability and harmony," advocating ideals of right conduct. "Jikigyo often spoke of the four classes, confirming both the hierarchical distinctions between them and their ultimate unity" (Tyler 1984, 115). Writings attributed to Jikigyō do not explicitly describe the means or nature of a social transformation. "There is, however, no call for a political revolution and no questioning of the Tokugawa political order. Nor is there an apocalyptic vision of violent social or religious reform. Jikigyō seems rather to have emphasized stability and to have believed that the world of Miroku would be brought about by human effort, discipline, and everyday moral values" (Collcutt 1988, 263). Jikigyō's motives and message are particularly difficult to reconstruct because of the highly restrictive constraints under which all people lived at the time: to criticize the government meant oppression, persecution, or even execution (K. Tamai 1983, 251). Jikigyō proved that he was willing to give his life so that others might eat, but he may not have wanted to risk imprisonment and execution for himself and his followers. Within Fujidō, as well as other movements, is found "the paradoxical relationship between adherence to accepted values and the drive for religious and social change during the nineteenth century" (J. T. Sawada 2006, 343).

The work of Miyazaki, while recognizing Jikigyō's support of common values and peaceful coexistence with the status quo, places Jikigyō and his direct descendants in a line of thought based on *furikawari,* "the concept of a revolution of the whole of society" (Miyazaki 1990, 287). Indeed, even though peaceful and persuasive, Jikigyō's transmission of Kakugyō's heritage as a Fuji-centric alternative to the mythology of the "age of the gods" was an indirect attack on this emperor-centered view. During Tokugawa times this theological attack may have been recognized more by Kokugaku writers than by *bakufu* bureaucrats, who probably were concerned more with the practical business of governing the country and paid less attention to religious (and mythological) orthodoxy. The shogunate did not tolerate anomalies in its rigid social order: commoners were to know their place and keep to it. Some Fujidō believers,

> hoping to inform the emperor and the shogun of their doctrine and thus gain official recognition of Fujidō so as to speed up the actualization of the Age of Miroku, had recourse to the Bakufu.
>
> As a result of this direct appeal, however, Fujidō was banned by the Bakufu in 1849. Instead of being destroyed by the decree, it continued to grow stronger under its ninth-generation leader, Gyōga. (Miyazaki 1990, 289)

The size of the movement was cause for concern by the authorities: "by the 1860s Fujidō had come to have the largest organization of religious followers of all the New Religions then in existence. According to records from 1863, the distribution of believers ranged over 995 villages in eighteen provinces from the Kantō area to northern Kyūshū" (Miyazaki 1990, 285).

In addition to this unwelcome intrusion into *bakufu* affairs, Jikigyō and his successors had challenged the fabric of Tokugawa life. "In their view of society . . . Jikigyō Miroku and Fujidō held extremely original ideas. One of these was their stress on the equality of the four social classes (warriors, farmers, artisans, and tradesmen) in the country and the equality of the sexes. Because they thought that all human beings were born from the same original father and mother, and that humans were reborn into this world any number of times, sometimes into different walks of life and different social levels, the difference between high and low birth or occupation was not recognized as an essential distinction. On the basis of this idea, some leaders did, in fact, criticize the overbearing attitude of warriors and the servility of commoners" (Miyazaki 1990, 287).

Jikigyō challenged the status quo both in words and in actions, boldly proclaiming the end of a degenerate era and the coming of the age of Miroku, and criticizing not only selfish individuals but also society as a whole for the unequal status among classes and the unequal treatment of women. In addition he flouted the authority of a major Shinto shrine and the generally accepted understanding of purity and impurity by carrying out his fasting to death on a sacred mountain. These actions of Jikigyō, invoking the dual legitimation of Fuji and Miroku, were precedents that inspired his later followers to justify their own writings and deeds.

Jikigyō's successor Sangyō Rokuō was outspoken in his criticism of the esteem placed solely on yang (male) to the detriment of yin (female), believing that this imbalance between yin and yang would lead to the destruction of the world:

> The movement of this world and the creation of all things are controlled by the principle of yin-yang and the five forces. Although there should be no distinction of essential superiority or inferiority between yin and yang, in the present world only yang (male) has come to be esteemed. Due to this imbalance of yin and yang, the present world has proceeded on the way to the ruin of raging fire and flood.
>
> To save the world from this kind of ruin, when Fuji's "rope of men and rope of women" are joined, then the world up to the present ends, and the "restoration of the world of Miroku" begins. In the new world the "rice *bodhisattva*," as the unity of Miroku and Konohana, is born in mutuality, supporting the proper cycle and harmony of the order of yin and yang.[10]

Here Sangyō Rokuō cites Jikigyō's prosaic phrasing of Fuji's "rope of men and rope of women" being joined, and yet the critique of male dominance has been recast in a more sophisticated argument based on yin-yang and the five forces.[11]

Rokugyō Sanshi, the successor to Sangyō Rokuō in the Fujidō lineage, put into action the ideas of Jikigyō Miroku and Sangyō Rokuō about abolishing the treatment of women as inferior: "One expression of this belief can be seen in the way Sanshi challenged the generally accepted religious idea that women were impure, by having one of the women believers stand on the top of Mt Fuji, where the presence of women had been prohibited" (Miyazaki 1990, 287).[12] Jikigyō broke a religious taboo on the upper slope of Mount Fuji; Rokugyō Sanshi fractured a gender taboo on the summit.

"From about 1854 til 1868, Fujidō was extremely active, for its followers were convinced that the world was at a crossroads: either the world would be renewed and become the Age of Miroku, or human beings would end up unable to satisfy the wishes of the original father and mother and would meet with catastrophe" (Miyazaki 1990, 289). Fujidō's challenge of the status quo also extended to the religious establishment. As Hisa Sen'emon, a disciple of Sanshi, commented, "The more Shinto, Confucianism, and Buddhism grow influential, the more they all become haughty and the more they look down upon and despise people; as a natural result, the hearts of the people become base, they lose compassion and kindness, they become avaricious and want only to amass for the present gold, silver, rice, and coins, and thus live a life of luxury" (cited in Miyazaki 1990, 305).

Jikigyō and Fujidō carved out a passageway leading back to a "pure Japanese" teaching, a reaction against the "ways of China and India." On this point Hisa Sen'emon was explicit: "Until now the Japanese have followed the ways of China and India when they set up moral codes, and as a result all those who are called wise, scholars, noted priests, and the learned are people who carry out the ways of China and India. This is a cause of regret for the people of Japan" (cited in Miyazaki 1990, 305). Fujidō shares the hope or nostalgia of most Kokugaku proponents for a "return" to an ideal or purely natural or completely Japanese way of life. This attitude may have been fostered in part by the gap between the common people and the upper classes in society (Miyazaki 1990, 305–6). However, this view of returning to a "pure Japanese" way was completely different from the kokutai (national-polity) theory and its stress on emperor worship. In fact the leaders of Fujidō must have felt their cause was superior to not only the three established religions but also the imperial institution.

Jikigyō's and Fujidō's egalitarianism was so inclusive that it embraced not only all four social classes but also the emperor and the shogun, because all were necessary for social order. "Jikigyō Miroku says: 'According to the oracle I received, from now on the Son of Heaven (the emperor), the shogun, and all of us are each to carry on with contentment the family profession that falls to our lot.' Therefore, being the emperor is recognized as a profession in the same way as being a farmer or a merchant is" (Miyazaki 1990, 298). Sangyō's writing echoes the same plan because for him, all of the parts of society are essential for the whole to exist, and "neither emperor, nor shogun, nor warrior, peasant, artisan, or merchant, 'when you go back to origins, is a way of life that ought to be superior or inferior'" (Miyazaki 1990, 298). Sangyō included in another of his writings "a secret prayer for the longevity of the emperor and the shogun transmitted to Fujidō from Jikigyō Miroku," but "this secret prayer was to be used only at times when the emperor and shogun have determined to fulfill their functions, even at the cost of their lives, to save their subjects. . . . Hence what is missing from these materials is the idea that the emperor's existence *per se* was something unconditionally exalted" (Miyazaki 1990, 298–99).

Jikigyō Miroku saw the emperor in the reflection of his own plan of self-sacrifice, insisting that "the 'role of the Son of Heaven' was to control these spirits by offering his life so that his subjects would escape from such misfortunes as natural disasters and poor harvests" (Miyazaki 1990, 299). Sanshi's disciple Hisa San'emon wrote along the same lines: "All the regular functions, and the special court banquets and other ceremonies the Son of Heaven performs to help all peoples on earth, all of these are his virtuous acts of great sacrifice for our sakes" (cited in Miyazaki 1990, 299). In Fujidō, "'great sacrifice' refers to a religious austerity performed for the purpose of obtaining universal salvation" (Miyazaki 1990, 299). Jikigyō placed the welfare of the people above the position of the emperor, and from this vantage point he could dare to criticize the emperor's job performance in serving the people. Jikigyō says: "The Son of Heaven does not even know his own duties; instead, he makes all kinds of new things, he gives money stipends to this official and that, he takes money, he lets all these officials he has appointed take things from the ordinary people, he lets them wring tears from his subjects" (cited in Miyazaki 1990, 300). Such daring ideas were not limited to Jikigyō: "we find Hisa Sen'emon, an ordinary believer, who felt authorized by a religious authority that transcended the present order, able to criticize the emperor and the shogun in these words: 'Even though they are the Son of Heaven and the shogun, when they have opposed the will of Heaven, they might suffer from calamities'" (Miyazaki 1990, 300–301). Jikigyō and his believers, not unlike much of Japan's folk community, shared an egalitarian notion of transmigration such that "it was entirely possible for someone from another family to be reborn as a member of the imperial family," and therefore "it was only natural that no importance was attached to the emperor's lineage by Miroku and his successors" (Miyazaki 1990, 301).

The views of Jikigyō and his spiritual heirs document just how radical a Fuji-centric "theology" (buttressed with other arguments) can be; they also highlight Miyazaki's argument of a "pure Japanese" view of Japan that preempts a whole repertoire of earlier notions dominating the post–Meiji Restoration scene—the Kokugaku (National Learning) privileging of the "age of the gods," the idea of *kokutai* (national polity) as centered in the emperor, and the view of a sacrosanct emperor as a divine descendant of the deities with an unbroken lineage. This Fuji-centric theology or ideology offered an alternative to the post-Meiji form of nationalism and imperialism centered around absolute loyalty to the emperor. Although Fuji-centric notions did not become the major Japanese ideology of recent and modern times, the potentiality of this "revolutionary" movement raises interesting questions.

PLATE 1. *A Shower below the Summit* (*Sanka hakuu*), from the series *Thirty-six Views of Mount Fuji* (*Fugaku Sanjūrokkei*), c. 1823, by Katsushika Hokusai (1760–1849). This woodblock print (ukiyo-e) is one of the recent images by which many modern Japanese and others identify Fuji as a hallmark of the country and a paradigm of "traditional Japan." In both photographs and artistic renderings, the color of the peak varies considerably depending on the time of day, weather, and season. Reproduced with the permission of the Brooklyn Museum

PLATE 2. *En no Gyōja.* Polychromed wood statue, c. 1300–75, from the Kamakura period (1185–1333) (55 × 32 × 26 in. diameter). En no Gyōja (En the Ascetic) is the legendary founder of Shugendō, revered for first entering and climbing Japanese sacred mountains. He combined Shinto, Buddhist, Taoist, and even Confucian elements into a distinctively Japanese "mountain religion." Here En no Gyōja is depicted with sinuous legs, in priestly robes, and with a cloak of leaves, a Buddhist-style staff, and sutras. His open mouth indicates that he is chanting. Reproduced with the permission of Kimbell Art Museum, Fort Worth, Texas

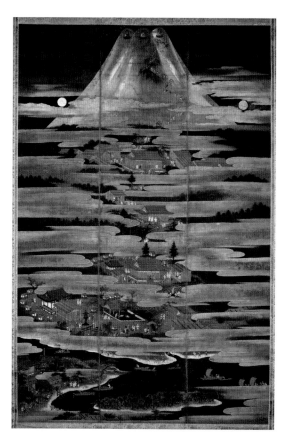

PLATE 3. *Fuji Pilgrimage Mandala* (*Fuji sankei mandara*), attributed to the noted painter Kanō Motonobu (1476–1559) or his workshop. This ink and color on silk scroll from the mid–sixteenth century shows Fuji pilgrims winding their way past Seiken Temple on the zigzag path up the mountain, flanked by the sun and the moon, and reaching the triple-domed peak (each of which is graced by a Buddhist deity). (Designated by the Japanese government as an Important Cultural Property.) Reproduced with permission of the Fujisan Hongū Sengen Taisha, Fujinomiya-shi, Japan

PLATE 4. This woodblock print, *Cave Tour in Mt. Fuji* (*Fujisan Tainaimeguri no zu*) (1858), by Utagawa (Gountei) Sadahide (1807–1878 or 1879) provides a fanciful version of the cave known as Tainai (Womb), with pilgrims carrying out their subterranean peregrinations and devotions. In the lower part of the print, some pilgrims avail themselves of the milk from the "breasts" hanging down from the ceiling of the Womb-cave. Reproduced with permission, photo © Yokohama Museum of Art

PLATE 5. This woodblock print, *New Fuji, Meguro* (*Meguro shin Fuji*) (1857), is no. 24 in *One Hundred Famous Views of Edo* (*Meisho Edo hyakkei*), by Utagawa (Andō) Hiroshige (1797–1858). The picture is presented from the perspective of Edoites standing on and looking over the man-made miniature Fuji to the snow-covered peak. *New Fuji, Meguro* is distinguished as "new" not from the physical mountain but from an older miniature Fuji (*fujizuka*). Reproduced with the permission of the Brooklyn Museum

PLATE 6. *Suruga Street* (*Suruga-chō*), no. 8 in the series *One Hundred Famous Views of Edo* (*Meisho Edo hyakkei*) (1856), by Utagawa (Andō) Hiroshige (1797–1858), is a wood-block print whose name indicates the Suruga District of Tokyo, Suruga being the earlier title of the province where Fuji is found. The clever use of diminishing perspective per-suades the viewer either that Fuji is drawn to Edo as its patron deity or that Edo is led to Fuji as its sacred guardian—or that there is a deliberate interplay of these two themes. Reproduced with the permission of the Brooklyn Museum

PLATE 7. An exquisite example of the outline of Fuji as a decorative motif is this seventeenth-century "campaign coat" (*jinbaori*) made of wool, at the time an exotic fabric imported from Europe. Fuji is represented in the classic three-peaked form, with a curlicue of sacred smoke (*shinka*) emerging from the mountain. The black circles at the bottom of the garment have been seen as pools of lava or water. Worn over armor on the battlefield, this coat draws on the power of fire and water (or lava) to protect the person and invoke military success. Reproduced with the permission of Osaka Castle Museum

PLATE 8. The main use of the image of Fuji in American propaganda leaflets during World War II was suasion, showing the lovely peak as a stimulus to homesickness and an inducement to surrender and return home (to Fuji). In this leaflet the message is a direct threat conveyed by the sight of many planes attacking Japan (with Fuji identifying the target). This image reproduced with permission from the Web site psywarrior.com, with thanks to retired United States Army Sergeant Major Herbert Friedman

PLATE 9. Shiba Kōkan (1747?–1818) emphasized what have come to be known as "true view pictures" (*shinkeizu*); here he depicts Fuji in this mode. In the color on silk painting *Mt. Fuji from Shunshū Kashiwara* (*Shunshū Kashiwara Fuji zu*), the highly stylized three-peaked or three-domed outline has given way to a more "natural" or "empirical" rendition of the mountain. Reproduced with the permission of Kobe City Museum

PLATE 10. This woodblock print, *Picture of the Korean Embassy* (*Chōsenjin raichō zu*) (1748), by Hanegawa Tōei (fl. 1735–1750), depicts Korean ambassadors or tribute bearers entering the Japanese capital of Edo during the nineteenth century. The artistic technique of diminishing perspective draws the eye between the buildings down the line of emissaries to Fuji, which crowns the picture. The peak has been used both domestically to unify the country and internationally to set Japan off from other countries; here Fuji, the unique mountain and symbol of Japan, reigns over a visiting Korean Embassy's procession. Reproduced with the permission of Kobe City Museum

PLATE 11. *Foreigner and Chinese Viewing Mt. Fuji* (*Nihon meizan no Fuji*) (1860 or 1861), more literally translated as "Japan's Famous Mountain Fuji," by Ikkōsai Yoshimori (1838–84), portrays two representatives of "outsiders" prominent in Japanese culture, Chinese and "foreigners" (Westerners), expressing curiosity and amazement at Japan's most lofty peak, which extends outside the rectangular border. Here the foreigners' interest in Fuji can be seen as a pictorial version of "reverse orientalism." Reproduced with the permission of Kanagawa Prefectural Museum of Cultural History

In the post-Meiji codification of national identity, the very land of the Japanese isles, including Fuji, was subordinated to the emperor, all but precluding the development of a Fuji-centric ethos and attendant institutional forms. As Maruyama (writing in postwar Japan) points out, "conditions of initial-stage nationalism also fostered a vicious circle which permitted the ruling class and reactionary segments to monopolize the symbols of nationalism" (Maruyama 1969, 143). Under less restrictive conditions a Fuji-centric ideology might have offered some form of political program; it did, of course, share a theme important to Kokugaku writers, the quest for a "pure Japanese" spirituality predating continental influence. In addition the claim for the superiority and uniqueness of Fuji held not only for other Japanese mountains but also for the whole world, amounting to a topographical legitimation of Japan's superiority over other countries. Yet the gist of this message is clear: "This teaching of Jikigyō Miroku's, that men are able to bring about the ideal world through their own efforts, became the most important belief, the cornerstone, of the Fujidō doctrinal system" (Miyazaki 1990, 288). This conviction even led some Fujidō writers to question the infallibility of the emperor and persuaded some Fujidō members to attempt to intervene directly with the shogun's government, a life-threatening act and remarkably "modern" in its import. Indeed, Fujidō's indirect statement that "even though they are the Son of Heaven and the shogun, when they have opposed the will of Heaven, they might suffer from calamities" (Miyazaki 1990, 300–301) anticipates World War II–era graffiti questioning the emperor system; one example asks: "Isn't the Emperor a human being just like the rest of us" (Ienaga 1978, 216). This Fuji-centric view advocated an egalitarianism of social classes and an equality of genders that was truly remarkable for the time. Fujidō certainly suggests many provocative (albeit never taken) routes to modernity other than those of the "Myth of Meiji" (to use the phrase of Gluck [1985]), with its ideology of an authoritarian government based on a sacred national polity (*kokutai*).

An interesting commentary on the potentialities of Fujidō comes from a very different perspective. The modern Japanese Christian theologian Koyama, who in his book *Mount Fuji and Mount Sinai: A Critique of Idols* has criticized "cosmological" Fuji and praised "eschatological" Sinai, nevertheless lauds the historical and ethical consciousness of Jikigyō Miroku: "Elaborating this new social ethics of neighbourly help, Jikigyō implied his criticism of the Tokugawa Shogunate. . . . This is one of the remarkable cases of the appearance of a 'liberation theology' in the religious history of Japan. In my view, it was the ethical emphasis which prevented this group from seeing history in terms of cyclical movement. Mount Fuji has its own right 'theology' which said something important to the people at that time" (Koyama 1984, 86, 93–94).

Despite the potential of Fujidō's radical call for reform, clearly at cross-purposes with postrestoration ideology, Miyazaki has detailed a gradual and, at least as perceived by most Fujidō believers, spontaneous shift to and assimilation of (and subordination to) Kokugaku (National Learning). The foundation for this accommodation or doctrinal reform was laid by the Fujidō successor Shibata Hanamori, who wrote, "I explained the traditional teaching in an imperial-country fashion"; in other words, he attempted to "re-interpret Fujidō doctrine in accordance with National Learning" (cited in Miyazaki 1990, 296–97). As early as 1863 Hanamori noted that the reason Western nations "respect Japan as the best nation in the world . . . [is because] it is the land of a most August emperor descended without any upheavals in a single line of emperors." By 1870 (just after the Meiji Restoration of 1868) he expanded this argument that only in the sacred land of Japan, "in fulfillment of the divine oracle from Amaterasu-omikami . . . the prosperity of the Throne will be as infinite as the heavens and the earth" (cited in Miyazaki 1990, 302–3).

Hanamori's views of the emperor as being indispensable to human society share much with Jikigyō's. However, Jikigyō and his successors "assumed a religious supreme being that transcends the emperor's and Amaterasu's authority, namely the original father and mother (the sun and the moon)," while "for Hanamori the authority of the emperor was viewed as absolute" (Miyazaki 1990, 303). Hanamori's new teaching was in line with "the revere-the-emperor and national-polity positions of National Learning and Mito Learning, and extremely close to the Meiji government's policies for educating the nation" (Miyazaki 1990, 303). The ties of Gyōga, the ninth-generation leader of Fujidō, to the emperor and court also influenced this shift; "Gyōga re-interpreted *furikawari*, which meant a renewal of society, to *furikaeri* [going back to ancient times]." For Hanamori, "'*Furikawari*' means going back to the world in which the August virtue of His Majesty the Emperor was prosperous" (cited in Miyazaki 1990, 306–7). Here Jikigyō's message is recast to agree with postrestoration policy, and the shift, which cleverly utilized Fujidō's own notions of returning to the original way, made it easy to reinterpret it as restoration of imperial rule.

Religious groups lived under harsh conditions during the early Meiji government's search for means of unifying and mobilizing the country, which discovered in the imperial lineage a convenient and effective rallying point. In the early 1870s, when the government was forcibly separating Shinto from Buddhism, banning Shugendō, and suppressing so-called superstition, religious groups were under the dual anxiety of escaping extinction and, in order to avoid this fate, trying to find ways of adapting to the policies of the new regime. Every group had its own solution to rejecting or accepting government pressure, or devising interpretations of their teaching compatible with the government's ideas (J. A. Sawada 2004). A number of religious movements found double happiness in gaining institutional recognition as (eventually thirteen) units of Sect Shinto (Kyōha Shintō) and somehow realigning their teaching to conform to Meiji policy and ideology. Fujidō moved in this direction by changing the group's name to Jikkōsha, which "in 1878 gained official recognition as a religious confraternity under the Office of Shinto Affairs, and in 1882 became independent as the Shinto Jikkōkyō, one of the thirteen recognized Shinto sects" (Miyazaki 1990, 295). This enabled the group to spread its teachings, free from oppression by the authorities and unhindered by interference from the established religions. Some Fujidō believers objected to this "Shinto-izing" and broke with Jikkōkyō to form the Fujidō Kōshinkō ("Faithful Fujidō Confraternity") but soon lost their vitality and their religious character (Miyazaki 1990, 295).

From a contemporary historical viewpoint, this story presents a curious denouement of Jikigyō's teaching: Fujidō—which had actively and successfully maintained its distinctive message by opposing the competing developments of Fuji asceticism and Fuji faith—passively and voluntarily surrendered to the combined Meiji forces of Kokugaku (National Learning), Shintoization, and emperor-centered nationalism. However, the conditions for institutional survival were quite trying, and the sociopolitical situation was extremely fluid; Fujidō's leaders may well have seen the Meiji Restoration as part of or means to the world reform that Jikigyō had foretold.[13]

Fujidō's newfound Meiji respectability bore unusual, even ironic, fruit. Apparently the first introduction of Jikkōkyō to the West was during the World's Parliament of Religions in 1893 at Chicago when Shibata Reiichi, the son of Shibata Hanamori, read a paper summarizing the teachings of the Jikkōkyō movement; he represented it as a mixture of veneration of the three creation deities found in the Kojiki (which he claims should be considered as one deity and not polytheism) together with token recognition of Fuji, "which is the shrine of our nation." The records of the parliament render the name as Reuchi Shibata and the religion as Zhikko; in the parliament proceedings Shibata's "Closing Address" urges Americans "to continue their struggle to achieve true universality."[14]

The press notices of the parliament were "almost painfully enthusiastic,"[15] as documented in a summary of the report from a contemporary (1893) newspaper account: "the Daily Inter-Ocean and other papers reported on the stir caused by the appearance of Reuchi Shibata, the Shinto priest, whose paper, at least as evidenced in the published record, was somewhat lackluster. Standing before an oil painting of sacred Mount Fuji in what was reported to be a 'statue-like attitude with his eyes fixed on the floor,' he received wave after wave of applause. . . . Shibata was 'the hero of the moment' . . . [with] the audience's exoticist fascination with the orient" (Seager 1995, 166–67).

The conversion of Fujidō into Jikkōkyō represents something of a doctrinal inversion of Fuji. In Fujidō the figure of Fuji as the primordial cosmic mountain towers over the emperor; within Jikkōkyō a much diminished Fuji cowers under the absolute sovereignty of the emperor and deities of the Kojiki. Whether the transformation from Fujidō to Jikkōkyō was an involuntary reaction to political pressures and more of an attempt to survive than a voluntary espousal of the aims and principles of the new Meiji government is impossible to determine today. Fujidō (or Jikkōkyō) was in good company: "The reactions of the New Religions at the time varied from religion to religion, from meek submission to defiant opposition, but by the beginning of the twentieth century almost all the New Religions that had arisen in the late Tokugawa or early Meiji period had adopted emperor worship and patriotic and nationalistic doctrines" (Miyazaki 1990, 283).

The permutations of Fuji spirituality from Fujidō to Jikkōkyō, strange as they may seem when juxtaposed so sharply, are hardly anomalies. Viewed with a jaded eye, history is full of irony and opportunism. Yet whatever Jikkōkyō's shortcomings may seem to be in hindsight, the group's successful adaptability should rightly be credited with preserving and passing down the heritage of Fujidō, albeit in a diluted form, to the present. Perhaps Shibata Hanamori was taking "preventive"[16] measures when he said, "I explained the traditional teaching in an imperial-country fashion" (cited in Miyazaki 1990, 296–97). If nothing else, the story of Fujikō > Fujidō > Jikkōkyō provides a case study of diversity and conflict in one lineage as an example of the heterogeneity within Japanese society (Najita and Koschmann 1982). We have followed the evolution (or devolution) of Fujidō from its heyday to its modern transformation and have seen how one movement can diverge sharply from its original principles, presenting an apparent inner contradiction. Now we return to other movements contemporary with early Fujidō, which portray a remarkably different set of Fuji beliefs and practices.

7

Pilgrimage Confraternities

People Come to the Mountain

THE "EIGHT HUNDRED AND EIGHT" FUJIKŌ

During the lifetimes of Kakugyō and Jikigyō, a wide variety of religious practices centered around Fuji, especially the emerging custom of Fuji pilgrimage. In the Tokugawa era, especially in the bustling city of Edo, numerous Fuji pilgrimage associations arose and were so active in their local meetings and pilgrimages that they dominated the religious setting of the mountain.

Religious ascent of Fuji has as its precedent the mythical-legendary flights of Shōtoku Taishi and En no Gyōja and then the historical figures of Matsudai and Raison within the pattern of Murayama Shugendō. The "mountain entry" of Shugendō helped establish both routes and routines for the religious trip up the slopes of Fuji: guides, fees, rites, and instructions were the template imposed on both the mountain and the climbers to regulate ascent of Fuji as a group ascetic experience. However, no uniform catechism governed the entire mountain: each climbing route and every shrine and temple along the route left its own imprint on the itinerary and its activities, providing its own set of beliefs and practices as well as issuing its own amulets. From the late fifteenth and sixteenth centuries a number of climbing routes had been opened when the dominant pattern was "Fuji asceticism."

The most conspicuous aspects of Fuji pilgrimage throughout the Tokugawa era are its high degree of organization and the participation of large numbers of people, especially commoners, in the confraternities known as Fujikō. News of Jikigyō's self-sacrifice near the summit of Fuji must have provided the stimulus spurring the rapid increase of individual believers and the expansion of these pilgrimage groups. Much of the personal motivation for revering and climbing Fuji comes from the model of religious founders such as Kakugyō and Jikigyō, and yet nonreligious factors were influential for making possible the growth of these groups and their (more or less) religious trips. The prior elite tradition of pilgrimage by the members of the imperial family and nobility gave way to the custom of travel by all classes, for recreation as well as for religious purposes. Pilgrimage to Fuji, not unlike pilgrimage in Japanese religion generally, has been a many-faceted phenomenon; it arose as part of the emergence of popular culture and the opening (and leveling) of travel and access to famous places for the lower classes. Fuji pilgrimage was a religious activity commingled with travel as recreation. In Tokugawa times, "the creation of a 'culture of movement' was an important stimulus for travel."[1] In the period when Fuji pilgrimage was becoming more fashionable and more highly organized, Japanese society was being filled with many forms of mass-produced travel literature, from woodblock prints to how-to-travel books.

Each pilgrimage site had or developed its particular attractions, be they scenic, historical, curative, or spiritual. A political decision that greatly enhanced Fuji's visibility and notoriety was the shogun's early seventeenth-century ruling of "alternate attendance," requiring feudal lords (daimyo) to spend every other year in Edo "in attendance" on the shogun. Although this requirement was a political device to maintain control over the hundreds of territorial rulers, it had wide-ranging economic and social consequences that enhanced the visibility and prominence of Fuji as a pilgrimage site. In order for these daimyo to come to Edo with their large retinues, the shogun maintained highways, which came to serve as vital arteries for travel in general, economic development, and social exchange. This pattern of alternate attendance anchored Edo and the surrounding area (rather than Yamato, Nara, and Kyoto) as the center of the country. The Tōkaidō (the Eastern Sea Highway) from Edo to Kyoto had been important since the twelfth century with the establishment of the shogun's headquarters at Kamakura. The number of travelers, especially commoners, increased markedly from the seventeenth century, and the fame of this route (over which Fuji's peak towers) was spread through the new media of mass-produced books and woodblock prints.

In the earliest perceptions of Fuji as a sacred mountain, the power of the volcano in fire and water was directly encountered only by those in the immediate surrounding area; it was the rare exception (such as the poet Saigyō) who left behind an impression of Fuji based on personal observation of the mountain, rather than formulaic expressions of poetic or artistic ideals. However, after 1600 when the political and cultural fulcrum shifted to Edo, and with the new requirement of alternate attendance, the number of people of all classes who actually saw Fuji with their own eyes increased dramatically. Within this setting Fuji was touted as the highest and most beautiful peak, the premier mountain in Japan, accentuating an earlier idiom that it was the first-ranking mountain of the world (in the "three countries," that is, India, China, and Japan).

As Japan's center moved to the east, Fuji became central to Japan's consciousness, helping promote the rise of Fuji pilgrims and pilgrimage associations. Within the lineage of Kakugyō and Jikigyō, especially among the uncompromising Fujidō leaders and believers, were people who, while mere mortals, were almost totally committed to religious goals. Some of the same religious purists must have trod the flourishing path of group pilgrimage to Fuji, but the majority of pilgrims freely mixed religion with pleasure. In the premodern era sightseeing and pilgrimage walked hand in hand. From Tokugawa times pilgrims have enjoyed the company of fellow travelers and the sensory delights along the way.

A description of pilgrimage to Ise may also apply to Fuji: "One diary kept by a member of a confraternity group of twenty individuals making a leisurely pilgrimage reads like an 'Eater's Guide to the Ise Pilgrimage,' noting the restaurants the group ate at, the more than one hundred types of food products tasted during the two-month-long trip, the inns stayed at, the various local speciality products seen or purchased, and the 'famous places' (*meisho*) visited" (Vaporis 1994, 238).

Usually pilgrims stopped at a number of holy sites rather than limiting themselves to just one religious destination. These nameless multitudes who figured in the woodblock prints of Hokusai and Hiroshige and filled the ranks of hundreds of confraternities give us a picture of Fuji faith. The Fuji piety of Fujidō is characterized by a single-minded ethic and intense commitment; the Fuji faith of Fujikō is acted out in diverse beliefs and practices in a more relaxed and open-minded atmosphere that typifies so much of Japanese popular religion (Jippensha 1960). Fuji piety and Fuji faith shared many features and developed during the same time frame, but they were parallel and competing dimensions of Fuji spirituality—even though they might, and often did, inhabit the same individual.

Fujikō represent a particular form of organization, *kō*, found throughout Japan in various forms and in different religious expressions. *Kō*, confraternities, have often been called pilgrimage associations since many of them existed for this purpose. However, some *kō* served to propagate and celebrate other religious commitments and even functioned as mutual aid societies (Davis 1977, 15, 27–30.). The original meaning of the word *kō* is "a Buddhist lecture," but *kō* gradually came to signify the gatherings of people who heard these lectures; similar meetings later spread to Shinto believers and gatherings. The term is usually found as a compound word, the first part of which names the holy site, such as Isekō (Ise and its large Shinto shrines), or the object of worship, such as Daishikō (for a saint, Kōbō Daishi). *Kō* arose among the aristocracy in the Nara and Heian periods and spread among the people during Kamakura times. Despite this abundance of confraternities in so many locales and in such a variety of religious modes, Fuji confraternities appeared surprisingly late on the scene and did not appear at all in some Fuji settings.

Equally surprising is the fact that none of the Fuji pilgrimage groups formed after the time of Jikigyō were in the Kōsei line: almost all of the confraternities and the throngs of pilgrims made famous in Tokugawa times, and still remembered today as Fujikō, belonged to the Jikigyō Mirokuha tradition. Perhaps the asceticism promoted by the Kōsei side of Kakugyō's transmission, which adhered to the *gyōja* emphases of Murayama Shugendō, was not conducive to the formation of lay groups as popular movements; or maybe the Kōsei people did not recruit powerful leaders as successfully as did the Jikigyō Miroku followers.[2] Also the momentum of popular/ mass culture in Edo probably was much more aligned with a lay movement such as Fujikō, in which the leaders had their own occupations and did not receive money for any services. A tenet of Fujikō that matched Fujidō's transmission of Jikigyō's teaching was the anticlerical stance forbidding any of their leaders from becoming professional religionists and accepting payment for services. Both Fujidō and Fujikō sharply criticized the Fuji *gyōja* for peddling Fuji as a commodity. Fujidō went the extra step of denouncing the rituals of *gyōja* as a contradiction of Jikigyō's ethical plan of self-cultivation, while Fujikō embraced all these practices as legitimate and complained only of their being performed for a fee. In Fujikō's teachings this removed *gyōja* from the authentic lay tradition of Fuji and placed them in the same debased compartment of services-for-sale as Shinto and Buddhist priests. While Fujidō flourished, the *gyōja* style of Fuji asceticism within Murayama Shugendō and in the Kōsei line following Kakugyō remained on the sidelines of the major new development of Fuji confraternities in the Jikigyō Miroku line.

Before Jikigyō those who climbed Fuji as "pilgrims" were called Fuji *dōja;*[3] the *Fuji Mandara* attributed to Kanō Motonobu (died 1555) is the oldest picture of Fuji *dōja* (see plate 3).[4] Those who continued Kakugyō's line were called Fuji *gyōja,* literally "Fuji ascetics"; yet they also qualified as ritualists or magicians because their primary function was to provide various rituals, healings, blessings, and amulets to believers who visited them, and whom they in turn visited. Apparently small circles of *gyōja* centered around the founder Kakugyō, but at that time there were no organized groups of believers called *kō.*

Before Jikigyō there were no groups like the later confraternities and no use of the name *kō.* In Jikigyō's day his followers had faith in him as a Fuji *gyōja,* and apparently a small number of people climbed with Jikigyō to carry out the practices of, and themselves to become, Fuji *gyōja.* Although the exact origins of *kō* for Fuji are difficult to trace, after Jikigyō's death these groups appeared in rapid succession, and once the term *kō* caught on, it was adopted by all of them (Iwashina 1983, 132–33).

In 1736, three years after the death of Jikigyō Miroku, his disciple Takada Fujishirō (whose religious name was Nichigyō) formed a group called Miroku Dōgyō. As noted previously, the term "Miroku" refers to the historical person Jikigyō Miroku while nuancing the Buddhist divinity Miroku (Maitreaya) and the folk beliefs associated with it. *Dōgyō,* literally "same practice," is a term used in other cult and pilgrimage situations, such as the Daishikō venerating Kōbō Daishi, to indicate a fellow ascetic or fellow pilgrim.[5] Takada and his group vowed to build in Edo a miniature

Fuji (*fujizuka*, literally "Fuji mound") for the thirty-third death anniversary of Jiki-gyō Miroku. Completed in 1779, this was the first of the miniature Fujis that soon dotted the landscape of Edo and neighboring regions. These mini-Fujis are treated in the next chapter, but worth noting here are the close interconnections among the increase in the number of commoner Fuji pilgrims, the formation of Fuji confraternities, and the construction of Fuji mounds.

After the death of Takada, this group changed its name from Miroku Dōgyō to Marutōkō. (The group continues to the present time and will be described later.) From this point in the late eighteenth century and into the next century, Fuji confraternities became quite large and powerful. Their fame was the stuff of legend, enshrined in the well-known phrase "the eight hundred and eight *kō* and eighty-thousand members." The numbers are figurative rather than literal. Over a hundred *kō* are documented, and there may have been as many as three hundred or more, counting the branch *kō* as well as the main *kō*.[6] The first public mention of Fujikō, unfortunately, was the government's 1795 notice suppressing the burgeoning movements, reinforcing an earlier notice against the same people and groups (but not using the term *kō*). The shogun's concern was the rapid rise of such large and widespread groups and the power they represented: from the authorities' viewpoint, "the worst thing about the cult was that the devotees were all workmen, day laborers, small tradesmen, etc., and that they mingled on terms of equality with the few warrior-class people who joined them. In all this the authorities detected potential subversion" (Tyler 1981, 157). The complaint was not against individual belief and practice but rather against performing rites (such as *kaji kitō*) for others, which the government saw as a dangerous practice because it led to the formation of large groups (Inobe 1928b, 216–20). No other folk religion was persecuted the way Fujikō was (Iwashina 1983, 351). The ban on such organizations attempted to suppress most of the ritual and magical practices associated with Fuji asceticism and Fuji faith, and the shogunate called in for questioning the representatives of Fujikō and Fujidō.

There were a dozen investigations of Fuji groups within a hundred years, eight resulting in bans. Just as the various leaders, groups, and individual members of these groups had difficulty selecting a standard set of beliefs and practices from the panoply of Fuji spirituality, so too did the authorities have difficulty in detailing their complaint.[7] A carryover from the early Tokugawa era persecution of Christians led to the government suspicion that these potentially subversive groups might be Kirishitan, a charge the Fujikō groups vigorously denied, proclaiming their Fuji-centric faith (Iwashina 1983, 303; Tyler 1984, 111).[8] The numerical size and geographical dissemination of Fujikō (like Fujidō) made all these groups the targets of government scrutiny, but the government's actions had little effect on the popular Fuji movements: just as the Tokugawa-era bans and restrictions on travel did not prevent people from engaging in tourism in ever larger numbers, the Tokugawa ban and limitations on Fujikō and Fujidō could not hinder their expansion and practices.

The confraternities reached their apex of expansion and activities during the early and mid–nineteenth century.

In the latter decades of the nineteenth century, following the Meiji Restoration of 1868, Fujikō suffered a number of telling blows. Its ancestral tradition, Shugendō, was disbanded by the new government because it was an admixture of Shinto and Buddhism, and Fujikō suffered under the burden of the same religious miscegenation (in the eyes of the government). The Meiji government's artificial split of Shinto and Buddhism also sundered much of Fuji's heritage. In the early Meiji persecution of Buddhism (Ketelaar 1990), many of the artifacts of the Fuji tradition were destroyed, moved, or lost. Still, many Fujikō survived until World War II, when the bombing of Tokyo and surrounding areas demolished not only the buildings but also the neighborhoods on which Fujikō depended. In postwar times a few kō have carried on, but they have few younger members, and the future of Fujikō is uncertain.

FUJIKŌ: PILGRIMAGE TO THE MOUNTAIN

Kō were of two major types: village-wide associations, to which every household belonged; and proxy groups, which were voluntary organizations (Iwashina 1983, 243). Fujikō are of the proxy type. People sharing a common belief in Fuji (among a host of other affirmations) formed a group, held occasional or regular meetings, and contributed (or pooled) money so that every year some of the group, the proxies, would receive the amount needed to make the pilgrimage to Fuji. For confraternity members, these funds, which covered lodging and meals along the way, fees on the mountain, and enough for purchasing amulets at Fuji (and other sites), were distributed upon the proxies' return. Some Fujikō (and other kō) were organized for a set number of years, long enough for each member to have a turn as proxy (Iwashina 1983, 243–44). Especially in Edo the Fujikō developed as strong neighborhood associations with permanent status. Some Fujikō were large and prosperous, becoming the "main confraternity" that spawned "branch confraternities."

Fujikō have been lay groups with simple and straightforward organization. The main officers are the head (kōmoto), the religious leader (sendatsu), assistants (sewanin), and the general members (dōja) (Inobe 1928b, 180–81). The head had to be rather well off financially since usually he bore much of the expense of meetings, which might be at his home. The leaders were in charge of religious instruction as well as guiding the group on pilgrimages to the mountain; to become sendatsu one had to make a number of ascents of Fuji. The assistants, in the absence of an ecclesiastical structure, took care of business matters. These offices could be expanded as the need arose. In the case of a main confraternity and branch confraternity, the leader of the former was daisendatsu (big or great leader), and the leader of the latter was kosendatsu (small or minor leader). The genius of these groups was their lay status, informal organization, neighborhood networking, and face-to-face contacts. The success of the Jikigyō Miroku line of Fujikō is largely owing to the presence of charismatic *sendatsu*, who were capable of softening the harsh teaching of Jikigyō to appeal to common people and adept at guiding them effectively on pilgrimages and ministering to their religious needs during the year through *kō* meetings (Iwashina 1983, 274).

Lumping together all Fujikō does a grave disservice to the concrete texture and dynamic vitality of these groups; in their own eyes they were quite different. Their individuality is borne out in the richness of their attractive crests or "confraternity marks," some of the most colorful identifying features of the Fujikō. Each *kō* created and proudly displayed its unique mark or crest on its *kō* flags and on its members' sedge hats; at some of the huts or climbing "stations" on the slopes of Fuji these flags were deposited as evidence of the passage of such groups. In 1842 a *kō* leader created a "one hundred and eight *kō* crest mandala": ninety-three from within Edo and fifteen from outside Edo.[9] Like the crests for warriors, aristocrats, and tradesmen, the *kō* crests embodied fine aesthetic taste. Within the currents of Tokugawa urban and popular culture, the use of distinctive crests by members of these confraternities (who mostly belonged to the lower levels of society) laid claim to some of the same status displayed by aristocrats and warriors.

Kō crests too were replete with symbolic meaning, each containing hidden, sometimes "inside" expressions of the complex symbolism associated with the sacred mountain. Several examples illustrate these marks and their significance. They come in two main types: the "mountain-shape," featuring the Sino-Japanese character for mountain (pronounced *yama* or *san*), with another character below it; and the "circle-shape," a single Sino-Japanese character inside a circle (pronounced *maru*). Maru-ichi (the character "one" enclosed by a circle) means "Nippon one"—in other words, "Japan first." Maru-fuji (the character *fuji* enclosed by a circle) means "Mount Fuji." Yama-hana (the two characters for mountain-flower), Maru-hana (the character *hana* enclosed by a circle), and Yama-sakura (the two characters for mountain cherry) all refer to Konohana Sakuya hime (the female *kami* associated with Fuji). San-san (the two characters for mountain-three) and Maru-san (the character "mountain" enclosed by a circle) are shorthand for the sacred phrase Sanmyōtō Kaizan, found in Kakugyō's *minuki* style of mandala. A branch *kō* used the crest of the main *kō* and added a character or two as its distinguishing mark (Inobe 1928b, 175–79). The use of the *kō* mark on flags and sedge hats (and later on the *hachimaki* or headband) lent the members a sense of group solidarity while giving the individual a badge of identity. Having an item bearing an artistically pleasing mark with an "inside" meaning was part of the pleasurable experience of belonging to a confraternity.

While on pilgrimages confraternity members not only sported their crests but also wore special outfits, clearly a continuation of the style of *yamabushi* (Shugendō) dress. From Muromachi times there are records of distinctive dress for the people on their ascent of Fuji, especially white cotton clothing, cotton surplices,[10] and round straw or sedge hats. By Tokugawa times the costumes included most of the Buddhist/ Shugendō paraphernalia, such as bells, rosaries, and the eight-sided "diamond stick." The diamond stick, originally a Buddhist ritual tool, became one of the favorite souvenir items of later pilgrims and tourists, who used it both as a walking stick and as a blessed memory of their trip by virtue of the various brands burned into the stick as they passed through the "stations" of the climb.

The clothing of a pilgrim was white only before he climbed the mountain and visited religious institutions, most of which had a red clay seal for imprinting the name of the temple/shrine and a blessing. Such stamps could cost a considerable sum, especially at the summit of Fuji, but the paintings and photographs of earlier times, as well as the sight of contemporary pilgrims, show that pilgrims spent freely on such visual blessings. These stamps were considered very sacred because the red clay mixed with oil for the stamps came from holy sites on the mountain. In earlier times the red clay of Hitoana was highly prized; to this day the amulets and stamp of the Shinto shrine at the cave called "Womb" (Tainai) are still favored, especially for protection during childbirth. The clothes themselves were sanctified both by having been worn on pilgrimage to a holy site and by having received stamps of blessings. No matter how dirty they became on the trip, they were never washed. On the contrary, the clothes were "pure," and even if they appeared stained and worn, a person had to purify himself[11] before donning them. This description of the Jikigyō Miroku style of pilgrim is the form usually associated with Fuji pilgrimage. The Fuji *gyōja* had their stricter form of (mainly Buddhist-derived) Shugendō regulations and dress, and they even maintained their ascetic tradition by observing a period of abstinence prior to pilgrimage that included a "separate fire"—in other words, food cooked on a fire separate from (impure) women. By contrast the members of Fujidō rejected the use of ritual tools such as rosaries and bells on their pilgrimages, just as they did not ascribe to the efficacy of the rituals themselves and the attendant gender disparity that defined women as impure (Inobe 1928b, 263–71, 61).

In Tokugawa times commoners gained access to limited travel, although it remained difficult, expensive, and sometimes dangerous. The main clientele for Fuji pilgrimage were wealthy farmers from the countryside and merchants from Edo; some samurai and individuals not belonging to *kō* apparently participated because of the ancient fame of the mountain and their individual beliefs. For the majority of Fuji pilgrims, both farmers and merchants, the confraternity was the group that helped spread and kindle faith in Fuji and also made possible the social and economic support for the trip.

The activities of Fujikō fall into the two convenient categories of the pilgrimage during the summer climbing season and the (usually monthly) meetings during the rest of the year (to be described in the next chapter). During Tokugawa times almost every aspect of Fuji pilgrimage was highly controlled, much different from the freedom of movement of contemporary tourism. Even the season of climbing

This sketch of pilgrimage dress shows, on the left, a Fuji *gyōja* and, on the right, a pilgrim's clothing. Note the *kesa* (surplice) around the neck, the diamond stick in the right hand, and the bell in the hand or hung at the waist. The pilgrim facing the viewer has a crest featuring the three-domed Fuji as part of his confraternity's crest; the man facing away has the characters *dōgyō* (pilgrim) on his hat. Reproduced with the permission of Kokon Shoin was restricted: Fuji was open for pilgrimage only for about two months, marked by an official "mountain-opening"on the first day of the sixth month and ended with a "mountain-closing"on the twenty-seventh day of the seventh month.[12] In Edo the "mountain-opening" was ritually inaugurated at the miniature Fujis; the entrances of various routes up the mountain, such as Yoshida, held their rites too. Each Fujikō had considerable latitude in selecting its own dates within the climbing season for ascent and in setting its route to the mountain, including stops at any number of shrines, temples, famous places, inns, and restaurants. Because the main mode of travel on the highway was walking, the trip took considerable time.

Preparation for the pilgrimage to and ascent of Fuji involved a number of forms of purification. Murayama Shugendō observed a rather strict form of abstinence including even a "separate fire" for cooking food, and such practices were not unusual for mountain austerities. Although other groups were less strict than Shugendō organizations, some form of purification was required to usher the ordinary or impure person into the extraordinary, holy realm of Fuji—an idea universally accepted by the various kō. The purification and abstinence could last as long as a hundred days or as few as seven days prior to pilgrimage (Inobe 1928a, 322–24). In the Ise area a seven-day set of "Fuji purifications" (fujigori) was observed by those who were unable to make the pilgrimage; these purifications were handled by leaders and required a fee. An interesting aspect of the Ise tradition is that these rites became an end in themselves rather than a preliminary to the ascent; these customs of the Kansai area were distinctively different from the Kantō practices following Jikigyō Miroku (typified in Fujikō) (Iwashina 1983, 36, 39). The Fujikō of Edo, in the Jikigyō Miroku line, observed their own purification of so many days or weeks prior to the departure, which included following a vegetarian diet. As with other pilgrimage associations, Fujikō too had a ritual send-off of their proxies. For the Fujikō of Edo, this meant a confraternity meeting soliciting the favor of Fuji and its host of divinities for the pilgrimage; the confraternity meetings feature a remarkable fire rite. The Fujikō still active today perform this rite to send off their members, in the process burning prayer papers in the fire and passing items of clothing and packs through the fire and smoke as a purification and blessing.

Pilgrimage to sacred mountains has long been recognized as a conspicuous dimension of Japanese folk religion.[13] Some pilgrims made their way to one of the headquarters of Shugendō at many mountains or at sites such as Ontake. There were also circuits of mountains, such as the "three-mountain meditation" of traveling to and ascending the three mountains of Tateyama, Hakusan, and Fuji (Iwashina 1983, 25), a trip that took about thirty-five days. Probably no more than one hundred a year made it in Tokugawa times, but in 1680, a propitious (kanoe saru or "monkey") year in the sexagenarian cycle when restrictions were relaxed for both purification and women, 350 circled these three sacred mountains.

Pilgrims to Fuji came from all directions and began the ascent from various entrances. The focus here is primarily on the Fujikō from Edo, who came from a northerly direction and arrived at the north side of Fuji, the Yoshida entrance. On the round trip there were many variations, even for these Fujikō, but two essentials were the "before" Fuji and "after" Fuji stops of Takaosan and Ōyama[14] (Iwashina 1983, 400–407). From Edo to Takaosan there were two routes, both called the "Fuji Highway" (Fuji Kaidō). Takaosan (Mount Takao) at 1,968 feet is not a lofty peak, but it has been worshipped since ancient times and is home to both Buddhist and Shugendō traditions. Its location just to the west of Edo (in present-day Hachiōji) made it a natural "before" or starting point for the trip to Fuji. At Takaosan behind the Buddhist temple Yakuōin is an old Sengen shrine where pilgrims paid their respects. From Takaosan the pilgrims proceeded through the "Small Buddha Pass" (Kobotoke Tōge) and on to the Kōshū Kaidō (the Kōshū Highway), and after other stops they arrived at Yoshida, the northern entrance to Fuji. All pilgrims passed through a special torii that also served as an inspection station, where every pilgrim paid an entrance fee. The leaders of Fujikō made prearrangements with guides (*oshi*), who ran their own lodging houses, to stay the night at the foot of Fuji in this facility. The *oshi* and the pilgrims (and their confraternity) had a kind of parish relationship, which usually extended beyond the pilgrimage season.[15] In reverse direction the *oshi* would travel to the area of his parishioners and distribute amulets and possibly also perform rituals for them; some *oshi* paid only one annual visit to their parish, while others performed spring and fall visits. Each lodging house had its own source of running water (sometimes specially constructed) for the pilgrims to engage in yet another purification. Before ascending the mountain the pilgrims visited a Sengen shrine for a purification ceremony, and they then climbed the mountain by following a narrow trail mostly of volcanic ash and rock. Traditional pilgrims who walked could advance only one "station" a day on the various highways; their time on the road depended on such variables as how many shrines, temples, and scenic sites they included in their itinerary; how long they tarried; and especially how much leisure and money they had to expend on the trip.[16]

This overview of pilgrimage starts from Edo and ends at Fuji via the Yoshida entrance, but the popularity of the mountain led to the opening of a number of entrances. Inobe (1928a, 197) provides a convenient overview of the entrances and the geographic origins of their visitors:

Entrance	Origin of pilgrims
Ōmiya (and Murayama)	Kantō
Suyama	Tōkaidō
Subashiri	Kantō
Yoshida	Kantō and northern Japan
Kawaguchi	Kōshū and Shinshū

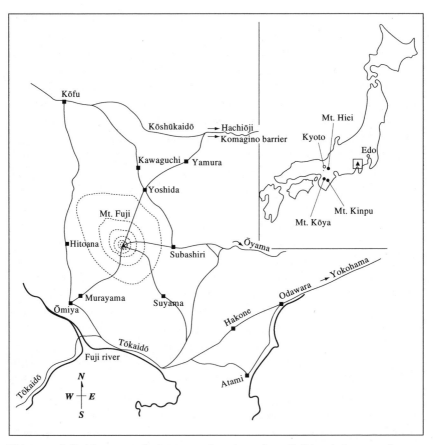

This map of climbing routes during premodern times shows Fuji in relation to major
highways (*kaidō*) and its location within Honshū. (See also the map of "Pilgrimage
Routes to Ōyama," which includes the nearby Mount Fuji, in Ambros 2008, 149.)
From Miyazaki 2005, 345; reproduced with the permission of *Monumenta Nipponica*
and Umezawa Fumiko

Three types of lodging held for these entrances: at Ōmiya pilgrims stayed at
shrines supervised by shrine priests; for Murayama, at Shugendō temples overseen
by *yamabushi*; and for Suyama, Subashiri, Yoshida, and Kawaguchi, at lodgings handled by guides (*oshi*). In addition just as Ōyama once outranked Fuji in popularity
before it became a post-Fuji visit, so too the fortunes of the various entrances vacil-
lated. Subashiri is the oldest entrance; from the sixteenth century there were many
sendatsu, lodgings, and guides (Inobe 1928a, 197). The Suyama entrance fell into disuse when its climbing route was destroyed by the 1707 Hōei eruption (on the side
of Fuji); later efforts to restore it were short lived, and this route fell into disuse.

Suyama, whose name is forgotten today, was once more prosperous than Ōmiya, Murayama, and Subashiri.

Exact figures for the number of annual pilgrims from each of these routes are difficult to reconstruct; a 1625 record of Murayama Shugendō's three main temples indicates about 900 pilgrims for the year; in 1624 (a lucky or auspicious "monkey year") there were about 5,000 pilgrims. For the most flourishing period of the 1800s, the average number of annual pilgrims was 1,450 for Suyama, 700 to 800 for Subashiri, and about 8,000 for Yoshida (Inobe 1928a, 32). For Murayama Shugen, 400 to 500 pilgrims climbed at the end of the eighteenth century and 2,000 climbed in a monkey year from that era. A record from the twenty-sixth day of the ninth (lunar) month in 1680 reports that 140 pilgrims were on the summit of Fuji to view and worship the moon (Iwashina 1983, 23–24). "In the early nineteenth century more than ten thousand pilgrims visited Mt. Fuji during the few months of the summer climbing season"; "No other mountain attracted such a large number of pilgrims" (Miyazaki 2005, 339). These relatively low figures count those who went solely or mainly for religious purposes; the huge numbers who climbed the mountain in recent years did so for a variety of recreational, tourist, and sightseeing intentions more than for spiritual fulfillment.

For Yoshida there are better records, especially for the number of *oshi* houses or lodgings for pilgrims there from 1572. Starting with 81 *oshi* houses in 1572, the number stays in the range of the 80s until 1775, when it drops to 60. It climbs again into the 80s and peaks at 100 in 1872 but then drops precipitously to 45 in the late 1800s and early 1900s. The number is down to 24 in 1939 and drops to a low of 12 in 1967. These figures give some numerical indication of the height of Fujikō fortunes in Tokugawa times, the blow to these organizations by the suppression of Buddhism and the disbanding of Shugendō in the early Meiji period, and the rapid decline of Fujikō in postwar times.[17] The existing lodging houses in Yoshida today cater mostly to individual tourists and tour groups such as schools. In modern times the opening of railroads favored those entrances close to train stations and greatly increased the number of annual visitors. The Subaru Line (completed in 1964 just before the Olympics in Tokyo), a highway to the fifth station of Fuji, transformed Fuji pilgrimage: a charter bus trip to this halfway point, a hike to a prearranged lodging near the seventh or eighth station, a light meal and a few hours sleep, an early morning final ascent to the summit to greet the rising sun, and the return trip to the waiting bus at the fifth station. This enabled travelers from Tokyo to easily make the round trip in two days, something unheard of before.

Fuji, like other sacred mountains in Japan, is divided into ten stations (*go*), and every climbing entrance leads to ten stations. The entrance is the first station (Ichigo), the next is the second station (Nigo), and so on, but the summit is not called the tenth station. A document from Murayama Shugendō from the Kan'ei era (1624–44) mentions one through nine *sō* (stairs or courses), the first recorded division of the climbing route into ten stages (which were later called *go*) (Iwashina 1929, 260). The stations had shrines and tea huts, and some had room for cramped overnight sleeping. Pilgrims might pay their respects at shrines along the way, purchase amulets, or have their "diamond sticks" branded with the mark of a station. Some of the hardier pilgrims would undertake the "middle-path circling," winding around the circumference of Fuji at about the fifth station. Iwashina cites figures for 1816 indicating that about ten thousand climbed from the Yoshida entrance, when only a hundred completed the middle path route—which, like everything else, required a fee, one benefit of which was a stamp certifying completion. A diamond stick carried while making the "round" or circumambulation of Fuji was taken home and used to push in a child's protruding navel to make it get better (Inobe 1928b, 283).

In late Tokugawa times during the repeated suppression of Fujidō and Fujikō, the government destroyed a Kakugyō shrine within the precincts of the Yoshida Sengen Shrine, a Mirokudō (a hall or chapel for Jikigyō Miroku) at the seventh station of the Yoshida entrance, and a stone monument at Hitoana.[18] Prior to this time pilgrims could venerate Kakugyō at the Yoshida Sengen Shrine before climbing and pay their respects to Jikigyō at the seventh station. Climbing was considered an ascetic practice, and as they ascended, many recited verses such as "purification of the six senses" (a Buddhist phrase adopted by Shugendō practitioners) to the accompaniment of the bells hung from their sashes.

In the Japanese literature on Fuji, the ban on women climbing Fuji is often mentioned when describing the ten stations since the first station (Ichigo) or second station (Nigo) is where women were turned back. A sign dating from late Edo times at Yoshida's second station announces, *nyonin zenjō oitate,* female ascent forbidden (or turned back).[19] Commentators note that this prohibition at Fuji was not unusual; in Edo times women were not allowed to climb any sacred mountains (Iwashina 1983, 164). Such restrictions existed in an age when even women considered themselves impure (Inobe 1928b, 326). As early as the tenth century at the Shugendō mountain Ōmine, females were excluded because this sacred mountain was where men sought a place free from women to cut off their own passion or desire.[20] Two different rationales were offered for prohibiting women on sacred mountains: first, the area was reserved for male ascetics seeking a mountain refuge free of women in order to pursue their practice free from the carnal desire stimulated by females; second, women were considered intrinsically impure, mainly because of menstrual blood.[21] Fuji is exceptional, not in the prohibition against women but in the periodic lifting of this ban and the attempt by Fujidō to do away with it permanently.

By contrast, Kumano pilgrimage is noted for its openness to women: "no other temple-shrine complex of the premodern era had such a high percentage of female pilgrims" (Moerman 2005, 182–83), but participation in pilgrimage did not automatically qualify women for equality. In fact the theme of women's impurity and inferiority was so central to this pilgrimage pattern that their presence in this activity reinforced the premises of their lowly status. Women participated in this pilgrimage to transform their lives and bodies ritually, but in the process they implicitly accepted the principle of their impurity and inferiority. "As the headquarters of women who preached to women the terms of their iniquity, the place of women's religious freedom was also, paradoxically, the place of their bondage" (Moerman 2005, 231). Some Fuji groups, notably Fujidō, argued that because women were inherently pure they should have equal access to Mount Fuji. Local variations in beliefs and practices and inconsistencies in both enforcing the strictures against women and permitting the various allowed practices at sacred sites such as Fuji present a complex picture of the attitudes toward and actual roles of women. As seen at Kumano, the mere fact of female access to sacred sites does not necessarily imply gender equality; and at Fuji, where a variety of beliefs and practices of exclusion existed, some voices spoke for equal ritual participation by women (Miyazaki 2005).

Jikigyō Miroku and his followers argued for greater equality of men and women: "At the summit of Fuji the rope of men and the rope of women are joined"; Jikigyō boldly claimed that even menstruating women were not impure and could offer prayers to Sengen (Iwashina 1983, 166). Feminist and more "democratic" observers today may point out several logical missteps, especially the contradiction of labeling women and menstruation impure, when all people, male and female, are born of women. Historically most Japanese sacred mountains displayed a pattern similar to Fuji, having as their main deity a female *kami*, while excluding human females as impure.[22] The cave on Fuji called Tainai (Womb) was revered and entered as a sacred practice, while a female body with an actual womb was not fit for climbing the sacred mountain.

Even within the prevailing worldview and customs, during the "monkey year" that occurred every sixty years in the sexagenarian Chinese calendar, women were allowed to climb Fuji, but some *oshi* would not lead them and some entrances would not accept them (Iwashina 1983, 439). Other restrictions were also lifted, including lengthy purification prior to climbing, although some minimal purification was observed. Fuji was closely linked to Kōshin or "monkey" faith. A folk legend attributes this connection to Fuji (which in ancient times was always shrouded in mist) first having appeared for viewing in the monkey year. This folk explanation hardly accounts for the close interplay between Fuji faith and the Kōshin cult; nevertheless, during the monkey year many women, and more men than usual, climbed Fuji (Tyler 1993, 259–60).

For pilgrims the ideal of reaching the summit was (and still is today) to stay at a lodging on the slope of the mountain and get some sleep in the early evening, arise in the dark of the early morning, and arrive at the top (or at least at the eighth station) to greet the rising sun. Worship of the rising sun at the summit was thought to enable the viewers to see the forms of the three Buddhist divinities Amida, Kannon, and Seishi within the sunrise.[23] No pilgrim who scaled Fuji would miss visiting the

Sengen shrine at the summit to pray there and either purchase an amulet or have the shrine's stamp imprinted on his white costume.

All pilgrims did the practice known as circling the crater.[24] The rim of Fuji's crater was likened to the eight petals of a lotus and endowed with a host of Buddhist divinities. The crater, known as the inner sanctum, was thought to be the dwelling place of Sengen Daimyōjin and the location of heaven, among other beliefs. Offerings were thrown into the crater. Among the most important of the manifold holy places within the crater were the two springs Kinmeisui and Ginmeisui, silver water and gold water. From the earliest days of Fujikō this highly valued water, called prayer water, was taken in bamboo containers back to Edo, to be used in prayers and healing.

Two requisite holy sites for visitors to the mountain were Hitoana and Tainai. Hitoana was famous from ancient times as the residing place of Sengen Daibosatsu and as a dangerous cave containing both heaven and hell—where Kakugyō performed his "tiptoe" asceticism. This earlier tradition of Hitoana as a mysterious place lived on within the Fujikō practices. Pilgrims could perform asceticism within Hitoana and could worship statues such as Dainichi (which were removed at the time of the suppression of Fujikō, apparently restored, and then destroyed in the persecution of Buddhism in early Meiji times—along with a "confinement hall") (Inobe 1928b, 307–9). The red clay of Hitoana, used like ink for stamping pilgrim's robes, was also taken home for use in healing. The sand of Fuji was thought to be good as a protective device for warding off fire, and a special flower growing on Fuji was good for easy childbirth. Pilgrims entering Kakugyō's sacred cave and at least performing a token ascetic practice after the fashion of the founder could then exit it and pay their respects at Kakugyō's memorial stone.

In the Fujikō tradition, Hitoana was immortalized first by the revelation to Kakugyō that he should practice there, and then by the divine message and *minuki* bequeathed to him while he performed asceticism in the cave. By contrast, while the cave known as Tainai (Womb) has no such illustrious precedent, an amazing accumulation of lore surrounds and inhabits it. On this volcanic peak are hundreds of caves similar to the Tainai, but tradition has singled this one out as the mother of all caves at Fuji.[25] The name of Tainai, or Womb, is quite literal, for the whole cave is likened to a womb. The symbolism applied to the cave is multivalent, for this terrestrial cavity is considered at the same time to be the birthplace of Sengen Myōjin and the place of appearance of Sengen Daibosatsu, and also a human womb with associated anatomical parts. One rock is called navel cord; another large rock is labeled the placenta. The protuberances hanging down from the roof of the cave, like stalactites, are called breasts, and the water dripping from them is milk. (See plate 4.) The ceiling of the large cavern of Hitoana allows those who enter to stand; by contrast, the Tainai is quite low, such that in earlier times the pilgrims put straw sandals on their knees to crawl through some parts of the cave. The candles used to light their way were thought to have miraculous power during childbirth. Pilgrims took them home and saved them for use when family members gave birth; the claim was that a short candle was the best, aiding in a short labor and quick delivery. While a person was crawling through the cave, a white cotton cord was used to hold up one's sleeves; this cord, a "womb purification," was taken back to serve as a pregnant woman's "belly band." Such belly bands with religious blessings for pregnant women have long been in use in Japan; noteworthy here is the "natural" blessing/protection emerging from the womb of the mountain. While pilgrims were in the Tainai they also used this cord to catch and dry the "milk" dripping down from the pendant rock breasts. In addition these cords were used for women in labor or new mothers with little or no breast milk; the cord (which may have been used as a belly band) was placed in water, which the mother drank, aiding in delivery or assuring abundant milk. In general the Tainai customs and beliefs originate with the folk traditions connecting Konohana Sakuya hime to the mountain and to Sengen Daimyōjin (Inobe 1928b, 293–97).

Each Fujikō had its own pattern for descending the mountain: some insisted that the descent follow the same route as the ascent, so as not to "split" the mountain, while others followed an alternate path and departed the mountain via a different point than their entry. Leaving Fuji, many pilgrims took the opportunity to visit Enoshima, a scenic island in Sagami Bay near Kamakura. Enoshima shrine has been a popular place of worship since Kamakura times. The proximity of Enoshima to the city of Kamakura, with its famous shrines and numerous temples, made both logical and convenient stopping places for returning pilgrims. Just as Takaosan was practically a mandatory "before" Fuji visit, so Ōyama became a necessary "after" Fuji stop. Ōyama, a mountain 4,088 feet in height, was well known for its temple-shrine complex, especially a Shingon temple and Sekison shrine (later Aburi shrine). The pilgrims paid respects at this shrine and then descended to worship the Ōyama Fudō before going on their way; some visited *oshi* (guides), who were abundant around Ōyama.[26] Although in Edo times Ōyama was relegated to a kind of afterthought of pilgrimage to Fuji, faith in Ōyama as a site of pilgrimage and purification preceded such practices at Fuji. The antiquity and depth of Ōyama faith is such that, even when Ōyama was outstripped by the popularity of Fuji, failing to visit Ōyama after Fuji became a proscribed custom that was called a "half-pilgrimage" (Iwashina 1983, 396–400).

Another good example of the complexity and multivalence of Fuji pilgrimage is found in the lakes surrounding Fuji and pilgrimage to these lakes for the purpose of purification. Indeed, Kakugyō, although practicing austerities within Hitoana, was so assiduous in performing ablutions and purifications in the surrounding lakes (where he received many of his charms or *fusegi*) that he has been called a "water *gyōja*" (Iwashina 1983, 57–59). Just as stones were placed along the route commemorating thirty-three ascents of Fuji, so were there stones around the lake marking

thirty-three rounds for the eight lakes around Fuji. Kawaguchi was the entrance closest to the lakes; while quite important in earlier times, it was eventually eclipsed by
the popularity of other entrances for climbing Fuji.

Although individuals went on pilgrimages as proxies for other members of the
confraternity, the many Fujikō and the families of the individuals also were indirect
but active participants in the process. The pilgrimage association might have a regular meeting or at least a "send-off prayer" to mark the departure of the proxies.
During their absence family members offered candles and daily prayers before the
household shrine. Some Fujikō also prayed for proxies during their pilgrimages. *Kō*
members anticipated their pilgrims' homecoming, meeting them with torches in
Tokugawa times and greeting them at railway stations in more recent times. Depending on the confraternity's customs, the returnees might reciprocate with a "prayer"
at each member's home. The send-off at the start of the pilgrimage was rather simple, but the homecoming or thanksgiving was more elaborate, usually with food and
drink for the confraternity. A highlight was the pilgrims' distribution of amulets
(especially from Sengen shrines) obtained on the trip to those who had not made
the journey (Iwashina 1983, 264–65). Fuji pilgrimage ended where it began, in Edo
at the confraternity meeting.

8

Miniature Fuji

The Mountain Comes to the People

FUJIKŌ: ENSHRINING THE MOUNTAIN

Pilgrimage involves movement of people, typically from home/village and profane space to center/temple and sacred space (Turner and Turner 1995). During the Tokugawa period and the rise of a "culture of movement," the dynamic of pilgrimage as travel for religious purposes became more popular, more widespread, and much more conspicuous. The confraternity's sending off and boundary greeting (and/or thanks ceremony) signaled the crossing from the ordinary world to an extraordinary space, and return therefrom. However, at Fuji, as at any sacred mountain in Japan, and in most religious settings, this round-trip route of pilgrimage was only one aspect of a complex pattern of images and actions as well as movements.[1]

Pilgrimage also is an elaborate process encompassing the passage of symbols and the travel of ideas. This pattern of beliefs, symbols, activities, and rituals is prefigured in the legendary experiences of Shōtoku Taishi and En no Gyōja, whose flights to and over Fuji transported them beyond the physical terrain to a mystical sphere and ascetic retreat: an Indian Buddhist peak paired with a Chinese Taoist height, superimposed on a Japanese sacred mountain. From ancient times Fuji's image has reflected the arrival of cultural and religious notions from other lands and their interaction with Japanese customs. Fuji pilgrimage also engendered the construction of physical replicas as well as the creation of homologies (utilizing both material entities and spiritual realities). The marriage of the foreign spirituality of Buddhism with the native divinities of Japan is honored in the tale of Matsudai Shōnin, the pioneer of Fuji faith, who pondered how Dainichi, a (Buddhist) male form, could be manifested at Fuji in the female form of Asama Daimyōjin. The revelation to

Matsudai of the buried crystal image of Fuji is an important precedent for the mountain presenting itself in miniaturized sacred form and coming to the people. The symbolism of Fuji is an interesting example of the permutation of a native sacred mountain into an intricate national and, eventually, cosmopolitan worldview.

Matsudai practiced asceticism *on* the mountain, which enabled him to remove a likeness of Fuji *out of* the mountain. His successor Kakugyō actually went *inside* the mountain, entering the cave Hitoana, and from this point the symbolic representations of Fuji became a mosaic of overlapping images. Fuji, one among many sacred mountains, was transformed into the pillar of Japan and source of both creation and deities. Kakugyō, by entering Fuji, was identified with this pillar (and with Sengen), and the pillar in turn entered Kakugyō. This enabled Kakugyō to extract from his body *minuki* as the essence of Fuji in the form of a mountain mandala; this stylized diagram captured the power of Fuji both in Sino-Japanese characters expressing the visual shape of the mountain and in written and spoken magical phrases invoking its spiritual blessing. Then Jikigyō, and his spiritual heirs within Fujidō, elaborated and internalized Fuji the cosmic mountain as an ethical source for self-cultivation, emphasizing the inner piety or heart of the message rather than its external trappings. Jikigyō's act of self-sacrifice on the slopes of Fuji made possible the coming of the age of Miroku and Fuji-centered life for the people. A number of deities in a variety of forms and under various names have graced the mountain, but in Tokugawa times Sengen/Konohana Sakuya was the goddess tantamount to a patron deity for Fuji.

The relationship of Fuji pilgrimage to the Fuji confraternities has been sequential, causal, and interactive. Fuji pilgrimage preceded the confraternities and was responsible in large part for the rise of these groups, and then the two formed a symbiotic tie. A major difference distinguishes the act of human pilgrimage, when people come to the mountain, from the event of the epiphany of Fuji, when the mountain comes to people: human pilgrimage is seasonal and occasional (and for some, a once in a lifetime experience), while the mountain's appearance to people makes it permanently present and perennially accessible. Climbing Fuji as a tandem act of pilgrimage and worship is limited to relatively few people during a rather brief span of the year; the Fujikō, by enshrining Fuji as their object of worship, make its power immediately available to anyone at almost any time, with little expenditure of energy, time, and funds.

Japanese scholars have defined Fujikō as "groups of people sharing faith in Fuji." This definition is paraphrased and amended here as "groups of people who enshrine models of Fuji as an object of worship." Although these groups were not completely uniform in belief and practice, they shared some essential features, especially their object of worship and the manner of representing it. The centerpiece of the altar of most Fujikō meeting places was a stone replica of Fuji, harking back to the quartz miniature revealed to Matsudai and establishing Fuji as the focus of faith and ritual. Usually three hanging scrolls graced the altar: in the center a *minuki* and to the right and left Sengen (or Konohana Sakuya) and Komitake Gongen (the avatar of the peak or Fuji). This altar is a statement—and restatement—of the fact that Fuji (and its symbolic world) has moved to and made its appearance in the Edo meetings of Fujikō, for the purposes of being worshipped and providing blessings to the people.[2]

Gatherings of Fujikō were informal and occasional, usually in the home of the head of a confraternity, where one room housed the Fuji-centered altar. Departure for pilgrimage might call for a meeting, and the return of pilgrims always was celebrated with such a gathering. Other meeting times depended on the specific confraternity; the new year and the equinoxes were popular. Confraternities also observed January 17 as the founder Jikigyō's birthday and July 17 as the anniversary of his death. Most confraternities during their heyday observed a monthly meeting, the seventeenth being a favorite day. Confraternities might adopt a name from the day of the month when they assembled. Other popular days for meetings were the third, the thirteenth, and the twenty-sixth.[3]

In the Jikigyō Miroku line of confraternities, the meetings were known by the name of a fire ritual, or *takiage,* that marked the climax of the performance. Historically the *takiage,* literally "light (kindle)-offer," goes back to the *goma* or fire ritual of Shingon Buddhism, mediated by Shugendō's acceptance and practice of it. The distinctive external features of the *takiage* today are twofold: first, instead of the *goma* sticks or slats of wood used in Shingon and Shugendō, the Fujikō utilize small sticks of incense; second, the Shingon priests and *yamabushi* (Shugendō practitioners) stack wooden slats in a crisscross square lattice pattern, while Fujikō leaders pile up the sticks of incense almost vertically to construct a Fuji-shaped cone. In Buddhism the definition of *goma* ritual has multiple significance: "the act of burning firewood, grain, etc., as an offering to a deity in esoteric Buddhism, in order to achieve such objectives as stopping calamities and increasing merit . . . symbolizes the destruction by wisdom of evil passions and karma" and is understood as both an external (physical) and an internal (spiritual) rite (Inagaki 1988, 76). Fujikō apparently borrowed or appropriated these manifold significations of their fire ceremony as an offering to the deities of Fuji, as a means of bringing their members to "enlightenment," and also as a ritual technique to avail themselves of the extraordinary resources of the mountain. The ritual creation (or re-creation) of the sacred form of Fuji has its own power: from the earliest historical times when it frequently erupted, Fuji was feared and revered for the power of fire and water. The head and leaders of the confraternity place slips of written prayers in the fire; the flames emerging from the Fuji-shaped incense cone ignite the prayer slips, and the heat and smoke waft them, still burning, to the ceiling of the room, where they turn into ash.[4] These prayers in effect are offered to and consumed by the fire of Fuji. This is the same fire through which the confraternity leaders pass the items of clothing and packs taken on pilgrimage to the mountain.

Each confraternity has its own liturgy; the most commonly used name for this liturgy or scripture, especially in the Jikigyō Miroku line, is *Otsutae*, literally "the tradition" (or "what is handed down"). The oldest existing *Otsutae* in the Jikigyō Miroku line was written down by his disciple Tanabe Jūrōemon just three years after Jikigyō's death. In all of the Fuji lineages these writings were considered sacred texts, the holy phrases transmitted from Kakugyō; the tradition following Jikigyō Miroku is the belief that Jikigyō and his disciple Tanabe recited some of these passages three times just above the seventh station of Fuji (at the rock called Eboshi Iwa) while Jikigyō was confined in his small shrine and fasting to death. In all of the Fuji groups the *Otsutae* and their counterparts were liturgies because these texts were recited in Fuji gatherings even in the time before the rise of Fujikō, and then later they were the key element of Fujikō meetings. The collective memory of these groups is that even in Jikigyō Miroku's time people gathered and recited these phrases to Sengen Daibosatsu.

Iwashina used eight *Otsutae* from the period 1736–1874 for his analysis of the contents of these manuals, disclosing four major aspects corresponding to four phrases handed down from Kakugyō: 1) a form of purification; 2) devotional intention; 3) strengthening the body through the five forces (of traditional Chinese philosophy); 4) giving thanks for the aid of eating the five grains from the time of one's conception and birth (Iwashina 1983, 298). At the present time the *Otsutae* is recited more than read, intoned as a ritual text rather than uttered as a creed, but the performance clearly is a celebration of the power of Fuji and its host of deities such as Sengen. Fuji is in evidence everywhere, not only in many forms on the altar but also stamped on the white clothes of the members and printed on their headbands.

The performance of this ritual is powerful and impressive because of the skillful blending of recitation, group chanting and singing, fire, the ringing of bells, and the leader's use of Buddhist and other gestures. In the meetings of the Marutō Miyamotokō observed in 1988 and 1989, the head and leaders recited the almost hour-long performance from memory, while most members followed a written text. During the recitation the head and his helpers piled up the Fuji-shaped cone of incense and lit it (the actual *takiage*) and fed the prayer papers into the fire.

The *takiage* is a premodern multimedia performance in a holy setting. Its power and importance for Japanese participants are demonstrated by the fact that some of the remaining Fujikō gather monthly to recite the *Otsutae* and perform the *takiage* as a self-justifying end, not as a prelude or postlude for pilgrimage to Fuji. At one contemporary Fujikō's performance in Tokyo, an older member was asked how often the group climbed Fuji, and he evasively answered, "Not very often." Questioned about when he last climbed Fuji, he replied vaguely, "More than twenty years ago." This 1988 conversation took place in a time when air-conditioned tour buses could whisk a person from central Tokyo (especially from Shinjuku) to the fifth station of Fuji in several hours. Apparently some Fujikō members today value the rite of *takiage* more than the mountain or pilgrimage to it; the aging membership of these groups might hinder some from the ascent of Fuji. However, in the Jūshichiyakō's 1988 pilgrimage a seventy-five-year-old man scaled the mountain with no diffi-culty, never complaining and thoroughly enjoying the climb and the trip. News-paper accounts describe people in their nineties making the ascent.

The *Otsutae* is the heritage of Kakugyō and Jikigyō, a sacred text, a liturgy, and a performance—and more. From earlier days this document was seen to hold spe-cial powers apart from its literal, textual meaning. In Tokugawa times this work was copied by hand, when Fujikō members usually requested that a *sendatsu* or *oshi* write it out, so that the holy man's power would be conveyed to the liturgical book-let. One traditional use of the *Otsutae* was placing it on the body or using it to rub the body for healing.

The preceding discussion of Fujikō meetings has, necessarily, focused on its historical background and formal structure, but this may give a too-dry and too-serious impression of these gatherings. If the meetings of the late 1980s were anything like those of the previous centuries, they should be characterized not as solemn assemblies but as joyous get-togethers, lively neighborhood sessions. In previous times, apparently, the head and particularly the *sendatsu* used this opportunity to socialize with and minister to the needs of the members. In recent times the atmos-phere seems to be that of a club, with plenty of time for greetings before the meet-ing and general conversation afterward. The fact that Fujikō meetings contain a wealth of symbolic detail and ritual action does not prevent them from being lively and pleasant gatherings; after all, the people who go on pilgrimage to Fuji and com-bine spiritual business and pleasure are the same ones who come to Fujikō meetings and mix sanctity with sociability.

Fujikō are composed of the groups of people who have domesticated "wild" Fuji. If Fuji pilgrimage is Fuji-centric, then Fujikō meetings are Edo-centric or Tokyo-centric: as Edo became central to Japan and Fuji became Japan's central or "number one" sacred mountain, Fujikō arose primarily in Edo and the surrounding area but also arose in more distant regions. Conspicuous by their absence are Fujikō in other large cities such as Osaka and Kyoto, which have no counterpart to the "eight hun-dred and eight *kō* of Edo."

FUJIZUKA: CREATING MINIATURE FUJI

Fuji pilgrimage and Fuji confraternities are so closely intertwined that their appar-ently contradictory, yet actually complementary, themes are not obvious: Fuji pil-grimage is Fuji-centric, while confraternities are Edo-centric (or Kantō-centric). Fuji pilgrimage originated, and continues today, as an activity focused on the peak as a sacred mountain, emphasizing travel to and ascent of Fuji as a religious practice. In earlier times the people (usually men) who lived in the Kantō area and also some in outlying regions believed that if they did not make the trip to and up Fuji at least once, they could not bask in the blessing of Sengen Daibosatsu. Women were at a distinct disadvantage, limited to the lower reaches of the peak and free to attain the summit only once every sixty years. For males, though, the rule of thumb for Fuji pilgrimage seemed to be to climb as many times as possible. Some carefree pilgrims probably enjoyed the travel as much as the religious practice; yet for those persistent pilgrims who aspired to or actually merited stones commemorating thirty-three (or more) ascents, intense piety was the guiding principle of Fuji-centric pilgrimage oriented more toward religious realization than toward mere sightseeing.

The Fuji confraternities represent an obvious and significant shift from Fuji as a natural mountain that is sacred (a destination people occasionally visit) toward Fuji as a symbolic mountain that has come to the people (and permanently resides with them). Within Fujikō the emphasis switched to a mountain that was miniaturized and encapsulated in a replica symbolizing the power of the "natural" sacred mountain. The presence of the Fuji-shaped altarpiece in the home of the Fujikō head shows that the mountain became domesticated, literally made into a household item; but the prime example of how wild Fuji became domesticated Fuji is the construction by confraternities of *fujizuka*, "Fuji mounds." As these *fujizuka* were developed in and around Edo, the agency and action of Fuji spirituality were transformed once more. In Fuji pilgrimage people came to the mountain. Then in Fuji confraternities the mountain came to the people as a replica to be viewed and worshipped. However, the creation of *fujizuka* shifts initiative even more dramatically from the mountain to the people; the people bring the mountain to the city, not just to be viewed but also to be climbed and worshipped.[5] In fact the confraternities urbanized or "civilized" Fuji by re-creating or reconstructing it within Edo as *fujizuka*. Devotees of Fuji, not content with just one facsimile, built about sixty in Edo; counting those in nearby areas, about two hundred were constructed, all by Fujikō.[6] (See the woodblock print of a *fujizuka* and Mount Fuji in plate 5.)

The construction of the first *fujizuka* was proposed by Jikigyō Miroku's disciple Takada Fujishirō (whose religious name was Nichigyō Seizan). In 1765 he and his fellow followers of Jikigyō vowed to erect a monument of gratitude for their master. Their monument was a small hill on the grounds of an Inari shrine. Jikigyō's followers shared his anticlerical conviction against professional religionists, and they continued to practice their secular occupations. Takada happened to be a landscape gardener, enlisting several hundred fellow believers to help him with his major project. His was the first construction of a permanent mound as a miniature Fuji (Takeuchi 2002, 39, fig. 15)

There was the custom, dating from Kamakura times, of enshrining a form of Sengen (such as Sengen Daijin) at a small mountain called a *fujizuka*. This was not an actual copy of Fuji, and the only religious activity held there was worship of Sengen—as at other Sengen shrines (Takeuchi 2002, 39, fig. 14). In the ancient folk customs of venerating Fuji in the Ise Peninsula, the pilgrims who went by boat to

Fuji first heaped up a pile of sand on the beach near their village, calling it a *fujizuka* (Iwashina 1928, 33). This was only a preparatory or send-off ritual, and the "Fuji mound" was as temporary as a sand castle on a beach. Clearly these other uses of the term *fujizuka* do not approach the form, scale, or structure of the *fujizuka* in and around Edo; more important they do not mimic the physical pattern and behavioral practice of Fuji pilgrimage. The following discussion reserves the terms *fujizuka* and "miniature Fujis" for the Fuji mounds built by and for Fujikō, distinguishing the religious constructs from the innumerable "garden variety" Fujis erected for scenic and landscaping decoration.[7]

The miniaturization of Fuji in Edo times was a relatively late example of "*simulacra or replicated sites*: The practice of absorbing the mana of famous places by replicating them began rather early in Japan.... The city of Edo relied on numerous such simulacra for authority. The site most replicated was Mount Fuji" (Takeuchi 1986, 262). The earliest Japanese precedent for creating miniature cosmic mountains comes from the *Nihon shoki*: in 621 a monk from Pekche (Korea) came to Japan with the claim of the ability to "make the figures of hills and mountains," and he drew figures of Mount Sumi (Sumeru). In the following decade several models of Mount Sumi were constructed.[8] However, these historical antecedents apparently have little or no direct connection to *fujizuka*.[9]

Takada was meticulous in his re-creation of Fuji, obviously drawing upon his skill as a landscaper as well as his firsthand knowledge of Fuji. In creating the first *fujizuka*, a new artistic and religious medium, Takada found the means of bringing the "reality" and "experience" of Fuji to the people more directly and more forcefully than the earlier traditions of courtly poetry and art could have. Takada did not attempt to duplicate a dormant volcano or a lofty peak as a natural phenomenon or as an aesthetic landscape/sculpture. Rather he strove to re-create the sacred mountain he had seen, climbed, and experienced—fashioning a miniature Fuji as it was perceived within Fuji faith and dressing the frame of the mountain with the distinctive features essential for pilgrimage and worship. The "natural" aspect of Fuji that he borrowed (literally) for this frame was black lava rock brought from the foot of Fuji, to imitate the appearance of the dormant volcano from the fifth station up. This rock was later used on many *fujizuka* to cover or "face" an existing hill or a constructed mound. The cultural or spiritual aspect of Fuji he copied was the post-Jikigyō perception of Fuji as a sacred mountain and route of pilgrimage. In fact at the peak of the *fujizuka* was buried some soil brought back from the summit of Fuji, in effect invoking the power of Fuji and creating a branch or offshoot of it (Smith 1986, 3). Major features of Fuji's pilgrimage route were included in the design and construction, down to the division of the mound into ten stations. A zigzag path of switchbacks led from the foot of the mound to the top; there was a "middle path" for circumambulating the mound at its midpoint. A tiny shrine at the fifth station mimicked the same shrine on Fuji. The cave known as Tainai (Womb) was included, as was the rock called Eboshi Iwa, marking the spot on the upper slopes where Jikigyō fasted to death.

In 1779 this new Fuji was completed, marked by opening ceremonies. Takada got permission from his family Buddhist temple to be buried at the foot of this mound so that he could watch over it even after his death. Appropriately it came to be known as the "Takada New Fuji" (Takada Shinfuji). The construction of this *fujizuka* not only fulfilled his vow to honor Jikigyō but also brought both the sacred mountain and the merit of pilgrimage to Edo: "Anyone, even old men, even women, can go on Fuji pilgrimage by climbing a Fuji mound" (Iwashina 1983, 269–70).

Part 3

FUJI AS VISUAL IDEAL
AND POLITICAL IDEA

[Hokusai considered *The Thirty-six Views of Mount Fuji*] almost as a set of unified illustrations, its purpose—as cited in the original blurb—to reveal the "full face" of the Sacred Mountain, from every likely angle, in every possible condition and mood. The unifying factor in all this, the protagonist, is towering Mt Fuji, within which Hokusai himself resides.

Lane 1989, 187

9

Woodblock Prints
and Popular Arts

Not only the builders of replicas of Mount Fuji but also the artists who crafted images of the peak had a wide variety of possibilities for fashioning their creative efforts:

> The Sacred Mountain had occasionally appeared in scroll-paintings as early as the eleventh century, and by the fifteenth century had become a standard subject for the painter—first of the Yamato-e, Tosa, Sesshū and Kanō classical schools—but most often as the adjunct to some travel-narrative: the *Tales of Ise*, the wanderings of St Ippen or the poet Saigyō, the *Soga Tales* and, later, the *Chūshingura* drama. With the eighteenth century Fuji became a theme even for such Nanga literati masters as Taigadō (one of whose painting-seals bears the proud inscription, "Climbed Mt Fuji, 1748"). Contemporary with Taigadō was the dilettante painter Minsetsu, another devotee, whose sketchbook *Hyaku-Fuji* (The Hundred Fujis) was published in 1771 and featured the mountain in all manner of times, milieux and seasons. Minsetsu's actual sketches are only records of famous scenic views, quite lacking in artistic power; but the *idea* he innovated may well have been a direct inspiration for Hokusai, who at last brought vigorous artistic focus on the mountain in all its aspects. (Lane 1989, 183–84)

From the seventeenth century, ukiyo-e ("pictures of the floating world"), first in painting and then in woodblock prints, developed into a major art form of the Tokugawa period. *Ukiyo*, originally a Buddhist term devaluing this painful or "ephemeral world" (Inagaki 1988, 355) as a realm to be shunned in favor of spiritual realities, was revalued or reversed as a hedonistic term in Tokugawa times, referring to this "fleeting" world a person should enjoy to the fullest, especially with pleasurable and sensual experiences. This floating world was depicted graphically in the ukiyo-e and in *ukiyo-zōshi*, books or novels interspersed with pictures. Early ukiyo-e depict human figures, such as kabuki actors and courtesans. In the West today ukiyo-e are best known in the landscape prints of Hokusai and Hiroshige, and yet landscapes appeared rather late in the history of this genre. In the eighteenth century, full-color woodblock prints had been perfected, and by the nineteenth century, Western perspective had been incorporated into ukiyo-e artistry—two developments utilized to perfection in landscape prints. As ukiyo-e came to include landscape, the stage was set for Fuji's dramatic appearance. The two outstanding artists of landscape ukiyo-e are Katsushika Hokusai (1760–1849), renowned especially for his *Thirty-six Views of Mount Fuji* (*Fugaku sanjūrokkei*), and Andō Hiroshige (1797–1858), famous for *The Fifty-three Stations of the Tōkaidō* (*Tōkaidō gojūsantsugi*) and his (posthumous) *Thirty-six Views of Mount Fuji* (*Fuji sanjūrokkei*).[1] Not only Hokusai and Hiroshige but also every other contemporary and subsequent ukiyo-e artist selected Fuji as a prominent landscape subject matter.

One Hokusai picture, an 1857 woodblock print, draws the viewer away from generalizations to concrete examples, at the same time pointing the way from the summit of Fuji to a *fujizuka* in Edo, and on to the popularization of the mountain that spread throughout Japan and then around the world. This print, *New Fuji, Meguro*, is created from the perspective of Edoites standing on and looking over the man-made miniature Fuji to the snow-covered peak.[2] (See plate 5.) The reversal of the direction of the gaze, assuming the viewpoint of Fuji facing the *fujizuka*, and the changing of the lens from telescopic to microscopic suggest that the sacred mountain has made its imprint on the local scene. Closer inspection of the print and the circumstances behind the idyllic setting of this particular mini-Fuji discloses a more mundane situation in which Edo has imposed its stamp on the sacred mountain and appropriated it for a multitude of less than sacred purposes.

The mini-Fuji we see here was built in 1829 on the estate of a shogunal retainer named Kondō Jūzō . . . ; the idea was said to have been Kondō's own, but he was assisted by local Fujikō organizations. The mountain depicted here is much more smooth and uniform than most mini-Fujis, which generally were built of rough lava transported from the skirt of Mount Fuji itself and presented a rather lumpy appearance. The zigzag path we see up the slope was typical, however, mimicking the switchbacked route up the real mountain, as was the location halfway up of a replica of the Eboshi Rock (named for its shape, like that of a courtier's cap), where Jikigyō Miroku, one of the saints of the Fuji religion, died at the end of a self-imposed thirty-one-day fast in the summer of 1733.

The Kondō Fuji came to be known as the "New Fuji," in distinction to the earlier mini-Fuji nearby. . . .

The New Fuji was the occasion of a scandal only seven years after its founding, when Kondō Jūzō's son killed a neighboring farmer and his family in a dispute over the right to sell souvenirs to mini-Fuji visitors.[3]

This gloss of the print of a mini-Fuji offers a glimpse into the process by which Edo captured, popularized, and commodified Fuji. Murder over the right to sell Fuji memorabilia may have been a unique instance; nevertheless it is early documentation of the commercial production, distribution, and hawking of captive Fuji that has continued unabated since late Tokugawa times.[4] Perhaps the earliest and best example of packaging Fuji for mass consumption is found in the woodblock prints featuring it.

As contemporaries and intensely competitive artists, Hokusai and Hiroshige vied with each other for fame and sales; art lovers and art historians have kept alive this debate over which was the greatest Japanese landscape artist. Hiroshige wrote his own uncomplimentary comparison of Hokusai's work, acknowledging Hokusai's forte in composition but preferring his own more natural or realistic rendering: "My own designs are different—the scene just as it lay before my eyes" (cited in Lane 1989, 241).

Some favor Hokusai's work for his lively scenes and inventive designs; others praise Hiroshige's more sedate and understated treatment. Lane claims that the protagonist of *The Thirty-six Views of Mount Fuji* "is towering Mt Fuji, within which Hokusai himself resides" and also says, "Quite literally the Mountain is Hokusai, the Artist is Mt Fuji" (Lane 1989, 187, 189). If Kakugyō achieved a spiritual unity with Fuji, Hokusai created an aesthetic identity with the mountain. "Hokusai, we can be sure, had no preconceived philosophic intent in depicting the life of these poor people against the immutable shape of Fuji, and yet the 'Peerless Mountain' becomes in this series of prints a symbol of permanency underlining the transience of the men and women of the 'Floating World' who gaze up to it with such reverence. Looked at in this way, it is far more than simply 'One Hundred Views of Fuji': it becomes a commentary on man's relationship to nature, and assumes the stature of an epic" (Hillier 1980, 225).

These comments on Hokusai's *One Hundred Views of Mt. Fuji* renew the discussion of the relationship of humans to nature mentioned at the beginning of this book; the debate about Hiroshige and Hokusai is actually an argument about who most accurately captured *nature* and who most creatively imagined/realized *Nature*. We follow the suggestion that "Hiroshige was perhaps less an artist of Nature than of the culture of nature" (Smith 1997, 33, 39). This is a valuable clue in approaching some of the woodblock prints of Fuji, to see how this cultural form reshaped the natural form of Fuji.

UKIYO-E: FUJI IN THE FLOATING WORLD OF HIROSHIGE AND HOKUSAI

This woodblock journey to Fuji begins with Hiroshige's view of landscape and Fuji "just as it lay before my eyes," a self-professed naturalism: "Hiroshige presents nature in a more or less naturalistic manner. . . . His view of nature was inhabited by people who were perfectly in harmony with it" (Woodson 1998, 43). However, this "harmony with nature" and the timeless character of traditional Japan may be wistful thinking. "Such an emphasis was a source of particular consolation to young urban intellectuals in the rapidly industrialising Japan of the early twentieth century, as well as to many Westerners, who observed the process from without, lamenting the destruction of Japanese 'tradition'" (Smith 1997, 35–36). Hiroshige's contribution to the image of Fuji as the icon of Japan becomes clearer when his pictures of Fuji are contrasted with the classical models of the mountain. As with his predecessor Hokusai, and some other Western-influenced artists, Hiroshige replaced the earlier "famous place" stereotype of Fuji (an isosceles triangle capped with three rounded peaks) with a more "natural" depiction. In fact the Hokusai-Hiroshige rendition of Fuji has established the perception of the mountain down to the present day. One thoroughly "Japanese" theme that Hiroshige continued and elaborated to perfection was concern for the seasons and "atmosphere," presenting Fuji in a wide range of settings at different times of the year and in varied weather.

Hiroshige's total work can be credited with at least two major contributions to Fuji's iconic status. First, by including Fuji pictures in his series *Fifty-three Stages of the Tōkaidō*, he provided graphic confirmation of Fuji's image as the dominant feature of this central landscape.[5] Second, in his series of Edo prints, his treatment of the mountain in many of these pictures shows Fuji reigning over Edo or Edo subsuming Fuji, although these themes frequently coincide. For instance in his print *Suruga-chō*, number 8 of *One Hundred Famous Views of Edo* (Bicknell 1994, 112–13), diminishing perspective is formed by a view down two rows of shops whose parallel lines begin to converge as they enter low-lying clouds; at the point where they would apparently meet in the distance, Fuji's cone emerges from and crowns the clouds (see plate 6). Ironically, Hiroshige the "naturalist" has shown that the road of commerce leads to Fuji, or that Fuji has taken this mercantile route to enter the bustling life of Edo. This print emphasizes that the Edoites' prosperity was derived from their geographical proximity to Fuji, the primary marker of eastern Japan and home of the shogun's seat. In the balance of city and countryside (Smith 1978, 47), Fuji is brought to Edo to legitimate or sanctify it, while Edo is transported to the realm of the ethereal peak.

This pictorial tour of ukiyo-e started with Hiroshige because, as the poet Noguchi Yone wrote, "We are already all Hiroshige," referring to the way Hiroshige created a timeless portrait of traditional Japan (cited in Smith 1997, 33). The visual voyage through woodblock prints continues with Hiroshige's predecessor Hokusai, who was largely responsible for establishing the international reputation of Fuji. Hiroshige's contemporary (although a generation older), Hokusai created a prolific body of work: he "left us a total *oeuvre* of more than thirty thousand designs" (Forrer 1991, 11). His treatment here is confined to his *One Hundred Views of Mt. Fuji* and his earlier *Thirty-six Views of Mount Fuji* series, appearing relatively late in Hokusai's long career.

One Hundred Views of Mt. Fuji begins with three prints directly bearing on Fuji as a sacred mountain. The initial plate is *The Goddess Konohana Sakuya Hime;* "In Hokusai's view here, . . . she is simply a generic Shinto deity." The second plate, *The Appearance of Mt. Fuji in the Fifth Year of Kōrei,*[6] gives the genesis of the mountain before awestruck observers. The third plate, *En no Gyōja Opens Mt. Fuji,* portrays the powerful form of the founder of Fuji asceticism; he is "posed on the edge of what we take to be the crater of Fuji"[7] These three prints of the sacred, the ancient, and the legendary opening of the mountain achieve a twofold purpose: exalting the subject matter by divine sanction and grounding it in received cultural memory of the miraculous origin of the peak and the (mythical) founding of its pilgrimage practices. Except for several pictures of pilgrims on the mountain, the bulk of the other prints deal with the aesthetic delights of the peak, but they presuppose this archaic/sacred subtext.

After the fourth print, *Fuji under Clear Skies,* in the fifth print, *The Opening of Fuji,* and in the sixth print, *Sliding Down* (Smith 1988, 181, 180), Hokusai shows pilgrims on the mountain. There are some historical inconsistencies: the title of the fifth plate, *The Opening of Fuji,* is given as *yamaaki,* but the term Fuji devotees use for the seasonal opening of Fuji is *yamabiraki.*[8] Nor are there any narrow rocky passages through which Hokusai's pilgrims pass, single file, as shown in plate 5. Another discrepancy is the depiction of a Fuji pilgrim in the same print blowing a conch shell, which was a *yamabushi* (Shugendō) practice not adopted by Fuji pilgrims. It seems that "Hokusai never climbed the mountain himself, for they [the pictures] are unrealistic to the point of abstraction."[9]

Hokusai included a pair of prints (plates 5 and 6) portraying the ascent and descent of Fuji. Plate 6, *Sliding Down,* depicts pilgrims "sliding down" the "sand run" (*subashiri*), which made for a very quick descent. This exit route was closed after 1980 when twelve people were killed in a rockslide there. The author, having descended the mountain in 1969 by this "sand run," can verify Smith's comment that it was indeed quite "thrilling." The instructions of the Fusōkyō believers leading this 1969 group, when facing this precipitous slope of ash, were to dig in one's heels and keep the toes up, "just like skiing," and drag the diamond stick behind like a tail to maintain balance. In 1969 the mode of "sliding" was quite different from the depiction in plate 6, where each of the pilgrims has his back foot tipped up and his front foot is dug into the loose lava; their diamond sticks are thrust into the lava in front of them. Two practical considerations recommend against using this plate as an instruction guide for descending the "sand run," should it ever be reopened. First, planting the front foot and diamond sticks into the lava would cause a person to tip forward and fall; second, the "sand" is actually fine lava, almost like ground glass, which would quickly shred the feet of someone wearing straw sandals such as in the plate. Hokusai's rendering of the descent does succeed in expressing the downward rush of the "sand run," but actual experience on the mountain supports Smith's argument that Hokusai probably never climbed (or descended) Fuji.

Two plates, 46, *A Rock Shelter on Fuji*, and 76, *Circling the Crater of Fuji*,[10] give additional support to the claim that Hokusai never scaled the mountain: the shelters on the slopes of Fuji where the climbers rested were not natural caves but crude huts; and "circling the crater" is the proper term but actually involved walking around the rim of the crater. Apparently, religious ascent of Fuji did not include entering the yawning abyss of Fuji's crater. In short, seen from the vantage point of Fuji spirituality, these five plates convey nothing distinctive of the practice of Fuji asceticism, Fuji piety, or Fuji faith. Clearly for Hokusai, Fuji religiosity was little more than another feature of the mountain, blending in with Fuji's many settings and forms, rather than its holy character or its many religious practices. Some authors claim that Hokusai was a Fuji worshipper;[11] but the evidence strongly suggests that he never made the pilgrimage to the summit. Although he was devoted to his subject, if he was a worshipper of Fuji, apparently he worshipped from a distance. Kano (1994, 81) concludes that there is no clear evidence of Hokusai's participation in a Fujikō; his closest link to Fuji is one of his many assumed artistic names, "tsuchimochi," literally "earth-carrier" or worker in wood and plaster, a term used for the construction of *fujizuka*. Hokusai was at least indirectly connected to these groups since the publisher of his *Thirty-six Views of Mount Fuji* was the head of a Fujikō.

People Climbing the Mountain (plate 34 in his earlier volume of color prints, *Thirty-six Views of Mount Fuji*) is the only image in the series to depict the mountain close up and minus the peak. All of the other plates (the title gives the number as "thirty-six," but the published version actually includes forty-six) offer a variety of perspectives for viewing Fuji: from Edo, from the Tōkaidō, from other areas, from season to season, in different light, and with a motley assortment of people engaged in sundry occupations. In some plates Fuji is front and center, as in one of the most famous of all, commonly known as *Red Fuji* but literally *South Wind, Clear Sky* (Clark 2001, 116, plate 53); in others it is diminutive in appearance and almost an afterthought.

Hokusai was riding on a relatively new wave of Western influence, including the use of perspective and even depending on the newly imported Prussian blue (or Berlin blue) pigment for his exceptional color; he borrowed creatively from Chinese, Japanese, and Western forebears to develop his own distinctive style. This subtly international or cosmopolitan approach in the depiction of Fuji was revolutionary. The much earlier but enduring image of Fuji as a "famous place" was presenting it as an isosceles triangle capped with three small peaks. Hokusai, like some of his predecessors and contemporaries (especially Shiba Kōkan) and like Hiroshige, who followed him, departed from this older model and allowed his imagination to play with the form and even the location of the mountain. Hokusai selected the size, shape, and coloring of the mountain to fit into his composition, freeing Fuji from the accretion of centuries of standard depictions (the triple-peaked triangle of the "famous place"). Indeed, Hokusai freely invoked aesthetic license to "open the mountain" for artistic expression.

Hokusai, the master of composition, boldly borrowed the triangle of Fuji to fit in with other angles in his pictures and balanced them with circles and arcs. Although in some of his Edo scenes Fuji demurely peeks at the city from the background, in other settings Hokusai seems to be toying with the mountain. Even a cursory look through his *One Hundred Views of Mt. Fuji* yields many instances of his playful innovation with the form of Fuji.

A perusal of Hokusai's pictures reveals that he certainly did move the mountain to suit his aesthetic designs and creative fancies. These prints show a quite literal "popularization" of Fuji; often common people at work fill the frame of the picture, and Fuji becomes almost a decorative afterthought. Hokusai's compositions attest to a level of intimacy and familiarity with the sacred mountain; his playful manipulation of it reflected and enhanced Edoites' friendly ties to Fuji. From an aesthetic vantage point, the series of prints on Fuji provided Hokusai with the opportunity to demonstrate his virtuosity and artistic vision; from a historical and religious standpoint, the significance of his choice of Fuji as the subject or medium for his performance can hardly be overstated.

The contribution of ukiyo-e to the iconic status of Fuji stands in sharp contrast to the precedents set down by the practice of Fujikō and the construction of *fujizuka*. Hokusai's graphic treatments include aspects of a holy peak, but what sets them apart is the manipulation of Fuji as an aesthetic component of design. All three of these phenomena—Fujikō, *fujizuka,* and ukiyo-e featuring Fuji—centered around Edo and were part of the urbanization of Fuji. Hokusai's rendering of Fuji is the most urbane expression of the mountain as a "civilized" design.

FUJI AS DECORATION AND SOUVENIR

The fame of Fuji was established and disseminated mainly through ukiyo-e, but this sacred peak has graced almost every genre of art and form of craft. A separate volume could be devoted to Fuji in a wide variety of artistic guises: it is a favorite theme in all the decorative arts, especially metalwork and lacquer but also in ink box, inro (containers), netsuke, brocade, bonsai, and every imaginable ornament. "It is like a signature tune denoting 'Japan'" (Hillier 1980, 215).

Hokusai aided and abetted the popular and commercial utilization/exploitation of Fuji's image, providing models for the production of these goods: "In the First Series of this illustrated guide for craftsmen in comb and smoking-pipe designs eight

Fuji illustrations are included for employment on decorated combs," and "a good part of the public for the series consisted of amateur painters" (Lane 1989, 184). Hokusai claimed, "Even though one might be a person living in a distant province, if one but buys and studies from this album, it is the same as having enrolled in the master's studio" (Lane 1989, 176).

Representation of Fuji slid down the slippery slope of artist to craftsman to dilettante/amateur to hack exploiter with such ease that the gradations are nearly indistinguishable. The popularization and commercialization of Fuji's image are prime examples of the development of popular arts and literature in mid- and late-Tokugawa times. There is no height of luxury that Fuji did not attain. One exceptional piece featuring Fuji is a "campaign coat (*jinbaori*) with Mount Fuji and 'divine fire,'" an early seventeenth-century coat of black and yellow woolen cloth with appliqué; this was a "dress" military overcoat to protect against the elements and also make a fashion statement. (See plate 7.) "A yellow wool appliqué in the shape of Mount Fuji stands out dramatically against the black ground. . . . A little curlicue of smoke, created from cut white cloth, emerges from the mouth of the active volcano; stylised pools of lava dot the base of the mountain. Mount Fuji has been the object of religious devotion throughout Japanese history—here the triple-peaked crown of the mountain recalls its depiction in medieval Fuji mandalas. The auspicious, life-giving symbol of Fuji seems an appropriate decoration for a garment designed for the battlefield" (Rousmaniere 2002, plate 25).

Fuji has been subjected to every imaginable indignity in decorative arts—as any modern tourist to Japan knows. The author's personal collection ranges from the tasteful and creative replicas of the lofty peak to crude and even pornographic reproductions. A paradox of popular or mass culture is that, on the one hand, it makes symbols and works of art available to all; on the other hand, it dilutes their meaning through anonymous mass replication, rendering them undesirable and impotent (in the most extreme cases). Some of the remembrances of Fuji are hardly memorable as art objects, not unlike the cheap souvenirs found throughout the world: such artifacts shamelessly beg, borrow, or steal whatever image or association will imbue a piece of paper, wood, cloth, metal, or plastic with a feature or resemblance making it appear worthy of purchase. The popularization of Fuji is played out within this paradoxical process. A plebeian or democratic example of Fuji's universal appeal is the fact that it is a favorite mural subject of public baths (Kano 1994, 63). Perhaps the real test of an icon is its ability to move across the spectrum of "high" art to crafts and even common trinkets.

Another quandary for Fuji as the "peerless" artistic image was the challenge of migrating from silk canvases and woodblock prints to photographic paper. Indeed not only did Fuji meet the challenge of being represented through the camera lens, but also the tradition of ukiyo-e actually influenced the camera angle from which it was viewed and the way the black-and-white photographs were colorized by ukiyo-e craftsmen. If ukiyo-e gave way to the technology of the camera, the aesthetic power of ukiyo-e made its own distinctive imprint on photography: "One of the most interesting aspects of 19th-century photography in Japan was the work of European photographers who studied the composition and line of ukiyo-e prints and later transmitted this 'vision' of Japan to Japanese photographers" (Worswick 1983, 185). One of the Western photographic pioneers in Japan, Felix (or Felice) Beato, who settled in Japan in 1863–64, created one of the earliest photographs of the peak with wide distribution. He provided a photograph of Mount Fuji for the November 12, 1864, issue of the *Illustrated London News*.[12]

The history of Fuji pilgrimage has shown that the pattern of pilgrims going to Fuji was followed by pilgrims taking the mountain back to Edo. In a similar fashion so too the photographers who initially trained their cameras on "wild" Fuji subsequently installed aesthetic re-creations of "civilized" Fuji in their Tokyo studios for permanent posing in a picture within a picture. A number of "samurai" and individual and group photographic portraits from this era feature Fuji on a backdrop or hanging scroll.[13]

"The first professional Japanese photographer was Shimooka Renjō (1823–1914), who set up a studio in Yokohama in the early 1860s" (Worswick 1983, 185). This pioneer of Japanese photography occasionally used a "Fuji stamp" with his name and a three-peaked Fuji to mark his pictures.[14] "When Shimooka Renjō opened a new two-story shop in Yokohama in 1868, it sported a huge sign in the shape of Mount Fuji, with the English word 'Photographer' running up the left side and again down the right side of the sacred mountain."[15] Shimooka's selection of the peerless mountain for his logo was an appropriate choice for the site made famous in centuries of artworks, internationally renowned through ukiyo-e, and destined to become one of the most universally recognized photographs of Japan.

Every pioneer Western photographer in Japan and the earliest Japanese cameramen were obligated to capture the lofty peak of Fuji: this badge of the country graced the covers of photo albums, in which it often occupied a place of prominence.[16] The task of tracing the immense photographic record of Fuji is left for others, but one exceptional case is worthy of mention. A modern photographer who has devoted his life to taking pictures of Fuji, Okada Kōyō, claimed, "All in all, I have photographed the mountain more than 150,000 times, but I fear that I have still not exhausted all its possibilities" (Okada 1964, preface). He even stamped the back of his prints with an emblem including his name and a sketch of the mountain. The government has used a number of his Fuji pictures on postal stamps, and he is credited with the picture of Lake Motosu and Fuji on the five-hundred-yen note.[17] The afterword of Okada's 1964 work (which contains a number of color photos) also includes his paean of love for Fuji in "Mt. Fuji and I": "I have given my body and soul to this mountain—to me it is a beautiful woman fortunate enough to have me devote my life to her."

Among countless Fuji photographs, two from the 1930s are too precious to pass up, remarkable both for their subject matter and their size. One is a fourteen-by-six-foot image that Hara Hiroshi composed with photographs by Kimura Ihe-e and Koishi Kiyosh and that was displayed at the Chicago Trade Fair in 1938. "This impressive piece of wallpaper contained every soft cliché known to have titillated Japanophiles in the twentieth century: cherry blossoms, Mount Fuji, a geisha with trailing sleeves, the classic symbols of quietist culture (Shintō torii, pagoda, the Kamakura Buddha), an ancient castle, the Diet building, a few modern edifices, and a modern ship."[18] The other photograph is even more monumental: "A mammoth photographic wall poster showing Mount Fuji from across Suruga Bay was constructed for display at the Japanese Pavilion at the 1939–1940 New York World's Fair as part of the theme, 'the Architecture of Tomorrow.' . . . Fuji was chosen because it was the 'symbol' (*shinboru*) of Japan."[19]

Like good wine, Fuji traveled well from the nineteenth century into the twentieth: in the 1867 Exposition Universelle de Paris, Fuji was present on a lacquer screen; in the 1938 Chicago Trade Fair, Fuji kept up with the times by making its appearance on a "wallpaper"-size photographic print—thus lending both national identity and traditional character to modern constructions. In addition Fuji was selected and projected on the scene of the 1939 New York World's Fair as the symbol of Japan.

10

Western "Discovery" of Woodblock Prints

UKIYO-E: FUJI IN THE FLOATING WORLD OF JAPONISME

Fuji became a more prominent icon of Japan in the feudal era, rising in fame and popularity as Edo flourished. A domestic national symbol, Fuji gained greater stature through a process of internationalization. Fuji's emergence as a universal symbol of Japan, a nineteenth-century phenomenon, owed much to the Western discovery of ukiyo-e, but Westerners encountered Fuji at least two centuries earlier, as revealed by European travelers' accounts of Japan. Western knowledge of Fuji begins with the earlier record of a Portuguese Jesuit missionary to Japan, João Rodrigues (1561?–1633). Rodrigues's account provides the essentials of the perception of Fuji in early Tokugawa times, noting that "Fuji-san is Japan's highest, loveliest and most renowned mountain," briefly describing pilgrimage practices and the peak's beauty and round shape, and even noting the cave Hitoana as a sacred site.[1] Rodrigues provides a precedent for a trinitarian view of the mountain that has currency to the present day: its superiority in height, its unmatched beauty, and its fame are all crowned by its holiness, and his characterization of Fuji endures.[2]

The record of Rodrigues was not widely circulated. Arnoldus Montanus in his *Atlas Japannensis* of 1670, though working from second- and thirdhand accounts, published a much more influential early work on things Japanese, including Fuji. Among the various Japanese mountains, he mentions that "the Hill *Fussinojamma*, which they saw in their Way, rising so high into a Spire, might be discern'd thirty Leagues off, its lofty Crown always cover'd with Snow."[3] Montanus apparently was the first to disseminate notions of the lofty Fuji to Westerners.

More important was the travelogue of Engelbert Kaempfer (1651–1716), written in "High-Dutch" but translated and first published posthumously in English as *The History of Japan* in 1727 in two volumes, with later editions in Latin, Dutch, French, and German and reprints in various editions; a new English translation came out in 1999 (Kaempfer 1999). This was long the standard Western work on Japan. Kaempfer has the highest praise for Fuji: "The famous Mount Fuji in the province of Suruga, which in height can be compared only to Mount Tenerife[4] in the Canaries" (57). Fuji "is conical in shape and so even and beautiful that one may easily call it the most beautiful mountain in the world. . . . The poets and painters of this country never end praising and portraying the beauty of this mountain" (340).

After Kaempfer's death his books and manuscripts were purchased by Sir Hans Sloane (1660–1753) and became part of the collection of the British Museum in 1759.[5] The 1999 translation of Kaempfer includes "a segment of Kaempfer's map of the Tōkaidō, with Suruga (*lower right*), Mount Fuji (*left*)" (Kaempfer 1999, 341). This sketch of "Fuji no Jamma" by Kaempfer is the most likely candidate for the earliest graphic depiction of the mountain by a Westerner. Kaempfer adds little descriptive detail to the account of Rodrigues, glossing it with the aesthetic comment about poets and painters—which seems to echo a *Man'yōshū* phrase lauding the mountain's beauty (van der Velde 1995). Kaempfer's own drawing of Fuji was reproduced by the translator J. G. Scheuchzer in the first edition of his *History of Japan* (Kaempfer 1929),[6] but neither the author's original nor the translator's reproduction does justice to the mountain.[7] The icon has been reduced to a marker for the location of the mountain.[8] Only on close inspection does this drawing show distinctive features: the summit has three peaks, and Fuji contains a miniature mountain within its triple-peaked triangle. Kaempfer's rendering is based on an empirical sighting of the mountain and does not reflect the ideal image of a "famous place"[9] in the classical Japanese fashion, except for the three fingerlike protuberances. This sketch of Fuji bears such resemblance to the steep-sided mountain-within-mountain, rather short and squat, found in the *Shōtoku Taishi eden* (discussed in chapter 2) that it raises the question of whether Kaempfer (or his Japanese informants) had seen a Shōtoku picture-scroll. Kaempfer's version of Fuji is smallish and unartistic, but even so, it is proof that this pioneering chronicler understood Fuji's importance enough to create probably the first Western representation of the mountain. After Kaempfer's volumes a host of those who journeyed from European countries to Japan in Tokugawa times left their own tales of this mysterious island nation, spurring interest among would-be Japonistes and the general public[10] and laying the groundwork for the enthusiastic reception of woodblock prints.

Two pivotal dates for the introduction of ukiyo-e into Western countries are the 1853–54 "opening" of Japan forced by the American ships of Commodore Matthew C. Perry and the 1868 Meiji Restoration, which implemented Japan's own decision to engage, trade, and compete with Western nations. From the 1850s, woodblock prints found their way to the West in greater numbers, first to Paris and then to England and other European regions before making their American debut.

Nowadays Fuji's form is universally recognized, and its appearance in late Tokugawa woodblock prints is unanimously praised, but such was not always the case. In Japan the career of ukiyo-e paralleled other popular, plebeian arts such as kabuki and novels, which appealed to the merchant class. For that reason they were viewed with disdain or suspicion by the warrior-class authorities. Nevertheless the printing of ukiyo-e (and *ukiyo-zōshi*) in vast numbers attests to their popularity; so many of these works were produced that they helped support a cottage industry of recycling the labor-intensive, handmade paper (for such purposes as wrapping material). The serendipitous "discovery" of these woodblock prints in France is attributed to Félix Bracquemond (about 1860),[11] who happened to find a Japanese album of prints in Paris that had been used as packing material for porcelain imported to Japan; delighted with this wastepaper, he avidly searched for more. Like Bracquemond, many Westerners who came into contact with ukiyo-e recognized their artistic value and their worth for collecting. Even in Tokugawa times while Japan was still closed to the West, some late-eighteenth- and early-nineteenth-century European travelers were attracted to the prints and went so far as to commission woodblock artists to produce works, which they took back to Europe, where they remained relatively unknown in private or museum collections (Lane 1989, 181).[12]

Not all Westerners were so taken in by ukiyo-e; some of the earliest and foremost Western (elite) commentators on Japanese culture and art were predisposed to agree with their aristocratic native tutors in favoring the "high art" of medieval Japanese paintings and spiritually uplifting temple iconography over lowly, common, vulgar woodblock prints. The first British minister to Japan, Sir Rutherford Alcock, who was noted for leading the initial (1860) Western group to scale Fuji, commented that Japan has no "'high art' to compare with that of Europe."[13] Both Ernest Fenollosa, the pioneer American expert on Japanese art, and Henry P. Bowie, an early Japanophile who studied (and created) classical Japanese artworks, looked down on popular art of the then still-recent feudal centuries. Fenollosa openly and scathingly disparaged woodblock prints such as "Hokusai's 'beastly obscenities.'"[14] In the latter half of the nineteenth century the French, and then the English and other Europeans, developed a taste for ukiyo-e from imported works—not all of high quality—that grew into an almost insatiable thirst. The artists who purchased, copied, imitated, and used the prints (and other Japanese decorative art) as inspiration for their own creative works did not make their way to Japan. However, a number of collectors and dealers, intrigued by the woodblock prints, actually boarded ships to Japan, where they purchased large quantities of prints; this expanded the range of available works from the rather "late" Hokusai and Hiroshige to the earlier "primitive" works of Moronobu and the "classical" prints of Utamaro and others (Berger 1992, 128–29).

The impact of Japanese woodblock prints on European artists was instantaneous and overwhelming: art historians have noted the coincidence of the crisis in Western art of the mid–nineteenth century, stressing "the impasse in which late naturalism and sterile academicism alike now found themselves. . . . One is impelled to the conclusion that the time was ripe for a decisive change. Japanese artistic principles emerged as the liberating factor, the stimulus that led to a new figuration" (Berger 1992, 19, 1). The affordability of ukiyo-e—"Hiroshige's colour landscape prints could be purchased for not much more than the price of a bowl of noodles" (Smith 1997, 36)—made them likely candidates for export (Berger 1992, 11, 89–90), as did their great variety and ready supply and the ease of transporting them.

A long list of artists, many of them major figures—Degas, van Gogh, and others "from Whistler to Matisse" (Berger 1992)—gained inspiration from these prints, as did lesser known figures in decorative arts and crafts. Degas said, "Hokusai is not just one artist among others in the Floating World. He is an island, a continent, a whole world in himself" (cited in Calza 2003, 400).

The two decades after the 1853–54 involuntary opening of Japan were eventful times in the formation and expansion of Japonisme, with active participation of both Japanese and Westerners; Fuji was a silent but powerful witness to these developments. The official record of Commodore Perry's stay in Japan was published in Washington, D.C., in 1856 in three volumes. Gracing the covers is an embossed scene of the Japanese coast with Perry's gunship dominating the harbor in the foreground and Fuji rising in the background, flanked by a samurai.[15] Several features of this picture are compelling: first, the ship represents the American government, which has come across the ocean and imposed its demand of "opening" Japan; second, Fuji stands for both the land and the country of Japan. As a government publication, initially printed for distribution to members of the U.S. Congress and Senate before being made available to the public, it makes an official statement that Fuji equals Japan and that America (Perry's gunship) dominates Japan (Fuji).

Following Perry's expedition, during the 1850s, trade treaties made possible the commercial export of Japanese arts and crafts, including ukiyo-e, and these prints slowly began to appear in Western markets and magazines.[16] In 1861 Charles Baudelaire wrote, "I have had a packet of *japonneries* in my possession for a long time now" (cited in Berger 1992, 16). During the 1860s artists such as Manet, Whistler, and Degas were influenced by Japanese prints. In 1862 an oriental curio shop, La Porte Chinoise, opened in Paris; the shop carried Chinese and Japanese items and also was a meeting place for Japonist artists, collectors, and traders (Berger 1992, 338). Among these Japanophiles was Philippe Burty (1830–90), "one of the earliest and most active Japonistes," with his collection of more than twenty-five hundred objects; usually he is credited with coining the term "Japonisme" in a series of articles beginning in 1872 (Floyd 1996). In 1867 Burty and a select group of Japonists in Paris formed the Jing-lar club or society (Société du Jing-lar), "a dining club devoted to Japonisme," the

This membership card for the Société du Jing-lar, one of the first groups dedicated to Japonisme, features a smoking Fuji. Reproduced with permission from the S. P. Avery Collection, Miriam and Ira D. Wallach Division of Art, Prints and Photographs, The New York Public Library, Astor, Lenox and Tilden Foundations

members of which "met in Oriental dress to eat Japanese food as a preparation for their aesthetic deliberations" (Berger 1992, 338, 7). Fortunately history has preserved "Philippe Burty's Membership Card for the Jing-lar Society," a color etching "issued in ten copies, possibly corresponding to the number of members in the Société. The name of the individual member appeared in the smoke above the volcano. Curiously, this print was suggested by numerous visions of Mt. Fujiyama as found in prints by Hokusai or Hiroshige."[17] The depiction of Fuji, far from flattering, was chosen as part of the hallmark of a society of the premier group of artists and collectors devoted to Japanese art. Burty received the Medal of the Order of the Empire of the Rising Sun from the Japanese government in 1884.[18]

From the 1860s a number of expositions in England, Paris, and America presented Japanese art and woodblock prints to the public.[19] In 1862 Alcock selected and displayed his Japanese prints in the Great Exposition at London, the earliest public exhibition of Japanese prints in the West (Berger 1992, 338). By contrast, in the Universal Exhibition in Paris (Exposition Universelle de Paris) in 1867, the section for Japanese decorative art included materials chosen and brought to Paris by Japanese representatives. The Japanese delegation was distinguished by the presence of Toku-gawa Akitake (1853–1910), the younger brother of the last shogun; and the choice of Japanese art was in the hands of the Japanese authorities under the direction of the shogun (T. Watanabe 1984, 667). In Burty's recollection of this exposition, he describes a magnificent lacquer screen with various scenes, including the smoking crater of Fuji.[20] Significantly the Japanese themselves, in one of the first official presentations of their country and art abroad, designated the "smoking crater"as an identifying symbol of Japan.

"JAPONAISERIE FOREVER"

Van Gogh quoted the words of Goncourt, "Japonaiserie forever,"[21] and made his own confession of faith in Japanese woodblock prints: "The more you see things with a Japanese eye, the more subtly you perceive colour. . . . Do you see, what these simple Japanese teach us almost amounts to a religion" (cited in Berger 1992, 125, 126). He and his brother Theo collected prints, and Vincent decorated the walls of his room with them; Vincent assigned Hokusai to "*la vraie période*" and wrote instructing Theo "to buy at least a few of the '300 [*sic*] prints of his Mount Fuji series'" (128; brackets in original). Vincent van Gogh's passion for Japanese art led him to view nature through a Japanese prism: he claimed that "the landscapes in the snow, with the summits white against a sky as luminous as the snow, were just like the landscapes that the Japanese have painted" (cited in Wichmann 1999, 281–83). A number of prints, especially those of Hiroshige, were duplicated or "copied" in van Gogh's paintings. Perhaps the most remarkable example of Fuji's presence in Japonisme is van Gogh's *Portrait of Père Tanguy*, which ostensibly is a painting of his mentor, the gallery owner Père Tanguy, using as a backdrop Tanguy's collection of Japanese prints.[22] To the left and right are the figures of an actor and a courtesan, respectively; in the upper right corner is a cherry tree in bloom, and at the top center above Tanguy's hat is the peak of Fuji. "It is as if he [Tanguy] and Japan were one, and the Ukiyoye motifs (actor, courtesan, sacred Mount Fujiyama) were there for him alone."[23]

Not to belittle van Gogh's universally acclaimed talent (Berger 1992, 134–35), Fuji seems to have served as a talismanic motif encouraging it. Indeed the appearance of Fuji in van Gogh's *Portrait of Père Tanguy* is an anomaly: "otherwise direct quotes of Fuji imagery in European Japoniste works are surprisingly rare. Ukiyo-e prints themselves exported to Europe extremely well, but the motif of Mt Fuji—symbol of Japan, not of European interest in Japan—could not make the cross-over into European art so well."[24] A second, significant aspect of Japonisme equally important as woodblock prints is the decorative and applied arts, including fabric design, jewelry, ceramics, metalwork, glasswork, and graphic art; much as in Japanese decorative materials, Fuji is represented endlessly (Wichmann 1999). Not only ceramic and glass works of art but also wallpaper borrowed Japanese stereotypes, including the famed snow-clad peak.[25]

Hokusai's impact extended beyond the visual arts, especially as seen in his *Great Wave* print, which "more than any other Japanese print . . . astounded and delighted artists in Paris around the close of the nineteenth century."[26] The extent and range of Japonisme are demonstrated by the inspiration this print provided for Rainer Maria Rilke's poem "Der Berg" ("The Mountain")[27] and Claude Debussy's orchestral piece *La mer*. Debussy loved the sea and also was enamored of Japanese woodblock prints: a 1910 photograph of Debussy in his home next to a seated Igor Stravinsky[28] reveals in the background two prints, one an Utamaro and the other the lower portion of Hokusai's *Great Wave* (Lesure 1975, 124, 125). Debussy's concrete memories of the ocean and seas were mediated by his visual contact with Hokusai's *Great Wave*, which made such a profound impression on him, and its vision, that he had a segment of this print used for the cover of the original score of *La mer*.[29] Debussy's close contact with this work apparently channeled his recollections of the "reality" of the ocean (Howat 1994, 72–77), a reminder that the "Nature" of Hiroshige and Hokusai is greater than "nature" itself. Ironically the cover of *La mer* focuses solely on the "great wave" by deleting from the scene the dwarfed fishermen's boats and their occupants in the foreground, as well as the triangular form of Fuji a little off center in the middle ground. Art historians and critics agree that the main subject of Hokusai's print is the permanence and power of Fuji in the midst of a scene in which a towering wave threatens to swallow diminutive boats and powerless humans (Forrer 2003, 30). However, the modified version of the "great wave" minus Fuji may be truer to Debussy's frequent comments on his fascination with the power of the sea.[30]

The influence of Fuji's image also is present in highly unusual, totally unexpected places. What many consider the American painter John La Farge's best mural, *Ascension* (1887), in the Church of the Ascension in New York City, is based in part on the artist's firsthand experience of Fuji. In 1886 "John La Farge had gone [to Japan] on a . . . quest: to find the proper background for his mural for the Church of the Ascension. . . . In the gently ascending slope of Mount Fuji, La Farge had discovered a vision of the sacred uncluttered with Western associations. . . . La Farge reproduced, on the left side of the mural, his careful sketch of Fuji's exact slope so that Christ hovers above the sacred mountain, one more 'view of Mount Fuji' to add to Hokusai's album."[31] By La Farge's time Japonisme had left the limited circle of art salons and entered the public domain of common knowledge about Japan.[32]

JAPANESE "REDISCOVERY" OF WOODBLOCK PRINTS

As early as the 1880s Oscar Wilde, amused with the faddishness of Japonisme, said that "the whole of Japan is an invention" (cited in Ellmann 1988, 303) created by artists. Bracquemond unwrapped a porcelain from Japan, but in the act discovered the greater treasure in the packing material and, in effect, rewrapped or repacked it as an exotic model.[33] The early Japonists, artists and collectors alike, were quite aware that they were using woodblock prints and decorative art to reinvigorate Western art. Art historians and critics have sorted through this process of selection and adaptation, especially in noting the terms for their creative process.

The original French term "Japonisme" and the English usage of "Japonism" and "Japanism" bear similar meanings, while "Japanesque" means "in the style of Japan," and "Japonaiseries" carries a pejorative notion of a knickknack or a trinket (Weisberg and Weisberg 1990, xxvii). The poet Baudelaire even disparaged Japonaiserie as a silly fad, a *niaiserie,* coining the term "Japo*niaiserie*" (Barrett 1999, 78). However it is labeled, the infatuation for things Japanese, and for things oriental, is part of the complex process that Edward Said has treated in his notion of orientalism: the Western construction of the notion and the control/manipulation of the nations of the "Orient" (Said 1978). More recently scholars have begun to examine the reverse process, whereby nations of the Orient utilize stereotypes about them to their own advantage.

From the second half of the nineteenth century through the present, ukiyo-e (and Mount Fuji) and Japonisme helped Japanese ideologues in their attempt to forge an oriental identity over and against the West or Occident. The prints of Hiroshige and Hokusai continue to epitomize the character of the "true" or "real" or "ideal" Japan. In short, Japanese have turned the tables on orientalism, devising a kind of "reverse orientalism."[34] This reversal utilizes the mystique of the Orient as the door opener to the distinctiveness of Japan, which serves as an indirect entrance to the uniqueness of Japan—in turn resting on the foundation of unstated or understated notions of the superiority of Japan. Part of the idea of Japanese uniqueness, or *Nihonjinron,* is the claim of harmony with nature and harmony within family and social groups, two features that early Western Japonists perceived as models for Western art and society (Dale 1986). Western romantic notions of nature meshed with the perception of "N/nature" in ukiyo-e, and this connection apparently merged with the Japanese conception of reverse orientalism.[35]

The ukiyo-e aspect of reverse orientalism features multiple ironies: in part the adoption of Western techniques of perspective made woodblock prints appealing to European and American eyes. In the case of ukiyo-e, Westerners did not travel to Japan to plunder the finest treasure available but retrieved the detritus of wrapping paper and discovered it as an art form; with the rise of Japonisme and the demand for ukiyo-e, in Japan there was a rediscovery of ukiyo-e as a legitimate art form and a re-cognition of it as an expression of the "true" Japanese spirit, especially for upholding such values as harmony with nature and harmonious human relationships. The beauty and values of ukiyo-e helped establish the idea of the Orient (and Japan) as a positive ideal to emulate—and return to.

Since Eric Hobsbawm and Terence Ranger's work *The Invention of Tradition* (1983), a host of books and articles have appeared on "invention" or "invented tradition" in many cultures, including Japan.[36] One recent volume on Japan includes articles on the invention of many aspects of the Japanese tradition, even the invention of Edo (Vlastos 1998a). A volume of essays, *Inventing the Classics*, edited by Haruo Shirane and Tomi Suzuki, focuses on literature and "canon formation," but one article contains the suggestion that "the canon of visual art, which came to represent Japan abroad at the turn of the century, was in fact largely determined, as in the case of ukiyoe, by its desirability as a commodity in the West, by the tastes and demands of *Japonisme*" (Shirane 2000, 3), helping the country establish national identity through cultural identity.[37] An article or book waiting to be written is "The Invention of Ukiyo-e."[38]

One hopes art historians and other scholars will fill in this gap in the understanding of the Japanese reevaluation or reinvention of ukiyo-e, but until they do, several points seem worth suggesting. First, the discovery/rediscovery of woodblock prints was made by Westerners who were eagerly searching for the exotic Far East / Orient; second, this Western recognition of ukiyo-e and Japonisme was confirmed and reconfirmed by Japanese officials and scholars who were actively engaged in nation building and promoting national identity; third, Fuji was a minor but important motif in Japonisme generally but in the long run a major recipient of the nuances of both Western orientalism and Japanese "reverse orientalism"; fourth, as the exotic character of woodblock prints and things Japanese became commonplace, they turned stereotypical, and through mass replication of their images on every type of cheap trinket, they grew tired and trivial. The symbolic career of Fuji, and episodes of "discovery" and "rediscovery," will no doubt continue long into the future.

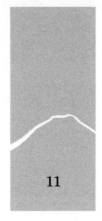

11

The Enduring Image of
Fuji in Modern Times

GIVING FORM TO JAPAN'S IDENTITY:
FUJI AND THE IDEOLOGY OF NATIONALISM

During the same general period when the visual ideal of Fuji was being framed in woodblock prints, the conceptual significance of the selfsame mountain was being formulated by artists and ideologues. Within Japan age-old notions of Fuji's aesthetic and religious character were key elements used by politicians, intellectuals, and artists to develop more elaborate ideas—ideology—using Fuji as a rallying point for national identity (Iida 2002). The earlier idea of Fuji as the supreme mountain of the three lands (*sangoku*) had been picked up and reinforced by religious leaders such as Kakugyō and Jikigyō: these figures parlayed the aesthetic and religious power of Fuji into a visual and conceptual legitimation of Japanese identity and supremacy.

Sangoku, the notion of three countries or "three realms," was an important concept in the promotion of Fuji from regional to national and universal status. Before the mid–sixteenth century, Japanese people saw the world as divided into three parts: "our country" (Japan), the continent (China and Korea), and India. There was tension between competing cosmologies, especially between the view of a Buddhist cosmology with India and Mount Sumeru at the center of the world, and a Shinto view that "focused on Japan's identity and space as *shinkoku*, the 'Land of the Gods' or 'Divine Land.'" The systems of both *sangoku* and *shinkoku* notions were fairly flexible, but this general worldview was dominant until the arrival of Europeans. Jikigyō's worldview presents an interesting blend of the *sangoku* and *shinkoku* cosmologies: he adopts the *sangoku* category to make his claim for Fuji universal (inclusive of the known world) but relies on the *shinkoku* tenet of Japan as the center of this world by invoking the "unique" status of Fuji. In Jikigyō's conceptual landscape, Buddhism's (India's) cosmic mountain (or *axis mundi*, pillar of the world), Sumeru, has been replaced by Fuji, Japan's own cosmic mountain. With the arrival of Europeans in Japan in the sixteenth century came "a shift in cosmologies, from a universe of Three Lands (*sangoku*) to a world comprised of Myriad Lands (*bankoku*)."[1] Maps on eighteenth-century porcelain dishes represent a creative accommodation of a Fuji-centric attitude in a myriad-realms (*bankoku*) context: the *sangoku* triad gives way to recognition of many other countries, but Fuji retains its preeminence and uniqueness by being the epicenter of Japan as the central country.[2] The works of artists such as Hokusai and Hiroshige helped place Fuji on an aesthetic pinnacle within Japan, and the cumulative effect of Japonisme was the elevation of Fuji to an ethereal ultimate for (or beyond) Westerners.

After two centuries of relative seclusion, in the latter part of the Tokugawa period Japan was faced with the dilemma of internal unrest and external pressure,[3] which strained the fabric of the status-regulated society and tested the ability of the shogunal government to ward off foreign powers. As Western nations increased their demand for trade with Japan, a political and ideological debate arose within the feudal government over whether to open the country. In the eighteenth and early nineteenth centuries, although most Japanese had a general awareness of Japan as a larger collectivity, as individuals they experienced their primary sense of loyalty and identity to the locality or domain in which they lived, not to a nation-state in the modern sense. To solve the problems of centralization and cohesion in the face of foreign pressure, Japan turned to "direct" imperial rule. "In the process, imperial loyalism, operating within a polity (*kokutai*) held to be uniquely Japanese, replaced feudal loyalty as the central feature of political Japaneseness."[4] This *kokutai* was particularistic: Fuji was part and parcel of this particularism that helped solidify and mobilize "Japaneseness."

With the arrival of Commodore Perry's black ships in the early 1850s and trade agreements at the end of the decade, the stage was set for the end of the shogunate and the establishment of a nation-state in Meiji times. To ward off domination by foreign powers, the newly established Meiji government acted to develop a unified nation, not only in political institutions but also in public awareness, by rallying people around common symbols for shared goals. The emperor and the imperial household were "restored" or "invented" (or reinvented) to unify and mobilize the Japanese people.[5] Fuji was another important symbol—perhaps outranked only by the emperor, the chrysanthemum seal, and the rising sun flag—in the effort to bring people of all classes and all regions together in a strong national bond against external forces. This process of visualizing and actualizing the Japanese nation-state has been described as creating "'Japan' as the aesthetic construct of the modern universal world" (Iida 2002, 11).

The foundation for Meiji nationalism rests on the bedrock of Tokugawa thought, which made use of Fuji as a rallying point for unifying and defending the country, placing it on an equal or a superior position with regard to the rest of the world. The Tokugawa ideologue Ogyū Sorai (1666–1728), a scholar remembered mainly for his Confucian studies and role as an adviser to shoguns (but who also was deeply influenced by Taoist writings), took Fuji as a central symbol. Sorai made only one major trip in his lifetime, a journey to the province of Kai in the service of the shogun, during which he and his party saw Fuji for the first time, "a moment of beauty that remained with him for the rest of his life" (Lidin 1983, 26). His travels in 1706 were his sole encounter with Fuji, and yet his perception of the mountain goes beyond a mere empirical description to a complex amalgam of sinicized protonationalism. "Mount Fuji occupied . . . a central place in Sorai's view of the world" (26), which equated Mount Fuji and the Chinese mountain Hōrai (Penglai) and also linked Fuji to legendary K'un-lun. His Fuji-centric Japanism in sinicized idiom is probably responsible in part for the inscription on his mentor's tomb, in which Mount Fuji's role is upgraded from being (the Chinese) Mount Konron's junior partner to being in the center of the world and being the heavenly pillar that compares with the pole star (41–42). Sorai is not motivated by the ideals of the age-old "famous place" imagery, dutifully describing the effects of an eruption of Fuji, and the actual appearance of the peak (lacking perfect symmetry). Sorai seems to sinicize Fuji in order to glorify and elevate it to a position of superiority, in the process appropriating its prestige for the government and people of Japan (5, 80, 86, 88).

Sorai "sees Japan in the centre of a cosmic geography" and is "consciously a Sinophile but feelingly and unconsciously a Fuji nationalist" who after the downfall of his own feudal lord switched his loyalty to the Tokugawa house. "It was thus easy to keep the Fuji faith. It needed only be redirected—in the direction of the Tokugawa family" (Lidin 1983, 42–43). Sorai participated in neither the ascetic ascent of Fuji nor the aesthetic activities of graphically depicting the mountain, and yet his life and thought reflect a worldview that was shared and utilized by others in the forging of a Japanese identity centered around Fuji.

In the late eighteenth century Mount Fuji became an increasingly important symbol in the national consciousness of artists and writers, especially as seen in the writing of Hiraga Gennai (1728–79), who helped articulate the notion of "Japan" (Haga 1983). In a posthumous biography of Gennai, "an account is given of Gennai's ascent of Mt Fuji and his praise of it as 'truly the highest mountain in the three lands.' . . . Likening this to statements such as 'Fuji is the source of the three lands' by the Fuji cult leader Jikigyō Miroku and 'Mt Fuji is a mountain not to be found in other lands' by the Western-style painter Shiba Kōkan, . . . and linking such statements to new expressions of Japanese cultural superiority versus China in popular language and fiction, Kanō creates a convincing case for the investment of Fuji imagery with a new level of national significance" (Clark 2001, 23).

Gennai complained that "Japan" (Nippon or Nihon) was an actuality or reality previously not given its due. Whereas formerly one's country (*kuni* or *koku*) was considered as consciousness of the domain (*han*) in which a person lived, "for him country meant recognition of 'Japan' as a nation (*kokka*)" (Kano 1994, 48). Gennai was concerned with the "national interest" (*kokueki*), specifically, material benefits for the Japanese nation (Nipponkoku). Gennai had a dream in which Fuji told him to protect the country, so for him, Fuji was the same as Japan. Gennai considered his dream a revelation, as real as Japan, but he was not an idle daydreamer: in his pragmatic realism he favored the Western style of painting that featured both natural perspective and an actual likeness of the natural scene. Gennai's free spirit led him to give up the headship of his family to continue his studies of herbal medicine and work as a naturalist; he pursued "Western learning," which at the time included European (especially Dutch) scientific knowledge and also Western painting techniques.

Gennai's fame as a naturalist earned him an invitation to inspect the copper mines in the Akita domain. On this trip he met a young painter, Odano Naotake (1749–80), of the Kanō school (the literati or "Chinese" style of painting) and gave him Western paintings to copy. He persuaded Naotake to take up a more naturalistic form of painting. Naotake, using Western techniques learned from Gennai and from further training in Edo, painted a remarkable likeness of Fuji in a quite naturalistic manner (Kano 1994, 49–51). Gennai's introduction of Western techniques to the outlying Akita domain also included the daimyo of Akita, Satake Shozan (1748–85), who founded the Akita school of Western painting (French 1983a). Shozan thought that paintings should be of practical use, and he criticized previous landscape painters of the literati as useless. He deplored the copying of paintings and emphasis on style and insisted that paintings of practical use should depict likenesses of the objects represented. He wanted to breathe a more scientific spirit into painting and favored the Western technique of perspective for this purpose.

Shiba Kōkan (1738–1818) may be considered the successor who carried out Shozan's artistic theories.[6] Kōkan started his career in the Kanō school but came under the influence of "Dutch" (Western) painting. He favored both true-to-life paintings and those serving the national utility (Kano 1994, 56). (See plate 9.) In this light Kōkan saw previous landscape paintings in the Chinese fashion as depicting nameless mountains, nothing more than dreams. He also leveled his condemnation of previous landscape artists at Kanō Tan'yū (1602–74), the foremost Kanō-school painter of the Tokugawa period, whose paintings of Fuji were universally acclaimed at the time (Kaputa 1983, 150–51). Kōkan lamented that although Fuji was a mountain found in no other country, paintings of this subject placed so much emphasis on style and manner that they did not resemble Fuji and therefore did not qualify as pictures. He said that while Tan'yū had created many paintings of Fuji, they did not look like Fuji; they were all emotion and brushstroke. According to Kōkan, Tan'yū's renditions of Fuji were only playthings and could not serve as "tools of national utility" (Kano 1994, 56–57).

Some painters of the time opposed the emphasis on Western techniques in depictions of landscape and Fuji, but their works evince correctly painting Fuji as the proper way of representing Japan. Nakabayashi Chikutō (1776–1853) painted a picture of Fuji in 1837, "treating it as a symbol of folk thought" and describing it in a poem as a lofty mountain from the age of the *kami,* constituting the "form of the country."[7] Even if Nakabayashi's approach is different from that of the Western-style painters, it reinforces the message of Western-style painters, such as Kōkan, who emphasized that Fuji is a mountain found in no other country. By this point, when "the form of Fuji is identical with the country of Japan," Fuji has risen to the status of "the core of Japanese identity" (Kano 1994, 58–59).

From late Tokugawa times the form of Fuji clearly served the function of national interests, with military overtones. An 1849 woodblock print by Utagawa Kuniyoshi (1788–1861) in the series *Taiheiki eiyūden* (Heroic Stories of the Taiheiki) is described as follows: "The general Fujiwara no Masakiyo, whose real name was Kato Kazue no Kami Kiyomasa (1562–1611), seated in full armor on a *shōgi* (folding campstool) on the shore of Korea, and pointing with his closed fan at Mount Fuji in the distance. . . . He and his men are feeling homesick, and Mount Fuji, which obviously cannot be seen from Korea, is included here as the symbol of their home country."[8] The greater-than-life-size general in armor, towering over the apparently subdued or submissive "local inhabitants" in Korea, is directing his fan at the national symbol that represents the source of power behind his foreign expedition. Fuji may not be visible from abroad, but the message here seems to be that its form—and the country's will—is embodied in military uniform.[9]

The combination of Korea and Fuji unites disparate external and internal symbols for the cultivation of Japan's national identity. The twelve official visits of Korean embassies (along with those from Ryūkyū) in Edo times "were an important element in the political legitimation of the Tokugawa shogunate in its early decades, and in later years helped to create a new Japanese conception of the organization of international space, and of Japan's role in the ordering of that space," providing a visual "means for creating 'Japan.'" By demarcating the "'alien' in Japanese culture" these activities were "part of the process of creating the national-cultural 'self': the early-modern Japanese national identity."[10] This is shown in the *Chōsenjin raichō zu* (*Picture of the Korean Embassy*) by Hanegawa Tōei (fl. 1735–50), which records the Korean Embassy's passage through Edo. (See plate 10.) This painting, known for its Western-style perspective with a vanishing point, frames the procession vertically within a street of the Nihonbashi district of Edo: "the twin rows of two-story buildings recede to a vanishing point in the off-center Mt. Fuji."[11] Several paintings adopt almost the same view, with a procession proceeding from the top of the picture toward the viewer and making a ninety-degree turn to the right in the foreground. The gist of this depiction of the Korean Embassy, an alien or foreign legitimation of the national polity, is that Fuji is the reigning emblem of the emerging national identity.

In the Tokugawa era Fuji's image was elaborated on and actively promoted as a symbol demarcating Japan as supreme over the three lands and/or the "myriad realms." Nineteenth-century textbooks for the education of women featured Fuji in scenes and poems (Nenzi 2008, 127–28). The genius of Meiji ideologues was to adopt and adapt this hallmark of Japanese identity and supremacy and to infuse it into the consciousness of the citizens of the new nation-state, especially through the engine of universal education.

An analysis of some recent Japanese publications gives detailed information on the textbooks and instructors' manuals that feature Fuji from Meiji times through World War II, noting the prominent role of Fuji in the development of geography as a discipline in modern Japan (Abe Hajime 2002). Behind the statement "Fuji is the symbol of Japan" are the assumptions of the consciousness of one land, one people, one country. Early geographers such as Shiga Shigetaka (1863–1927) and Kojima Usui (1873–1948) helped foster such attitudes. Shiga "expounded his notion of *kokusui hozon* (preservation of the national essence) in the face of indiscriminate modernization" and "reawakened an aesthetic sensibility and appreciation of the physical environment that was to become an important aspect of Japanese nationalism" (Neuss 1983, 91).

Shiga's work was important for Kojima, who in 1905 published *Nihon sansuiron* (Theory of the Japanese Landscape). Both works coincided with wars and heightened patriotism: Shiga's work appeared just before the Sino-Japanese War; Kojima's came out at the time of the Russo-Japanese War. Shiga called Fuji a standard for considering the world's famous mountains; Kojima viewed Fuji as representative of all Japan's famous mountains. Shiga is another example of the trend of reverse orientalism, citing foreigners' admiration of Japan's natural beauty as confirmation of Japan's venerable aesthetic heritage focused on nature. He saw in all this an affirmation of the bond between nature and humans that elevates humans and bestows sacredness —qualities and virtues he credits to famous mountains, and paramount among all famous mountains is Fuji. For this claim he cites the dual evidence of the literary works of foreigners praising Fuji and the ancient custom in Japan of naming a local mountain "X-Fuji" (Abe Hajime 2002, 58–59, 62–63; see plate 11 in this volume).

Many school textbooks, especially those for the lower grades, utilized Fuji to instill national consciousness. Geography was a required subject, beginning with the early Meiji curriculum, but Fuji appeared also in the lessons of Japanese language, art, and poetry. Students read and wrote poetry about Fuji, viewed and drew pictures of Fuji (both the photographic or "true-view" likeness and the classic "three-domed" peak), and read accounts of ascents of Fuji. They were encouraged to climb

Fuji; for those who never climbed, nor even saw Fuji, the recurring images of Fuji familiarized them with the lovely shape of the mountain and instilled in them yearning for the peak as a beautiful symbol of Japan.

Meiji education fostered loyalty to *kokutai*, the national polity; yet the educational materials utilizing Fuji were not so explicit and logical when presented to students, more in the line of acquainting them with the sight and appreciation of this "natural" symbol of Japan. The drawing, reciting, reading, and composing of Fuji imagery were actions intended to incorporate within the individual an unconscious and emotional attachment to Fuji, which was linked to *kokutai* (Abe Hajime 2002, 82, fig. 10). "Fuji" is much more than a mere signpost for the physical mountain: the significance of these educational materials is that they convey, instill, and cultivate a particular image uniting the people around a concrete symbol representing *kokutai* and all its attendant values (such as loyalty to emperor and state).

FRAMING JAPAN'S IDENTITY: MONEY AND POSTAGE STAMPS

From the Meiji era on, the government used the rubric of Fuji in various measures intended to enhance the newly minted nation-state. This was most readily apparent in money and stamps, obvious and significant markers of cultural and national identification. The images on currency, coin, and postage are chosen by government bureaus and officials because of their recognition factor among the populace; the circulation of these tropes in daily life spreads and reinforces the knowledge and popularity of the subjects. The prominence of Fuji as a symbol of modern Japan is demonstrated by its appearance on many forms of money and on numerous issues of postage stamps. (The chrysanthemum seal of the imperial household was incorporated into all Japanese monetary instruments from early Meiji times until 1946.)

In premodern times Japan depended for many centuries mainly on coinage imported from China, Korea, and other countries; coins minted in Japan imitated those of foreign origin. In Tokugawa times some privately minted coins and the shogunate's own coinage circulated; many domains used their own paper currency. It seems unlikely that Fuji appeared on any of these early modern forms of Japanese money.[12] Attention is directed here to modern money dated from 1871 with the Meiji government's establishment of the yen (*en*) as the basis of national exchange, because only in Meiji did currency and postage stamps become important tools of heightening consciousness of national identity. In modern times Fuji has been a prominent symbol on both paper currency and coin as a representation of Japan.

The early Japanese currency of Meiji times featured mythical themes, such as dragons and the phoenix, and popular divinities (Daikoku and Ebisu); later important rulers, political figures, cultural figures, and famous shrines and temples were featured on banknotes. Fuji's form first appeared on currency in the modern era in 1872 on a form of local currency in foreign silver exchange notes issued "By Government Permission" at Yokohama.[13] Two aspects of this issue are noteworthy: the value is in dollars, in increments from five dollars to one thousand dollars; and the writing is a combination of Japanese and English. The dollar amount indicates that the notes were intended for international trade, making the picture of Fuji more conspicuous as a representation of Japan to the rest of the world.[14] Fuji's silhouette did not appear on a national banknote until 1938, when it graced a fifty-sen bill, illuminated by a golden sun and flanked by clouds and cherry blossoms in a "natural" or photographic setting associating Fuji with the mythical founding of Japan.[15] "This resorting to Fuji as a national symbol in times of foreign threat, perceived or real, resurfaced during the Meiji era (1868–1912) and the continuing aggressive colonial expansion that culminated in the disasters of the China and Pacific Wars" (Clark 2001, 23); the cue for Fuji's entrance as a subject for a banknote seems to be the heightened nationalism of the late 1930s. (Fuji also was a standard prop for promoting tourism, as a symbol of Japan's natural beauty, and was used for this purpose when Japan expected millions of tourists in 1940, the twenty-six-hundredth year since the "founding" of Japan.) However, in 1942—well into the Fifteen Year War of 1931–45—Fuji was replaced on the fifty-sen note by a photographic likeness of Yasukuni Shrine, the Shinto shrine honoring the soldiers and sailors who died in the service of the country.[16] Fuji reappeared on the postwar 1969 five-hundred-yen note[17] and is used on the reverse of the five-thousand-yen note from 1984.[18] and on the reverse of the one-thousand-yen note from 2003. Fuji's prominence on bills from the late 1930s to the present day is clear evidence of the conspicuous role of this mountain for representing the nation, especially during and after World War II.[19]

Coins of foreign origin were present in Japan from the protohistoric age, and Chinese coins were dominant for most periods up to Tokugawa times; coins minted in Japan imitated Chinese patterns. In ancient and medieval times barter continued to be the main form of exchange among the lower classes. Not until Tokugawa times did coin and paper currency come into more common usage. However, the mix of foreign and native coins, both governmental and private, and the variation of weight and purity were major concerns both for individuals and for merchants; the government had difficulty establishing a policy of using foreign coinage or creating and controlling native mintage. As with paper money, the Meiji government's establishment of the yen as the basis for the national currency was a means of unifying both monetary policy and national identity; older currency and coinage were removed from circulation.[20]

Modern Japanese coins share with currency the borrowed imagery from China, such as the dragon and the phoenix, and Japanese themes such as the sun and rice plants. Coins too have adopted Fuji's image to label Japan. The earliest example, apparently, is the 1941 one-sen coin with the chrysanthemum crest crowning the peak of the mountain.[21] In mid-1945, just before the end of the war, the scarcity of metal forced the government to resort to baked clay for coins; one was a one-sen piece with the outline of Fuji on it.[22] As with paper currency, the surfacing of Fuji on coins coincides with the war effort and the attempt to coalesce and mobilize the people for support of military goals. The greater role of Fuji on coins in postwar times is seen in the selection of this symmetrical cone on commemorative coins. The first was the thousand-yen silver issued for the eighteenth summer Olympic games in 1964;[23] one side features the five circles of the Olympic logo, and the other side shows Fuji in a semicircle of foliage. More striking is the hundred-yen coin commemorating the 1970 Osaka Expo; this image, even in its miniature form, shows up as Hokusai's rendition of the mountain and his stylized ribbon-shaped clouds surrounding it. Fuji next appeared on a 1999 coin commemorating the tenth anniversary of the enthronement of the present emperor; the mountain rises up above a bouquet of chrysanthemums.[24] In coin as in paper currency Fuji made its entrance at times of wars but has been more prominent in the postwar period as a deimperialized natural and national icon.

Postage stamps, because of their more frequent issue and greater graphic possibilities, provide a richer historical narrative of Fuji's role as a national symbol.[25] The initial Japanese postage stamps, dating from 1871, featured geometrical designs and were not popular at the time. A departure from the geometrical pattern in 1908 was the portrait of legendary Jingū Kōgō (Empress Jingū, 170–269 C.E.); as "the consort of the Emperor Chūai, the fourteenth sovereign of this country," when the emperor died and could not carry out his punitive expedition to the early Korean kingdom of Shiragi or Silla, Empress Jingū, "disguising herself as a man, set forth on the planned expedition" and "succeeded in subduing the enemy."[26] One of the first portraits on a Japanese stamp—shortly after the Russo-Japanese War of 1904–5—was a ruler victorious on a foreign battlefield. In Japan, as in other countries, postage stamps served the national interest. In 1922 a set in use through 1937 featured a triple motif of the (imperial) chrysanthemum crest over an outline of Fuji and with a deer;[27] the imperial crest in effect granted Fuji visual authority as representing the emperor and the country.

After the Great Kantō Earthquake of 1923, when the government printing office along with stamps and printing machines were destroyed, "the need for stamps necessitated emergency measures," with resort to private printing companies. A new design utilized the triad of the imperial chrysanthemum crest over Fuji against a background of cherry blossoms, seeming to invoke national symbols to restore the country.[28] In 1926 a stamp with a landscape view of Fuji was issued (Yamamoto 1962, 52); this is described as one of a "Famous View Series" (*Sakura* 1997, 25).[29] In the "1st Showa Series" Fuji appears in the background with cherry blossoms in the foreground (*Sakura* 1997, 26).[30]

A 1934 set of four airmail stamps, which *Sakura* labels "Establishment of Communications Day," features a trimotor plane filling the foreground and Fuji nestled in the distance under the landing gear of the plane.[31] Another airmail stamp, "Kamakura Buddha,"[32] is dominated on the left by the towering Buddha; a small plane appears at the upper right and a small Fuji is seen below.

In 1935, when the exchange of New Year greetings reached 700 million pieces of mail, a "design appropriate to the occasion" was sought: one design was "the graceful Mt. Fuji enclosed in a frame ornamented with an ancient combination pattern of pine, bamboo and plum-blossom."[33] In 1936 four stamps portraying Fuji were issued as part of the national park series, this one for Fuji-Hakone National Park.[34] Japanese postage stamps from the early Meiji era to 1940 progressed from geometrical designs to portraits and landscape scenes, with Fuji presented as a national symbol. Fuji stamps from before 1941 were reissued later during the war.[35]

Yamamoto designates a special category for "Propaganda Stamps (1942–1948)."[36] "During the Pacific War of 1941–45 the Japanese Government issued 12 stamps for the purpose of whipping up the people's fervor and desire to prosecute the war." Of these twelve, "the design of the 4 sen stamp shows peerless Fuji and that monumental tower which was erected in the province of Hyūga (Miyazaki prefecture), the legendary cradle of the ancestors of the Japanese Emperors, in commemoration of the 1940 celebration."[37] The tower commemorates "the 26th Centennial of the accession to the Throne of the first Emperor of Japan, Jimmu Tennō," who subdued the local "stubborn resistance to the Imperial forces."[38] This mythical account from the eighth-century records of the *Kojiki* and the *Nihon shoki* was used by the Meiji government and its successors to legitimate imperial rule, unify the country through loyalty to the emperor, and mobilize the country during the Pacific War.[39] The 1942 stamp pairs the peak of Fuji and the top of the tower, and these two symbols (together with the ever-present imperial chrysanthemum) compound the power of the imperial logo, the sacred peak, and the tower in support of the war effort.[40]

The linking of Fuji with the commemoration tower of Hyūga certainly qualifies Fuji for service in the category of imperialistic propaganda. A group of stamps issued during Japan's World War II occupation of the Philippines, which pairs Fuji with a local volcano, employs Fuji as a tool of colonialism and chauvinism.[41] On April 1, 1943, fourteen regular stamps were issued, three of which Yamamoto identifies simply as "volcano Mayon"; however, the stamp clearly pictures two mountains, one slightly lower to the right emerging out of a tropical setting of palm trees and the other to the left and a little above, resting on a layer of clouds. The higher mountain appears to be Fuji, and this is confirmed by the *Sakura* catalog description of "Fuji and Mount Mayon." The setting is "Philippine Islands," but the twinning of Fuji with Mayon—Fuji in a slightly superior position—is reminiscent of the Japanese government's use of Confucian ideology on the Asian continent to urge cooperation of subordinate "little brother" Asian countries with their "big brother" Japan. This theme is predominant in imperialistic propaganda and postage stamps disseminated in the Japanese colonies and regions that came under Japanese control during the Fifteen Year War (1931–45).[42]

Within the same Philippine series, "On May 7, 1943, two stamps . . . were issued to commemorate the first anniversary of the fall of Bataan and Corregidor. . . . The design is a sort of montage showing map, sun-flag, airplane, warship and soldier";[43] this stamp makes explicit the military and colonial domination only implied in the twinning of Fuji with a Philippine mountain. Fuji's colonial service was not limited to the Philippines: "Eleven kinds of stamps were issued in May, 1943, by the Japanese Naval Administration in the Moluccas and Lesser Sunda," four of which feature "Mt. Fuji, golden kite, sun-flag and map of East Indies."[44] The image of the stamp expresses even more vividly than the caption the dominance of Fuji, which appears in the upper half of the stamp; the "sun-flag" is in the middle, and the map of the East Indies is at the bottom. Another colonial stamp of earlier date (issued by authority of what the *Sakura* catalog labels "'Manchukuo' Puppet Government," is the 1935 set "Visit of Emperor to Japan," here referring to Henri Pu-yi, the (puppet) emperor of Manchukuo. The stamp shows puffs of clouds over the steep slope of Fuji, labeled by the catalog as "auspicious clouds on Fuji," implying that Japan's close relationship with its newly established satellite, Manchukuo, bode well for Fuji/Japan.[45] Conversely, Fuji seems to welcome—and authenticate—the puppet emperor of Manchukuo. The service performed by Fuji's postal images of the 1930s and 1940s is reminiscent of the ideal of the late Tokugawa ideologues who insisted that pictures of the mountain should be "tools of national utility." Fuji certainly did function as an instrument of imperial, colonial, and military goals.[46]

An interesting footnote to Fuji in philately is provided by Baron Takaharu Mitsui's short 1940 article "Japan Portrayed in Her Postage Stamps." Appearing in the semiofficial English-language trade journal *Tourist*, the brief piece is a straightforward attempt to attract Western visitors to Japan, touting postage stamps as "illustrating noteworthy features of her scenery, history and national life." The article begins: "Even those Westerners who have not been to Japan know that Japanese nature is symbolized by Mt. Huzi [Fuji] and the Japanese character by her cherry-blossom." He waxes eloquent on the appropriateness of volcanoes and Fuji to grace stamps since they are "a manifestation of masculine power, and . . . the mother of hot springs. . . . The snow-crowned Huzi [Fuji], the charming cherry blossom, the frost-braving plum blossom . . . —these are to be taken at a higher connative worth than their mere ornamental value."[47] Mitsui's appraisal of Fuji's merits for appearing on stamps, based on his own attitudes and cultural heritage, are very close to the image of the peak conveyed in the early chapters of this work, especially the power of the volcano in fire and water and its beauty as a natural feature and symbol of the nation. This apolitical view of Fuji on the eve of World War II would be revisited and revived in the immediate postwar period.

Postwar Japan underwent many changes, notably the discrediting and banning of ultranationalistic and militaristic policies, along with the disestablishment of Shinto and the promulgation of freedom of religion. An interesting postal commentary on this process is an April 15, 1946, issue: "The 1 yen stamp has a design of the Yasukuni Shrine. The design was adopted presumably to do honor to the souls of the war dead. The sale of this stamp was banned on May 15, only a month after its issue."[48] Similar stamps honoring Yasukuni Shrine had been issued during wartime, but after the defeat Yasukuni was purged, even from postage stamps. The chrysanthemum seal (or "arms," as the *Sakura* catalog states), representing the imperial household and the supreme authority in the land, was another casualty of the occupation and its reforms.

By contrast the image of Fuji, although it had been used in wartime propaganda, was not banished; in fact, once rehabilitated, it became more popular than ever, even a symbol of peace. A Japanese stamp catalog notes, "Postwar efforts at postage stamp making in Japan were marked by the implementation of a program for revising designs so as to symbolize a country out for peace. The first step toward the attainment of this avowed object was the issuance on August 1, 1946, of a stamp, 1 yen, blue, R 217. The design is taken from the 'Shower at the Foot of Mt. Fuji,' one of the masterpieces of Hokusai Katsushika (1760–1849), color-print artist celebrated the world over for his '36 Views of Fuji' and many other color prints."[49]

Several points highlight the significance of this stamp. The date is important, marking the first move after the war for the postal service to shift from wartime militaristic themes to a peaceful motif. The choice of Fuji as one of the symbols to further peace documents the fact that it continued to represent Japan. The selection of an ukiyo-e print, in effect if not in explicit attempt, is a clever use of reverse orientalism to take advantage of the Western romantic attachment to Hokusai and Fuji in the process of appropriating it for peaceful aims.[50] The imperial crest, although moved from the center to the upper left corner, affirms that the emperor was still the nominal head of state, although this would change the following year with the adoption of a new constitution relegating the emperor to a nondivine status as a mere "symbol" of the nation. The removal of three characters—*Dai Teikoku*, "Greater Empire"—from the stamp transforms both emperor and mountain from rallying (imperialistic) symbols of a war effort to emblems of a nation, defeated and stripped of the gains of fifty years of colonial expansion, seeking peaceful relations with former foes. Today, as a shrine, Yasukuni is prospering, having regained and even exceeded its prewar glory; as a symbol, however, it continues to attract domestic and international criticism, being a lightning rod of divisiveness and controversy about lingering war issues.

In striking contrast, Fuji emerged relatively unscathed and untainted by the war, once more the enduring and malleable icon of Japan. Indeed during the occupation a commemorative stamp was issued for the centenary of the death of Hokusai in 1948, again utilizing stamps (and a centenary block) with a Hokusai print of Fuji (Yamamoto 1962, 175–76).[51] In 1949 the Fuji-Hakone National Park was featured for the second time in an ongoing series of national park stamps launched in 1936 (the first set devoted to Fuji-Hakone) and suspended during the war; in other words, Fuji as representing Japan and Nature in prewar times served the same role in the postwar era. In peacetime Fuji has surfaced again and again on stamps as reissues and revisions, as photographs and paintings, and as both reproductions and clever reworkings of Hokusai and Hiroshige.[52]

The heritage of Tokugawa ideology for Fuji to serve the needs of the nation has been expressed and realized in coins, banknotes, and stamps of Meiji times and later. Both in war and in peace Fuji has served the country.

Part 4

FUJI DEVOTION IN CONTEMPORARY JAPAN

In postwar times when Tokyo was rebuilt and new families moved in, they did not grow up with the sight of Fuji morning and night, and did not learn the old customs.

Iwashina 1983, 8

12

A Contemporary Fujikō

THE DECLINE OF FUJIKŌ IN MODERN TIMES

Fuji spirituality peaked in mid and late Tokugawa times, but thereafter the star of this sacred symbol dimmed considerably, even though some groups have tried valiantly to keep alive the religious character of Fuji that was so prominent in previous centuries. The fuller picture of Fuji faith today must be found in the existing Fuji pilgrimage groups, which retain, each in its own way, the religious practices of the past in a contemporary setting.

After the Meiji Restoration, Fuji pilgrimage groups suffered from the policies of the new government, which was intent on unifying the country under a "restored" Shinto and in the process temporarily persecuted Buddhism and permanently disbanded Shugendō. During the early Meiji years, when the attack on Buddhism was at its height and Buddhist institutions and artwork were the target of looting and destruction, many of Fuji's sacred sites, being of mixed heritage, were also targets of the same religious zealotry. Indeed some of Fuji's history is obscured because priceless statues and other artifacts were moved, lost, or destroyed during this time. Although not officially banned, the Fuji confraternities lost momentum and never fully recovered. However, during the Tokugawa era—the golden age of Fuji belief and Fuji confraternities—government suppression of Fuji groups could neither prevent their growth nor hinder their activities. The fact that in Meiji times oppressive governmental policies affected Fujikō so severely shows that these groups were already on the wane, owing to a number of social, political, and religious developments.[1]

In late Tokugawa times Fuji faith had a number of lively competitors for the hearts and minds of the people. Popular movements such as Shingaku, which taught Confucian ethics mixed with Buddhist and Shinto teachings and practices, drew large numbers of followers[2] (and may have influenced some forms of Fuji

practices, such as in Fujidō). From the early nineteenth century, new religions, especially the pioneer movements of Tenrikyō, Kurozumikyō, and Konkōkyō, recruited
many members. The trend of the times was definitely moving away from loosely
organized neighborhood groups (such as pilgrimage associations) and toward more
tightly structured nationwide voluntary organizations.

The end of World War II in 1945 was accompanied by the specific disestablishment of Shinto and the general banning of all state-sponsored religion. All religious
groups were set back by the massive destruction of the country. However, the policy
of complete freedom of religion ushered in an era of phenomenal growth for existing new religions and new religions that developed in the postwar era. With the
lifting of the ban on Shugendō, some groups reorganized formally as Shugendō
institutions. Within this setting the remaining Fujikō were free to organize and oper-
ate as they wished, the same as new religions and Shugendō, but conditions were not
favorable for their revival.

In prewar times the "mountain opening" ceremonies were still held at *fujizuka*,
a practice seldom observed in postwar times. Those *fujizuka* that have become local
tutelary divinities are still active. Scholars attribute the decline of Fujikō and their
activities mainly to the loss of homes and neighborhood identity (Iwashina 1983, 8),
particularly in the Fujikō stronghold of Tokyo. In postwar times Tokyo's skyline grew
higher, obscuring the sight of Fuji for many Tokyoites; furthermore the influx of new
people meant that the old customs died out. These certainly were daunting conditions for Fujikō to surmount in reorganizing, but even in areas that survived the war
unscathed, *fujizuka* and Fujikō did not prosper. An already diminished Fuji religiosity was hampered by the changed social conditions and the momentum of the
new religions.

One of the ironies of Fuji "pilgrimage" is that increasingly in modern times,
when fewer people climbed for religious reasons as members of Fujikō, many more
made the ascent as a recreational or sightseeing activity. A 1920 newspaper (*Yamanashi Nichinichi Shinbun*) reports that 48,300 people climbed Fuji that year (Iwashina
1983, 20–24). A telephone call to the Fujiyoshida City Hall yielded figures indicating
that from just under 100,000 to over 200,000 people passed through the Yoshida
entrance and moved through the sixth station safety center (Anzen Shidō Senta)
annually from 1981 through 1988. Earlier figures were not available, but these relatively high numbers were recorded after the development of the Subaru line in 1964.
Figures for climbers from Fujinomiya provided by the Fujinomiya City Hall ranged
from 20,000 to almost 40,000 during the years 1965–69 and jumped to 300,000 for
1970 when the Fujisan Skyline (to the fifth station on the south) opened; for the years
1971–88 the numbers stayed in the mid-200,000 range except for two years when
the figures were in the mid-100,000s. The opening of highways and the ease of bus
transportation have dramatically altered not only the mode of travel but also the
kind and number of travelers, as well as the ambience of Fuji and the experience of

the ascent. In this and the next chapter we will follow three contemporary groups in their practice and pilgrimage of Fuji spirituality, starting with the most traditional example, Miyamotokō.

MIYAMOTOKŌ: EDO CUSTOMS IN TOKYO

Despite the many challenges of postwar times, Miyamotokō, the continuation of one of the oldest Fujikō, has proudly tried to maintain the beliefs and practices of Tokugawa-era Fuji religiosity. Miyamotokō was selected for fieldwork and participant observation because it was clearly the oldest and most "traditional" Fujikō still active. Ida Kiyoshige, the head of the Marutō Miyamotokō, traced his family heritage to the people and Fujikō who created the first *fujizuka*. At age seventy-one, "Ida . . . had climbed the mountain 146 times. Mr. Ida . . . made his first ascent of Fuji at the age of seven with his father, the previous leader of the group. A stone statue of the latter, dressed in pilgrim's garb, stands beside the Shinto shrine that marks the beginning of the traditional climbing route from Fuji-Yoshida. The statue was erected to commemorate his 150th ascent of the mountain. One of Ida-san's ancestors was the first person to construct a Fuji replica."[3] Ida, an unassuming man, gladly agreed to a four-hour interview in his "Fuji Mansion" residence, a treasure trove of Fuji memorabilia as well as a meeting place of his Fujikō with its own distinctive Fuji altar (seen previously in chapter 7). This 1988 interview offers insight into the personal motivation behind the valiant attempt to keep alive the ancient customs of Fujikō in modern Tokyo.

Ida proudly displayed his group's liturgy, *otsutae*, which retains the pre-Meiji language; after Meiji (with the government's suppression of Buddhism and establishment of state Shinto), most of the Fujikō changed their liturgy into a Shinto style of recitation patterned after Shinto prayers. This was the first of numerous claims that the Marutō Miyamotokō retained the older, traditional ("true") customs and did not compromise with newer practices for the sake of gathering members or taking in money (or giving in to governmental pressure). He regretted that occupying a modern building, with fire alarms and walls that stain easily, meant that his group had to give up the age-old form of fire ritual, *takiage*, for the simpler style using incense.

Ida outlined the monthly meetings and the pattern of annual pilgrimage as well as the officers and membership, most of whom come from the nearby area. When asked if people enter from other Fujikō that are dying out, he was taken aback and answered that most of the people in Miyamotokō were originally in the *kō*, a family heritage going back generations. He emphasized repeatedly that his group is not a "business." In the informal setting of his own home he was very critical of Japanese religion in general, saying that Buddhist priests and others are involved in religion for money and that this Fujikō too might flourish if he and his members were in it for money because these days people will do anything for money.

Because on a nearby table lay a flyer from Fusōkyō announcing a nationwide Fuji group, the conversation turned to Fusōkyō. Ida said that Fusōkyō engages in these activities to recruit members, from Hokkaido to Kyushu. However, "pure Fujikō" (like Miyamotokō) are few. According to Ida some leaders of Fuji groups are mere *ogamiya* ("faith healers"); such people join Fusōkyō.[4] He stressed that he is not an *ogamiya,* and Miyamotokō has no intention of joining Fusōkyō. In a rambling discussion covering many topics, he returned again and again to two points. First, some people are involved in religion for commercial, financial reasons, and they may be "successful" in terms of numbers of believers and accumulation of money, but Miyamotokō is not interested in this. Second, some people such as the Fusōkyō leaders and their nationwide group are interested in empire building, in order to gather in many members and develop a large organization (*kyōdan*), but this tends to water down the ancient Fuji practices by letting in *ogamiya* and everyone else, while retaining the umbrella name of Fuji faith. Ida personally and Miyamotokō as a group reject all of this. In this sense Ida and Miyamotokō may be seen as antiestablishment.

Ida said that during Meiji times, because of government pressure, Miyamotokō temporarily came under the supervision of Fusōkyō, but Miyamotokō never officially joined it; because Miyamotokō is an original Fujikō, there is no reason to join now. He stressed that Fusōkyō has no direct connection to Fujikō; the intention of Fusōkyō is just to surround and incorporate these groups in order to increase its own organizational strength. When asked about giving out ranks, Ida said that Fusōkyō does give out religious ranks to followers (apparently to attract members), but Fujikō never had such ranks.

As the talk shifted to what traditional practices Miyamotokō retained, Ida admitted that many of the old customs and practices have fallen by the wayside. It was the *oshi* (guide) who gave out titles such as *daisendatsu* (great leader). When asked about the traditional "practice names," Ida said that *oshi* also gave these out but that they are not used now. If a person asked, he or she would probably be given such a name, but these days people do not ask. He pointed out that the people who serve as *oshi* today are not *oshi* in the traditional sense, having become Shinto officials. These Shinto-style *oshi* could give out practice or ascetic names, but it is a moot point because no one makes this request. In earlier times leaders and members of Fujikō had extraordinary experiences on the mountain, but according to Ida, these are rare today. He emphasized that because they are not running a "business," they do not push this kind of thing.

In earlier times each Fujikō performed its own *nanasha* (seven-shrine) observances at the beginning of the climbing season; the specific shrines or sacred sites varied for each *kō,* and the number was not always exactly seven. In recent times Marutō Miyamotokō was one of the very few Fujikō carrying out the *nanasha* observances. Formerly the Miyamotokō members made their *nanasha* "round" by walking the circuit of seven sacred sites. In 1988 the Miyamotokō made an automobile tour in two cars; the diminished scale of the rite is measured by the fact that researchers and television crews equaled or outnumbered the Miyamotokō members. The first two stops of the day were not at shrines but at two cemeteries to honor the grave of the founder of this Fujikō, whose practice name is Nichigyō, and the grave of the next leader in this lineage. These services were brief and to the point. Following the usual Japanese custom, they used wooden buckets of water to clean the memorial stone, decorated it with fresh sprigs of greens, and lit incense; then they recited a short prayer.

From the second cemetery they traveled to the Senju Fujizuka, within the shrine compound of the Hikawa Jinja. Here the Miyamotokō paid their respects at the small shrine next to the *fujizuka* and recited part of their liturgy. They climbed and descended the miniature Fuji, after which the shrine priests gave out ceremonial sips of sake, followed by cups of green tea. The group then motored to Fuji Sengen Jinja, whose celebration was in conjunction with a large flower fair in the neighboring markets. Here the members lined up for a brief recitation but did not climb the *fujizuka*.

The group rode to the next stop, Onoterusaki Jinja, where they were greeted at a side entrance by a television crew that had made an agreement to film them at the shrine. The crew asked the members to reenter from the (wider and more impressive) main shrine entrance where they customarily entered. As they circled around the shrine and started down the main entrance, the author walked backward ahead of the *kō* filming the performance, wondering where the television crew was. After they arrived on the shrine grounds proper, the television crew was in full action with cameras in all the best angles, capturing the *kō* in their liturgy before the shrine and following them up and down the miniature Fuji. These *fujizuka* are usually closed except on such festive occasions, and nearby families made the most of this open access by frolicking on the mountain. Children were surprised and amused at the white-clad pilgrims on this local landmark and mimicked the *kō* members' finger gestures (*in*, or *mudra*). The television staff became makeshift traffic-control officers, shushing the children and shooing people away from these pilgrims during their close-up interviews. The lead interviewer's final question was a request: they had not gotten a good shot of the group making their procession into the shrine grounds and asked for the group to repeat their entry. The obvious but unstated fact was that they could not show a "traditional" Fuji festival with a foreign researcher backstepping his way ahead of the group with outstretched video camera. The Miyamotokō obliged and made their entrance for the third time. The element of a "spectacle" was not lost on Ida and his friends. Back in the car they joked about the camera crews and the fact that Japan is so full of money, that it is *miru-miru* ("looky-looky") everywhere you go.

As this anecdote makes clear, members of the Miyamotokō were keenly aware of their own almost desperate attempt to continue customs and practices centuries old in a highly changed social and geographical setting. In their effort to communicate their heritage and values to a wider public, they were also cognizant of the fact that they allowed themselves to be used by the modern technology of cameras and the sophisticated communication medium of television. However, if the television staff arranged, staged, and selectively edited the event to present it, in all likelihood, as a "traditional" occurrence, then the Miyamotokō brought to this event the accumulation of centuries of beliefs and practices. Fuji religiosity is thus a good example of the perils of essentialism and of the tension between the modern and the traditional, themes that will be taken up again in the final chapter of this work.

The last stop of the day was the Komagome Fuji Jinja, where a lively street fair and festival was in progress. The crowded shrine grounds and carnival atmosphere of booths made it difficult to move. The Miyamotokō entered, said a prayer at a small shrine at the foot of a steep stairway, and then climbed the stairs and repeated their prayers in front of the main shrine before descending via the "down" staircase. The shrine officials served tea to the group before they went to the cars and ended the day. Here, as at other shrines, the officials were well aware of the historic character and notoriety of Miyamotokō, but most festival participants ignored them and seemed oblivious to the connection of the day's festivities to this group or to the notion of the opening of the climbing season for Fuji.

The *nanasha* "round" marks the official beginning of the climbing season, but each *kō* specifies its own time for its ascent. Miyamotokō has its own ceremonial send-off for the annual pilgrimage at Ida's residence; a lengthy recitation of the *otsutae* (liturgy) and performance of the fire rite *takiage* were held the evening of August 1, 1988. Worth noting are several incidental details. The altar was graced by large bottles of sake from various contributors, including NHK, the government broadcasting agency, apparently as thanks for earlier filming or an advance gift for future cooperation. At the end of the almost hour-long recitation, conviviality and joking ensued. One aside by Ida—advising people to bring along lunch for the bus and not to worry about food since there is plenty on the mountain—warned that "the mountain is high, and so are the prices." His earthy humor is reminiscent of the nineteenth-century travel book *Shank's Mare*, which also poked fun at pilgrimage: "When your debts pile up to Fuji's height / That is the time to fly by night" (Jippensha 1960, 369).[5]

The walking pilgrimage of Edo times has already been described. In recent times groups take charter deluxe buses directly to the fifth station, thanks to a modern highway. The Miyamotokō left Ida's apartment building about 7:30 A.M. on August 4 and, counting several people picked up along the way, totaled forty-three passengers. At 9:55 A.M. the group arrived in Fujiyoshida at the pilgrimage lodging called Daikokuya, where most of their belongings were left; they kept only what was needed on the mountain (clothing, rain gear, snacks). Prior to the trip the author received permission to hand out copies of a brief questionnaire, which Ida had read and enthusiastically approved. At the Daikokuya, after his general information on the ascent and safety requirements, he asked the members' cooperation with the questionnaire, which was distributed. They departed the Daikokuya at 10:40 A.M. for the Kitaguchi Sengen Jinja, where the group lined up for formal purification by Shinto priests, after which Ida made formal offerings of sprigs and papers to the shrine. Everyone received a ceremonial sip of sacred sake. In earlier times the "old route" ran through this shrine to the nine stations and the summit. In 1988 Ida's group paid respects to both the old route and a statue of Ida's father at the beginning of this former entrance to the mountain. Ida climbed up on the pedestal of the statue (which commemorates his father's 150th ascent) and replaced the old headband with a new one.[6]

At 11:30 A.M. they left this shrine via the bus and the highway to the fifth station, passing the Tainai (Womb) cave, which would be visited on the way down. Markers indicated the first through fourth stations, until the bus arrived at the fifth station, a bustling center of lodgings, restaurants, and souvenir shops. People paid respects quickly at the Komitake Jinja at the fifth station, were caught in the lenses of some filmmakers, and then ate their packed lunches in a nearby shop. Shortly before 1:00 P.M. the group, numbering thirty-nine, left the fifth station. The oldest member was eighty-eight. Ida and some others chanted the "purification of the six senses." Walking at a leisurely but steady pace and with occasional rests, they passed the sixth and seventh stations and arrived at the hut called Gansomuro about 6:00 P.M.

The Gansomuro is the site of the Eboshi Iwa, where Jikigyō Miroku starved himself to death. An interview with Ida explains the key significance of this site: "On the yearly ascent of the volcano, he carries up a ritual mirror inscribed with the word *Sengen,* the name of the deity of Mount Fuji, and places it in front of the rock where the saint martyred himself. He regards this place as the most sacred feature on the entire mountain, a focal point of the pilgrimage. The teachings that Jikigyo dictated there as he was fasting to death for the sake of others encourage people to care for each other. As Ida-san puts it, 'The most important thing in climbing is the inner strength to help each other, so that not just the strongest but all the members of Fujiko reach the goal. Mount Fuji, from our religious point of view, is a mountain that accepts all comers.'"[7]

A Fusōkyō priest from the neighboring small shrine entered the hut, received an offering from the Miyamotokō people, and invited the group into the small shrine. About twenty or thirty people crowded into the tiny shrine, where the Fusōkyō representative gave a standard overview of Fuji pilgrimage, emphasizing how difficult it was in earlier times. The overview began with the patriarchs Matsudai and En no Gyōja, who performed asceticism and received the deity Sengen and Motochichihaha (the original father and mother), the source of the mountain. Moving quickly to Meiji times, when Fuji practices were in decline, he described the organization of the Fuji Issankyō, leading to the adoption of the name Fusōkyō in 1878. He explained the idiosyncratic term *fusō*, which originated in China and refers to a land to the east with a mountain in the center: this "treasure mountain" is called Fusō no Yama; so Fuji is identical to Japan.

This priest gave other details of Fuji from a Fusōkyō perspective and claimed that because Jikigyō Miroku starved himself to death here at the Eboshi Iwa, it is called the "little summit," as opposed to the physical summit of the mountain. After his talk he invited all the audience to participate in a rite of purification, protection, and healing performed in the darkened room by placing a wooden box from the shrine's altar on the head of each person.[8] Following the ceremony in the shrine, they returned to the hut for a light evening meal and then went to sleep on the "shelves" lining the walls of the hut. They arose at 4:15 A.M. to greet the rising sun, a marvelous sight from this lofty vantage point, and welcomed it with a brief prayer. After breakfast in the hut, the authorities deemed the high and rising winds too dangerous for further ascent. Because the charter bus was waiting for them, they could not delay the ascent until the wind calmed and so had to descend. From this point the pilgrimage was anticlimactic. Leaving Gansomuro at 6:00 A.M., they made the trip down quickly and with no ceremonies. They arrived at the fifth station after 8:00 A.M., rejoining Ida and several others who had not gone to Gansomuro.

After rest and refreshments the group boarded the bus and left the fifth station at 10:00 A.M. for the Tainai. In the bus on the way to the cave, Ida gave the background and rationale of the Tainai. Jikigyō Miroku died at Eboshi Iwa, but first he practiced in the Tainai. The founder of the Miyamotokō, Nichigyō, went every day looking after Jikigyō Miroku; hence his practice name of Nichigyō (literally "daily" *nichi* "practice" *gyō*). He also developed the first *fujizuka* on a site now occupied by Waseda University. He explained that Tainai means "inside a woman's body" and also "where a child is born," as can be understood when viewing the cave. When the bus arrived at the Tainai at 10:30, people quickly went through the shrine to enter the cave. Some who had been there before were disinterested and sat waiting for the others to re-emerge. Some bought amulets from the Tainai Shrine, whose specialty is easy childbirth. (See plate 4.)

They left the Tainai at 11:00 and were able to make an unscheduled stop at the Shiraito ("White Thread") Falls, a wide rim with many separate "threads" or falls. They wandered around this popular tourist site with its many vendors. Ida took them aside and showed them a stone dedicated to Jikigyō Miroku near the falls. The members had their obligatory commemorative photograph taken against the background of the falls, ate lunch at nearby shops, left at 2:00 P.M., and arrived at the lodging Daikokuya at 3:00. After a hot bath, several members walked to a nearby Mirokudō (Miroku Hall) and viewed statues of Miroku, Konohana, and other historical objects. That night the Daikokuya provided a lavish meal for all the Miyamotokō participants in their large dining area. Ida gave a talk noting his regrets about not making it to the summit and hoping for better weather the next year. As is customary at such group events, beer and sake were consumed, to the accompaniment of karaoke.

The next morning after breakfast, while waiting for the bus, a woman who participated in the *nanasha mawari* complained about the cameramen at the Onoterusaki Jinja who for their television show had them climb the *fujizuka* a second time and reenter the shrine grounds. She said that she had been intrigued with Fuji and wanted once to see that mountain. Although she had been afraid that she could not climb Fuji, she went with Miyamotokō and made the ascent. She and the other women with her—discussing the regular meetings of the *kō*, the monthly fees, the *nanasha* "round"—emphasized that it took time, money, and energy to be a part of the group and said that if not for the deep faith (*shinkō*) they found in this group, they would not continue. Such explicit expressions of religious commitment during the pilgrimage were rare, since religious faith is taken for granted rather than overtly mentioned, but they are significant evidence that even without active proselytizing, some individuals are still attracted into the *kō*.

The party boarded the bus to go to the local nature museum, which featured archaeological materials; then they viewed a film of the mountain. In several places the film showed clips of Miyamotokō from previous years climbing the mountain; this provoked laughing and clapping. One of the closing comments of the film was that because Fuji exists in the hearts of the Japanese, those who have never seen Fuji feel as if they are missing something important.

From the museum the bus took the party to an *onsen* (natural hot spring) for a hot bath, followed by a lunch. In this pleasant atmosphere the group relaxed and became more conversational. One woman said that she had climbed the mountain forty years ago, following the "old route," which was a "weird"[9] experience unlike the trip from the fifth station to the summit. An elderly man in the group, a photographer who had published a book of photos on Fuji, agreed heartily with her. One of the *kō* leaders asked for other impressions, but there were no volunteers, so they fell back on the standard Japanese practice of having individuals sing. They left the *onsen* for the last stop before Tokyo, a "you pick" grape farm. The *sendatsu* of the *kō* seemed a bit embarrassed by this diversion and took me aside to explain that they used to climb from the first station all the way to the summit and then go back to Tokyo, but that was too tiring, and these days people want to relax a little. With few opportunities to travel, nowadays they take advantage of the Fuji ascent to stop here for grapes. Several times during the pilgrimage Ida had been apologetic about the itinerary, complaining that to attract a busload he had to make the trip "interesting" with the *onsen* and the grape farm. However, the history of Fuji pilgrimage reveals an ongoing tension between the more hardcore "Fuji asceticism" and the more relaxed "Fuji faith." Ida's rationale also contains much of the ethical overtones of "Fuji piety," with his anticlerical and anticommercial critique and his insistence on self-cultivation as the true goal of Fuji pilgrimage.[10]

The members boarded the bus one last time for the trip to Tokyo, where the group disbanded. A "thanks" meeting with *takiage* was held on the tenth of the month. This meeting was similar to the send-off meeting, except that clothes and packs were not held over the fire for purification, and this time a congratulatory meal followed. Ida reiterated what had been said at the lodging Daikokuya: he regretted that the group had not been able to make it to the summit; but he said, "You don't have to reach the summit when you climb Fuji to achieve your goal: more important is the spirit in which you climb."

13

New Religions and Fuji

MARUYAMAKYŌ: THE CRATER OF FUJI AS A MECCA

Popular wisdom states, "There are many paths up the mountain but they all lead to the top." Fuji controverts this truism: the summit is not necessarily the most significant point on the mountain; the peak does not have the same meaning for all pilgrims; and completing the ascent is not as crucial as looking inward and achieving a spiritual goal. Indeed the specific rationales and particular procedures for climbing Fuji are directly related to the distinctive notions that different groups attach to the mountain and its ascent. While all of the so-called Fuji cult movements share the common emphasis on religious pilgrimage to and ascent of Fuji, each espouses quite different ideas of the character and organization of Fuji spirituality. These ideas are reflected in their respective modes of approaching and climbing the mountain.

Maruyamakyō[1] ("Maruyama religion") is a new religion that emerged from a *kō* (Maruyamakō) to become a large established religious institution. This development amounts to a rejection of Ida's fundamental principle of preserving a "pure" Fuji faith untrammeled by the compromises of organized religion. The reverse of Maruyamakyō's institutional history is seen in Jūshichiyakō, a Fujikō that developed after World War II within one branch of a new religion called Gedatsukai. In the case of Maruyamakō a Fujikō spawned a new religion; in Jūshichiyakō a new religion gave birth to a Fujikō. In sharp contrast to Miyamotokō, Maruyamakyō and Jūshichiyakō share the same institutional status as new religions, but each presents a distinctive spiritual itinerary in its own pilgrimage patterns.

The close relationship between confraternities (*kō* and Fujikō) and new religions is seen in the relative ease with which the Fujikō named Maruyamakō helped give rise to Maruyamakyō. Confraternities are smaller, more localized voluntary organizations that paved the way for the larger, nationwide voluntary organizations known as new religions, which feature uniform creedal and ritual forms along with their bureaucratic structure. Another feature that distinguishes most new religions is the presence of a strong founding figure who deliberately created a group of followers and established doctrinal and ritual patterns for their corporate worship. In the case of Maruyamakyō, the founding figure was Itō Rokurōbei (1829–94), a charismatic leader who bridged the gap from confraternity to large-scale religious institution. Itō came from a family of hereditary Fujikō guides of Maruyamakō in an area close to present-day Tokyo. Itō grew up in a household of Fuji beliefs and practices and had several deep religious experiences of Fuji's power to heal. He became an avid believer especially after the last such recovery, at the age of twenty-five. After this experience Itō began to contemplate the word "mind" in the phrase *kōkūshin*.[2]

It was not until later, however, that Itō initiated his own form of religious practice and belief. In 1870 his wife Sano became critically ill. An ascetic devoted to the worship of Fudō Myōō was brought in to pray for Sano's recovery, and in the course of his rituals the ascetic was possessed by Sengen Daibosatsu, the deity of Mount Fuji. Subsequently, Sano recovered, but as Itō was carrying out rituals to thank the god, he himself was possessed by Sengen. The deity complained about having been constrained to use the body of the "inauspicious" Fudō ascetic and ordered Itō to act as his "intermediary" (*toritsugi*) from then on (J. A. Sawada 1998, 117).

As part of his religious career, Itō underwent various ascetic practices and developed healing techniques, some of which were taken from the heritage of Fuji spirituality. For example "he performed the *shikimi* discipline in order to reestablish the 'original condition of the world and humankind.' The practice involved circumambulating Mt. Fuji on tiptoe (*tsumadate* [*sic*]) for a period of fourteen days while holding a banner that displayed the saying 'Great Peace in the World' (*tenka taihei*). This act was, in effect, a ritual re-creation of the world originally intended by the god of Fuji; it signaled the commencement of the new Maruyama teaching."[3] Itō felt called to go beyond merely participating in and transmitting the beliefs and practices of his family's confraternity; he took the first steps that would eventually lead to the establishment of the new religion Maruyamakyō.

Itō, steeped in Fuji beliefs and practices, was moved to extreme measures to carry out his calling within this tradition. Even though he was arrested in 1873 and 1874 by the authorities for "illegal religious activities" and was criticized by relatives for neglecting the family business, he persisted in pursuing his commitment: "Faced with these challenges to his faith, in 1874 Itō ascended Mt. Fuji once again, this time determined to fast to death (*danjiki nyūjō*)—no doubt inspired by the example of the Tokugawa Fuji leader, Jikigyō Miroku (1671–1733)." However, another Fuji devotee, Shishino Nakaba, who was in the process of establishing an umbrella organization for various Fujikō and other movements (which he called Fuji Issan Kōsha), persuaded Itō to break his fast and meet with him. "Itō formally affiliated himself with Fuji Issan Kōsha, and when Shishino subsequently created a Fuji group called Fusō-kyō, in 1876, Itō became one of its senior guides." Entering an officially approved religious organization protected him from persecution. However, with Shishino's death in 1885, Itō left Fusōkyō and "placed his group under the jurisdiction of the Shintō Jimukyoku (Bureau of Shinto Affairs)" (J. A. Sawada 1998, 118).

Itō was rigorous not only in his ascetic practices but also in his social campaigns; although he was not personally involved, some of the members of his movement helped support "a revolt against bankers and wealthy farmers." He also went so far as to insist "that the Emperor was responsible for the sociocultural chaos of the times." The fortunes of Maruyamakyō went from early success to sharp downturn. Estimates of Maruyamakyō membership in 1892 range from a hundred thousand to more than a million. "But the movement had already begun to suffer from a lack of internal organization, and by Itō's death in 1894, the group was in serious decline." With its emphasis on "'common moral values'" and a loss of its critical attitude toward the state, its membership shrank: "Today's group, still headquartered in Kawasaki, has a membership of about 11,000." Maruyamakyō (like most Japanese religious groups) comes from a complex heritage: Maruyamakyō inherited the wealth of previous Fuji beliefs and practices and also emphasized Fuji's relationship to the sun and agricultural fertility. Itō also received and practiced the tradition of Fuji asceticism, but he "lived a good portion of his life in the anti-Buddhist climate of the early Meiji, and his writings vividly record his ongoing polemic against Buddhist institutions and ideas" (J. A. Sawada 1998, 118–20).

The founder's religious development, major activities, and key teachings set the context for treating Maruyamakyō's relationship to Fuji. The founder and his group emphasized his "independent stance with regard to all established religion; his alien-ation from Buddhism is paralleled by an explicit critique and reinterpretation of long-held Shinto traditions (120). . . . Itō's ethics were thus dominated by Confu-cian moral notions" (125), and yet in the teaching of Itō "the mind of human beings is fundamentally the same as the mind of Fuji, or the original Parent God" (121). Maruyamakyō, viewed from the perspective of the long tradition of the Fuji heri-tage, displays the full range of Fuji asceticism, Fuji piety, and Fuji faith. In addition, of course, the older confraternity Maruyamakō was the repository of the lineage of Kakugyō Tōbutsu and Jikigyō Miroku and their ascetic practices, as well as myriad beliefs, customs, ethical ideas, and deities that these founders and their followers honored and transmitted. Narrowing the focus to the place of Fuji within Maru-yamakyō, many roles can be identified: it is a sacred mountain to be venerated; a cosmogonic source from which they believe the world emerged; an ascetic site of practice (and for receiving revelations); a dwelling place for deities and ancestors; and a holy ground for continuing pilgrimage and worship. All of these features were present when the author accompanied Maruyamakyō's annual ascent of Fuji.

An afternoon spent with the head (*kyōshu* or *kyōshusama*) of Maruyamakyō, Itō Kōkai,[4] and two members of his staff gave these representatives of Maruyamakyō the opportunity to share their views of the group and for informal conversation. High-lights of this meeting provide useful background for understanding Maruyamakyō's pilgrimage practices and also offer an interesting comparison with the statements of Ida of Miyamotokō.[5]

In contrast to Miyamotokō's homey meeting place, Maruyamakyō, although rather small by new religion standards, boasts a sizable headquarters with a number of imposing buildings, including the Hondō ("main hall"). This meeting took place in a formal reception room; the *kyōshu* and his main assistant were dressed in tradi-tional Japanese clothing.[6] The other man, who had written a book on the founder, was in casual Western attire. He dominated the first part of the meeting by giving a standard overview of the founder's life, emphasizing that Maruyamakyō originated out of the hard Japanese farm experience of the founder, who developed this religion in response to the needs of the people. In stressing the asceticism and suffering of the founder, he mentioned a number of other new religions and their founders, claiming that the founders Nakayama Miki of Tenrikyō and Deguchi Onisaburō of Ōmotokyō did not undergo extensive asceticism like that of Itō. This man gave other details of the founder's life and described the founder's fasting in a cold cave at the eighth station as an ascetic practice so severe that it would have been fatal to ordi-nary persons; in effect the founder experienced a kind of rebirth.[7]

After the lengthy talk by the writer, the meeting turned into a free exchange of questions, with answers mostly from the *kyōshu*. In response to a question about why the national flag is so prominent in this religion, the *kyōshu* said that Maruyamakyō had honored and circumambulated the *hi no maru* (flag with the sun) even before the Meiji Restoration. In summing up the gist of Maruyamakyō, the *kyōshu* said that its objective is to change the human heart—not mere purification but actually re-forming one's heart. He stressed that Maruyamakyō is a religion "descending from the mountain": more important than the mountaintop experience is what happens in one's heart after coming down from the mountain. This was true for the founder and is true for each member's experience.

According to the *kyōshu*, the separation of Maruyamakyō from Fusōkyō occurred when Maruyamakyō was developing rapidly but Fusōkyō was standing still and its leader, Shishino, was a hindrance. Maruyamakyō left Fusōkyō and stopped being merely a group worshipping Fuji; it became a religion in its own right. When asked about the Fujikō named Maruyamakō that preceded this religion, the *kyōshu* acknowledged that his religion still honors the local shrine (Sengensha) with its *fujizuka* and sends celebratory sake for the annual tutelary deity festival. This is the shrine and *fujizuka* where the founder played as a child. The writer mentioned again that although the founder was originally connected to the mountain, he descended the mountain and did not climb Fuji so often. In other words Maruyamakyō be-came a religion of the plains, a religion "separated from Fuji." After an overview of Maruyamakyō rituals and festivals,[8] the three representatives summed up the Fuji pilgrimage, which starts at the headquarters and climaxes with a key ceremony within Fuji's crater.

The 1988 annual Fuji pilgrimage (*tozan*) began at 7:30 A.M. on August 8 in the city of Kawasaki from Maruyamakyō headquarters. Some members from distant prefectures travel to the headquarters on these annual pilgrimages and stay overnight; in 1988 six people stayed overnight and joined a busload of thirty-six.[9] Another bus from Aichi Province would meet the Kawasaki group at the Kigen Dōjō, a new Maruyamakyō building at the foot of Fuji.

The pilgrimage practice of Maruyamakyō is simpler in form than those of Miyamotokō and Jūshichiyakō. The ceremony marking the start of the *tozan* was held at the Hondō, where a priest blessed and purified the people gathered in front of the hall. He then very deliberately brought from the hall and handed to the *kyōshu* a long cylinder with a carrying strap; it contained a scroll of the founder's portrait. The *kyōshu* personally carried this cylinder all the way to the summit and back. From the main hall the people walked across the grounds to the founder's memorial stone, which they honored before walking to the waiting bus. As the bus made its way to the foot of Fuji, the *kyōshu* gave a talk over the speaker system. This talk included practical advice for the climb and the overall schedule, with mention of the founder's asceticism on Fuji and his decision to stop short of starving himself to death. This is the reason for going to Fuji, worshipping the *kami*, and greeting the rising sun—to follow the founder's practice. The *kyōshu*'s assistant handed out the author's questionnaires (which had been approved and duplicated) and asked for them to be filled out on the way to Fuji.[10] The bus included a mixed group: some were in special blue clothing, and others wore everyday clothes; the most conspicuous feature was the number of parent-child and husband-wife groupings.

At 10:30 the group arrived at the foot of Fuji, stopping at the Kigen Dōjō, a Maruyamakyō meeting and practice hall built three years before (formerly located in the city of Fujiyoshida). The Kawasaki group had a light lunch early to make way for the people soon to arrive on the bus from Aichi Prefecture. The two busloads, especially the Aichi bus, included quite a few children ages six to ten and also high school students and young adults (in contrast to Miyamotokō's older clientele). Shortly before noon a simple ceremony was held for all participants. It concluded with the *kyōshu*'s blessing with his outstretched fan. After a commemorative photo outside the hall, the group boarded the buses and went straight to the fifth station without stopping at the Sengen Jinja or the Tainai.

Arriving at the fifth station a short while later, the group used the restrooms and shopped a little but did not visit the Komitake Jinja. The group had been instructed at the Kigen Dōjō that they would chant their sacred phrase *tenmei kaiten;*[11] this was their main activity during the ascent. The *kyōshu* was asked if Maruyamakyō had ever carried out any religious practices at the Sengen Jinja in the days before the highway took them directly to the fifth station. Rather surprised by the question, he replied that in the old days they had walked all the way from Noborito (present-day Kawasaki, a suburb of Tokyo), passed through this shrine, and maybe bowed their heads in respect, but that is all because Maruyamakyō has no connection of faith with Sengen Jinja.

A little after 7:00 P.M. the group arrived at the lodging Tomoekan above the seventh station, where they were to stay for the night. There was a brief ceremony at the altar of the Tomoekan and chanting of *tenmei kaiten* in honor of the founder's practice at this spot. They had gone from the Kigen Dōjō below Fuji almost to the summit without any rituals or worship except for the chanting of *tenmei kaiten*. At the point when they passed the Gansomuro (near the site of Jikigyō Miroku's final fasting, which Miyamotokō considered more important than the summit), the *kyōshu* was asked if they stopped there to honor Miroku, but he said no, there was no connection to this place—their lineage of faith was different. In the only ritual observed while going up the mountain, one leader (called a *sendatsu*) performed a healing rite on a sick member: he pressed a sacred book against her stomach, had her breathe rhythmically, and then used the sacred book to strike her lightly on the back several times.

Members of the group went to sleep with clothes on, lying on the "shelves" around the outer wall of the lodging. They were awakened about 2:15 the next morning and left for the summit about 3:00 A.M. Even at that early hour the narrow path up the mountain was crowded and moved slowly. The *kyōshu* had told people that safety was paramount and that the sunrise could be greeted from any point on the mountain. Therefore they should not worry about making it to the summit before dawn. Even so he and the others were eager to reach the top before daybreak. Some in the long line of climbers simply sat on the steps and waited there to watch the sun appear. The *kyōshu* and others in the group called out to let them pass, threading their way up the packed path to reach the summit just before the sunrise and then lining up and welcoming it with a prayer and the *tenmei kaiten* chant.

After the sunrise ceremony they went for tea at a shop, which was an opportunity to ask the *kyōshu* about various practices and sites not observed while climbing. He acknowledged that Maruyamakyō did not participate in these customs since the most important part of the pilgrimage for them, the ritual of *tenpaishiki* ("heaven-worship-rite") was held within the crater. He said that behind the shop was the crater of Fuji, the world of the *kami*. The importance of the mountain is that here the founder personally experienced asceticism and received the direct revelation of the *kami;* the aspects of Fuji belief that are valued by traditional Fujikō people are merely incidental. After tea they walked behind the shop and up over the lip of the crater and then descended a short way into a flat space within the crater, where a temporary altar for the *tenpaishiki* was set up.[12] The *kyōshu* had been carrying the cylinder with the scroll of the founder's portrait all the way up the mountain; the scroll was now removed from its container. A walking stick from which to hang the founder's picture was set in place by piling rocks around it.

The *kyōshu* had explained in the tea shop that this place was opposite the "eternal snow," where the parent *kami* (*oyagamisama*) was revealed to the founder. Their rite of worship, while kneeling on towels, facing the founder's portrait, and looking past it to the eternal snow, was in honor of the founder and the spirits of all their ancestors. In his brief speech the *kyōshu* told his group what to take with them down the mountain to enrich their lives: the importance of the mountain, the significance of the founder and the *kami,* and meeting with the ancestors.[13] A small watermelon and a bottle of sake that had been carried up the mountain were placed under the founder's scroll; the watermelon was cut up to give each member a small piece, and small cups of sake were passed around. At the conclusion of the ceremony, the scroll was carefully rolled up and reinserted in its special container; the leftover sake was poured over the rocks forming this makeshift altar. At the conclusion of this worship service, the *kyōshu* blessed the group with his folding fan and declared them "reborn" (*umarekawatta*).[14]

With this ceremony the *tozan* was completed; those who wished to walk around the rim of the crater did so, while others began the descent to the fifth station. When the group had almost completed this circuit of the crater, a young man from our group struck up a conversation. He had climbed the Alps and the Matterhorn in Europe, and he asked the purpose of the author's study, volunteering that Fuji is the symbol of Japan. The gist of his religious commitment is that he had no religion at all, Buddhist or Shinto, until two years earlier, when he joined Maruyamakyō. His parents belonged to Maruyamakyō. When asked why he joined, he said that there were all kinds of reasons. After he turned thirty, he began asking a lot of questions, and this led to his joining. He did not seem to want to say more (perhaps since another man had joined us and was walking alongside and listening closely). The first man changed the subject, saying he had heard that when the famous conductor Herbert von Karajan of the Berlin Philharmonic was in Japan and traveled from Tokyo to Kyoto on the bullet train, he let out a cry of joy when he saw Fuji out the window.[15] As someone who had traveled to Europe and even scaled several Alpine peaks, he seemed overjoyed that a European celebrity would view Fuji so enthusiastically. His brief anecdote is testimony that Maruyamakyō is able to attract relatively young adults, and in this case a quite cosmopolitan man, as members.

No observances took place around the rim of the crater, on the way down the mountain, or at the fifth station, where the group boarded the buses and went to the Kigen Dōjō. Some of the Maruyamakyō members and leaders have their own jackets, blue or black, but they did not have the red stamps placed on their clothing, as is the custom for Miyamotokō and even some nonreligious climbers; some Maruyamakyō pilgrims did have their "diamond" walking canes emblazoned with the hot irons marking the stages or summit. After the noon arrival at the Kigen Dōjō, there was a brief ceremony, with the *kyōshu* reiterating the importance of the parent *kami* (*oyagami*) and ancestors. Later the *kyōshu* and his aides prepared amulets for the participants to take home with them. A celebratory banquet followed, and then buses were loaded and departed. The buses arrived at Maruyamakyō headquarters about 4:30 P.M., and members headed for home.

The Maruyamakyō writer had stressed repeatedly that this religion is a "descend the mountain" religion, "separated from Fuji." For the most part this is true, but there are always differences between formal pronouncements and actual practices in any religious organization. At the Kigen Dōjō, after the celebratory banquet, one person, in the course of a lengthy conversation, emphasized that Maruyamakyō has a long history and a deep connection with Fuji, which is the symbol of Japan. Traces of folk piety and Fuji faith seem to have been preserved among some members, even though the leaders present their movement as "separated from Fuji." Maruyamakyō is much more complex than can be summed up quickly, but looking only at the relationship between this religion and Fuji, two major conclusions are warranted. First, Maruyamakyō does not bring Fuji into its place of worship the way Miyamotokō enshrines several forms of Fuji in its meeting place; rather Maruyamakyō brings its own altar and makeshift worship site to the mountain. Second, if Miyamotokō is Fuji-centered, then Maruyamakyō seems to be founder- and ancestor-centered since the importance of the mountain is defined by the founder's having practiced and received his revelation there and by members' ancestors residing there. Just as the founder was reborn there, so the members can find rebirth there. The crater of Fuji can be called a Mecca for this group: members make their pilgrimage here to follow the pattern of their founder and to come into contact with him; to draw near to and worship the parent *kami* revealed to the founder and still dwelling here; and to honor and be reunited with family ancestors in a rite of rebirth.

GEDATSUKAI: OLD TRADITIONS IN A NEW RELIGION

In light of Fuji's long history, Jūshichiyakō is a recent Fujikō, having been formed in postwar times by the Nakano branch of the new religion Gedatsukai.[16] When compared to the historical development of antiestablishment Miyamotokō and full-service religion Maruyamakyō, Jūshichiyakō is the anomaly: a pilgrimage association spawned by a new religion. Jūshichiyakō affirms the beliefs and practices of both the new religion and the older confraternity.

Gedatsukai was founded by Okano Eizō (1881–1948), whose father had been a *sendatsu* in a local Fujikō in Saitama Prefecture.[17] Okano apparently assimilated his father's penchant for mountain pilgrimage, also accepting the prevailing religious values of Confucian ethics, veneration of local *kami*, and worship of Buddhist deities. He expressed no particular religious leanings until a midlife crisis, an illness, shortly after his father's death, during which he had a vision of his own death and rebirth and experienced a calling to devote his life to religion. He visited many shrines and temples, talked to a number of religionists, and eventually confined himself on Mount Tanzawa[18] to continue his spiritual quest. This experience together with a revelation at his family's local tutelary shrine led him to found Gedatsukai in 1928 as a return to traditional religious values. While he quickly gathered followers, the authorities investigated, harassed, and even briefly imprisoned him, but he continued his newfound vocation, even accepting Buddhist ordination from (and affiliation with) a recognized Buddhist group in order to carry out his work.

After World War II, Gedatsukai was free to organize and exist as an independent body. Okano died in 1948, and yet his new religion continued to develop, especially under the organizing guidance of his main disciple, Kishida Eizan, who opened many new branches. Kitamotojuku, Saitama Prefecture, is the site of the headquarters (known as the Sacred Land, Goreichi), including the former parish shrine for the Okano family, where Okano Eizō received his definitive revelation. Gedatsukai has called itself "suprareligion" in the sense of encouraging people to return to traditional religious values: diligence in worshipping at their own parish Shinto shrine and faithful devotion to their own hereditary Buddhist temple, as well as the cultivation of Confucian values such as filial piety. Okano and his followers created their own teachings and a full round of rituals: a basic teaching is repayment of debt;[19] a distinctive practice is a rite using sweet tea in the home for twice daily veneration of ancestors.

The minor role Fuji plays in Gedatsukai, both as a mountain and as a symbol, is reflected in the group's headquarters compound, the Sacred Land, which has a number of buildings and objects for veneration: from Shinto shrines to Buddhist halls and other stones and monuments. Lost among these more imposing structures is a diminutive Fuji only several feet high. Gedatsukai calls this small mound "Sengen Jinja Yōhaijo,"[20] the site for worshipping from afar Sengen Shrine. This replicated Fuji recognizes the faith of the founder's father, but it does not play a prominent role in the teaching or practice of Gedatsukai.

The Nakano[21] branch in Tokyo (one of the oldest and most flourishing in Gedatsukai) is apparently the only one sponsoring a Fujikō. The idea for inaugurating a Fujikō came from the Nakano branch leader at the encouragement of Okano, who visited the branch frequently. When Okano learned that the grandfather of this branch leader had been a *sendatsu* in a Fujikō, Okano encouraged him to revive the *kō* and honor the long tradition of pilgrimage to Fuji. Although the current branch leader was not personally familiar with the particular practices of Fujikō, through his business connections he was acquainted with Ida and knew that Ida and the Miyamotokō were regarded as the personal and group repositories of the oldest and most traditional Fujikō. He learned the basic practices of a Fuji confraternity from Ida, including the performance of the fire rite *takiage*, and formed his Fujikō centering around regular performance of the *takiage* and annual ascent of Fuji. Recruiting *kō* participants from his branch membership, he blended Gedatsukai practices with elements of Fuji faith he knew and the customs he learned from Ida. He retained the name of Jūshichiyakō from his family's *kō; jūshichiya* is literally "the seventeenth day," which honors the day of the month when Jikigyō died.[22]

Arrangements for contact with the Nakano branch and its Jūshichiyakō were made through the Gedatsukai executives who had first provided information about the Fuji activities of this group. A few days after a meeting at Gedatsukai's Tokyo offices,[23] an official set up a meeting with the head[24] of the Nakano branch at his nearby home. On the lane leading to his home is a small but well-kept Shinto shrine, Gosha Inari Jinja, with a smaller shrine for Benzaiten and a miniature Fuji. A towering gingko tree about three feet in diameter was the natural marker for the long history of the recently renovated shrine; a stone monument for the small Fuji mound dated it to 1936.[25]

The branch leader's house is a quiet island within the hubbub of Tokyo, with a large entryway to accommodate many shoes and slippers for the regular branch meetings. The house boasts not only a standard Gedatsukai altar but also a number of "mini-shrines" on the altar enshrining the founder's own handwriting. After the author's self-introduction and explanation of his research, the branch leader gave his own overview of Fujikō. He said that after the war there have been many publications about these beliefs and practices, but not all are reliable since they do not capture the ancient tradition. He brought out many books describing Fuji, including a lineage of the Murakamiha and the Mirokuha, but he was humble about his own ignorance of Fuji spirituality, even of his own Fujikō, and recommended Ida of Miyamotokō for expert advice. According to the branch leader, his *kō* goes to Fuji four times a year: on June 30 for the Shinto ceremony of great purification at Yoshida Sengen Jinja, which is the same as the mountain opening; on the ascent in late summer, the exact date of which varies from year to year; on August 26, the fire festival (*hi matsuri*) marking the end of the official climbing season; and at the new year for the ceremonial first visit at Yoshida Sengen Jinja.

The Jūshichiyakō meets every month on the seventeenth (*jūshichiya*) for a worship service after the branch's monthly day of thanks.[26] The branch leader (*shibuchō*) is known as a *sendatsu* (leader), but the austerities that *sendatsu* used to perform are no longer continued, and their *kō* uses incense instead of wood for the *takiage*. He proudly displayed a very old banner of the Jūshichiyakō and also three scrolls they always take with them on their ascent: Miroku, Kakugyō, and Konohana Sakuya were on the central one, and the two side scrolls featured a number of Shinto *kami* (but no Buddhist figures). He mentioned the five Fujikō that had participated with them the previous year at the mountain opening, and he lamented the fact that the confraternities have become formal groups motivated more by tourism than belief. The Jūshichiyakō used to spend one night on Fuji and the next night at an *onsen,* but this became expensive and few could afford it. That year they would just spend one night on the mountain and would not stay at an *onsen.*[27]

The branch leader's talk rambled about topics, including the difficulties of running both a Gedatsukai branch and a Fujikō, which at times tended to "collide." He played a video of the presentation of a large plaque from Jūshichiyakō to the Yoshida Sengen Jinja; the plaque in large characters announced *"kansha,"* a key Gedatsukai concept of thanks or gratitude for life and its blessings. In the video the head of the board of directors of Gedatsukai gave a long talk about the founder Okano and how his father was in Fuji and hence the miniature Fuji at the Sacred Land; there is a karmic interconnection of Sengen Jinja, Jūshichiyakō, Fuji, the founder, and his father. In effect the plaque of thanks, or gratitude, is a recognition of this blessing. In the video the branch leader spoke about difficult times after the war when young people did not enter the *kō;* not until about 1968 or 1969 did they revive the Jūshichiyakō, with encouragement from Gedatsukai officials (who were reinforcing the founder's earlier suggestion). The branch leader said that after the war everything changed. There is no longer asceticism (*gyō*) except among a few older *sendatsu.* In the old days there were many who practiced rigorous austerities, similar to Shugendō, but the branch leader has not undergone this training (which must be received from a master), so he does not engage in the rather severe traditional form of *gyō;* he merely makes the ascent.

The branch leader focused on three basic aspects of Fujikō: ascent (*tozan*); asceticism (*gyō*); and worship (*ogami*). Each of the three has become severely attenuated. The ascent is still carried out, but it is more like tourism (anyone can climb the mountain, with or without faith), and he called most Fujikō today "ascent-*kō*" (*tozankō*), who neglect or omit both asceticism and worship. *Gyō* (austerities) are almost nonexistent. Even in the rare cases that worship (*ogami*) is performed, it may be more of a mechanical chanting than a heartfelt utterance. He candidly admitted that practices have deteriorated, and he regretted not knowing more about *kō* faith, practice, and history, but he has done his best to maintain the connection of faith to Sengen Jinja and revive the Jūshichiyakō, in accordance with the wishes of the founder Okano. The video concluded with a moral that seems to be the spirit of the branch leader: Gedatsukai members should be absolutely thankful in their hearts for Fuji—keeping alive a heritage that is a faint shadow of the practice in its heyday.

On May 17 the Nakano branch held its monthly thanks meeting, followed by the Jūshichiyakō's performance of the fire ritual. All members attending the meeting followed the same routine at the nearby shrine: first paying their respects at the larger Inari shrine, then at a small shrine to the right, from there to the Benzaiten shrine, and finally to the small Fuji. Gedatsukai's own variation of worship, bowing the head and clapping four times, was observed at each of the sites. Levity accompanied piety in these activities: middle-aged and elderly women smiled and laughed like children as they climbed the steps of the Inari shrine and rang the bell. The lengthy thanks meeting, with sixty to seventy in attendance, lasted from 1:30 to 4:30 P.M.[28]

At about 4:45, as the last people left the Gedatsukai formal service and light refreshment period after it, the Jūshichiyakō began its fire rite in another room that doubled as sleeping quarters for some of the branch leader's family. In addition to the branch leader, nine men and seven women were present. The Fuji altar had the three scrolls mentioned earlier (the ones taken on the ascent of Fuji). Noticing that the author's video camera was recording the rite, one woman pointed out a calendar with a picture of a scantily clad female and turned it to the wall, saying that it should not be in the pictures. The group joked good-naturedly, some expressing the opinion that the pinup girl was actually a female *kami* and others chiming in that even if she was a *kami*, she could not be there because Konohana would not like it.[29] The Jūshichiyakō *takiage* is modeled after that of Miyamotokō but is shorter, lasting only about twenty-five minutes. The *takiage* concluded with chanting of the Buddhist scripture *Hannya Shingyō*, praise of the founder, and the distinctive fourfold clapping. The Jūshichiyakō is composed entirely of branch members willing to stay an additional half hour after a three-hour Gedatsukai worship service; no one came just for the brief *takiage*.

On June 30 the branch leader and several members of his Jūshichiyakō traveled to the annual "mountain opening" at Yoshida Sengen Jinja. The branch leader mentioned that he had gone to the same shrine on June 19 for the dedication of a stone monument honoring Jinben Daibosatsu, the formal title the emperor conferred upon En no Ozunu in 1799 as the founder of Shugendō.[30] Upon arrival at Yoshida Sengen Jinja, the Jūshichiyakō members made their way around the shrine compound, paying respects at the major shrine, the many small shrines, the statue of Ida's father at the beginning of the climbing path, and also the newly erected monument for Jinben Daibosatsu. The Shinto ceremony began at 3:00 P.M.; it was actually a purification rite that used paper cutouts of a human form rubbed on the body to remove impurities (and later burned); they passed through a large reed circle three times.[31] These features plus the formal offering of sprigs by the dignitaries and the reading of a Shinto prayer were part of the general purification rite. Nine Fujikō were present and made offerings. These people were ushered outside and lined up, and there a waiting television crew filmed a masked man using a wooden mallet to "cut" the straw rope hanging across the torii leading to the old climbing path. This was the official opening of the mountain to climbing from the northern route; other routes have their own ceremonies. This ceremony seemed to be a standard Shinto purification rite; the mountain opening was more of an afterthought and concession both to Fujikō and to the television crews.

Two trips up Fuji have been described; therefore this account of the Jūshichiyakō pilgrimage of July 27–28 will be abbreviated and only its more distinctive features noted. The pilgrimage began in the lane leading to the branch leader's residence, where participants individually "paid their respects" (*omairi*)[32] to the Inari shrine, the small Fuji, and related shrines, as they did at the time of the branch meeting and *takiage*; before boarding the bus the branch leader lined up the participants for a group *omairi*. This routine of repetitive group and individual *omairi* set the tone and pattern for the entire pilgrimage, with members worshipping at every available shrine, temple, and monument. The branch leader spoke briefly, mentioning the connection of the founder and Gedatsukai to Fuji and emphasizing the importance for their ancestors that they go to this mountain that never changes. Of the forty-four who boarded the bus, only three were young people. According to the branch leader there were usually more young people, but this year Gedatsukai's own annual pilgrimage[33] was so close to the Jūshichiyakō trip to Fuji that members could not spare the time and expense for both. When the group arrived at Yoshida Sengen Jinja, they all washed hands and faces before going to the main shrine, where a Shinto priest officiated over offerings, purification, and a sip of sacred sake. After a commemorative photo the group assembled to honor the memorial for Jinben Daibosatsu and then dispersed for a flurry of individual *omairi* to every site within the shrine compound.

From Yoshida Sengen Jinja the bus proceeded to the Tainai; only fifteen minutes were allowed for individuals to pass through this cave and shrine and to purchase amulets. At this shrine, as at Yoshida Sengen Jinja, an envelope containing money was handed over to the shrine officials for admission of the group (and everyone received amulets). From the Tainai the bus went to the fifth station, where a group *omairi* was performed at the two main shrines, followed by individual *omairi* to a number of smaller sites. Only ten of the group planned to make the trip to the summit with the overnight stay in a mountain hut, and they would bring back amulets for the majority, who spent the night in hotel rooms at the fifth station.

Ten continued the climb to a lodging, the Hōraikan.[34] The price of the lodging included the fees of front and back "guides," who were, unlike the traditional spiritual leaders known as *oshi*, college students making money during their summer vacation. One of them said that he took the job because he thought it would be interesting, but then he admitted that it was boring to climb the mountain everyday.[35] The Hōraikan (near the eighth station) was reached by early evening with no incident; there were no rituals except for the branding of a few walking sticks at several stations. Several people performed *omairi* at the elaborate altar within the Hōraikan.[36] The woman in charge of the Hōraikan confirmed the branch leader's statement that his people had been coming to this lodging for about thirty years. When asked about other Fujikō who would be coming, she quickly named four Fujikō—two with thirty members, one with fifty, and another with a hundred— booked at the lodge. Otherwise they were all unaffiliated "general climbers." She was proud that this was a Meiji-era lodging, a "shrine" (*miyasan*) originally founded by

Kakugyō. She pointed out the names of the various deities enshrined at the altar, which was adorned with fresh offerings brought by her "guests."

They went to bed on the shelves of the lodging, sardine-style, about 7:30 P.M. After a restless night (with many complaints of "noisy" and "can't sleep" voiced), they got up about 1:30 A.M. and began the ascent. They passed the Gansomuro and Eboshi Iwa with no observance and arrived at the summit about 4:30, in time for greeting the rising sun. After tea two members made formal visits to the two main shrines. They went to the office of the Chōjō Jinja, where amulets were deposited and a sizable contribution was left with the shrine priest. When he was asked how many kō came there every year, he responded that about twenty did. Some of the kō perform their own recitations, but they are the exception; most just pay their standard respects (omairi). At one time, according to this priest, there were about five hundred kō, and recently some are being renewed. Most pilgrims come from Yoshida, especially after the Subaru Line highway was built, but some come from Kawaguchi and Subashiri.

Next they went to the Chōjō Jinja and the Oku no Miya, where the routine was repeated: handing over of amulets, purification of the three scrolls (brought from Nakano to the mountain), purification of the kō members, and a sip of sacred sake. The Jūshichiyakō members recommended a red stamp from the Oku no Miya as the "best" one. They descended to the fifth station and went directly to the Komitake Jinja for omairi before joining the other members in a meal. From the fifth station they took the bus back to the Yoshida Sengen Jinja, with a repetition of the purification and offering of sprigs at the beginning of the ascent, a group omairi before Jinben Daibosatsu, and as before, individual omairi. The ethos of this Fujikō's pilgrimage is captured in one member's response to the questionnaire item asking the reason for climbing Fuji: "A Japanese does not need a reason to climb Fuji!"

On the bus trip back, everyone was tired, but several speakers took advantage of a captive audience. A Gedatsukai official congratulated the group on their climb and was glad for the good weather. The branch leader too was grateful for the good weather and said that the sunrise was wonderful. He talked at length about ongoing discussions over whether to include a side trip to an onsen in the future; he reported that the people present were split about fifty-fifty, so next year they would keep it to one night without an onsen and then the following year would make it a two-night trip with an onsen. He reminisced that once there were four buses, then two, and now one. Because many members are now older, the trip is difficult to organize, so he encouraged everyone to try to get new members. He directed his remarks to those on the trip who were not yet members, inviting them to join. A treasurer's report was circulated to everyone on the bus; it listed seventy-three members and a million yen in the treasury. A request was made for the researcher's questionnaires to be turned in. With the formalities over, the bus attendant broke out the beer and juice and turned on the karaoke. The bus arrived back in Nakano (Tokyo) in late afternoon. The pilgrimage ended with a final *omairi* at the Inari shrine and the small Fuji.

On August 17, after the Nakano branch thanks-day meeting from 1:30 to 4:30, the Jūshichiyakō performed the *takiage* fire ritual from 4:30 to 5:00. Following these two meetings, the author sat down to a meal and a lengthy conversation with the branch leader. When asked if his group had ever held any celebration at the Eboshi Iwa, where Jikigyō Miroku starved himself to death, he said that there used to be a religious practitioner (*ogamiya*) there and that the Jūshichiyakō unfurled their scrolls and had a service there. This question put him on the defensive, having to admit that his group did not observe all the old customs. He conceded that in the Miyamotokō they carry on a lot of the traditional procedures, but "they are not a *kyōdan* (religious organization)," and so they can continue these things. The old practices are difficult to maintain because Gedatsukai is a *kyōdan*. His branch continues the *kō* and makes the pilgrimage to Fuji because the founder Okano told them to treasure these old traditions, and they do so, within Gedatsukai. They interpret the meaning of the ascent in terms of Gedatsukai's rubric of preserving the old faith, even though they do not carry out all the traditional observances. After all, they are not ascetics (*gyōja*). He mentioned again that he has the title *sendatsu* (leader), but in the old days a *sendatsu* had to learn a lot of rules as the disciple of a master and undergo many difficult practices as he passed through the lower ranks before earning this title.

In this context he brought up the discussion about the *onsen* that had been mentioned on the bus ride from Fuji to Nakano. The group had changed their minds and decided after all to go to an *onsen* on next year's Fuji trip. When a pilgrimage is too much like asceticism (*gyō*), it is not enjoyable, and the group leader admitted, a pilgrimage is a form of recreation for the group. Thus for Jūshichiyakō too the challenge is to strike the right balance within the age-old tension between the spiritual and the sensual while maintaining old traditions within the framework of a new religion.

14

Surveying Contemporary
Fuji Belief and Practice

STATISTICS AND PERSONAL STATEMENTS
ON FUJI SPIRITUALITY

A multitude of individual and collective parties are still climbing Fuji for religious purposes, but limitations of time and energy made it impractical to observe and climb with more than the three pilgrimage associations already discussed. The danger of overgeneralizing about these three disparate Fuji-focused movements and the difficulty of assessing their common heritage were foreseen in the research plan, which included a brief questionnaire to help give concreteness and at least minimal numerical references to supplement participant observation notes and anecdotal evidence.[1] The same questionnaire was approved by the head of each group and distributed on the bus by representatives of the respective groups with a request to cooperate.[2] This questionnaire provides an overview of the makeup of these pilgrimage groups and their activities, beliefs, and future prospects. Here the general order of the questionnaire is followed to discuss the statistics of the three groups; following the treatment of the questionnaire, some comparative remarks on the three groups are offered.

	Miyamotokō	Maruyamakyō	Jūshichiyakō
Return rate*	74.3% (29/39)	71.9% (23/32)	84.1% (37/44)
GENDER			
Male	17 (58.6%)	15 (65.2%)	12 (32.4%)
Female	12 (41.4%)	8 (34.8%)	25 (67.6%)
Total	29 (100%)	23 (100%)	37 (100%)
AGE			
(average)	59.3 (n=28)	40.6 (n=23)	59.3 (n=35)
RESIDENCE			
Tokyo (23 wards)	24 (82.8%)	3 (13.0%)	30 (83.3%)
Tokyo (outside wards)	1 (3.4%)	2 (8.7%)	2 (5.6%)
Other prefectures	4 (13.8%)	18 (78.3%)	4 (11.1%)
No response	0	0	(1)
Total	29 (100%)	23 (100%)	36 (100%)
Fuji group member	8 (27.6%)	15 (65.2%) (Mkyō)	31 (86.1%)
Not member	21 (72.4%)	8 (34.8%)	1 (2.8%)
	—	—	4 (11.1%)(Gk)
Total	29 (100%)	23 (100%)	36 (100%)
FUJI CLIMBING EXPERIENCE			
First climb	7 (24.1%)	10 (43.4%)	3 (8.3%)
Multiple climbs	22 (75.9%)	13 (56.6%)	33 (91.7%)
Most climbs	30	30	31
Avg. no. climbs	7	7.6	10.3
Earliest first climb	1931	1937	1938
Avg. year first climb	1966–1967	1962–1963	1968–1969
GOAL OF FUJI PILGRIMAGE			
Sacred mountain	14 (42.4%)	8 (29.6%)	20 (33.9%)
Close to kami-Buddhas	0 (0.0%)	1 (3.7%)	2 (3.4%)
Benefit from kami-Buddhas	0 (0.0%)	0 (0.0%)	2 (3.4%)
Purify own heart	9 (27.3%)	12 (44.4%)	14 (23.7%)
Asceticism	2 (6.1%)	5 (18.5%)	16 (27.1%)

BUS QUESTIONNAIRE RESULTS *(continued)*

	Miyamotokō	Maruyamakyō	Jūshichiyakō

GOAL OF FUJI PILGRIMAGE *(continued)*

Other	8 (24.2%)**	1 (3.7%)	5 (8.5%)***
Total (responses)	33 (100%)	27 (99.9%)	59 (100.0%)

REASON FOR CLIMBING FUJI

Written response	17 (58.6%)	4 (17.4%)	15 (40.5%)
No response	12 (41.4%)	19 (82.6%)	22 (59.5%)
Total	29 (100%)	23 (100.0%)	37 (100.0%)

* *Although some younger members returned questionnaires (as will be obvious from the ages on some of the profiles), apparently most younger people did not fill out and return them.*

** *Of 8 "other," 2 strengthen body, 1 sports, 1 pleasure, 4 no written reason.*

*** *4 of 5 "other" are "thanks."*

The uniformly high return rate for the questionnaires was not surprising, given the captive audience and the encouragement of group leaders. Jūshichiyakō with its 67.6 percent female participation reflects the makeup of its parent group Gedatsu-kai;[3] noteworthy is the predominance of males in Miyamotokō and Maruyamakyō. Both Miyamotokō and Jūshichiyakō are older groups with an identical 59.3 years average age; Maruyamakyō is a much younger body at 40.6 years average age. By residence, Miyamotokō and Jūshichiyakō are overwhelmingly Tokyo phenomena; Maruyamakyō has only a few participants from Tokyo.

Membership figures tell more about these groups than can be recognized at first glance on a full bus. The Miyamotokō, which has the reputation of being the oldest continuous Fujikō, shows up with only 7 members (27.6%) of its group and 21 non-member participants (72.4%); this reinforces the leader Ida's remark that filling a bus is difficult. These figures are important not only for membership per se but also because they reduce percentages for climbing experience and lower the average year of first climb. Maruyamakyō rates higher with 65.2 percent membership. Jūshichi-yakō comes in highest with 86.3 percent membership in its *kō*, and with the additional 11.1 percent indicating membership in Gedatsukai, their total affiliation is a remarkable 97.4 percent; this combined higher membership percentage elevates the Jūshichiyakō results for climbing experience.

The figures for climbing experience highlight remarkable differences among the three: Jūshichiyakō, the "new" Fujikō within a new religion, comes up as the seasoned veteran with only 8.3 percent making their first climb in 1988, while 91.7 percent already had completed a number of ascents. The "traditional" Miyamotokō has the middle percentage for first climbs, at 24.1 percent, which reflects the majority of their participants being nonmembers. Maruyamakyō, with 43.4 percent first-climb participants and a high membership rate (and also the duty to climb Fuji to honor the spirits of dead parents), will surely maintain its annual Fuji ascent. Apart from these differences, two figures stand out as almost identical: "most climbs," ranging only from 30 to 31; and "earliest first climb," ranging only from 1931 to 1938. However, Jūshichiyakō comes out significantly higher in the average number of climbs at 10.3, while Miyamotokō and Maruyamakyō are almost the same at 7 and 7.6 respectively. (The Miyamotokō bus figures for average number of climbs certainly is lowered by the predominance of nonmembers.) The results for average year of first climb reveal the institutional strength of Maruyamakyō, which comes in as the earliest, 1962–63, while the two other groups are a few years later.

The item for the goal of Fuji pilgrimage provides indications of the nature and extent of religious faith associated with these movements. The answer "to climb a sacred mountain" found responses from Miyamotokō at 42.4 percent, followed by Jūshichiyakō at 33.9 percent, and trailed by Maruyamakyō at 29.6 percent. (Maruyamakyō leaders emphasize that their movement is a "descend the mountain" or "separated from the mountain" religion.) That these responses constituted the single highest category under the goal of Fuji pilgrimage indicates statistically that Fuji is still considered a sacred mountain today (at least by these groups), lending credence to leaders' statements and members' activities to that effect. The percentages for "come close to kami-Buddhas" and "benefit from kami-Buddhas" are both lower than expected, statistically not significant.[4] The responses for "purify my own heart" are the second-highest category, ranging from 44.4 percent for Maruyamakyō to Miyamotokō at 27.3 percent and Jūshichiyakō at 23.7 percent. For "asceticism" (gyō) Jūshichiyakō ranks highest at 27.1 percent, with Maruyamakyō following at 18.5 percent and Miyamotokō quite low at 6.1 percent. The Jūshichiyakō results are unexpected, especially in light of the leader's repeated apologies that he and his group do not really practice asceticism: in this case denial of an actuality may reflect aspiration of an ideal.

By its very nature a questionnaire is a cryptic document with inherent ambiguities: the disadvantage of using prescribed answers is that they channel responses into neat compartments. However, previous research in Japan demonstrated the necessity, practicality, and utility of this shorthand approach, owing to a number of factors: the diplomacy required to get approval for distribution; the need for brevity (a single sheet); the simplicity enabling respondents to fill out quickly and return the questionnaire (rather than to complete it partially or discard it). One unscripted, open-ended question was saved for the query "reason for climbing (Fuji)" in order to allow freer expression of the respondents. Here the results were good for Miyamotokō and excellent for Jūshichiyakō; as mentioned previously, the haste with

which the Maruyamakyō representative distributed and gathered up the questionnaires resulted in few and short answers for this question. Even so, these free responses help frame and sharpen three views of Fuji.

THREE VIEWS OF FUJI

The preceding statistics make possible a comparison and contrast of these three contemporary examples of Fuji spirituality and the identification of a common heritage as well as distinctive differences. These groups' relationships to Fuji are analyzed
through the categories of perception, realization, actualization, regeneration, and
organization.

The three movements exhibit similarities in each of the categories. All share a
perception of Fuji, Japan's highest and "number one" peak, as a sacred mountain.
While the natural and national characteristics of Fuji are important to these groups,
they see Fuji primarily as a religious reality. The questionnaire's results in the "goal"
(for climbing) item and in the open-ended "reason" show dramatically that these
people have a clear picture of Fuji as a sacred mountain. Each group has its own
emphasis on which particular part or parts of the mountain are most sacred, which
is inevitably linked to the founding figures and seminal events in their respective
histories.

Although their definitions of this sacred mountain vary, the groups are united
in their insistence on personal recognition and realization of the sacred reality of
Fuji; this awareness is a means of transforming human life generally and individual
humans specifically. The goal of climbing that got the highest number of responses
on the questionnaire was "to purify my own heart." The perception of these Fuji
pilgrims identifies Fuji as a sacred mountain; their realization of this sacred reality
leads to a salvific transformation of human life. In other words, identifying with the
sacred peak can change human character.

Another matter of consensus is that actualization follows from this realization
and in effect implements transformation: acting out one's awareness of Fuji's sacred
character means going to the mountain on pilgrimage and carrying out worship.
The specific activities of pilgrimage and the particulars of the ritual vary remarkably,
but they confirm that "pilgrimage" is much more than an abstract concept of or
meditation on a mountain: one must go to the mountain at specified times under
controlled circumstances and perform prescribed ritual acts. This action is repeated
—annually for the groups and at odd year intervals for an individual. As a number
of questionnaires indicated, respondents reported that they had wanted to climb
Fuji for a long time and only now were able to. They write about seeing Fuji from a
distance, which inspired them all the more to make the climb.

The effect of this actualization, or in other words, the fulfillment of the realization, is the regeneration of human life, as seen in the dominance of the goal of purifying one's own heart. Many written "reasons" for climbing give the same rationale:

for example, "To know myself, and to realize peace with myself within nature"; and "I climb in order to renew myself." The benefit may also be more concrete: they mention blessings, material goods, and protection. The statistics for "goal" show that respondents are reluctant to indicate such benefits, which may appear too selfish, but their written results show that they give thanks for these very things.

Each of these groups also takes for granted that the process of recognizing and acting out veneration of Fuji is best done not as individuals but as part of an organized body. In fact getting to know their fellow members better and helping them was the stated reason for climbing Fuji on some questionnaires and accorded with reports from the leaders on their conversations with the pilgrims. Although the manner of organization most effective for Fuji spirituality is perhaps the most divisive of all the categories, the three groups stand together in favoring corporate activity.

The same set of categories reveals striking contrasts for each of the items. Perception of Fuji as a sacred mountain is a many-splendored affair. Miyamotokō, looking back to the founding figure of Jikigyō Miroku, places most importance on the site of the Eboshi Iwa, where he carried out his self-immolation. Maruyamakyō bypasses the traditionally revered places to concentrate all its attention on the crater where the parent *kami* was revealed to Itō and where the *tenpaishiki* is performed. Jūshichiyakō is the most comprehensive and persistent of the three, stopping for *omairi* at every possible site. Miyamotokō and Jūshichiyakō both focus on Yoshida Sengen Jinja as a beginning point for their ascent; Maruyamakyō does not even acknowledge this shrine marking the beginning of the old (ten-station) climbing path. In this sense "Fuji," "ascent," and "pilgrimage" take on decidedly different meanings for each of these movements.

Realization of Fuji's reality also takes on a wide range of significances for the respective parties. Miyamotokō has a more "classic" view of Fuji, looking at it through the founder Jikigyō's eyes and experience, as the mountain made sacred by his self-sacrifice; hence Miyamotokō promotes the ascetic ideal that helps people serve others. Miyamotokō is Fuji-centered (because it brings Fuji back to its Tokyo altar), whereas Maruyamakyō is founder-centered (because it takes a scroll of the founder to Fuji for its temporary altar). Maruyamakyō advocates the realization of the presence of the parent *kami* who was revealed to Itō within the crater of Fuji and the awareness of the closeness of family ancestors. Jūshichiyakō encompasses a wide spectrum of aspirations covering the whole gamut of Fuji asceticism, Fuji piety, and Fuji faith. The Jūshichiyakō leader regrets the loss of asceticism, but his members rank the highest for "asceticism" as a goal of climbing. In addition Jūshichiyakō encourages *omairi* to every available holy site while teaching that pilgrimage to Fuji not only purifies the heart but also helps one serve others.

Actualization follows on the heels of realization. Miyamotokō places importance on reciting its old liturgy and performing its *takiage* (fire rite) as a way of permanently enshrining Jikigyō's teaching and the sacred mountain where he gave his life;

members honor the father of the Miyamotokō leader Ida near Yoshida Sengen Jinja as they begin their climb, and they revere Jikigyō at the Eboshi Iwa. Maruyamakyō avoids all of the customary sacred sites and heads straight for the crater, where, not just recognizing the sacred site of their "mecca," they actually consecrate the crater area with their temporary altar (one respondent mentioned this as his reason for climbing, to participate in the *tenpaishiki* at the crater). If Jūshichiyakō's activities had to be summed up in a single word, it would be *omairi*. The Jūshichiyakō leader admits that his *takiage* is a shorter, paler version of the Miyamotokō original and admits that asceticism is no longer practiced; his group is oriented around a rather diffuse pattern of *omairi*, worship of every available sacred site.

Regeneration is a renewal of spiritual life for these people. One Miyamotokō member wrote, "From long ago Fuji has been close to our existence, and by climbing Fuji we become physically and spiritually refreshed." Here the sacred mountain seems to reinvigorate the pilgrim. In Maruyamakyō this regeneration is the new life granted by the parent *kami* and ancestors, especially in the climactic *tenpaishiki*: the term "reborn" (*umarekawaru*) is a key Maruyamakyō category. Maruyamakyō respondents wrote that they climb to renew their lives, and they do so with the understanding that the ancestors climb with them. These themes overlap from group to group; in fact a Jūshichiyakō member responded: "I am allowed to climb Fuji together with all my ancestors who climbed Fuji, and those who wanted to but were not able to climb Fuji." Just as Jūshichiyakō's *omairi* is more diffuse than those of the other two parties, so is the source of blessing: Fuji is the general benefactor, but Jūshichiyakō has close ties to Yoshida Sengen Jinja.

Organization is the point that most sharply separates these three groups. Miyamotokō stubbornly clings to what it sees as Jikigyō's model of a Fuji-centered, strongly anticlerical lay group. Ida views the transition from Fujikō (*kō* or confraternity) to *kyōdan* (large-scale organization) as a betrayal of the founder's principles, a sellout to financial and commercial ambitions. Maruyamakyō sees itself centered more around its founder Itō and considers itself separated from the physical mountain itself and from all the traditional trappings of "Fuji faith." For Maruyamakyō, the move from *kō* to *kyōdan* was a positive and essential move to become a full-fledged religion. Jūshichiyakō is a paradox, in effect affirming both *kō* and *kyōdan* status while recognizing that the two styles often "collide." The Jūshichiyakō leader apologetically concedes that Gedatsukai's *kyōdan* status is one reason his *kō* cannot maintain all the traditional practices that the Miyamotokō does, and he appreciates the irony of his position. On the one hand, Jūshichiyakō would not exist without Gedatsukai's founder, Okano, having encouraged its revival. On the other hand, it operates within the framework of Gedatsukai as a religion and the physical and ritual space of a branch, circumstances constricting its growth and limiting its activities.

Fuji religiosity, with its strands of piety, faith, asceticism, and pilgrimage—and its various forms and organizational structures—displays a great variety of spiritual activity inspired by the same mountain. That Fuji continues to stimulate so many people in so many ways, despite the series of violent upheavals experienced in modern Japanese society, attests to the durability of Fuji as an object of veneration and worship. This religious dimension of Fuji, its status as a sacred mountain, remains a timeless facet of its status as icon of Japan. There are many paths up the mountain, and they all arrive at the summit, but the groups and individuals traversing (or contemplating) these paths carry with them (personally and collectively) distinctive patterns of Fuji belief and practice.[5]

Part 5

FUJI THE FLEXIBLE SYMBOL

I tried to see Mt Fuji as a symbol of a particular beauty, a particular being
... in addition I thought of Fuji as free spiritual food for the people.

... just as poets of old (classical poets) have given me a number of outstanding literary creations about Fuji I thought I would like to give some to the future. Furthermore I would like, even now, that a large number of different works about Fuji be created in the future.

The poet Kusano Shinpei, quoted from Fukasawa Chūkō,
Kusano Shinpei—kenkyū josetsu (1984)

15

War and Peace

THE MOBILIZATION OF FUJI

Fuji, which has proved remarkably flexible and enduring as a source of aesthetic and religious inspiration through the centuries, has been shown to be equally resilient and powerful as a national symbol and political trophy. That Fuji was recruited for wartime morale is not as surprising as its quick refurbishing in the postwar period as a poster for peace.

Wartime propaganda is filled with vicious images and hyperbolic verbiage. All nations fighting World War II had extensive propaganda machinery, and Japan was no exception. Propaganda can be divided into three categories. The first two types, domestic propaganda for civilians and patriotic propaganda for the civilians in allied, friendly, or occupied countries, both aim to inspire support for the war effort and military campaigns. The third type, sometimes called psychological propaganda, is directed at (or dropped over) opposing forces and is designed to undermine their morale. Fuji was a stock symbol of home-front propaganda in Japan. As seen in the image on the next page, the imposing outline of Fuji is an example of "domestic" propaganda used to buttress the invitation to Japanese youth to train for war and prepare to enter military service. The government-sponsored magazine in which this photo appeared, *Shashin Shūhō* (Photographic Weekly Report), published other photos and texts utilizing the power of Fuji. A 1944 cover of this magazine[1] features a photograph of a boy peering out of a tank, which was taken from a low angle so that the tank dominates Fuji. The text identifies the tank as belonging to the Iron Bull (Tetsugyū) Corps of the Army Youth Soldiers (Rikugun Shōnenhei), the caption noting that Fuji "watches over" this youth as he trains in his tank. The synergy of such photos goes far beyond what the text explicitly states: although Fuji is invoked as a guardian, at the same time the image encourages and inspires the boy soldiers

The November 11, 1942, issue (p. 17) of *Photographic Weekly Review* (*Shashin Shūhō*), an official government publication, features a photograph titled "Fujisan Fumoto" (At the Foot of Mount Fuji), illustrating the article "One-day Boot Camp for Bantam Tank Troop" and showing how boys were taken to Fuji for military training in tanks. The article does not need to state explicitly what the staged photograph demonstrates: a phalanx of boys in (outsize) uniforms, tanks, and Fuji as the crowning touch present a united war front. Courtesy of the David C. Earhart Collection of Japanese Primary Sources from the Asian-Pacific War

to guard and preserve not only this national symbol but also the nation as the physical land and political entity nuanced by Fuji. That this deeper message need not be spelled out speaks to the power of Fuji's iconic status.

The pages of *Shashin Shūhō* also portrayed Fuji as the emblematic bearer of Japanese imperialism across much of the vast territory of occupied Asia—what the Japanese called Dai Tōa Kyōeiken, or the Great East Asia Co-Prosperity Sphere (D. C. Earhart 2008, 261–307). The putative rationale for the Japanese war machine was to relieve Asians of the colonial yoke of the European powers, simultaneously liberating these nations and uniting "one billion" Asians in this "Co-Prosperity Sphere" initiated and overseen by Japanese leadership. Following closely the highly successful

Japanese blitzkrieg of 1941 and early 1942, grandiose plans were made to implement this co-prosperity sphere. One such project was the envisioning of the Shōnan Express, Shōnan being the Japanese name for Singapore, and the "Express" being a train that would run from Tokyo to Singapore. The cover story of the October 14, 1942, issue of *Shashin Shūhō*, honoring the seventieth anniversary of the establishment of the Japan National Railway, describes with delight: "Imagine. 'We're on our way,' we say with bag in hand, boarding a train that goes to Shimonoseki, Keijō [Seoul], Mukden, Beijing, Canton, Hanoi, Saigon, Bangkok, and finally, without ever having gotten off, we arrive in Shōnan." A map traces this imaginary journey, but an actual train is depicted as the physical substance behind the dream: "The photograph at top right shows the Fuji Express (with Mount Fuji–shaped emblem) at Tokyo Station" (291, illus. 79). In effect Fuji was selected as the traveling logo-in-motion for the Great East Asia Co-Prosperity Sphere, recruited as the ambassador in Japan's overseas propaganda campaign.

Aside from propaganda proper, Fuji was also yoked to the military effort in more than emblematic fashion, serving as the mark of an airplane suicide force. The cover of *Shashin Shūhō* 349 for November 29, 1944, is the photograph of an airplane tail with "the classic three-peaked Fuji and a lightning bolt painted on it. The large caption praises the Army Special Attack Forces in Leyte, Philippines, and the smaller caption says, 'A member of the Fugaku (Mount Fuji) Squadron paints Fuji's sacred peak and a lightning bolt on his beloved plane.'"[2] (The Special Attack Forces is known in English as the suicide, or kamikaze, units.) This particular unit has been described in some detail by Warner and Warner: "The Army's air force had organized two special attack units, the Banda (Ten Thousand Petals) and the Fugaku (Mount Fuji). . . . The Fugaku unit began with nine Peggys, specially modified for suicide missions, carrying two eight-hundred kilogram bombs, and equipped with explosive nose fuses. The Peggys were twin-engine heavy bombers, with a crew of six to eight." The send-off of one of these suicide forces is remarkable because of its conclusion with the invocation of Fuji. Before takeoff on their suicide mission, in a ceremony including wine cups and "poems addressed to 'the god troops of the Banda unit,' . . . General Tominaga told the pilots. 'You are members of the Banda unit, about to display the spirit of Japan, the land of the gods, and the righteousness of Japan, and thereby become cherry blossoms in full bloom after which your unit was named. A man's life is lighter than a feather, and the mission with which you are charged of destroying the enemy is heavier than Mount Fuji.'"[3]

If the photos of the boy soldiers and tanks against the backdrop of Fuji portray an alliance of mutual protection between mountain and military, this example of the link between Fuji and aviators/planes demonstrates a joint collusion between mountain and air force as a combined unit attacking the enemy. In ancient times the power of Fuji was a force to be feared and worshipped; in medieval times Fuji was a decorative motif for samurai (as in the campaign coat seen in plate 7). In the Pacific

War of the 1940s, however, apparently for the first time Fuji's power was employed as an offensive weapon.

Fuji played essentially the same role in the domestic propaganda of Japan and America. American as well as Japanese propagandists used the triangular outline of the sacred mountain as a marker for the Japanese homeland, its unstated and understated presence speaking all the more eloquently as a universally recognized symbol that signifies without explanation. Several examples from Japanese propaganda and wartime American cartoons illustrate how Fuji served these mutual foes. On the Japanese side, two wartime leaflets disseminated to the Japanese public demonstrate how the government used the image of Fuji to promote the war; these leaflets carry the gist of the Japanese home-front propaganda mission. "Most graphic renderings of the demonic foe bore the face of the U.S. president or British prime minister. ... [One] appeared in October 1944, when Japanese propaganda concerning alleged allied atrocities was accelerating. [It] portrays Roosevelt and Churchill as debauched ogres carousing within sight of Mount Fuji, and was accompanied by an exhortation to kill the devilish Americans and British" (Dower 1986, 195, fig. 23).

This picture presents the two Allied leaders as "debauched ogres," common characters in Japanese folklore connoting brutish, selfish strength (rather than satanic evil) vanquished by a smaller but more intelligent and tenacious hero. In this particular cartoon, a rough-looking minion behind Roosevelt has one hand on the president's shoulder, and the other hand points toward the middle of the picture where American military forces are advancing over the globe toward Fuji, which rises majestically above the horizon and touches the top of the picture. Even in propaganda guise Fuji displays a curving, pleasing asymmetrical profile. The left side of the picture with the debauching demons has ominous dark clouds, but Fuji's triangle is pure white, and to the right where the text appears the sky is clear. The morality play is obvious. Fuji represents Japan and purity, both of which are threatened by the dark, sinister forces of the Allied leaders and their troops (208–11).

Another Japanese propaganda picture including Fuji, from a November 1944 popular magazine, bears a similar message: "Cartoons in [the magazine] *Hinode* depicted the Americans as gangsters lusting after overseas lands and committing racist outrages at home. In one extraordinary panel, the righteous bayonet of 'the divine country Japan' speared cartoon-thug America in the posterior as he tried to lasso Mount Fuji." Propaganda draws on the unconscious but leaves little to the imagination: here America is trying to capture the sacred mountain of Fuji, and "the divine country Japan" retaliates with a well-placed bayonet. Fuji was a useful tool for Japanese homeland propaganda but of course did not appear in Japanese material designed for Americans and the Allies.[4]

Two aspects of the American and Japanese war of language and pictures are significant in the discussion of Fuji and World War II. The first is that, although the popular Western media lampooned the emperor, official Allied military propaganda

—for purely political purposes—avoided maligning him. The second is that the image of Fuji served both sides in basically the same fashion. On the first point, American anthropologists and social scientists who worked in the war as applied scientists, or planners of propaganda, recommended "that the Allies refrain from attacking the emperor and the imperial institution, the consummate symbols of the culture system as a whole. To do otherwise would harden Japanese resistance to surrender, for attacking the throne would be seen as a threat to destroy the entire Japanese 'way of life.'"[5] Although there were disagreements within the American government and military (especially because of localized control of propaganda in the field) on the extent, nature, timing, and content of propaganda, one scrupulously followed principle was delivering the message to Japanese civilians and combatants that the militarists ("Gumbatsu") had subverted the ideals of the country and misled the emperor into an unjust and unwinnable war. On the second point, apparently there was no official American policy on not disparaging Fuji,[6] and whether it was simple neglect of Fuji (and other symbols such as cherry blossoms) or a tacit understanding not to criticize this symbol, American military propaganda used the form of the mountain only as an identifier of Japan.

An American newspaper cartoon published during the 1942–43 Japanese occupation of two of the Aleutian Islands presents an interesting foil to the Japanese cartoon of the carousing demons Roosevelt and Churchill overseeing the attack of Allied forces on Mount Fuji. In the American cartoon the viewpoint is reversed, with an apish Japanese soldier poised on the end of a long diving board that has "The Aleutians" printed on the end. The point of the cartoon is spelled out in its title, "KNOCK HIM OFF THAT SPRINGBOARD." A tiny smoking Fuji and a miniature torii identifying Japan anchor that springboard. In this cartoon the dominant figure is the monkey-soldier: Fuji is just a minor prop (Dower 1986, 6, fig. 5). This is in sharp contrast to the Japanese graphic, which positioned a lofty Fuji from the midground of the picture to the top. In both cartoons Fuji is immediately recognizable as both a physical mountain and a symbolic representation of Japan and the Japanese people.

American propaganda directed at Japanese forces took the form of leaflets dropped by planes on civilians and troops. This leaflet program was extensive, both in the university training of personnel on the home front and in the use of high-speed presses in the field capable of printing millions of leaflets per month.[7] "In their attempts to demoralize Japanese troops Allied propagandists in the Southwest Pacific alone disseminated nearly 400 million propaganda leaflets and witnessed the capture of approximately 19,500 Japanese prisoners" (Gilmore 1998, 2). Fuji played a minor but revealing role in a handful of the multitude of individual leaflets. American leaflets have been classified into the four categories of divisive propaganda, subversive propaganda, enlightenment propaganda, and propaganda of despair (Gilmore 1998, 11). The leaflets depicting Fuji, when considered with the accompanying text on the reverse, include most or all of these features, but the major import of Fuji is playing the card of homesickness and nostalgia, as the following discussion demonstrates.[8]

"Leaflet 114a depicts a Japanese mother and child in the forefront, dead Japanese soldiers behind her with what appears to be cherry blossoms, and the towering presence of Mt. Fuji in the background."[9] The picture is a photographic print, apparently a montage. The translation of the text on the other side of the image blames "militarists" for starting the war, "which continues to destroy your homeland," and encourages the Japanese serviceman, "Deliver your homeland." The visual, including Fuji, is an obvious marker of this "homeland."[10]

The same picture was used on leaflet 1049; "The back has a long message meant to encourage the Japanese Wake Island garrison to surrender," written "in the form of a letter from a Japanese prisoner of war" and emphasizing the "starvation and despair" he experienced on an isolated island in the Marshalls, as contrasted with the fine treatment he is now receiving as a prisoner of war. In the picture used on both leaflets Fuji, cherry blossoms, and the mother and child pair all serve to stir up homesickness and sap the will to fight. The photographic image used on leaflets 114a and 1049 is clear evidence that American "psywar" practitioners perceived Fuji as an appropriate visual stimulus for calling up feelings of homesickness.

In another American propaganda leaflet using Fuji for the purpose of identifying Japan, the audience is the Japanese soldier and the time later in the war, when the Japanese military was suffering heavy losses. The attacker was now the attacked. "Leaflet 519 depicts Japan [as indicated by Mt. Fuji] being attacked by multiple American aircraft and ships. The purpose of the leaflet is 'to show that American forces are closing in on Japan.'" (See plate no. 8.) The text provides information (to "enlighten") about American bases less than fifteen hundred miles from Tokyo, the U.S. Navy operating off the shores of Japan, and submarines sinking Japanese ships; it concludes with the advice, "Free your country from the Gumbatsu [militarist] tyrants who control it."[11] The graphic design on the leaflet places Fuji in the very center, like a bull's-eye. The lower third of the drawing is a phalanx of battleship guns and naval ships pointing at Fuji; the upper third of the leaflet is the underside of a large four-engine bomber and many twin-engine bombers all headed for Fuji, with two bombers returning from their sortie. Here Fuji serves to identify Japan, the unrepentant foe, as the recipient of air and naval bombardment. Obviously the point is to evoke fear and despair.[12]

One leaflet touches on the religious dimension of Fuji. "Leaflet 2064 is a very stark dark blue and white leaflet that depicts a Japanese pilgrim standing at the foot of Mt. Fuji at the intersection of two paths marked by road-stones reading 'Duty' and 'Humanity.' The leaflet is designed to lower Japanese morale and create a desire for peace. Text at the upper right of the leaflet is: 'There are two roads but only one goal.'"[13] The text on the back begins with the statement "Japanese people have been praised and respected for their sense of duty. A true Japanese knows his obligations to his country as well as his family." It cites a medieval precedent that "a true Japanese will conquer ninjo [human feeling][14] and give his all to his country" and suggests, "Your duty is to bring peace and to save your country from ruin," praising the emperor and his desire for peace. Emperor, family, and nation are linked together with the soldier's duty, and blame for the war is heaped on the Gumbatsu. The image is striking. An imposing three-domed Fuji dominates the upper half of the picture, highlighted by a white sky and billowy clouds. The pilgrim in traditional outfit complete with pilgrim's hat is centered in the picture, with his back to the viewer. He is flanked by the two "road-stones," aligned with the peak of Fuji, and apparently is looking at the summit as his "goal." From each of the stone posts a ribbon of road winds up each side of the image toward the slopes of the mountain. This leaflet shows some acquaintance with the notion of Fuji as a sacred mountain as well as the custom of climbing Fuji as a pilgrimage linked to personal, social, and national values.[15]

In the eyes of the American psychological warfare practitioners, Fuji was a convenient marker for identifying Japan, in effect serving the same signaling purpose as in popular media directed at the American audience. In the leaflets dropped on Japanese military personnel, Fuji was utilized as both sign and symbol, not only to denote Japan but also intended to call up the notions of homeland and the emotions linked to emperor and national identity as well as family and social belonging. Although Fuji was used by Japanese propagandists as a patriotic logo to bolster militarism and the war effort, apparently this role of Fuji was never attacked by American psyops personnel, who used the mountain only as a signifier of Japan. From panoramas of fierce bombardment to peaceful woodblock print scenes, from frightening "mom and Mount Fuji" graphics (replete with dead soldiers) to the joy of homecoming, Fuji went to war in the American battle of phrases and graphics. Japan's sacred mountain played a double role in World War II, enlisted for service in both Japanese and American propaganda. One of the supreme ironies of Fuji's indirect role in the war is that the physical form of the mountain was a landmark for the U.S. bombers as they made their way to their targets in and around Tokyo, while during the air raids the spiritual power of Fuji was invoked by some of the sendatsu of Fujikō to protect their neighborhoods and members from destruction and injury.[16]

FUJI AS THE EMBLEM OF PEACE

In the American propaganda against Japan, hostility was directed especially at the militarists (Gumbatsu) and the head of the military, Tōjō Hideki, but no single symbol stood for Japan as the swastika did for Nazi Germany. The rising sun on the Japanese flag (hi no maru) was a prominent feature of Japanese imperialism and as such even today is opposed by Japanese peace activists and people in Asian countries who see it as an extension/revival of Japanese militarism (Field 1993, 33–104). In postwar Japan the emperor and the emperor system, which some Allied representatives

hoped to abolish, have received considerable criticism. The preservation of the emperor as the "symbol of the country" and his exclusion from responsibility for the war
were in large part because of the pragmatic policy of the Allied occupation and Gen.
Douglas MacArthur's strategy of using the emperor to control the people and reform
Japan (Dower 1999, 292–301).[17] The rehabilitation of the emperor coupled with the
imperfect justice of the Tokyo war crimes trial created a dubious legacy, and to this
day the debate over responsibility, guilt, and punishment for the war continues.

In the immediate postwar period, Shinto was disestablished, the emperor was
persuaded to formally renounce his divinity, and chauvinistic versions of Shinto
mythology and Confucian ethics—advocating superiority of the Japanese people
and absolute loyalty to emperor and nation—were removed from the school curriculum. This transformation was far reaching: "Scathing criticism at home and abroad
went to the very heart of the 'national polity' [kokutai] idea, and the national polity
was altered" (Maruyama 1969, 148).

In the midst of all this postwar purging, cleansing, and reform, the symbol of Fuji
remained intact, only temporarily hidden from public view. By order of the occupation censors within the headquarters of the Supreme Commander, Allied Powers
(SCAP), Japanese filmmakers were not allowed to show Fuji.[18] This prohibition was
not without its self-contradictions, which led at least one filmmaker to protest.

Mt. Fuji, a powerful symbol of Japanese nationalism, was . . . taboo. During
the war, the Japanese government had tried to promulgate a sacred, mystical
image of the mountain. However, the occupation's linking of Mt. Fuji with
nationalism and militarism might seem somewhat paranoid. Director Masahiro
Makino had an argument with a Japanese-American censor at CIE [Civil Information and Education within SCAP] who insisted on this point, and thus forbade him to show Mt. Fuji in his Sophisticated Wanderer [Ikina furaibo] (1946).
The director was distressed. The story was about cultivating land on the slopes
of Mt. Fuji, and avoiding shooting the mountain itself would be most difficult.
Makino replied that Mt. Fuji was not a symbol of nationalism but of the Japanese people; however, the censor was not persuaded. Makino continued: "If you
really believe so, why didn't you drop atomic bombs[19] on Mt. Fuji, and not on
Hiroshima and Nagasaki?" The American officials . . . admitted that he was right,
but nonetheless insisted that he not include Mt. Fuji in his film. During the occupation period, Mt. Fuji only appeared on the Japanese screen in the Shochiku
Studio logo.[20]

This ban by the American occupation was not the first instance of bureaucratic
rationalization to censor and control the film roles of Fuji. The left-wing antiwar
director "Kamei's script for The Geology of Mt. Fuji [Fuji no chishitsu] (1941) was
never allowed to be filmed because its rational, scientific analysis angered the government, which had sought to maintain the mystique of Mt. Fuji as a solemn national

symbol" (K. Hirano 1992, 116). Wartime Japanese censorship blocked a film about Fuji because it was not nationalistic; postwar American censorship banished the mountain's form from the screen entirely because even a "natural" scenario of farming on the peak's slope was presumed to be nationalistic. In both cases the physical object automatically served as a tool of nationalism.[21]

If Fuji was excluded from films during the occupation, it was not blackballed from other media. A photograph of the mountain was used to drive home a newspaper's front-page 1946 New Year's editorial: "The era of imperialism, aggression and tyranny has been wiped off the national slate and the entire Japanese nation, today, faces with eager hope the coming of Democracy and the Four Freedoms promised in the Atlantic Charter. The glistening peak of Mt. Fuji, the blue shadows of the pine mottled with whiteness, reflect a peacefulness that augurs well for the future . . . a future that holds forth for Japan a golden opportunity to enter once again the comity of world nations as a worthy and respected member."[22]

On the opposite side of the Pacific Ocean, not all Westerners were favorably inclined toward the sacred mountain as a harbinger of democracy. A postwar newspaper cartoon from the *Detroit News* portrays Fuji not as the voluntary bearer of but as the involuntary recipient of democracy (Dower 1988, 121). The cartoon is dominated on the left side by an American GI who holds open a book, *Democratic Way of Life*, forcefully admonishing with his index finger a much shorter, Japanese man holding a scabbarded sword with one hand and an offered flower in the other. The right side of the cartoon is a grab bag of Japonalia: a stone lantern, a Buddhist statue (like the Kamakura Buddha), an Inari fox, a torii, a Shinto priest, hanging diagonally across this pastiche a paper lantern, and also—the crowning touch—snow-covered Fuji. Here the implication is that all of Japan, including Fuji, needs the American lesson of democracy. The diminutive Japanese is wearing geta (wooden clogs), further emphasizing the point that America is modern and civilized while Japan is backward and uncivilized (Dower 1988, 110).

Even the apelike stereotype of the Japanese soldier could be tamed: "The cover of *Leatherneck's* September 1945 issue, celebrating Japan's surrender, revealed the malleability of wartime stereotypes, as the simian caricature was almost immediately transformed into an irritated but already domesticated and even charming pet" (Dower 1986, 186, fig. 9). The cover, rendered cartoon-style, shows a laughing marine, who has hoisted on his shoulder a frowning monkey in a Japanese uniform.

Fuji was never maligned or demonized in the fashion of the animalistic soldier. Indeed the anomaly in this episode of Fuji's career is that the punishment for wartime service was so light and inconsistent and lasted for such a short time. Of course the occupation's censors looked to military leaders and governmental institutions (and organized religion) in assigning responsibility for the war; Fuji, neither an organized institution nor an embodied person, could more easily be manipulated (and exorcized/exoticized) by means of both Japonisme in the West and reverse orientalism in Japan.[23] In general, noninstitutional symbols such as the stereotypical dyad of Fuji and cherry blossoms were immune to the Allied purges, even though each had its own part in the unfolding political drama that culminated in World War II.[24] Flowering cherries, because they were intimately connected with national identity, inevitably became intertwined with the military campaigns of the nation.[25] In hindsight the ease with which Fuji's symbolic meaning shifted from uniqueness and superiority justifying an aggressive war to the harbinger of peace and universalism promoting democracy is, mildly put, ironic.

The ultimate incongruity in Fuji's postwar career is the fact that this image sometimes banned by occupation censors for its association with Japanese nationalism and militarism soon became the design of choice for representing a united Japanese and American national and military effort. The American military presence in postwar Japan has embraced Fuji, even adopting it as part of its official regalia. The adoption and display of Fuji on American military insignia connotes domination and domestication; prewar Japonisme seems to be overlaid with postwar exoticism (and may retain traces of colonial aspirations and fantasies).

Several examples illustrate these "Fujified" American military badges. An official army release best tells the story, first giving a capsule overview of the history of "The United States Army Japan" and then elaborating:

> The Distinctive Unit Insignia (often referred to as a "unit crest") for USARJ is a gold color metal and enamel device, 1-1/4 inches in height overall, consisting of a stylized representation of Mount Fuji in light blue, with a white peak silhouetted against a red demi-sun on a blue background. All is enclosed by a circular gold scroll of five segments, bearing in the upper three segments the words "Omnia Fieri Potest" (literally: "It is possible to do all things" and can be translated as "All things are possible.") in blue enamel.
>
> The location of USARJ in Japan is symbolized by the representation of Mount Fuji, a world famous symbol of Japan.[26]

Every other American military group in Japan has been represented in some form with the shape of Fuji. The Command Submarine Group Seven, the American submarine group stationed in Japan, has a cap with a badge featuring a light blue Fuji (with the classic three-domed snow-clad peak) in the background, a red Shinto torii (sacred archway) in the middle ground, and in the foreground a submarine flanked by two dolphins.[27] In other words, the dolphins (attendants of the Greek deity Poseidon) are joined by a classic Japanese holy/ideal mountain and a Shinto sacred archway to oversee an American submarine group based in Japan.

Fuji also appears on (at least) five postwar American military coins in Japan. These minted medals, more commonly called "challenge coins" or "unit coins," are unofficial materials designed and purchased by military personnel. The items are created by the rank and file of the respective units, who apparently agree that Fuji represents Japan. One coin, described as a "US Armed Forces in Japan Challenge Coin,"[28] has snow-clad Fuji at the bottom, an orange sun just above center, and the Shinto sacred archway at the top; five circles surrounding the sun represent army, navy, air force, coast guard, and marines; the imprint identifies the coin (above) as "Yokota Air Base" and (below) "Tokyo Japan." The Fuji on this coin is more like the U.S. Army Japan insignia, which has a "natural" crater, unlike the "classical" three-domed peak of the Comsubgru Seven badge. Four other challenge coins feature variations of Fuji, military equipment, and unit names.[29] The official army insignia, submarine badge, and armed forces challenge coins all demonstrate the way in which postwar Fuji has come to represent Japan even for American military on the official level and among lower-ranking military personnel.[30]

In one sense these American military insignia demonstrate how Fuji has helped usher in peace. In another sense the emblems are not necessarily benign or without ambiguity. Just as Commodore Perry's mid-nineteenth-century memorial volumes had the outline of Fuji embossed on their covers, the adoption of Fuji by the U.S. military may also be seen as a "capture" of Japan's preeminent symbol. This brings to mind the Japanese wartime propaganda graphic depicting "the cartoon-thug America" who "tried to lasso Mount Fuji" (Dower 1986, 249). One of Japan's worst wartime fears has been realized: Fuji has become a trophy of the victorious Americans.

Several of the most dramatic American wartime pictures of Fuji show the mountain "captured" by the camera through American submarine periscopes. Winston Churchill selected one such photograph, pairing it with a photograph of a Japanese ship that has been torpedoed and is sinking, for inclusion in one of his books about the war. The two photographs, under the title "The Massive Blow from the Sea," carry the caption "Periscope views of Mount Fuji (top) and a sinking Japanese destroyer (bottom) recall the far-ranging activities of the 226 big, hardy submarines which harried the Japanese throughout the war" (Churchill 1959, 2:570). The photographs illustrate the capabilities of submarines that sank destroyers and "captured" Mount Fuji, taking it home as a photographic souvenir of war.

A different publication glosses this same periscopic view of Fuji: "This unusual shot rather dimly captures Japan's most famous mountain," rendering it more as a landscape than a warscape (Steichen 1980, 117).[31] Another wartime periscope photograph of Fuji is credited to the submarine *Skate,* and a Web site boasts of it: "During one patrol, they came near enough to the Japanese coast to photograph Mt. Fuji through the periscope. The picture (scope reticle and all) made it into Life magazine."[32] The Web site for the submarine *Icefish* makes a similar claim: "His [the *Icefish* commander's] daring proximity to the coast of Japan was documented by his famous photograph, published on the cover of Life magazine, of Mount Fuji, taken through the periscope of his submarine."[33] The braggadocio of these claims resembles the "counting of coup" by Native Americans, who strove to strike or touch their enemy and thereby display their own courage while robbing the power of the adversary. Here the derring-do of the sub commanders and crews was to approach and seize the hallmark of Japan through photography.

The periscope "capture" of Fuji was dramatized in the 1943 Warner Brothers film *Destination Tokyo*, which featured Cary Grant and earned an Oscar nomination for the writer Steve Fisher. The mostly fictional film has an American submarine land in Tokyo Bay to prepare for Doolittle's 1942 bombing of Tokyo. In the film, as the submarine finally makes its way to Tokyo Bay, the crew raises the periscope to confirm its position, and a huge Fuji appears right in front of them (as the sound track rises to a dramatic crescendo). This film uses Fuji as a marker for Japan viewed through the periscope, from the deck of the submarine when a landing party goes ashore, as well as in a brief aerial shot as Doolittle's planes begin their bombing run on Tokyo.[34]

Companions to the periscope shots of Fuji are the numerous aerial photographs of the mountain by American war planes both during and after the war.[35] Steichen (1980, 124–25) also includes a striking photo of the "sunset over Fujiyama—U.S. Fleet in Tokyo Bay, August 29, 1945," with the caption: "Mt. Fujiyama, as symbolic of Japan as are Tokyo and the Islands, well deserves its romantic background. Everyone in the American Navy hoped to see Fuji, preferably aboard ship." This photo, capturing the glowing outline of a backlit Fuji rising above Tokyo Bay, which is filled with U.S. warships, is reminiscent of the image of Fuji and the "black ships" on Commodore Perry's commemorative volumes of the mid–nineteenth century. Here too American ships dominate Fuji/Japan, and yet the caption softens the conquest with admission of the "romantic background" and the (presumed) wish of every sailor to see it.[36]

The most blatant instance of the American utilization of Fuji to depict simultaneously the defeat of Japan and the capture of the mountain was having the surrender ceremony take place in Tokyo Bay with Fuji as a backdrop. An eight-page brochure issued by the Joint Intelligence Center, Pacific Ocean Areas and titled "U.S.S. Missouri: Scene of Japanese Surrender" was originally distributed to naval personnel shortly after the surrender.[37] The brochure consists mainly of postcard-sized photographs and features an aerial shot of the battleship *Missouri* and the American and Japanese signatories of the surrender. The back of the pamphlet features a photograph of the U.S. fleet anchored in Tokyo Bay with the sun setting over the silhouette of Fuji; the title, "The Setting Sun," seems to be a deliberate pun, a fitting conclusion to the war and the end of "the rising sun" (Japan). The picture certainly recalls the imagery of Commodore Perry's commemorative volume with the American fleet dominating Tokyo Bay and Fuji, and it conveys the message that America has again dominated Japan—as symbolized by Fuji.

In the West the association of Fuji with claims of Japanese uniqueness and superiority, in turn linked to both national identity and ultranationalism (and imperialism and colonialism), is known primarily by students of Japanese history. For the most part the postwar image of Fuji is a continuation of prewar Japonisme, updated with elements of the postwar "economic miracle." Favorite tourist advertisements or postcard photos show the bullet train racing past snow-clad Fuji: the best of both worlds—high tech industry and traditionally romantic naturalism. On one Japanese postage stamp is a revision of Hokusai's *Great Wave* woodblock print, which replaces Fuji with the Philately Hall. As mentioned earlier, one of the first postwar Japanese postage stamps featured an ukiyo-e of Fuji as an attempt to put a peaceful face on the Japanese map. The international reputation of Fuji, filtered through a long legacy of Japonisme and revived after the war in the new era of peace and friendship, has been reborn—with the mountain presented as a natural wonder of beauty and a beautiful emblem of harmony with nature.

Nowhere is this renaissance of Fuji more conspicuous than in the appearance of its photograph and woodblock images on the postage stamps of the world. In fact the very notion of what "Japan" represents to non-Japanese is conveyed by the stamps their countries print (Naitō 2003, 4–5). In the postwar era new trends in creating postage stamps of greater variety and more interesting design tailored to the philatelic market resulted in many "Fujiyama-samurai" postage stamps being marketed by foreign countries. In 1953 the U.S. Post Office issued a stamp commemorating the hundredth anniversary of the opening of Japan by Commodore Matthew C. Perry. The timing of this stamp is also significant, in that it was released just a year after the end of the 1945–52 occupation of Japan. The design of the stamp incorporated the anchorage of American warships in Edo Bay (Tokyo Bay) and a portrait of Perry, with Fuji in the center field and a samurai in the lower right. These are the same elements found embossed on the official reports of Perry's Japan mission published in 1856. The stamp also suggests the greater geopolitical role assumed by the United States after its victory in World War II. From a Japanese perspective, Japanese ports were really opened in 1858, coinciding with the so-called Harris Treaty (United States–Japan Treaty of Amity and Commerce), and so the Japanese issued their hundredth anniversary commemorative stamp of the opening of Japanese ports in 1958. In light of the previous discussion of the Perry volume's Fuji image and the utilization of the mountain's picture in both American wartime propaganda and in postwar American military insignia, the 1953 stamp may be considered an unintentional and unconscious but for that very reason an even more powerful statement of American dominance over Fuji and its land and people.

Although "Fujisan" is the more proper term, Naitō's treatment of Fuji on foreign stamps deliberately adopts the frequent Western perception/misperception of "Fujiyama" to emphasize the foreign viewpoint, in effect mocking the Western stereotype of Japan as "Fujiyama-samurai." With Japan's postwar economic recovery and acceptance as an industrial-commercial power together with Japan's attempts to forge international ties, a flood of foreign stamps with the subject of Japan appeared. A 1966 ukiyo-e stamp from the government of Sharjah marks a first not only for Arab nations but also for all other countries outside Japan. Ironically at the bottom of this stamp is a credit that it was printed in Japan by "Govt. Printing Bureau Tokyo" (Naitō 2003, 72–73); in fact it was a made-in-Japan foreign stamp.

From the 1970s onward various countries issued stamps about Japan, many with ukiyo-e and among those quite a few depicting Fuji. The appearance of such stamps is the result of a resurgence of Japonisme and an exoticizing of Japan coinciding with the discovery by small countries of the ease with which cash could be extracted from the wallets of avid philatelists. The themes on the stamps reflect the image of Japan in Western countries, which was still perceived through the eyes of Hokusai and Hiroshige. Although in Japan these two artists did not necessarily represent "Japan," the collectors who bought stamps seemed to think they did. Fuji was one of the major subjects on these ukiyo-e stamps; other popular (and lucrative) subjects were the Olympics and Disney characters à la Japanese. The themes intermingled: a 1964 Albanian Olympic stamp superimposes an Olympic torch on Fuji's triangle; a 1991 Gambia Disney stamp shows "Mickey [Mouse] as a hawk hunter Tagari in Japan," with the hawk hovering over the distant image of Fuji; a stamp from New Caledonia and Dependencies honoring the Osaka Expo 70 is a horizontal rectangle accommodating the front cars of the bullet train speeding along an elevated track against the background of snow-domed Fuji, another melding of the technological and the traditional.[38] Because of the financial motive for their production, not all of these stamps were successful in their designs, but a sure bet was simply to copy a woodblock or use a photograph (France issued a series of woodblocks from a collection of early ukiyo-e in the Louvre). These are but a few examples illustrating a dubious but recent chapter in Fuji's career as icon of Japan.

In this chapter a seemingly disparate collection of materials has been discussed: Japanese and American wartime propaganda (especially American leaflets); postwar American military regalia; and postwar foreign stamps portraying Japan. What holds them together is their utilization of the image of Fuji as a convenient and effective representation of Japan. That this symbol can serve both sides in war and peace and then become transformed into an internationally disseminated hallmark of a country demonstrates the versatility and power of Fuji.

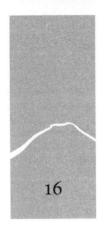

16

The Future of an Icon

The images of Fuji in modern times are so plentiful and omnipresent that they defy complete cataloging. The snow-covered peak of Fuji has been reproduced so mechanically in such great numbers—repeating the trite formula with little or no originality—that popular writers and academics alike agree that the towering mountain has been reduced to a commercial stereotype. Even in Tokugawa times, in Hokusai's *One Hundred Views of Mt. Fuji* the name Fujiya ("Fuji Store" or "Fuji Shop") appeared in a woodblock print.[1] The ancient and medieval visage of Fuji combined with the Tokugawa heritage and modern perspectives of Japonisme and reverse orientalism were fostered and nurtured by the Japanese government's deliberate plan of representing Japan domestically and internationally in the twentieth century. To cite just one 1930s example, the government, through publications such as the magazine *Nippon,* used a number of "markers" such as Fuji to promote tourism to the "museum" of the "real Japan." "*NIPPON*'s kaleidoscopic view of the Japanese empire promoted a timeless land with verdant peaks, typified by the national symbol of Mount Fuji; friendly natives (the idealized 'happy' people of the countryside and the colonies; and refined cultural sensibilities, [alongside] an urban, industrialized, expansionist imperial power. . . . [A] two-page spread titled 'At the Foot of Mt. Fuji'" presents photographs of "country people and their majestic environment near Japan's primary spiritual symbolic marker, Mount Fuji," accompanied by a highly romanticized text of happy farmers inspired by the "noble mountain. . . . 'The spirit of the mountain is their guide in life, its mysterious influence fills their days with happiness from childhood to old age, and they are never discontented, nor forget to thank Fuji-san for the deep comfort it gives'" (Weisenfeld 2000, 747, 759, 760–61).

As with propaganda language, the visual and textual aspects of stereotypes are quite malleable and flexible, readily adaptable to wartime or peacetime, colonialism or commercialism, and Fuji is just as visible in postwar times as in prewar tourism. "It is so much a national symbol, Mount Fuji is lumped together with geisha in the phrase *fujiyama-geisha* to refer to anything that is an overused Japanese stereotype" (Cutts 1994, 35). The trite image of the mountain has even led some Fuji-weary Japanese to encourage people "to find alternative images of Japan to replace *Fujiyama, Sakura* and *Geisha*, all well-known symbols of Japan."[2]

Even though some Japanese may be indifferent to the sight of Fuji, it is still so popular that a record is kept of how many days it is visible from Tokyo. Although tall buildings block its silhouette and weather may obscure its form, still "the Japanese can see it in their mind's eye every time they bite into a Fuji apple, load a roll of Fuji film, tune into the Fuji TV network, or make a deposit at the Fuji Bank" (Cutts 1994, 35). The companies and goods associated with this peak range from "natural" items such as the "natural water"[3] bottled from Fuji's springs to the enterprises such as Fuji Heavy Industries that make use of the abundant nearby water to manufacture automobiles, trucks, and airplanes.

An incisive critique of Japanese advertising's use of the "natural imagery" of "Mount Fuji and the Cherry Blossoms" as "orientalist and nationalist stereotypes" argues "that orientalist and nationalist stereotypes are simultaneously perpetuated and undermined in the media," rejecting the dichotomy of Westerners' distance from nature and Japanese closeness to nature. For example two global advertising campaigns (for a Hermès scarf and a Cadillac Seville) include the backdrop of Fuji to authenticate Japan as "the land of elegance" and to validate the products.[4] In effect Fuji the icon of Japan has become an international logo of "global stylistic continuity." An interesting conclusion of this study is that "Mount Fuji means 'Japan'" and "specific cultural settings, then, are focal points in a *global stylistic continuity*, and as such, images of Japanese nature tend to be the same regardless of whether they are produced in Europe or in Japan" (Moeran and Skov 1997, 181, 182, 188, 193).

A contrast of the American cowboy "Come to Marlboro Country" cigarette ad with the Hermès ad (showing a petite woman gazing at Fuji through binoculars) evokes the comment "a sexual contrast was built into orientalism with its imperialist image of the Occident as a man who—rightfully and hero-like—set out to conquer the supposedly receptive Orient" (Moeran and Skov 1997, 191). The sexual undertones of Fuji are so pervasive and self-evident that even in a local American newspaper, an ad for "Fuji Spa Massage" required only the explanation "We Do It Best."[5] In other words, the popular notion of the term "Fuji" has also come to imply a sexually available *oriental* (not necessarily Japanese) female, apparently a fringe benefit of the perception of the mountain when viewed from the perspective of Western orientalism through the lens of the "Fujiyama-geisha" stereotype.

A striking example of Fuji's crossing the boundary from exotic to erotic is found in the 1957 rock and roll (or rockabilly) tune *Fujiyama Mama,* with lyrics by Earl Burrows. Its explosive phrases were made famous by Wanda Jackson in a provocative sexual delivery. As the "Fujiyama Mama" who has been to Nagasaki and Hiroshima and is "about to blow my top," she belts out the message that when she starts erupting, no one will make her stop.[6] Through five stanzas the explicit references to energy and stimulants—sake, dynamite, "tobaccey," nitroglycerine, atom bomb— reinforce the sexual innuendo of the lines about "Fujiyama Mama."

If this stereotyping can be attributed to Western orientalism, it also owes a certain debt to reverse orientalism since Wanda Jackson toured Japan and her rendition of this song was well received.[7] Wanda Jackson, widely recognized as the first sex symbol of country music, and her performance of this song amount to a white singer's appropriation of the sexual allure of an oriental woman—a "Fujiyama Mama." For the American public of the 1950s, Wanda Jackson's song had two surprises: its overtly sexual content and the Japanese source. However, given the long-standing orientalist view of the sexually submissive Asian woman (Madam Butterfly) and the dominance of the Japanese sex industry by American GIs after World War II, this development is hardly an anomaly. Musically, Fuji has run the scale from classical (Debussy's *La Mer*) to rock. Capitalizing on the energy and power of fire in Fuji, this country/rock song crystallizes the postwar image of Fuji in a concatenation of nuclear energy with orientalism/eroticism.

Westerners have no monopoly on the sexuality of Fuji, a theme in Japanese culture at least since medieval times, with the volcano's heat and eruption being linked to sexual desire and heat. A nineteenth-century sexual guide uses innuendo to compare the caves of Fuji to female genitalia (Nenzi 2008, 173–74). A recent issue of a Japanese comic book (*Biggu komikku*) made an erotic connection with Fuji quite explicit in a sketch titled, simply and appropriately, "Fuji." A young man and his girlfriend, named Fujiko, spent a weekend at an inn near Mount Fuji. The morning after a night of sexual pleasure, the man awoke and looked out the window at the gently sloping triangle of snow-covered Fuji, which reminded him of his girlfriend's fulsome white breasts. He commented that now he knew why her name was Fujiko (Saitō 1989).

Most Japanologists, Japanophiles, and even occasional travelers to Japan have felt compelled to write about Japan and Fuji as the exotic. Of all the non-Japanese who have romanticized Japan, perhaps no one has lavished more love and praise on the land of the rising sun than Lafcadio Hearn, who reserved for Fuji the highest accolades. The first sentence of his book *Exotics and Retrospectives,* in the chapter "Fuji-no-yama," begins, "The most beautiful sight in Japan, and certainly one of the most beautiful in the world, is the distant apparition of Fuji on cloudless days" (Hearn 1898, 3). He continues in this chapter with the more prosaic account of "my own experience of climbing it [Fuji]" (6) and notices, once he actually is on the mountain, that "Fuji . . . is black—charcoal-black,—a frightful extinct heap of visible ashes and cinders and slaggy lava" (14). The sensation and sound of lava crunching under his own feet made him all too aware of the nightmare behind the dream: "one of the fairest, if not the fairest of earthly visions, resolves itself into a spectacle of horror and death. . . . But have not all human ideals of beauty, like the beauty of Fuji seen from afar, been created by forces of death and pain?" (14). Hearn used as the heading of his book a proverb about Fuji: "Seen on close approach, / the mountain of Fuji / does not come up to expectation" (3). The hyperbole that has been lavished upon Fuji is not without its modern detractors, including the famous writers Dazai Osamu and Nagai Kafū.[8]

If Fuji were not so lofty and so tightly wrapped in centuries of aesthetic, religious, and political ideals, it would not be the object of expectations so easily dashed by crass commercialism. The image of Fuji encompasses the majestic, the magical, the mystical; the stereotypes of Fuji range from the sublime to the ridiculous and skirt the ludicrous and the lewd. Magnificent Fuji has become trivialized in every imaginable form of souvenir. Monumental Fuji has been reduced to an advertising ploy and commercial logo; the natural form has been personalized into the exotic and erotic.

SECULAR IMAGE AND PATRIOTIC MANTRA

Two examples, one poetic and the other graphic, illustrate the national and patriotic service of Fuji in recent times: the poetry of Kusano Shinpei and the paintings of Yokoyama Taikan. They are labeled "secular" images of Fuji for lack of a better term. The religious undertones or overtones of Fuji never completely disappear in modern times, but a wide gap separates the few white-clad Fujikō pilgrims from the multitude of "mountaineers" on the peak who not only dress differently but also have contrasting perceptions of the mountain and their ascent.

"One of Japan's most distinguished twentieth-century poets . . . Kusano Shinpei [1903–1988] may well be unique among his peers in pursuing one theme [Fuji] so intently throughout the course of his career." Shinpei led a remarkable and adventurous life, first "escaping" from Japan as a teenager during the 1920s and spending five years in China, "the start of a long emotional attachment to that country." A friendship developed during that stay led to his being invited back to China in 1940 "as an adviser to the Ministry of Publicity in the puppet government of Wang Ching-wei (1883–1944)."[9]

Shinpei's translator gives the benefit of the doubt to this poet's participation in this puppet government, claiming that he was one of the Japanese and Chinese who "believed in a genuine form of pan-Asianism, in a genuine reconciliation between a generous Japan and a China freed from the shackles of foreign oppression" and that he utilized this "pan-Asianism" both in his Fuji poems and in his official work in

China 1940–1945.[10] Regarding the symbolism of Fuji in Shinpei's poetry, at the very least it is consistently nationalistic from prewar through postwar times. One wartime (1943) poem ties Fuji to the Chinese mountain range K'un-lun (a connection dating back to Heian times):

> At the limits of the sea.
> Fuji calls to far K'un-lun.
> At the limits of the sea,
> K'un-lun responds to our far-off Fuji.[11]

In this poem Shinpei has linked to Fuji a legendary Chinese mountain "believed to extend into heaven," which his translator interprets as "a rather obvious way to promote Sino-Japanese comity" (Morton 1985, 48). Another contemporary example of the pairing of Fuji with a foreign mountain for possibly "pan-Asian" ideals was the Philippine "Occupation" postage stamp linking Fuji to Mount Mayon, which was issued in 1943, the same year Shinpei penned his poem. However this poem by Shinpei is interpreted, it involves "ideology"; his translator attempts to balance "the nationalistic strain in Kusano's rhetoric" with "an older view of Fuji, of Fuji as symbolic of Japan, as a numinous presence" (Morton 1985, 48, 42.)

Shinpei's poems echo imagery from the *Man'yōshū* and draw on mythological themes such as the dragon associated with Fuji; at other times his lyrics are almost iconoclastic, as expressed in this 1968 poem:

> Fuji is not a sacred mountain.
> Fuji is a mountain.
> Just a mountain.
> Just a mountain but the symbolic existence of Japan. (Kusano 1991, 33)

Here he makes a forceful case for Fuji as a secular image that is the symbol of Japan: this poem epitomizes the modern Japanese notion of Fuji as somewhat less than sacrosanct but still fully symbolic of Japan.

Shinpei's lifetime of writing poetry about Fuji cannot be compressed into a few excerpts and generalizations; his career and work are difficult to characterize. His service in Japan's puppet Chinese government remains ambiguous, putting him in the awkward historical position of supporting Japan's failed combination of colonialism and militarism. Yet in the 1980s, when politicians were posturing about a crack on Mount Fuji and even proposed to fix this fissure in the natural monument and national symbol, Shinpei blasted their impertinence for daring to tamper with it:

> It is not a subject for debate by representatives.
> In that tiny stone hut called the "Diet."
> Ferroconcrete.
> With that Fuji is Fuji (irreparable). (Kusano 1991, 77)

Shinpei, iconoclastic in denying that Fuji is a sacred mountain, becomes anti-establishment in declaring Fuji too precious to be used as a political ploy. No matter how Shinpei's vision of nationalism and "pan-Asianism" is viewed, his poems, like Fuji, will remain for future generations to ponder.

Yokoyama Taikan (1868–1958) was a painter whose life, nationalism, and art—especially his preoccupation with Fuji—overlap chronologically and intersect thematically with the career and work of Kusano Shinpei. Taikan's work is positioned within the context of "'Nihonga' (literally 'Japanese painting'), which combines traditional themes and brush techniques with elements from abroad." Nihonga was founded by "the historian-ideologue" Okakura Kakuzō (1862–1913): "Its primary goal was to restore confidence in local traditions and to counter the widespread adoption of Western modes by talented Meiji-period painters." The Nihonga school of painting was supported by the imperial institution and the establishment generally, although it has received criticism from those who favor more strictly traditional art, as well as from those who espouse modernism. Mostly ignored by Westerners, Nihonga has remained quite influential in Japan. Some "have raised political objections [to Nihonga], claiming that it has been too deeply bound up with right-wing nationalism" (Rosenfield 2001, 163–64).

Okakura's nationalism was overt and outspoken.[12] Okakura traveled to India in 1901 and was welcomed by the famous poet philosopher Rabindranath Tagore (1861–1941). Okakura's work *Ideals of the East* begins with the manifesto "Asia is one"; and although he mainly pursued artistic cooperation, he saw the unity of Asia being realized not by the painting brush but by the military sword (Rosenfield 2001, 169, 183).

Taikan's early painting "embodied certain cardinal principles of the Nihonga school: an intense (even narcissistic) preoccupation with national identity; a focus on cultural roots." A parallel of irony between Shinpei and Taikan is that each honed his domestic nationalism while on foreign soil, supposedly cultivating Asian unity—Shinpei in China and Taikan in India. Taikan first went to India in 1903, but he and his Japanese colleague returned to Japan at the outbreak of the Russo-Japanese war. Okakura made a second trip to India, and Rabindranath Tagore was received in Tokyo by Taikan as well as by Japanese government officials; "but the warm welcome soon cooled, for Rabindranath openly attacked Japanese militarism, and aggression in China. . . . The cosmopolitan side of Nihonga coincided with Japan's long-range ambitions on the Asian mainland," and Taikan was certainly not timid in supporting these plans. He had developed strong ties with the imperial household, having been commissioned in 1926 to do several paintings; one of these, *Dawn Over Sacred Peaks*, "was taken to be an allegory of Japan entering under the reign of the 125th monarch [Hirohito]" (Rosenfield 2001, 166, 169, 173).

Later he was an ardent backer of the war: "Taikan firmly supported the policies of his country and its allies. In 1938, for example, he spoke in Tokyo on the spiritual content of Japanese art to visiting members of the Hitler Jugend. In 1940, he held a benefit exhibition in Kyoto of ten paintings of Mount Fuji and ten of the ocean, donating the proceeds of a half-million yen (a vast sum in its day) to pay for fighter planes. In 1943, he organised the Japan Patriotic Art Society (Nihon Bijutsu Hōkokkai) to encourage artists to support the war effort" (175–76).

"Despite his intense patriotism, Taikan's published works contain nothing more overtly propagandist than his countless views of Mount Fuji—as though by painting it over and over again he was reciting a patriotic mantra."[13] Taikan had his long upward ride on the roller coaster of nationalism and militarism and then experienced a much quicker drop in 1945 when his Tokyo house and studio burned in an air raid and defeat put his brand of super patriotism in disfavor.

Like Tokyo and Japan rising again from the ashes of destruction, Taikan too emerged from the war with his intense nationalism intact. Taikan's 1952 sketches for the painting *Pacific Ocean on a Specific Day* (*Aru hi no Taiheiyō*) reveal the depths of this patriotism: "Each of the sixteen sketches depicts Mount Fuji, pre-eminent emblem of Japanese nationhood, looming serenely over wildly turbulent waves; almost lost in the agitated sea is a dragon, the ancient Sino-Japanese symbol of royal authority. Eighty-two years old when he began the series, Taikan must have intended a major statement about war and nationhood. . . . [H]e submitted them [the sixteen sketches] as an allegory of Japan's emergence from the storm and turmoil which had engulfed it in World War II" (Rosenfield 2001, 174). The date of these sketches is hardly coincidental, as 1951 marked the signing of the peace treaty between Japan and the United States, and 1952 was the last year of the Allied (mainly American) occupation of Japan.[14]

The works of Shinpei and Taikan are two examples of how the image of Fuji has helped keep alive attitudes and commitments toward "war and nationhood" in postwar times. These notions and postures can be labeled as national identity, nationalism, ultranationalism, nativism, and/or patriotism, and perhaps even chauvinism. No simple characterization will suffice to handle the complex figures of Shinpei and Taikan, and no single-frame depiction of Fuji can capture its ever-moving, many-splendored richness.

Epilogue

Descent from the Mountain

Now that the natural, cultural, spiritual, and symbolic drama of Fuji has played out, what is a fitting close to this account of constantly shifting images? In the preface these permutations were compared to the workings of a kaleidoscope, whose finite physical pieces yield an infinite number of visual patterns. However, unlike the kaleidoscopic variations, which are arbitrary, the changing perceptual scenes of Fuji are linked closely to the alteration of social, economic, political, artistic, and religious developments. A skeptic may conclude that the only permanent feature of Fuji is its function as a kind of Rorschach flash card that serves to reveal the underlying currents of Japanese history that are imposed or stamped on the mountain. In fact in one of the many Western literary works that drew inspiration from Fuji, the main character records her reflections: "It may indeed be that I am using Hokusai's prints as a kind of Rorschach for self-discovery" (Zelazny 1991, 23). In meditation and concentration techniques, the direction of activity can be at least twofold: either the meditator can be drawn into the target of concentration (as with a mandala) or the target can be incorporated within the consciousness and life of the meditator. Fuji can be considered as a tabula rasa upon which are etched the changing seasons of Japanese culture and identity; or Fuji can be comprehended as a reservoir of images an individual can (selectively) incorporate and utilize as personal resources.

Not only the vision but also the illusion of Fuji may well be in the eye of the beholder, as with the interpretation of Hokusai's *Fuji in a Window:* "An old man seated at a desk stretches his arms up in an arch that echoes Fuji through the window. Western viewers since Dickins have all agreed that the gesture is one of ecstasy as he catches Fuji in a particular light, while Japanese inevitably see this as a yawn."[1]

In this panoramic survey of Fuji, the intent has been to listen to and record gasps of delight as well as yawns of boredom in an attempt to recognize both the sacred and the prosaic.

Even if one admits the fear of, and is never able to rule out the possibility of, self-deception, perhaps one may also be allowed to harbor the hope of, and the potential for, self-discovery. Admittedly the negative side of stereotypical and exoticized views of Japan can obfuscate the comprehension of the actualities of Japan (for example by interjecting essentialist notions of nature). An alternate view is one that portrays "the exotic as a creative stimulus."² In other words, the exotic is neither necessarily nor totally negative but may also have a positive side. Citing cultural difference and "the other" as crucial for cultural creativity, this viewpoint seeks "to recover the exotic" within a framework of "critical self-reflection."

With all this history in view, several reminders may serve to prepare the next generation for the future of Fuji. In the first place, although all of these perceptions are the heritage of the past, they are available to everyone to appreciate in the present—from the ancient poems and medieval artworks to the spiritual ideas of various groups. In modern times the luster of Fuji as an artistic and religious icon has given way to the more tarnished appearance of a secular logo or patriotic mantra. Such a fate may be inevitable for traditional icons in any country as highly industrialized and commercialized as Japan. The many facets of Fuji's image, from sacred to secular, stereotype to logo, are available for enjoyment as well as reflection and criticism.

In the second place, it would be premature to consider the present moment to be the last chapter in the story of Fuji. The natural history of Fuji is open ended, with future eruptions always a possibility. Government officials in Japan monitoring seismic activity on the mountain realistically caution that it is not a matter of if but when Fuji will erupt, and plans have been drawn up to try to evacuate the surrounding area and minimize the human and physical damage. The *prospect* of eruptions as cataclysmic events is more than scientific forecasting of natural occurrences and crosses over the boundary of contemporary cultural expressions to the anticipation of aesthetic and religious realities. One Tokyoite, learning of the research for this book, wrote the author a letter warning that someday Fuji will erupt, and when it does, it will destroy most of Tokyo. Indeed a major eruption might so thoroughly alter Fuji's nearly perfect conical shape that the silhouette so familiar today could become the remembered symbol of a past age, lost forever (like Mount Saint Helens). Whatever the future holds for Fuji, the expectation that something earth shattering will happen to it is part and parcel of the cultural baggage this mountain carries into the next age. The fact that this icon has become integral to the identity of Japan is no guarantee that it will maintain its position in the limelight. However, because Fuji has been so prominent in the life of Japan for two millennia, it is not likely to be forgotten and soon disappear.

In the third place, cultural perceptions of Fuji in the future will inevitably couple it as a national hallmark and an internationally recognized symbol. Perhaps the most remarkable development in the peak's cultural history during the past few decades has been the effort to secure recognition of Fuji as a UNESCO World Heritage Site. The first proposals to UNESCO were unsuccessful because of pollution around the mountain: garbage and sanitation on the mountain—several hundred thousand climbers ascend it annually—were severe problems. Grassroots organizations in Japan teamed up with environmentalists around the world to clean up the mountain and improve sanitary facilities. Makoto Motonaka of the Agency for Cultural Affairs made the cultural argument for Fuji's candidacy: "Mount Fuji [is] a symbol of the Japanese spirit. . . . Mount Fuji is indeed the most representative symbol of Japan . . . rooted in the deepest foundations of the uniqueness of Japanese culture" (Motonaka 2003). Yasuhiro Nakasone, former prime minister of Japan, chaired the movement to clean up the mountain and make the argument for Fuji's acceptance with UNESCO. Nakasone stated, "Mt. Fuji has been not merely a natural object, but has been a spiritual home and a source of courage for all the Japanese people throughout Japan's history. I believe that it is a mission for us Japanese people living today to make Mt. Fuji a world's treasure."[3] These two quotations by government officials lend a formal—political—stamp of approval to Fuji as a natural, cultural, spiritual symbol, combining national pride anchored in "the uniqueness of Japanese culture" with international appreciation (à la Japonisme) of this cosmopolitan symbol.

Whatever Fuji's role on the world scene, in Japan the facets of the mountain will probably continue to reflect and color the new developments of Japanese society, art, and religion. The old depictions of Fuji will never completely vanish, even as new images appear. Fuji should not be relegated to the dust heap of history; just as some pilgrims today still honor their ancestors who have climbed Fuji in the past, so poets and artists hark back to the lyrics of the *Man'yōshū* and the previous scenarios of Fuji.

Even as this book ends on the note of "secular logo" and "patriotic mantra," the nuances of the ancient sacred mountain remain. No one can predict when Fuji will erupt—be it decades or centuries in the future—or what new shape it will take. However, there is no doubt that the momentum of cultural and religious history will color the perception of the future "new Fuji"; at the same time, in ways no living human can anticipate, the changed appearance of the mountain will alter previous perceptions.

One Fujidō leader, emphasizing inner piety over the sacrality of a mountain, said that when you reach the summit of Fuji, nothing is there. In the nineteenth century Lafcadio Hearn, who though not Japanese was in some ways the most Japanese of all, reminded us that on close inspection Fuji may not live up to expectations. These two diverse viewpoints reinforce the notion of Fuji as a tabula rasa or a Rorschach foil. Even so, the perfectly shaped triangular peak has endured through the ages—flexible, malleable, adaptable, in a wide range of artistic genres and religious milieus, as well as in diverse social and political settings—and is likely to persevere in its iconic role. Like the poet Kusano Shinpei, modern observers may look back at Fuji "as a symbol of a particular beauty" and share his optimism that "a large number of different works about Fuji [will] be created in the future."[4]

APPENDIX

Sino-Japanese Characters

1. 富士 (contemporary characters for Mount Fuji)

2. 不二 (not two, peerless)

3. 不死 (not dying)

4. 不尽 (not exhausted)

5. 仙元 or 仙見 (Sengen)

NOTES

Preface

1. *Pachinko* is a popular Japanese gambling device; the player attempts to drop metal balls through a vertical wall of pegs into winning slots.

2. *Fuji: Sacred Mountain of Japan* is available online, in two parts, at http://bit.ly/fuji-sacred-mountain-pt1 and http://bit.ly/fuji-sacred-mountain-pt2 (accessed May 16, 2011).

1. The Power of the Volcano

1. Aramaki 1983, 193; Teikoku-Shoin 1989, 2–3, 9; Kokudo Chiriin 1990; Shiki 1983; Takai et al., 1963; Tsuya 1968.

2. See *We Love Fuji / Furusato no Fujisan* 1988; and Morita 2001.

3. See plate 1 for one example of Fuji in a dark reddish hue.

4. Here "real nature" refers to the material world; Asquith and Kalland 1997, 25.

5. Later other Sino-Japanese characters read only Sengen, as in Sengen Daibosatsu, will be seen.

6. Endō Hideo (1987, 19) cites a number of Japanese terms similar in sound to Asama (all of which are associated with volcanoes or hot springs), which may be related to terms such as *aso* in the South Pacific, meaning "volcano," and similar terms in Ainu language meaning "volcanic rock." Endō does not mention that the term "Fuji" is popularly linked to a similar Ainu term, *huchi* or "volcano," even though in ancient times Japanese *H* must have been *P*, making "Fuji" more like "Puji." See also Inobe 1928a, 124–25; and Batchelor 1905, 133.

7. *Ara mitama.*

8. Fickeler 1962, 95; Deffontaines 1948, 100–101.

9. Plutschow (1990, 26–32) is paraphrasing Motoori; the more calm or benevolent aspect is *niki,* and the more wild or rough aspect is *ara.*

10. Kelsey (1981, 218) and Palmer (2001, 218) have treated the nature of *araburu kami* (in the ancient writings *Fudoki*), which Kelsey translates as "raging deity" and Palmer as "malevolent deities."

11. Even "in Hokusai's view here, . . . she is simply a generic Shinto deity" (Smith 1988, 195, plate I/1).

12. Chamberlain 1882, 115–19; Philippi 1968, 144–47, 500.

13. Endō 1987, 12–14; Collcutt 1988, 251–52; Tyler 1993, 265.

14. Thal 2005; Ambros 2008, 175–205.

2. The Beauty of the Ideal Mountain

1. Miner at al. 1985, 5; Levy 1981, 23; quotation from Carter 1991, 2.

2. Carter 1991, 3–4. For a reproduction of the nineteenth-century woodblock print of the famous eighth-century poet Yamabe no Akahito standing with his servant on a hill with view

over the Bay of Tago and with Fuji in the background, see Uhlenbeck and Molenaar 2000, 6, plate 1.

3. *Fudoki* are eighth-century reports on the natural conditions and oral traditions of the current provinces.

4. Japan's many sacred mountains had their own local (and regional) devotees with their own claims to greatness. Ambros (2008, 25–26) cites the 1532 *Ōyamadera engi* about the superiority of Mount Ōyama: "Isn't [Ōyama] truly the greatest mountain in Japan?"

5. Plutschow 1990, 106–17, 108; Levy 1981, 25.

6. The Heian-era *Taketori monogatari* (The Tale of the Bamboo Cutter) will be taken up later, in the discussion of the influence of Chinese mythological elements on the image of Fuji.

7. Morris 1964. This refined court life is captured in *Tale of Genji* by Lady Murasaki (Murasaki 2001).

8. See the appendix of Sino-Japanese characters. For the standard characters for Fuji, see no. 1; for the homonym *fuji* meaning "unparalleled" (not two, peerless), see no. 2; for another homonym with the meaning of "not dying," see no. 3; for yet another homonym, meaning "not exhausted," see no. 4.

9. For Fuji's appearance in other works and genres, see McCullough 1968; Kominz 1995; Cogan 1987; Tyler 1981; and Bell 2001.

10. For a reproduction of the color woodblock print *Monk Saigyō Gazing at Fuji* by Isoda Koryūsai, from about 1770, see Clark 2001, 97, plate 32.

11. In a much later work, the early nineteenth-century *Shank's Mare* (*Hizakurige*), the writer Ikku Jippensha quotes the song of postboys on the road who give a naughty description of Fuji's smoke as the effervescence of sexual life (Jippensha 1960, 51).

12. This work is the best volume in English for viewing the variety of Japanese pictorial depictions of Fuji; see also Uhlenbeck and Molenaar (2000) for woodblock prints of Fuji. The standard work in Japanese is Naruse 2005.

13. Naruse's argument that the artistic representation of Fuji as three peaked must be based on empirical observation will be treated later.

14. Takeuchi 1984, 40. In China, too, literature and poetry were what inspired painters (Soper 1962, 166; Frodsham 1967, 205).

15. This painting is based on the *Shōtoku Taishi danryaku* of 917 by Fujiwara no Kanesuke, which in turn is a compilation of earlier traditions of the illustrious prince, who lived 576–622 (Naruse 2005, 5, 7, 8, illus. 1).

16. Shōtoku's image too shifts from age to age; see Ito 1998.

17. Tyler (1993, 283) notes, "A standard passage in his [Shōtoku Taishi's] legendary biography tells how he flew over Mt. Fuji on the 'black horse of Kai,' but versions of the story that are centered on Fuji instead of the prince—including [*Gotaigyō no maki*] *The Book of the Great Practice*—naturally have him stop on the mountain."

18. Klein 1984, 17. In the writing *Gotaigyō no maki*, the claim is made both that "mountain pilgrimage was Shaka's [Buddha's] practice for twenty-two years" and that "of old, Shaka upon this Mountain [Fuji] received texts, preached the myriad sutras, realized the inner meaning of the Buddha-Dharma, and became the great teacher and saint of this world" (Tyler 1993, 292).

19. Snellen 1934, 178–79; Rotermund 1965; H. B. Earhart 1965b, 1970, 16–19; Nakamura 1973, 140–42.

20. *Shinsen, shenxian* in Chinese.

21. Takeya cites Miyako no Yoshika (834–879) in *Fujiden* as calling Fuji the realm of the immortals; in one version of the Heian work *Taketori Monogatari*, the peak of Fuji is linked to the elixir of immortality and the theme of transcendence (to heaven).

22. Ambros (2008, 26) notes that Mount Ōyama was also likened to the Chinese sacred mountains of Penglai and K'un-lun.

23. Naruse (2005, 7–25) provides black-and-white illustrations of many of these pictorial biographies of Shōtoku, commenting on the great diversity of the depictions of Fuji, all of which feature the great prince soaring over the peak on a black steed. He notes especially the Chinese

influence on these images. Only a few of these early graphic renderings of Fuji exhibit the later standard three-peaked (or domed) mountain outline.

24. The typology is from Takeya 2002. See Takeuchi 1984, 41–43; and Naruse 2005, 14–24, for black-and-white illustrations of many pictorial biographies of Shōtoku, with Naruse's artistic sketching of Fuji's outline for each example.

25. For a description of "The Standard Taoist Mountain," see Hahn 1988. For K'un-lun, see also Stein 1990, 223–46; important for the Japanese borrowings in the context of Fuji is the basic notion "that the word *k'un-lun* refers to a 'hill with three levels'" (226). See also ten Grotenhuis 1999, 27.

26. For possible Chinese precedents of three peaks, see Soper 1962, 28, 50; for Korean precedents, see 100.

27. Takeuchi 1984, 44–45. See also Takeuchi 1992; and Ienaga 1973.

28. Uhlenbeck and Molenaar 2000, 15. For Buddhist influence on the perception of the Japanese landscape, see Grapard 1986. Naruse (1982, 2005, 25–29) insists that "image" precedes "symbol," arguing that the three-peaked representation of Fuji must have some basis in visual observation. He provides several photographs that he claims support his thesis that Buddhist (Tendai) notions of triads were superimposed on this actual observation of Fuji having three peaks (with a higher middle peak).

29. Klein 1984, 18; Clark 2001, 11–12.

30. Clark (2001, 11) writes, "As a result of its iconic status, the painting was frequently copied by later artists, particularly those of the Kanō school."

31. This scene was replicated in every imaginable form, from woodblock prints to netsuke; for the eighteenth-century print *Monk Saigyō Gazing at Mt Fuji* by Isoda Koryūsai, see Clark 2001, 97, plate 32.

3. Asceticism

1. H. B. Earhart 2003, 81–96; Hakeda 1972; Kiyota 1978; R. Abe 1999; Groner 1984; Swanson 1987.

2. Eliade 1959; Fickeler 1962, 109; Deffontaines 1948, 100–101.

3. See the appendix of Sino-Japanese characters, no. 5. See Tyler 1993, 265, for variations of the term *Sengen*.

4. See plate 2 for a statue of En no Gyōja.

5. See H. B. Earhart 1965b. For statues of En no Gyōja, see Sawa 1972, 115–16, figs. 130, 131. For a woodblock rendition of En no Gyōja, see Smith 1988, 184–85, plate I/3, and the commentary, 195–96.

6. See H. B. Earhart 1970, 20–21, for discussion of these titles.

7. Endō 1987, 25; Inobe 1928a, 176–77.

8. As recorded in the *Honchō seiki* (Endō 1987, 27).

9. According to a legendary Kamakura-period account, *Jizō bosatsu reigen ki*.

10. According to Tyler (1981, 149), "The crystal mountain found by Matsudai Shōnin clearly alluded to Fuji as Hōrai" (Peng lai, a sacred mountain in China).

11. Inobe 1928a, 177; Endō 1978, 26.

12. Collcutt 1988, 253; Hardacre 1988, 275; Guth 1988, 203; Moerman 2005, 79.

13. H. B. Earhart 1965a, 1970; Miyake 2001.

14. Although various names such as *hōin* (in Murayama Shugen) were used for these practitioners of Shugendō, they are referred to herein by the generic name *yamabushi*.

15. For a traditional scene of pilgrims circling the crater, see Miyazaki 2005, 137, fig. 9.

4. The Mountain Becomes the World

1. Endō dates these climbing routes as follows: Subashiri, 1500; Suyama, 1486; Kawaguchi, Muromachi times (but no clear historical record); Yoshida, 1502. Other climbing routes were opened later. A map of these routes is provided in chapter 7.

2. H. B. Earhart 1970; Davis 1977; Reader and Swanson 1997; Reader 2005; Moerman 2005; Ambros 2008, 144–47.

3. The significance of the name will be mentioned later. The traditional dates for Kakugyō give him a Methuselah-like life span; Miyazaki (1976, 81) calls Kakugyō a semilegendary figure.

4. Inobe 1928b, 6; Tyler 1984, 101–2.

5. Tyler 1984, 101–2; Miyazaki 1990, 283.

6. Inobe 1928b, 6–29; Iwashina 1983, 42–75; Tyler 1981, 1984, 1993; Collcutt 1988.

7. Royall Tyler kindly provided me with his translation of the *Gotaigyō no maki* from Murakami and Yasumaru's text before it was published (Tyler 1993). Tyler's title is "The Book of the Great Practice." Collcutt 1989, 256, renders this title as "Record of Great Austerities." This chapter owes much to Tyler's translation, notes, and commentary. For convenience the work is cited herein as *The Great Asceticism*.

8. For a painting titled "Mt Fuji and Shiraito Falls" by Suminoe Buzen, see Clark 2001, 77 (cat. 9). Tyler 1993, 274, points out that the Shiraito waterfall was a site of purification for Kakugyō; water ablutions or purifications were as important for Kakugyō as his cave asceticism and ascent of Fuji.

9. "Tiptoe" is *tsumadachi*; a leader of Maruyamakyō demonstrated his understanding of this practice for me, which was not standing on tiptoe but actually tucking the toes under and standing on the bent toes. Tyler 1993, 313, calls this the "practice of the block."

10. Tyler 1981, 148; 1993, 270–71.

11. See Tyler 1993, 256–57, for his treatment of the name.

12. The noun *fusegi* comes from the verb *fusegu*, "to defend or protect, to ward off" (Tyler 1993, 294, 300–302, 321).

13. In Kakugyō's writing, as presented by Tyler, this represented a support of the status quo; especially with Jikigyō and the development of the movement of Fujidō, there was the appeal for greater equality among these four classes, and even a "reversal" both in gender and class roles.

14. See Tyler 1993, 281, for his discussion of possible Christian influence on Kakugyō.

15. See also the work of Grapard, especially Grapard 1986.

16. For the sun and moon as a paired "iconographic convention," see Moerman 2005, 33n62. See also Bambling 1996; and ten Grotenhuis 1999, 172–73, 175.

17. Those familiar with Japanese will recognize *nuki* in the publishing term *nukizuri*, an offprint of an article "extracted" from a journal. A less well-known use of *nuki* in a religious context is the *toge-nuki* Jizō, referring to the bodhisattva Jizō as a "thorn-pulling" or "thorn-extracting" deity—in other words, removing/relieving pain and suffering.

18. Murakami and Yasumaru 1971b, 483; ten Grotenhuis 1999, 3–5.

19. As in *kuni-mi* and *mono-mi*, "seeing" a sacred object is a ritually empowering event. The *mi* of *minuki* refers to the body; the *mi* of *kuni-mi* and *mono-mi* is a different word referring to seeing.

20. The explanation of the *minuki* is based mainly on Inobe 1928b, 89–96; see also Tyler 1993, 255, 290–91, 300, 302.

21. Tyler 1984, 105; 1993, 278, 283.

22. Chamberlain 1882, 1:15; Aston 1896, 1:5.

23. For studies of Kokugaku, see Koyasu 1983; Harootunian 1988; Nosco 1990; McNally, 2005; and Burns 2003.

24. Inobe 1928b, 96; Iwashina 1983, 64; Murakami and Yasumaru 1971b, 483.

25. For Japanese amulets, see H. B. Earhart 1994; H. B. Earhart 2004, 11–12; Tanabe and Reader 1998, 183–86, 192–97; Iwashina 1983, 59; and Miyake 2001, 100, and fig. 33.

26. Tyler (1984, 101, 104) points out that Kakugyō "dropped almost all Buddhist language from his discourse." Kakugyō's ascetic practices retain a strong Buddhist character.

27. For the ethical teachings of Kakugyō, see Collcutt 1988; and Tyler 1984, 1993.

5. Touchstone of Ethical Life

1. Tyler 1993, 253; Inobe 1928b, 95–96; Iwashina 1983, 83, 93–95, 108–9; Tyler 1984, 111.

2. Iwashina 1983, 77; Inobe 1928b, 36.

3. Tyler 1984, 113; Iwashina 1983, 142, 155.

4. Iwashina 1983, 95, insert 108–9.

5. For the notion of repayment of *on* (gratitude), see Bellah 1985; J. A. Sawada 1993; and H. B. Earhart 1989. Kakugyō also mentioned *on* in *The Great Asceticism*. Janine Anderson Sawada has also published under the name Janine Tasca Sawada.

6. Iwashina 1983, 4; Bellah 1985; J. A. Sawada 1993.

7. Iwashina (1983, 5) goes so far as to say that Miroku's notion of *furikawari* (revolution) was a prediction of the collapse of the class system and the advent of democracy.

8. Tyler 1984; Collcutt 1989.

9. Tyler 1984, 113. Tyler notes the alternate account that Jikigyō lived a few days longer and gave some final parting instructions to his disciple.

10. See J. A. Sawada 2004, 47–50, for another late Tokugawa instance of frugality, fasting, and the "agrarian idealism" of the sacrality of rice.

11. Ambros (2008, 120–23) writes that the Ōyama cult was not driven by charismatic figures such as Jikigyō.

12. Tyler 1982, 140. The notion of *sangoku* will be treated at greater length in chapter 11.

6. Cosmic Model and World Renewal

1. For "Fuji asceticism" there is no exact Japanese equivalent. The literature refers to Fuji *gyōja* ("Fuji ascetics"), the Shugendō (*yamabushi*), and freelance practitioners who performed various prayers, rites, and healings for fees. Fuji asceticism can be rendered into Japanese as Fuji *shugyō* or shortened to Fuji *gyō*.

2. Although asceticism and mendicancy were themes present throughout Japanese religious history, their practice and importance varied from site to site. Ambros 2008, 88, notes, "In the 1660s, the tradition of mountain asceticism largely disappeared from Ōyama."

3. This is a term close to Iwashina's *fuji no shinkō*, literally "the faith of Fuji," used in a broad sense such as the English "cult of Fuji."

4. This chapter relies on the work of Inobe and Iwashina and (in English) the work of Tyler and Collcutt and especially Miyazaki's publications, based on her study of Fujidō documents. Thanks to Professor Miyazaki (who also publishes under the name Umezawa) for making available her Japanese articles on Fujidō.

5. Yasumaru Yoshio has called this common Tokugawa set of values *tsūzoku dōtoku;* see Hardacre 1986, 43; and J. A. Sawada 1998, 109–10, 127.

6. See Kuroda 1981, for the claim that "Shinto" as an organized religion and formal institution is a creation of the Meiji era.

7. Susan Burns's characterization of Motoori Noringa's threefold periodization provides an interesting contrast with the three ages of Fujidō (Burns 2003, 91–92).

8. Davis 1977, 57–62; White 1995, 116–22.

9. J. A. Sawada 2004, 32; Ambros 2008, 90.

10. This is my translation of an excerpt of Sangyō Rokuō's writing *Sangyō Rokuō kū otsutae,* as quoted in Miyazaki 1976, 78–79.

11. See J. T. Sawada 2006 for an overview of "Sexual Relations as Religious Practice in the Late Tokugawa Period: Fujidō."

12. Moerman 2005, 199–203, describes the general phenomenon of women violating sacred boundaries as an act that reveals the sacrality of these sites: "The Buddhist literature of medieval Japan abounds with evidence of women who trespass on hallowed ground."

13. Kokugaku had a nationwide impact, but its local acceptance and application varied considerably. See Ambros 2008, 111–15.

14. Shibata Reiichi, quoted in Seager 1995, 118.

15. Seager 1995, 166, is quoting Ketelaar 1989.

16. Steinhoff 1991, 206, in treating the recanting or "conversion" (*tenkō*) of former Japanese communists in the 1930s who became ardent supporters of a rightist state, mentions, in addition to the categories of voluntary and involuntary conversion, the notion of "preventive *tenkō*."

7. *Pilgrimage Confraternities*

1. Vaporis 1994, 1, 14. "Culture of movement" is the translation of *kōdō bunka*, a term developed by Nishiyama Matsunosuke.

2. Iwashina 1983, 234, notes that in the Murakami tradition there were no branch *kō*, with the founder controlling all of one lineage, a pattern that may have been a major factor keeping the Murakami heritage from experiencing rapid expansion.

3. Inobe 1928b, 194, dates the term *dōja* for Fuji pilgrims to Muromachi times, prior to the formation of *kō*. Ambros 2001, 342, uses the transliteration *dōsha*, which she translates as "traveler."

4. Iwashina 1983, 14; he notes that the *Fuji Mandara* shows the older style of climbing, with a cord for tying the hair hanging down.

5. Reader 2005, 53, 57–59. Reader translates *dōgyō* as "companion" (53) and "being together" (57).

6. Iwashina 1983, 247–48. Tyler 1981, 157, cites one claim that there were as many as four hundred Fujikō within Edo, which he thinks may be true for the Tenpō era (1830–44) at the height of their popularity; he cites another claim of seventy thousand members in Fujikō in 1823.

7. Iwashina 1983, 237, says that the authorities' account of Fujikō activities—focusing on Shugendō, *yamabushi,* the fire ritual (*saitō goma*), and healing rites—differs sharply from Jikigyō's teaching.

8. Ambros 2008, 90, notes the *bakufu*'s restrictions on "marginal religious specialists" from the 1660s. She says that the regulations against pilgrimage to Ōyama were issued partly to "prevent pilgrims to Mt. Fuji from continuing their already lengthy journey to Ōyama" (173).

9. Iwashina 1983, 247. Inobe (1928b, 180–81) cites an incomplete record of 130 *kō* crests. Dower has provided both a handbook of Japanese crests (1971) and a brief encyclopedia article (1983).

10. The *kesa* or surplice is a standard item of dress for a Buddhist priest and is usually of a finer material such as brocade; *yamabushi* adopted it for their costumes.

11. Most pilgrims were male. Miyazaki (2005, 382) has documented the fact that "the exclusion of women had a relatively short history at Mt. Fuji."

12. Variation of these dates (according to the lunar calendar) depended on the era, the entrance, and the convenience of the pilgrims (Inobe 1928a, 314–15). In the lunar year, marked by the first full moon of the solar year, these dates fell a few weeks to more than a month later than in the Gregorian calendar.

13. Kishimoto 1960; Kitagawa 1967.

14. Ambros 2008 has provided a detailed description of the "Ōyama cult."

15. *Oshi* is the general term for a widespread role of "lay religious specialists who contributed to the spread of regional pilgrimage cults in the Tokugawa period" (Ambros 2001, 329, 354, 369; 2008, 84–116).

16. Ambros 2008, 16, gives one week travel time from Edo, two weeks from more distant starting points to Ōyama, and the longer periods of travel for pilgrimage to Ise and Shikoku (160).

17. Ambros 2001 describes the varying fortunes and careers of lodgings and guides (*oshi*) and innkeepers at Ōyama.

18. Inobe 1928b, 251; Iwashina 1983, 366–69.

19. Miyazaki 2005, 364, 365, figs. 4 and 5; Tyler 1993, 326.

20. Iwashina 1983, 164; Miyake 2001, 150; Ruch 2002; J. T. Sawada 2006, 349–55.

21. For the complex question of the impurity of women in Japan, especially within Buddhism, see Iwashina 1983, 427–28; Namihira 1977; Miyata 1987; Paul 1985; Takemi 1983; Ruch 2002; Nagata Mizu 2002; Moerman 2005, 181–231; and Ambros 2008, 45, 223–24.

22. Miyake 2001, 153, treats this apparent contradiction as the polarity of "Goddess of the Mountain versus Profane Mother of the Village."

23. This triple appearance is called *sanson goraikō* and was also said to be experienced at other mountains such as Tateyama and Yudonosan (Iwashina 1983, 279–81).

24. *Hachi meguri.* See Miyazaki 2005, 376, fig. 9, for a drawing of the "summit of Mt Fuji, showing the pilgrims' route around the crater." Smith 1988, 56–57, plate III/76, includes Hokusai's

rather fanciful version of "Circling the Crater," although Smith (216) concludes that "Hokusai . . . surely never saw it [the crater] in person."

25. Hahn 1988, 151, notes on the standard Taoist mountain in China an overabundance of caves, but one that is singled out: "a mid-mountain temple of some importance is usually associated with a cave."

26. Ambros 2001, 349, 366; Iwashina 1983, 412.

8. Miniature Fuji

1. Reader and Swanson 1997; H. B. Earhart 1989, 198–206; Reader 2005; Moerman 2005.

2. Takeuchi 2002, 34, figs. 9 and 10. For views of an altar in the setting of a confraternity meeting, see my documentary video, *Fuji: Sacred Mountain of Japan*.

3. Inobe 1928b, 311–17; Iwashina 1983, 248–49.

4. This is a description of the *takiage* witnessed a number of times at the Marutō Miyamoto-kō during 1988–89. See my video documentary, *Fuji: Sacred Mountain of Japan*.

5. Peter Brown has noted about Christianity that "translations—the movement of relics to people—and not pilgrimages—the movement of people to relics—hold the center of the stage in late-antique and early-medieval piety" (1981, 88). The replicas of Fuji as altar pieces for Fujikō can be seen as "translations" of the mountain, and the *fujizuka*, which contained soil from the sacred peak, are comparable to relics. In the case of Mount Fuji (as a sacred center) and the local Fujikō and *fujizuka*, there was both a symbiotic relationship and an alternation of movement between the center and its "translation."

6. Smith 1986 has provided an overview of *fujizuka* and a map of surviving examples within the 23 *ku* (wards) of Tokyo: "No Fujizuka have been built since 1935, but 56 still survive, 47 of them within the 23-ku area" (4). Thanks go to Professor Smith for providing a copy of this article. Iwashina 1983, 268–73, at the time of his writing counted about 200 existing *fujizuka* built by Fujikō, including those in nearby prefectures.

7. Some of the latest *fujizuka* were of ferroconcrete construction. One of the most unusual modern renditions of the "garden variety" is a "tailored" version of Fuji "sewn" onto a museum lawn (O'Brien 1986, 22–23).

8. Aston 1956, 2:144, 251, 259; Takeuchi 2002, 26; Stein 1990, 258–59.

9. For other interesting examples of "Building the Sacred Mountain: Tsukuriyama in Shinto Tradition," see Nitschke 1995.

9. Woodblock Prints and Popular Arts

1. See Stewart 1979, 3–16, who credits some of the works to his pupil Hiroshige II.

2. Smith et al. 1986, plate 24. See also Uhlenbeck and Molenaar 2000, 13, plate 4, and 14, plate 6; and Takeuchi 2002, 24, fig. 1 and fig. 2.

3. Smith et al. 1986, text for plate 24.

4. For other examples of the pattern of how all Japanese religious life is closely tied to economic conditions and practices, see Thal 2005, 36; and Reader 2005, 128–31. Nenzi 2008, 136–38, has commented on how Fuji was reinvented as a marketable commodity, even as a board game (136, fig. 12).

5. Traganou 2004, 4, argues that "the Tōkaidō—either by its being imagined as the realm of the margin in Edo Japan, or by its being appropriated under the auspices of the 'central' ideology in the Meiji era—has been a locus of identity formation, if not for the whole of Japan, at least for the residents of the main urban centers (Tokyo, Kyoto, Osaka) and their intermediate areas"; Fuji was an integral part of this "identity formation"(45). See also Berry 2006, 98–99, fig. 17 and fig. 3; and "Travellers on the Tōkaidō Highway" in Clark 2001, 12–13.

6. The fifth year of Kōrei corresponds to 219 B.C.

7. Smith 1988, 188, 195, 186–87, 184–85; quotation from 195.

8. It could be, as Ronald Toby has suggested in correspondence, that Hokusai, ever playful, had been toying with a deliberate use of a different term.

9. Smith 1988, 181, 180, 196; quotation from 196.

10. Ibid., 110, plates 56–57, 216; quotation from 216.

11. Woodson 1998, 52; Lane 1989, 184.

12. Tucker et al. 2003, 313; Bennett 2006, 143.

13. See the Nagasaki University Library collection of photographs from the Bakumatsu-Meiji period at http://oldphoto.lb.nagasaki-u.ac.jp/unive/word/main.htm (accessed December 17, 2010), especially numbers 1320, 3933, 4042, and 4044 for examples of Fuji backdrops. (This Web site contains many old photographs of Fuji.) Crombie 2004 has devoted a slim volume to *Shashin: Nineteenth-Century Japanese Studio Photography;* plate 15 notes, "Photographers followed the tradition, established by the master printmaker Hokusai (1760–1849) of showing Mount Fuji in all its aspects. Here a drawing of the mountain is used as the scenic backdrop for the two women spinning on an old-fashioned wheel." See also plates 17, 28 ("Pilgrimage go up Fujiyama 1880s"), 29, and (possibly) 39.

14. Ishiguro 1999, 277–81; Tucker et al. 2003, 18, 360.

15. Dower 1980, 6; Yokohama Kaikō Shiryōkan 1987, 188. Shimooka too used Fuji as the background for some of his photographs (Tucker et al. 2003, 18–19).

16. Tucker et al. 2003, 31, plate 9; Sharf 2004, 12; T. Tamai 1992, 344; Hockley 2004, 66, 76, 77.

17. See the "DirectoryZone" page, compiled by Philbert Ono, on the Web site *PhotoGuide Japan,* http://photojpn.org/dir/index.php (accessed December 17, 2010).

18. Nihon Shashinka Kyōkai 1980, 320–21, plate 457, 20; quotation from 20.

19. D. C. Earhart 2008, 330n3. See also Tucker et al. 2003, 322: "*Graceful Mount Fuji,* described as the largest photo mural ever produced (approximately 107 ft. long), is presented to the city of New York."

10. Western "Discovery" of Woodblock Prints

1. Cooper 1965, 8–9, quoting Rodrigues.

2. Ibid., 9. For other references to Fuji by Jesuits during the "Christian Century," see Cooper 1974, 18, 214, 376n46; and Schurhammer 1923, 121–22.

3. Montanus 1670, 62, 118–19.

4. Montanus 1670, 469, makes an earlier comparison with Tenerife.

5. Kaempfer 1999; Massarella 1995.

6. The copy used here is a Tokyo 1929 reprint of the London first edition of 1727. For a discussion of Kaempfer's skill as a cartographer, see Lazar 1982.

7. Schmeisser 1995, 138, 150–51; Kaempfer 1999, 341.

8. Kaempfer's map can be compared with two Japanese maps on porcelain dating from 1840–43. The rather simple, "outline" drawings of Fuji on both are quite similar to the unadorned rendering of Fuji by Kaempfer. On the world map, "Japan was placed reassuringly at the center, surrounded by water and islands and various landmasses," and this puts Fuji at the epicenter of this Japanocentric map (Singer with Carpenter et al. 1998, 284–85, plates 141 and 142).

9. Kaempfer did collect and bring home with him pictures of such famous places (Schmeisser 1995, 143; Bodart-Bailey 1992, 44, 1–11).

10. See Weisberg and Weisberg 1990, 3–29, for lengthy descriptions of the various editions of these travelers. Berger 1992, 21, includes also the Dutch East India publication by Montanus, *Atlas Japannensis;* Berger notes that "Philippe Burty probably had the French edition published in Amsterdam in 1680."

11. The dates for this discovery vary—1856, 1859, 1862. See Berger 1992, 13; and T. Watanabe 1984, 670.

12. See also Lane 1989, 188n4; Tsuji 1994; Calza 1994, 165, 166; Weisberg et al. 1975, 2, 16; and Berger 1992, 9, 17.

13. Berger 1992, 100–101, quoting Alcock; T. Watanabe 1984, 680.

14. Fenollosa was apparently referring to Hokusai's *manga,* comic sketches (Berger 1992, 110; Meech and Weisberg 1990, 95–100).

15. Among the earliest, if not the first, woodblock prints introduced to an American audience are two color Hiroshige reproductions in this publication (Hawks 1856, 1:462–63). Also see T. Watanabe 1984, 673.

16. Berger 1992, 338–44, provides a convenient "Chronology" of events related to Japonisme.

17. Weisberg et al. 1975, 29–30, plate 19.

18. Ibid., 8, fig. 6.

19. Kornicki 1994, 167, disabuses us of the grander aims and claims of such gatherings, whose context was "the nationalisms and colonialisms of nineteenth-century Europe."

20. The source for this material is an Internet document by Laurent Buchard, "Japonisme et Architecture: Ouverture—Perceptions du Japon" http://laurent.buchard.pagesperso-orange.fr/Japonisme/OUVERT.htm#Perceptions%20du (accessed February 21, 2011). Buchard is quoting Burty: "paysages où fume le cratère du Fousy-Hama."

21. In van Gogh's day *japonaiserie* and Japonisme were not distinguished.

22. For a published reproduction of this painting, see Walther and Metzger 1993, 1:282–99. The painting can be viewed online by searching for "pere tanguy," for example, http://www.van-gogh-on-canvas.com/images/portrait_of_pere_tanguy.jpg (accessed December 17, 2010).

23. Walther and Metzger 1993, 1:297; they are describing the slightly different later version of this portrait. See also *Self-Portrait with Bandaged Ear* (Wichmann 1999, 41–44, plate 68).

24. Clark 2001, 21–22. Another impressionist, Cézanne, although he denied knowledge of or influence from Asia, certainly was familiar with the ukiyo-e of his circle of painter friends. In spite of Cézanne's statement to the contrary, the shadow of Hokusai's revered peak may well be cast on the sacred mountain in Cézanne's series of paintings of Montagne Sainte-Victoire. See Berger 1992, 112–15; Clark 2001, 22; and Guth 2004, 23–24.

25. Weisberg et al. 1975, 209–10, plate 298.

26. Lane 1989, 192; Calza 2003, 400–401.

27. Lane 1989, 192; Rilke 1964, 291; Rilke 1987, 210–11.

28. Stravinsky too was inspired by both Japanese lyrics and woodblocks, and he once owned prints of "views of Mount Fuji" (Funayama 1986, 274).

29. The cover of the original score of *La Mer* with the *Great Wave*—minus Fuji—is reproduced in several French publications (Lesure 1975, 166–67); the same cover is in Calza 2003, 423.

30. A recent compact disc release of Debussy's work, including *La Mer,* Deutsche Grammophon's recording of the Cleveland Orchestra, conducted by Pierre Boulez, has on its dust jacket and cover a modern rendition of the *Great Wave* scene, credited to Pham van My. This version restores Fuji to its centermost position and smooths out the overpowering wave but does not resurrect the missing boats and fishermen. This item is worthy of the cosmopolitan reputation of Fuji: a French musical composition played by an American orchestra, led by a French conductor, recorded by a German company, with a faux-Japanese scene illustrated by a Vietnamese artist. See Debussy, *La Mer, Nocturnes,* the Cleveland Orchestra, Pierre Boulez, Deutsche Grammophon 439 896-2 (1995) (Universal Classics Group 2003). Thanks go to Cynthia Darby for help locating these materials on Claude Debussy.

31. Benfey 2003, 159–61. La Farge wrote about Japan and Fuji (1897, 9, 32, 228; 1904, 217–49).

32. Slaymaker 2002; Matsuda 2002. In the preface to his catalog *Mount Fuji: Sacred Mountain of Japan,* Martin Dorhout has provided a personal account of how he became interested in ukiyo-e and eventually became a collector of Fuji prints (Uhlenbeck and Molenaar 2000, 7).

33. For Japonist artists in America, see Meech and Weisberg 1990, 95–234. In this context discussions about "wrapping culture" (Hendry 1993) and "unwrapping Japan" (Ben-Ari Moeran, and Valentine 1990) are interesting. For Bracquemond, the treasure was in the wrapper, not the wrapped: the disposable packing he unwrapped was "rewrapped" when it was exoticized and revalued.

34. Faure 1995; Heine and Fu 1995; Skov 1996.

35. Lehmann 1984; Iida 2002, 272.

36. For a postmodernist interpretation of Japonisme (or Japanism), see the remarks of Karatani 1989, 261–62; and Karatani 1994.

37. For one example of a book using the title *Inventing Japan*, see Buruma 2003; references to Mount Fuji are on pages 5, 135, and 138.

38. Meech and Weisberg 1990, 233–34, note that the American-educated wealthy Japanese entrepreneur Matsukata Kōjirō (1865–1950) not only amassed one of the finest collections of French impressionist works but also "purchased a collection of more than eight thousand . . . ukiyo-e prints . . . in France around 1920 with the hope that by returning them to their native land, he would give Japanese artists and scholars the opportunity to study an aspect of their culture that was still little known to them." See also Meech 1988, 10–24. Matsukata's "reverse importation" of ukiyo-e would seem to be a major event in the assessment of reverse orientalism. For some reservations of the notion of "invention" (shared by this author), see Burns 2003, 709; Vlastos 1998b; Chakrabarty 1998; and Iida 2002.

11. The Enduring Image of Fuji in Modern Times

1. Toby 2001, 17–19.

2. See also Ayusawa 1953 for "the types of world map made in Japan's Age of National Isolation."

3. Beasley 1984a, 563; Burns 2003, 3; J. A. Sawada 2004, 211; Iida 2002, 11–13.

4. Gluck 1985, 286; Beasley 1984a, 564.

5. Beasley 1984a, 556; Gluck 1985; Fujitani 1996; Bix 2000.

6. Kano 1994, 55–56; French 1983b; Roberts 1976, 88.

7. Graham 1983. Melinda Takeuchi 1992, 192n53, notes that "Chikutō himself painted an extraordinarily naturalistic picture of Mount Fuji, which might seem at first a violation of his own proscription" of Western painting, except for the fact that it was an exercise in copying another work.

8. Uhlenbeck and Molenaar 2000, 13, plate 5.

9. Robinson 1982, 144–45; see also Smith 1988, 60, 61, 215, plate 73.

10. Toby 1986, 415, 423.

11. Ibid., 424, plates 1, 2, 6; Singer with Carpenter et al. 1998, 297, plate 155.

12. No instance of Fuji has been found on premodern coins. See *Kodansha Encyclopedia of Japan*, 5:242–43; Kodansha 1993, 2:999–1000; and Pick 1994–95, 2:671–72.

13. Described in a catalog as "#S205-211 Mt. Fuji in frame of 2 facing dragons at top ctr." (Pick 1994–95, 1:676).

14. A Bank of Japan Web site, http://www.imes.boj.or.jp/cm/English_htmls/feature_gra2-7 .htm (accessed December 17, 2010), describes this "Yokohama *kawase-gaisha*" as a banknote.

15. Pick 1994–95, 2:678n58.

16. Ibid., 2:678, no. 59.

17. Ibid., 2:680, no. 92.

18. Ibid., 2:681, no. 98.

19. A scan of Pick 1994–95 and a Bank of Japan Web site for Japanese military and occupation currency turned up no images of Fuji.

20. *Kodansha Encyclopedia of Japan*, 5:242–43; Kodansha 1993, 2:999–1000.

21. Krause and Mishler 2004, 1229, no. 59.

22. Ibid., no. 110.

23. Japan's hosting of the 1964 Olympics helped restore its international reputation. Japan was scheduled for the twelfth Olympic summer games in 1940, but they were cancelled because of the outbreak of war. A Japanese poster associated with the 1940 Olympics prominently features Fuji. See D. C. Earhart 2008, 54 and illus. 25. See Krause and Mishler 2004 for examples; the 1964 Olympics coin is 1236, no. 80; the Expo 1970 coin is 1234, no. 83.

24. Krause and Mishler 2004, 1236, no. 123.

25. Horodisch 1979. Thanks go to the late Hyman Kruglak for the gift of the article "Mount Fuji Prominent on Japanese Stamps" (Rogers 1993); this article cites Robert Spaulding Jr.,

"Fuji from Various Viewpoints," *Japanese Philately* 20, no. 1, which was not available to the author.

26. Yamamoto 1962, 43–44; see stamps R93 and R94 on p. 43 for the portraits of Empress Jingū. Hereafter the stamps in Yamamoto are cross-listed with *Sakura* 1997 and *Scott Standard Postage Stamp Catalogue, 2005*, vol. 4 (cited as *Scott* 2004). For Empress Jingū, see *Sakura* 1997, 21, stamps 87, 89, 88, 90; and *Scott* 2004, 18, ("Jingo") stamp A33. Yamamoto's is an earlier work, useful for identifying stamps through its publication date of 1962. *Scott* is the basic English-language reference for all stamps of the world; the volume including Japan covers the earliest to the latest Japanese stamps. Yamamoto illustrates stamps in rather low-quality black and white; *Scott* 2004 provides illustrations in better-quality black and white, but a later edition is upgraded to color plates. *Sakura* includes the earliest stamps up to its publication date of 1997, with high-quality color illustrations; the work is in Japanese but includes some general categories in English.

27. Yamamoto 1962, 49, R123, R124, R125; *Sakura* 1997, 24, all of the "Mt. Fuji & Deer Series"; and *Scott* 2004, 18, stamp A49.

28. Yamamoto 1962, 54, 55, stamps R126–32; *Sakura* 1997, 25, "Earthquake Series," stamps 160–66; *Scott* 2004, 19, ("Cherry Blossoms") stamp A51.

29. Yamamoto 1962, 49, stamp R138; *Sakura* 1997, 25, stamps 173, 176; *Scott* 2004, 19, ("Mt. Fuji") stamp A56.

30. *Sakura* 1997, 26, stamp 192; Yamamoto 1962, 59, stamp 185; *Scott* 2004, 20, ("Mount Fuji and Cherry Blossoms") stamp A94.

31. *Sakura* 1997, 55, stamps C56, A2-5; Yamamoto 1962, 241, stamps A-M1–A-M5 (1929 and 1934); *Scott* 2004, 102 (listing it as "Passenger Plane over Lake Ashi-AP1), stamps C3–8 (1929–34).

32. *Sakura* 1997, 48, stamps A33–36; not found in Yamamoto; *Scott* 2004, 103 ("Great Buddha of Kamakura-AP6"), stamps C39–42.

33. Yamamoto 1962, 237–38, 237, stamp N-Y1; *Sakura* 1997, 189, stamp N1; *Scott* 2004, 19, ("Mt. Fuji") stamp A70.

34. Yamamoto 1962, 201–2, stamps N-P1, N-P2, N-P3, N-P4; *Sakura* 1997, 177, stamps P1–4; *Scott* 2004, 19, stamps A71–74. Kondō 1987, 169, writes, "When areas were first designated for the national park system in 1934, Fuji was not nominated; that it took two more years for Fuji to become a national park was mainly because the Japanese Imperial Army had a training camp on the eastern slopes of the mountain."

35. Yamamoto 1962, 62–63; see stamp R193 on p. 63 and stamp R212 on p. 65. The same stamp in different denominations was issued in 1946: see Yamamoto 1962, 65, stamp R213; *Sakura* 1997, 27, stamps 220, 229, 230; and *Scott* 2004, 22, stamp A52.

36. Apparently the date "1942–1948" is a typo for "1942–1945."

37. Yamamoto 1962, 68–69, stamp R188; *Sakura* 1997, 27, stamp 209; *Scott* 2004, 21, stamp A146.

38. Yamamoto 1962, 135–36. This tower is also shown on a ten-sen banknote of 1944, without Fuji (Pick 1994–95, 2:678, "50, 10 sen, ND [1944]. Black on purple unpt. Tower monument at l").

39. The *Sakura* catalog classifies this stamp as part of the "2nd Showa series" and includes with it a stamp showing Fuji and cherry blossoms (*Sakura* 1997, 27, stamp 220); it is described (in Japanese) as "revised printing (*kaihan*) of stamp 192" and sports stylized ribbons of clouds. This stamp has not been located in Yamamoto under "Propaganda Stamps (1942–1948), a. Wartime Issues." See *Scott* 2004, 22, stamp A152.

40. *Sakura* 1997, 222–23, "Philippine Islands," provides a similar set corresponding to those in Yamamoto. These and other Japanese occupation stamps have not been located in *Scott*.

41. *Sakura* 1997, 222, stamps 18, 20, 24, 26; the identification is given in Japanese as "Fuji to Mayonzan" (Fuji and Mount Mayon). See Yamamoto 1962, 290, stamps 7, 9, 13, 15, 25. The natural likeness of Fuji and Mayon is remarkable. This stamp was reissued in 1943 for flood relief, overstamped; "'BAHA' is Tagalog for 'flood'" (Yamamoto 1962, 293, stamp 25). See also *Sakura* 1997, 222, stamp 38.

42. For an example, see *Scott* 2004, 22, stamp A156, showing "Boys of Japan and Manchukuo," issued on September 15, 1942, "for the 10th anniv. of Japanese diplomatic recognition of Manchukuo." As a 1942 Japanese government document explains, "the various countries of East Asia

would be bound together in reciprocal relationships like 'parent and child, elder and younger brother,'" and "the puppet state of Manchukuo, often cited as a model for Japan's relationships with other Asian countries, was described as a 'branch family' in the ministry study and a 'child country' in other sources" (Dower 1986, 283). *Shashin Shūhō* 266 (April 7, 1943): 17, includes an article that calls Mount Mayon "the Philippine Fuji" (D. C. Earhart 2008, 289, illus. 74).

43. Yamamoto 1962, 289 (quotation), 291, stamps 18, 19; *Sakura* 1997, 222, stamps 29–30.

44. Yamamoto 1962, 296–97, stamps 8–11; *Sakura* 1997, 221, lists stamps 8–11 under "Japanese Naval Control Area."

45. *Sakura* 1997, 216, stamps 71, 73. The second group of stamps in this set (stamps 72, 74) is labeled "auspicious clouds over twin phoenixes." A scan of these catalogs brought up no additional instances of Fuji.

46. In World War II (or the Pacific War) the linkage of Fuji with military might was continued in the air: "The Japanese Navy ordered the construction of Nakajima G10N1 'Fugaku' (Mount Fuji), an ultra-long range heavy bomber, for bombing the United States mainland. The bomb-load capability of the bomber was 20,000 kg for short range sorties; 5,000 kg for sorties against targets in the U.S." This information comes from http://en.wikipedia.org/wiki/Attacks_on_United_States_territory_in_North_America (accessed January 31, 2011). See also Mikesh 1993, 180, for "Popular Names of Japanese Naval Aircraft. Attack Bombers—Mountains. Fugaku (Mount Fuji) G10N1." Another source claims, "The Meiji elite found it [Fuji] useful as a symbol of the unified nation and considered expanding the concept to Asia during World War Two by instituting a string of Mount Fuji's across the Greater East Asian Co-prosperity Sphere to encourage the colonized to identify with the fatherland." This information comes from http://metropolis .japantoday.com (accessed January 31, 2011).

47. Mitsui 1940, 9–10. This article is courtesy of the David C. Earhart Collection of Japanese Wartime Publications, 1931–48.

48. Yamamoto 1962, 73, stamp R216. This stamp has not been located in *Sakura* 1997, 28–29, "New Showa Series" of 1946–47, or in *Scott*.

49. Yamamoto 1962, 75–77. See *Sakura* 1997, 28, stamps 239, 240; and *Scott* 2004, 22, stamp A167.

50. This may be the first instance of an ukiyo-e to picture Fuji on postage.

51. Yamamoto 1962, 175, item S-S10; *Sakura* 1997, 58, item C115; *Scott* 2004, 23, item A189. (Both *Sakura* and *Scott* list this lithograph as 1947.)

52. A quick scan yielded this tentative listing of recent Fuji stamps from *Sakura* 1997 and *Scott* 2004, cited by (matching) page number and stamp number: *Sakura*, 64, stamp C201; *Scott*, 27, stamp A285; *Sakura*, 71, stamp 297; *Scott*, 31, stamp A412; *Sakura*, 72, stamp C319 (the Diet building superimposed on Hokusai's "Red Fuji"); *Scott*, 32, stamps A435, A436; *Sakura*, 73, stamp C346; *Scott*, 32, A437 (not shown); *Sakura*, 76, stamp C399 (the "Great Wave" of Hokusai); *Scott*, 34, stamp A506; *Sakura*, 78, stamp C422; *Scott*, 35, stamp A525; *Sakura*, 78, stamp C423; *Scott*, 35, stamp A530; *Sakura*, 79, stamp C434; *Scott*, 79, "Design: No. 850" (not shown); *Sakura*, 80, stamp C462; *Scott*, 37, stamp 50y (not shown); *Sakura*, 81, stamp C482; *Scott*, 38, stamp A593; *Sakura*, 81, stamp C483; *Scott*, 38, stamp 50y (not shown); *Sakura*, 85, stamp C544; *Scott*, 41, stamp 50y (not shown); *Sakura*, 88, stamp C595; *Scott*, 43, stamp A723; *Sakura*, 100, stamp C776; *Scott*, 50, stamp A914; *Sakura*, 100, stamp C783; *Scott*, 50, stamp A921; *Sakura*, 105, stamp C836; *Scott*, 52, stamp A967; *Sakura*, 118, stamp C1077; *Scott*, 60, stamp A1239; *Sakura*, 133, stamp C1301; *Scott*, 65, stamp A1571; *Sakura*, 138, stamp C1378; *Scott*, 67, stamp A1625; *Sakura*, 140, stamp 1399; *Scott*, 68, stamp A1644b; *Sakura*, 153, stamps C1577, C1579, C1581; *Scott*, 73, listings 2541, 2543, and 2545 (not shown).

Special-issue stamps from *Sakura* 1997 follow. National Park issues are *Sakura*, 177, stamps P1–4; *Sakura*, 179, stamps P45–48; *Sakura*, 182, stamps P91–94. New Year's greeting stamps include *Sakura*, 189, stamp N1. International mail postal cards include *Sakura*, 230, items FC16–17, FC20–21, FC22–23; 231, items FC34–35, FC26–37, FC38. New Year's postal cards include *Sakura*, 234, item NC13; *Sakura*, 235, item NC59. "JPS Original Philatelic Materials" include *Sakura*, 248, item JUP2 (the Great Wave of Hokusai, with Fuji replaced by the Philately Hall [Yūshu Kaikan]);

Sakura, 249, item JUP22 (the Great Wall of China, the Temple of Heaven, and Fuji), item JUP28. No doubt this tentative list has overlooked some issues and certainly will be added to in years to come.

12. A Contemporary Fujikō

1. The decline of Fuji pilgrimage groups is paralleled by the "demise" of similar groups such as at Ōyama, due to "several interrelated factors that reflected larger societal changes and upheaval" (Ambros 2008, 242).

2. Bellah 1985; J. A. Sawada 1993.

3. Bernbaum 1990, 67. This is the *fujizuka* leveled to erect a building on the campus of Waseda University. Since the time of this research Ida passed away and was succeeded by his son as the new head of the group.

4. See the description of one such freelance practitioner in Dore 1958, 368.

5. The author paid the same fee as other participants, 27,000 yen, which included a deluxe charter bus round trip from Ida's building, lodging in a hut on Fuji one night, lodging at a pilgrimage inn in Fuji Yoshida the next night, and a stop at an *onsen* (hot spring), with most meals included.

6. View this statue in the author's documentary video, *Fuji: Sacred Mountain of Japan.*

7. Bernbaum 1990, 67. This rite with the mirror was not observed by the author in 1988; it may not have been performed because ill health forced Ida to return to the fifth station to wait for the group.

8. This rite was first observed by the author in 1969 on his initial climb of Fuji with the Fusōkyō group. One of the Miyamotokō participants in their *nanasha mawari* mentioned that their *kō*'s participation in this ritual dated only from the previous year. Ida said that until a few years before 1988 they had stayed at a mountain hut called Taishikan; apparently the change to the Gansomuro hut made this rite available to them. The rite is comparable to the *kaji kitō* performed in Shugendō.

9. Her phrase was *kimi ga warui,* literally meaning "have a bad feeling about something." The author's experience of the old route concurs with her impression. On a field trip to Fuji with Miyake and his students from Keio University, upon arrival at the fifth station the weather was so foggy that the police closed the climbing path up the mountain, so the group descended on foot via the old route. Even the students were "spooked" by this strange place and so shocked when they saw two hand sickles crossed and nailed to a tree (a folk hex or curse technique) that they yelled in unison "curse!" (*noroi*).

10. See also Iwashina 1973, 244.

13. New Religions and Fuji

1. To this day Maruyamakyō uses an identifying emblem composed of a circle (*maru*) enclosing the character for mountain (*yama*); apparently this was the mark of the Maruyamakō.

2. For this term, see J. A. Sawada 1993, 2; and T. Hirano 1972, 115.

3. J. A. Sawada 1998, 117; brackets in the original. Tyler 1984, 105, cites this as *tsumetachi-gyō,* or "tiptoe practice." See also Tyler 1993, 273–74.

4. For convenience the founder is referred to as Itō, the present head as *kyōshu.*

5. The 1988 meeting took place on the afternoon of July 15.

6. As J. A. Sawada points out, the founder Itō was an opponent of Japanese imitating Western customs, such as Western clothing.

7. *Umarekawatta,* translated as "reborn," is a term repeated in a key ritual within the crater of Fuji.

8. Maruyamakyō can be considered a "full-service" religion, complete with marriage and funeral services as well as a memorial hall (Shōryōden) where members' ancestors are honored.

9. The fee for the trip was thirteen thousand yen; the leader's assistant politely but firmly refused to accept it from the author. This sum included the round-trip bus from Kawasaki to Fuji, an overnight stay in a Fuji lodging, and a few meals.

10. This efficiency was counterproductive for survey results because writing was difficult on the bus, and the assistant collected the surveys as people got off the bus at the Kigen Dōjō; few people filled in the open-ended question about "reason" for climbing.

11. Iwashina 1983, 376, calls this Maruyamakyō's sacred phrase (*shingo*). Thanks go to J. A. Sawada for referring me to the note on *tenmei kaiten* in *Nihon shisō taikei*, 69:560. In early Maruyamakyō the chant was *namu amida butsu* (the *nenbutsu* of Buddhism) and then a variation on this phrase (J. A. Sawada 1998, 63, 119–21) before the adoption of *tenmei kaiten*. The first two characters, *tenmei*, refer to the sun as the original parent deity and its brilliance; the last two characters, *kaiten* (sea-heaven), refer to the splendor of that brilliance on the surface of the sea and to the minds and bodies of the people who receive this vitality from the parent *kami* and work hard. The term is a symbol of unity between humans and the parent *kami*; chanting this term, regulating one's breath, is a practice to achieve the unity of heaven and earth. See also T. Hirano 1972, 123–24.

12. Some of the *tenpaishiki* can be viewed in the author's documentary video, *Fuji: Sacred Mountain of Japan*.

13. Veneration of ancestors is central to Maruyamakyō faith and practice; hence the elaborate memorial hall (Shōryōden) at the religion's headquarters. Ancestors are also directly linked to Maruyamakyō's Fuji pilgrimage since Japanese religion emphasizes honoring spirits of the dead, and Fuji is a special place where Maruyamakyō members believe the spirits of their deceased family members reside.

14. As J. A. Sawada 1998, 118, has pointed out, "Maruyama has been considered an early Meiji example of the 'world renewal' (*yonaoshi*) movements, often associated with peasant rebellions, that began to appear during the late Tokugawa." This theme of world renewal meant not only spiritual rebirth but also a social change; after Itō's death the group came to emphasize common moral values. This 1988 ceremony provides concrete evidence of contemporary Maruyamakyō's emphasis on personal renewal (or spiritual rebirth) rather than social reform.

15. Not all Westerners have been favorably impressed by the view of Fuji from a passing train. Richie 1994, 99, 98, commenting on "Honorable Visitors," cites the offhand dismissal of Fuji by Aldous Huxley.

16. For an overview of Gedatsukai as a new religion, see H. B. Earhart 1989.

17. For an overview of Okano's life, see ibid., 13–41.

18. Tanzawa is a rugged mountain in the Tanzawa–Ōyama Quasi–National Park. Ōyama appeared in chapter 7 as a mountain that preceded Fuji as a pilgrimage site.

19. *Hōon kansha.*

20. *Yōhaijo* is a standard term for a site for worshiping from afar; see chapter 1.

21. The branch takes its name from its location in the Nakano ward of Tokyo.

22. Some honor the thirteenth as the anniversary of Miroku's death (Iwashina 1983, 193). Other Fujikō were named Jūsanyakō, "the thirteenth day confraternity."

23. The formal meeting at Gedatsukai's Tokyo offices was on April 17, 1988; the meeting at the Nakano branch took place on April 22, 1988.

24. Gedatsukai's branches are called *shibu*; the branch leader or head is *shibuchō*.

25. The leader said that the characters engraved in the stone were modeled after Okano's writing.

26. Gedatsukai branches usually meet twice monthly, for a *hōonbi* (Repayment of Debt Day) and a *kanshabi* (Thanks Day).

27. The fee for the 1988 pilgrimage was fifteen thousand yen and included the chartered luxury bus round trip from the branch leader's residence to the fifth station, the side trip to the Tainai, some refreshments, a meal, and lodging in a mountain hut, as well as fees for amulets and the shrines.

28. For descriptions of *kanshabi* and *hōonbi* in other Gedatsukai branches, see H. B. Earhart 1989, 121–51.

29. This is an indirect reference to the well-known belief that the mountain *kami* (*yama no kami*) is female (Konohana is a *yama no kami*) and is jealous of women on her mountain.

30. The founder Okano had practiced within the Shugendō tradition and at the Buddhist temple Shōgoin where this title was conferred. In Gedatsukai there is a linkage among En no Gyōja (or En no Ozunu), mountain austerities, Shugendō, Fuji, and the founder Okano.

31. For an earlier description of such a rite, with illustrations of the human form (*hitogata*, also called *katashiro*) and the reed circle (*chi no wa*), see Satow 1879, 122.

32. *Omairi* is a general term for making a visit or paying respects at a shrine or temple; it is a favorite expression in Gedatsukai, which prides itself on honoring, respecting, and worshiping all traditional religious sites.

33. Sanseichi Junpai, pilgrimage to three holy sites: Sennyūji (ancestral temple for emperors); Ise Shrine; and Kashiwara Shrine (honoring the ancient imperial line).

34. The name is an adaptation of Hōraisan, the mythical Chinese mountain (Penglai shan) associated with the Isle of Eternal Youth.

35. Kawabata in his short story "First Snow on Fuji" has one character, who has been obsessed with the view and snow on Fuji, remark, "Even looking at Mount Fuji must get boring if you see it all the time" (Kawabata 1999, 151).

36. The plan had been for a group *omairi* here; it may have taken place, but in the crowded quarters and confusion the author did not observe it.

14. Surveying Contemporary Fuji Belief and Practice

1. Special thanks go to the late Nakamura Kyōko, who kindly helped with the Japanese text of the questionnaire and also prepared a master copy with a computer printout.

2. There were actually four sets of questionnaire, because the Maruyamakyō group had two buses, one from the Kawasaki headquarters and one coming from Aichi Prefecture. However, the data showed that the Aichi bus was mainly a youth group, making its responses less useful; a few interesting items from the Aichi materials will be mentioned in the text and footnotes, but this material is not included in the bus questionnaire results.

3. In a nationwide survey of Gedatsukai branches in 1979, the female membership of this new religion was 64.5 percent, which seems to be typical for new religions (H. B. Earhart 1989, 80). Reader 2005, 77–78, reports that for the modern Shikoku pilgrimage, several studies show participation of females at 60 percent or more.

4. The results here should not necessarily be taken literally: Tanabe and Reader (1998) have shown that practical benefits are important in all Japanese religion.

5. For examples of the extreme range of modern attitudes and conceptions about Japanese mountains and Fuji, see the sharply contrasting views of Daisetz T. Suzuki (1973, 334), the well-known popularizer of Zen Buddhism, and Kosuke Koyama (1985, 9), a famous Christian theologian.

15. War and Peace

1. *Shashin Shūhō* (*Photographic Weekly Report*) 341, October 4, 1944. The image appears in D. C. Earhart 2008, 210. Additional images illustrating the wartime and postwar role of the mountain are found in my article "Mount Fuji: Shield of War, Badge of Peace"; see H. B. Earhart 2011.

2. D. C. Earhart 2008, 440, illus. 51. Fuji's link to militarism has a long pedigree: the sacred mountain lent its name to one of the first modern Japanese warships: see Nihon Shashinka Kyōkai 1980, 264, 381, plate 377: "Sailors and retainers of the Shōgun on the deck of Mount Fuji, a warship built in the United States, 1868." As in war, so in peace: Fuji also provided the name for "Japan's Largest Oceangoing Liner," the *Fuji Maru*, as pictured in the *Asahi Evening News*, Friday, December 9, 1988, 3.

3. Warner and Warner 1982, 123. Thanks go to David C. Earhart for providing these quotations.

4. Dower 1986, 249. See also Gilmore 1998; Rhodes 1976; and the Web site psywarrior.com, especially articles by Herbert A. Friedman: "Vilification of Enemy Leadership in WWII"; "Japanese Psyop during WWII"; "OWI Pacific Psyop Six Decades Ago"; "The United States PSYOP

Organization in the Pacific during World War II"; and "Sex and Psychological Operations" (these Web-site articles are updated periodically). Special thanks go to retired U.S. Army Sergeant Major Friedman, an expert on U. S. psychological operations, for locating and providing images of Fuji on American propaganda leaflets.

5. Dower 1986, 121–22. Some anthropologists were critical of the simplistic characterizations of the Japanese by these scholars at the time; see Dower 1986, 128–29, 138; and Leighton and Opler 1977; as well as Winkler 1978, 142–46; and Friedman, "Vilification of Enemy Leadership in WWII." Kyoko Hirano 1992, 108, notes a shift in American propaganda films for home consumption: 1942–43 films depict the emperor as a symbol of Japanese militarism, but from 1944 this theme is avoided.

6. Personal communication from Herbert A. Friedman; he knows of no formal policy about how to treat Fuji but thinks that it was utilized as an obvious visual for representing Japan. American wartime popular literature has not been searched, but one 1942 literary caricature compares the violence of Japanese with the volcano of Fuji, the link being surface beauty and underlying frenzy: "Beneath the elaborate structure of bows and nervous giggles there simmers a Mount Fuji of dark frenzy" (Simon Harcourt-Smith, *Japanese Frenzy* [1942], p. 6, quoted in Littlewood 1996, 163).

7. See Friedman, "OWI Pacific Psyop Six Decades Ago"; and Winkler 1978, 146. Dower 1986, 337n1, writes that "the best work on the subject is Suzuki Akira and Yamamoto Akira, eds., *Hiroku: Bōryaku Senden Bira—Taiheiyō Sensō no Kami Bakudan* [Propaganda Leaflets—Paper Bullets of the Pacific War] (1977: Kodansha)," a work not available to the author. A scan of the 1990 publication *Kami no sensō dentan: Bōryaku senden-bira wa* brought up most of the leaflets appearing on the Web site psywarrior.com.

8. Friedman consistently interprets the leaflets as attempting to engender nostalgia and homesickness in the Japanese soldier, with the intended result of surrender.

9. Leaflets are referenced by the numbering in Friedman's article "OWI Pacific Psyop Six Decades Ago."

10. Ibid., translation given in the article.

11. Ibid. This leaflet is also reproduced (in black and white) in Heiwa Hakubutsukan o Tsukuru Kai 1990, 115.

12. Another leaflet "designed to induce Japanese troops to surrender" and featuring a picturesque landscape of Fuji is leaflet 520 (on Herbert A. Friedman's Psywarrior Web site, "OWI Pacific Psyop Six Decades Ago," http://www.psywarrior.com/OWI60YrsLater2.html [accessed February 21, 2011]). It cites the Russo-Japanese War, when two thousand soldiers taken prisoner by the Russians were returned to Japan. Leaflet 101 offers a similar nostalgia-inducing panorama of Fuji and an appeal for surrender. Leaflet 101 (also on Friedman's site) resembles a one-page surrender appeal included in *Psychological Warfare* (Linebarger 1948, 134, fig. 29). This leaflet features two columns of three panels following a Japanese soldier through the process of surrender, leading to a large panel at the bottom showing the soldier returning to his home and family, with Fuji in the background.

13. Friedman, "OWI Pacific Psyop Six Decades Ago."

14. Brackets in the original.

15. The emphasis on *giri* and *ninjō* on the two "road-posts" is similar to the perceptions of Ruth Benedict, one of the anthropologists active in the war effort who favored the "national-character approach." For discussion and critique of this approach, see the references in Dower 1986, 338–39n5.

16. Iwashina 1983, 276–78, cites the examples of *sendatsu* who wandered the darkened streets during bombing attacks, praying to Fuji and chanting the same sacred phrases used while climbing Fuji. Web sites by and about U.S. aviators from World War II abound in photos of Fuji taken from fighter and bomber windows, as do narratives about flying from Pacific islands to central Japan that mention Fuji as the first (sometimes the only) landmark visible.

17. K. Hirano 1992 provides a balanced overview of the occupation and its film policies; for discussion of cartoons, see Sodei 1988, 93–106; and Dower 1986, 107–23.

18. K. Hirano 1992, 44–45, gives this list of "Prohibited Subjects" for film: militarism, nationalism, chauvinism, xenophobia, discrimination. Specific content, such as Fuji, is not mentioned.

19. Makino could not have known that, according to one source, "the US Air Force was toying with the idea of trying to bombard Fuji back into activity to harness it's [*sic*] explosive potential as a huge natural bomb." This anecdote, which the author has not been able to document, is from http://metropolis.japantoday.com (accessed January 31, 2010). An online search for "Fuji and atomic bomb" called up a listing by Lisa Katayama from March 12, 2010, titled "An alternative to the atomic bomb?" She points to a wartime article: "A geologist proposed bombing Japan's volcanoes to win the war in a January 1944 issue of Popular Science." A black-and-white figure of American bombers (hypothetically) bombing volcanoes has the caption: "American bombers, swarming in from the sea, are depicted dropping blockbusters into the craters of Japan's volcanoes to set them into fiery eruption." Taken from http://boingboing.net/2010/03/12/an-alternative-to-th.html (accessed January 31, 2011). Censorship during the occupation was rather arbitrary; the rationale for censoring Makino's film may have been linked to suspicions about Makino himself and not just the image of Fuji.

20. K. Hirano 1992, 52–53 (my bracketed explanation follows CIE; *Ikina furaibo* was in brackets in the original). See also Richie 2001, 10; and Richie 1997, 12. A 1942 issue of *Shashin Shūhō* (232 [August 5, 1942]: 14–15) shows one-legged soldiers, physically incapable of returning to battle, valiantly climbing Fuji as an act of supporting the nation and the war, reminding people of the sacrifices made by Japan's fighting men, and encouraging civilians to follow this example and do their utmost. Thanks to David C. Earhart for providing this information.

21. For Kamei Fumio, see K. Hirano 1992, 33, 104–45. In prewar times he may have been the only one punished for his "natural" views of Fuji, but he was by no means the only one who saw the mountain that way. For example, a character in Natsume Sōseki's 1908 novel *Sanshirō* describes Fuji to Sanshirō as they are on a train heading north to the capital: "Oh, yes, this is your first trip to Tokyo, isn't it? You've never seen Mount Fuji. We go by it a little farther on. It's the finest thing Japan has to offer, the only thing we've got to boast about. The trouble is, of course, it's just a natural object. It's been sitting there for all time" (Natsume 1977, 15). Washburn 2007, 74–75, comments on this passage that the novel's character "sarcastically pronounces Mount Fuji to be the only thing Japan has to boast about as a way to belittle the Japan that blindly strives to be the equal of the Great Powers." See also the "natural" imagery of Fuji in the bleak postwar short story of Kawabata (1999, 152).

22. *Nippon Times,* January 4, 1946, p. 1. Thanks to David C. Earhart for providing this reference, courtesy of his Collection of Japanese Primary Sources from the Pacific War.

23. For a nineteenth-century graphic interpretation of reverse orientalism in a Japanese woodblock print, see plate 11.

24. Japanese and American historians of the occupation have commented on the inconsistencies in postwar purges, especially in the arts. For inconsistency in the treatment of cartoonists, see Sodei 1998, 94–95; Sodei 1988; Burkman 1988; and Mayo and Rimer 2001.

25. Parallels of national symbols and their patriotic utilization or manipulation can be drawn from any other country, so Japan's case is by no means unique. Ohnuki-Tierney 2002 includes extensive treatments of the aestheticization of cherry blossoms (27–58), the militarization of cherry blossoms (102–24), and "soldiers' death as falling cherry petals" (111–15).

26. This information is taken from an Internet article, "History of the US Army in Japan," http://aboutfacts.net/War13.htm (accessed December 17, 2010). Thanks to David C. Earhart for locating the Internet article (and for making a gift of the medal). Note that in this USARJ "unit crest," not only Fuji but also the "red demi-sun" are rehabilitated for peaceful purposes.

27. The cap is part of the author's personal collection, as is a tie clasp with the same design. Thanks to the author's son Kenneth C. Earhart for the gift of these items.

28. This is the description of the coin on eBay.

29. The names of the coins as listed on eBay are "Camp Zama Japan Challenge Coin Red," "Camp Zama Japan Challenge Coin Orange," "US Japan Challenge Coin," and "Yokota AFB Japan Challenge Coin." All these coins were purchased on eBay.

30. A search of various Internet Web sites for Japanese armed forces insignia turned up only one with the image of Fuji, which a Web site lists as "Japanese Opinion Medal" (http://digger history.info/pages-medals/jap_medals-ww2.htm [accessed December 17, 2010]).

31. The photo is credited to USS *Trigger* (SS-237) on war patrol May 24, 1943. See http://americanhistory.si.edu/subs/history/subsbeforenuc/ww2 (accessed December 17, 2010).

32. See http://www.subsim.com/ssr/simcomm1998.html (accessed December 17, 2010).

33. See http://www.ussicefish.com/Pages/officers.html (accessed December 17, 2010). A perusal of wartime covers of *Life* turned up no photo of Fuji; this run of magazines has not been searched for a print of Fuji.

34. For *Destination Tokyo*, see Morella, Epstein, and Griggs 1973, 164–67, and the Internet Movie Database http://www.imdb.com/.

35. See, for example, Steichen 1980, 116, for a photo captioned "Strike on Tokyo—52 Carrier-based Planes Pass Mt. Fujiyama, February 1945."

36. Without benefit of their records of the event, it is impossible to reconstruct the original "intent" of photographers who took such pictures. Steichen, a veteran of World War I, who volunteered in spite of his advanced age, was clear about his motives: "I had gradually come to believe that, if a real image of war could be photographed and presented to the world, it might make a contribution toward ending the specter of war" (Steichen 1980, 12). Steichen's book (which also includes the periscope "capture" of Fuji) is significant because of its original release in 1946 as a souvenir publication for navy personnel.

37. From the author's personal collection, a gift from his father, Kenneth H. Earhart, who was stationed on the *Missouri* at the time of surrender..

38. Naitō 2003, 64, illus. 1–13; Naitō 2003, 91, illus. 1–30. One entire series that Naitō does not mention is the many stamps commemorating the 1971 Boy Scout World Jamboree held in Japan. See http://www.iomoon.com/fujideaux.html (accessed December 17, 2010) for twelve stamps showing Boy Scouts against Fuji, from the issuing countries of Umm Al Qiwain, Fujeira, Senegal, Mali, and Mauritania, "none of which are listed in Scott."

16. The Future of an Icon

1. Smith 1988, 219. See plate 92 on p. 39 (the numbers for plates 91 and 92 have been interchanged).

2. Unsigned editorial, *Understanding Japan* 1, no. 3 (June 1992): 7.

3. The famed Asahi brand distributes plastic bottles of drinking water labeled "Fujisan no banajiumu tennensui" (Mount Fuji vanadium natural water); the bottle's English label is simply "natural mineral water," but it sports a color rendition of the snow-covered mountain.

4. The image of Fuji has been used on many American magazine covers for a variety of purposes. To take just one example, see *Time*, August 1, 1983, a "Special Issue" devoted to "Japan: A Nation in Search of Itself." A Japanese woman with traditional "geisha" style coiffure and outstretched arms displays a kimono with a pine and a seascape at the bottom of the garment, capped by a snow-covered Fuji and a red sun. This cover can be viewed at http://www.time.com/time/covers/0,16641,01-08-1983,00.html (accessed February 21, 2011).

5. *Kalamazoo Gazette*, Monday, September 4, 1989, C4, in a column of advertisements for massage and spa parlors.

6. First released on Capitol record 3843, 1957; reissued on various anthologies. A recent version is a 1996 Capitol reissue, "Vintage Collections, Wanda Jackson"; "Fujiyama Mama" was recorded by Wanda Jackson on September 17, 1957. The full lyrics can be viewed on various Internet sites by Googling "Fujiyama Mama."

7. See the biography of Wanda Jackson, which includes an overview of her work and reference to her Japanese tour, at http://www.missioncreep.com/mw/jackson.html (accessed December 17, 2010). Wanda Jackson was a contemporary (and acquaintance) of Elvis Presley, who is seen as borrowing the sexual power of black musicians. Thanks to David C. Earhart for pointing out this work and the Web site.

8. Kondō 1987, 162; Dazai 1991, 73, 84; Lyons 1985, 12; D. C. Earhart 1994, 496.

9. Morton in Kusano 1991, 89, 90, 42.

10. Ibid., 89, 90. For the controversial nature of the "Pan-Asianism" of Shinpei—and artistic figures such as Okakura—see Miyoshi 1994, 281–82; Karatani 1994, 39n18; Kaneko 2002, 3, 4–5; and Iida 2002, 16.

11. Kusano 1991, 20; Morton 1985, 48.

12. For another view of Okakura, see Karatani 1994, 36.

13. The phrase "patriotic mantra" is borrowed from Rosenfield's 2001 work on Yokoyama Taikan. Rosenfield attributes the lack of overt conflict in Taikan's paintings to the combined influence of Nihonga, with its emphasis on creating "a soothing, comfortable iconography," and also "the idealism of ancient Chinese principles of propriety and righteousness" (ibid., 176). Maruyama in his postwar assessment of patriotism and nationalism notes that "it would not be quite right to say that the old nationalism had either died out or qualitatively changed. It would be more precise to say that it had vanished from the political surface only to be inlaid at the social base in an atomized form" (Maruyama 1969, 151).

14. Naruse 2005, 237–39, comments that *Dawn on a Specific Day* shows that the Fuji that Taikan had always worshiped rose above the defeat of World War II, opening the eyes of the world to Japan's postwar reconstruction.

Epilogue

1. Smith 1988, 210, 84, plate II/60.

2. *Recovering the Orient* (Gerstle and Milner 1994, 2, 6).

3. From http://mtfuji.or.jp/en/index.php (accessed December 17, 2010).

4. On March 11, 2011, as this book was going to press, a massive earthquake on the seafloor off Sendai caused a catastrophic tsunami. The devastation was widespread and included the disabling of nuclear power plants in Fukushima. Early reports indicate that the engineers who located the nuclear reactors close to the shore and who planned the height of the protective sea walls took into account earthquakes and tsunamis dating back only to the late nineteenth century. However, some of Fuji's biggest eruptions occurred in the eighth and ninth centuries. By ignoring earlier records of more powerful seismic events, especially the immense earthquake and accompanying tsunami of 869, they underestimated both the potential severity of natural calamities and the need for safeguards. No one, not even vulcanologists or geologists, can predict earthquakes or eruptions, but past events remind us that future incidents are inevitable. It is not so much a question if Fuji will erupt, but when. The next chapter of Fuji's natural history, and the cultural response to it, is yet to be written.

BIBLIOGRAPHY

NOTE: Short articles from the *Kodansha Encyclopedia of Japan* (Tokyo: Kodansha, 1983) are listed by volume and page numbers.

Abe, Ryuichi. 1999. *The Weaving of Mantra: Kukai and the Construction of Esoteric Buddhist Discourse.* New York: Columbia University Press.

Abe Hajime. 2002. "Kindai nihon no kyōkasho to fujisan." In *Fujisan to nihonjin,* edited by Seikyūsha Henshūbu, 58–86. Tokyo: Seikyūsha.

Akashi, Mariko, et al., trans. 1976. "*Hitachi Fudoki.*" *Traditions* 1, no. 2: 23–47; 1, no. 3: 55–78.

Alcock, Rutherford. 1863. *The Capital of the Tycoon: A Narrative of Three Years Residence in Japan.* London: Longman, Green, Longman, Roberts & Green. Reprinted, St. Clair Shores, Mich.: Scholarly Press, 1969.

Ambros, Barbara. 2001. "Localized Religious Specialists in Early Modern Japan: The Development of the Ōyama *Oshi* System." *Japanese Journal of Religious Studies* 28, nos. 3–4: 329–72.

———. 2008. *Emplacing a Pilgrimage: The Ōyama Cult and Regional Religion in Early Modern Japan.* Cambridge: Harvard University Asia Center.

Andō, Hiroshige. 1965. *The Fifty-three Stages of the Tokaido, by Hiroshige.* Edited by Ichitarō Kondō. English adaptation by Charles S. Terry. Honolulu: East-West Center Press.

———. 1974. *Hiroshige: The 53 Stations of the Tokaido.* By Muneshige Narazaki, English adaptation by Gordon Sager. Tokyo: Kodansha International.

Aramaki, Shigeo. 1983. "Volcanoes." In *Kodansha Encyclopedia of Japan,* 8:193–95.

Arntzen, Sonja. 1997a. *The Kagerō Diary: A Woman's Autobiographical Text from Tenth-Century Japan.* Ann Arbor, Mich.: Center for Japanese Studies, University of Michigan.

———. 1997b. "Natural Imagery in Classical Japanese Poetry: The Equivalence of the Literal and the Figural." In *Japanese Images of Nature: Cultural Perspectives,* edited by Pamela J. Asquith and Arne Kalland, 54–67. Surrey: Curzon.

Asquith, Pamela J., and Arne Kalland, eds. 1997. *Japanese Images of Nature: Cultural Perspectives.* Richmond, Surrey: Curzon.

Aston, W. G., trans. 1956. *Nihongi: Chronicles of Japan from the Earliest Times to A.D. 697.* London: George Allen and Unwin. Originally published in *Transactions of the Japan Society,* Supplement 1 (1896) 2 vols., London. Reprinted 2 volumes in 1 with original pagination in 1956.

Ayusawa, Shintaro. 1953. "The Types of World Map Made in Japan's Age of National Isolation." *Imago Mundi* 10: 123–28.

Baldrian, Farzeen. 1987. "Taoism: An Overview." In *The Encyclopedia of Religion,* edited by Mircea Eliade et al., 14:288–306. New York: Macmillan.

Bambling, Michele. 1996. "The Kongo-ji Screens: Illuminating the Tradition of Yamato-e 'Sun' and 'Moon' Screens." *Orientations* 27, no. 8: 70–82.

Barnes, Gina Lee. 1983. "Haniwa." In *Kodansha Encyclopedia of Japan,* 3:97–98.

Barrett, Marie-Thérèse. 1999. "*Japonaiserie* to *Japonisme*: A Revolution in Seeing." In *The Trans-actions of the Asiatic Society of Japan*, 4th series, 14: 77–85.

Batchelor, John. 1905. *An Ainu-English-Japanese Dictionary*. 2nd ed. Tokyo: Methodist Publishing House.

Beasley, W. G. 1984a. "The Edo Experience and Japanese Nationalism." *Edo Culture and Its Modern Legacy*. Special issue, *Modern Asian Studies* 18, no. 4: 555–66.

———. 1984b. "Introduction." *Edo Culture and Its Modern Legacy*. Special issue, *Modern Asian Studies* 18, no. 4: 529–30.

Befu, Harumi. 1997. "Watsuji Tetsurō's Ecological Approach: Its Philosophical Foundation." In *Japanese Images of Nature: Cultural Perspectives*, edited by Pamela J. Asquith and Arne Kalland, 106–20. Richmond, Surrey: Curzon.

Bell, David. 2001. *Chushingura and the Floating World: The Representation of "Kanadehon Chushingura" in "Ukiyo-e" Prints*. Richmond, Surrey: Curzon.

Bellah, Robert N. 1985. *Tokugawa Religion: The Cultural Roots of Modern Japan*. New York: Free Press.

Ben-Ari, Eyal, Brian Moeran, and James Valentine, eds. 1990. *Unwrapping Japan: Society and Culture in Anthropological Perspective*. Manchester: Manchester University Press.

Benfey, Christopher E. G. 2003. *The Great Wave: Gilded Age Misfits, Japanese Eccentrics, and the Opening of Old Japan*. New York: Random House.

Bennett, Terry, comp. 2006. *Japan and "The Illustrated London News": Complete Record of Reported Events, 1853–1899*. Folkstone, Kent: Global Oriental.

Berger, Klaus. 1992. *Japonisme in Western Painting from Whistler to Matisse*. Translated by David Britt. Cambridge: Cambridge University Press.

Bernbaum, Edwin. 1990. *Sacred Mountains of the World*. San Francisco: Sierra Club Books.

Bernstein, Andrew. 2008. "Whose Fuji? Religion, Region, and State in the Fight for a National Symbol." *Monumenta Nipponica* 63, no. 1: 51–99.

Berry, Mary Elizabeth. 2006. *Japan in Print: Information and Nation in the Early Modern Period*. Berkeley: University of California Press.

Bicknell, Julian. 1994. *Hiroshige in Tokyo: The Floating World of Edo*. San Francisco: Pomegranate Artbooks.

Bix, Herbert P. 2000. *Hirohito and the Making of Modern Japan*. New York: HarperCollins.

Blacker, Carmen. 1984. "The Religious Traveller in the Edo Period." *Modern Asian Studies* 18, no. 4: 593–608.

Blong, R. J. 1982. *The Time of Darkness: Local Legends and Volcanic Reality in Papua New Guinea*. Canberra: Australian National University Press.

Bock, Felicia Gressitt, trans. 1970. *Engi-Shiki: Procedures of the Engi Era, Books I–V*. Tokyo: Sophia University Press.

———, trans. 1972. *Engi-Shiki: Procedures of the Engi Era, Books VI–X*. Tokyo: Sophia University Press.

Bodart-Bailey, Beatrice M. 1992. "The Most Magnificent Monastery and Other Famous Sights: The Japanese Paintings of Engelbert Kaempfer." *Japan Review* 3: 25–44.

———. 1995a. "Introduction: The Furthest Goal." In *The Furthest Goal: Engelbert Kaempfer's Encounter with Tokugawa Japan*, edited by Beatrice M. Bodart-Bailey and Derek Massarella, 1–16. Sandgate, Folkestone: Japan Library.

———. 1995b. "Writing *The History of Japan*." In *The Furthest Goal: Engelbert Kaempfer's Encounter with Tokugawa Japan*, edited by Beatrice M. Bodart-Bailey and Derek Massarella, 17–43. Sandgate, Folkestone: Japan Library.

Bownas, Geoffrey, and Anthony Thwaite, trans. 1964. *The Penguin Book of Japanese Verse*. Baltimore: Penguin Books.

Boxer, C. R. 1967. *The Christian Century in Japan 1549–1650*. Berkeley: University of California Press.

Brandon, James R., and Samuel L. Leiter. 2002. *Kabuki Plays on Stage*. 4 vols. Honolulu: University of Hawaii Press.

Brazell, Karen, trans. 1973. *The Confessions of Lady Nijō*. Garden City, N.Y.: Anchor Books.

Brower, Robert H., and Earl Miner. 1961. *Japanese Court Poetry.* Stanford, Calif.: Stanford University Press.

Brown, Peter. 1981. *The Cult of Saints: Its Rise and Function in Latin Christianity.* Chicago: University of Chicago Press.

Burkman, Thomas W., ed. 1988. *The Occupation of Japan: Arts and Culture.* Norfolk, Va.: General Douglas MacArthur Foundation.

Burns, Susan L. 2003. *Before the Nation: Kokugaku and the Imaging of Community in Early Modern Japan.* Durham, N.C.: Duke University Press.

Buruma, Ian. 2003. *Inventing Japan, 1853–1964.* New York: Modern Library.

Calza, Gian Carlo, ed. 1994. *Hokusai: Selected Essays.* Venice: International Hokusai Research Centre, University of Venice.

———. 2003. *Hokusai.* London: Phaidon.

Carter, Steven D., trans. 1991. *Traditional Japanese Poetry: An Anthology.* Stanford, Calif.: Stanford University Press.

Chakrabarty, Dipesh. 1998. "Afterword: Revisiting the Tradition/Modernity Binary." In *Mirror of Modernity: Invented Traditions of Modern Japan,* edited by Stephen Vlastos, 285–96. Berkeley: University of California Press.

Chamberlain, Basil Hall, trans. 1882. "*Ko-ji-ki,* or Records of Ancient Matters." *Transactions of the Asiatic Society of Japan* 10, supplement. Reprinted as separate volume, new edition, with "Additional Notes by William George Aston," Kobe: J. L. Thompson & Company, 1932. Reprinted in 2 volumes, Tokyo: Asiatic Society of Japan, 1973.

———. 1971. *Japanese Things: Being Notes on Various Subjects Connected with Japan.* Rutland, Ver., and Tokyo: Charles E. Tuttle. Reprint of 5th rev. ed., 1905.

Churchill, Winston, and the editors of *Life.* 1959. *The Second World War.* 2 vols. New York: Time.

Clark, Timothy. 2001. *100 Views of Mount Fuji.* Trumbull, Conn.: Weatherhill.

Cogan, Thomas J., trans. 1987. *The Tale of the Soga Brothers.* Tokyo: University of Tokyo Press.

Collcutt, Martin. 1988. "Mt. Fuji as the Realm of Miroku: The Transformation of Maitreya in the Cult of Mt. Fuji in Early Modern Japan." In *Maitrya, the Future Buddha,* edited by Alan Sponberg and Helen Hardacre, 248–69. Cambridge: Cambridge University Press.

Cooper, Michael. 1965. *They Came to Japan: An Anthology of European Reports on Japan, 1543–1640.* Berkeley: University of California Press.

———. 1971a. "Japan Described." In *The Southern Barbarians: The First Europeans in Japan,* edited by Michael Cooper, 99–122. Tokyo: Kodansha International, in cooperation with Sophia University.

———, ed. 1971b. *The Southern Barbarians: The First Europeans in Japan.* Tokyo and Palo Alto, Calif.: Kodansha International in cooperation with Sophia University.

———, trans. and ed. 1973. *This Island of Japon: João Rodrigues' Account of 16th-Century Japan.* Tokyo: Kodansha International.

———. 1974. *Rodrigues the Interpreter: An Early Jesuit in China and Japan.* New York: Weatherhill.

Cortazzi, Hugh. 1987. *Victorians in Japan: In and around Treaty Ports.* London: Athlone.

Cortazzi, Hugh, and Terry Bennett. 1995. *Japan, Caught in Time.* New York: Weatherhill.

Crombie, Isobel. 2004. *Shashin: Nineteenth-Century Japanese Studio Photography.* Melbourne: National Gallery of Victoria.

Cutts, Robert L. 1994. "Magic Mountain." *Intersect* (December): 34–39.

Dale, Peter. N. 1986. *The Myth of Japanese Uniqueness.* London and Sydney: Croom Helm; Oxford: Nissan Institute for Japanese Studies, University of Oxford.

Davis, Winston. 1977. *Toward Modernity: A Developmental Typology of Popular Religious Affiliations in Japan.* Cornell East Asia Papers 12. Ithaca, N.Y.: Cornell China-Japan Program.

Dazai, Osamu. 1991. "One Hundred Views of Mount Fuji." In *Self Portraits: Tales from the Life of Japan's Great Decadent Romantic,* translated and introduced by Ralph F. McCarthy, 69–90. Tokyo: Kodansha International.

de Bary, Theodore, et al. 2001. *Sources of Japanese Tradition.* 2nd ed. New York: Columbia University Press.

Deffontaines, Pierre. 1948. *Géographie et religions.* Paris: Gallimard.

Dobson, Sebastian. 2004. "'I been to keep up my position': Felice Beato in Japan, 1863–1877." In *Reflecting Truth: Japanese Photography in the Nineteenth Century,* edited by Nicole Coolidge Rousmaniere and Mikiko Hirayama, 30–39. Amsterdam: Hotei.

Dore, R. P. 1958. *City Life in Japan: A Study of a Tokyo Ward.* Berkeley: University of California Press.

Dower, John W. 1971. *The Elements of Japanese Design: A Handbook of Family Crests, Heraldry & Symbolism.* With over 2,700 crests drawn by Kiyoshi Kawamoto. New York: Walker/ Weatherhill.

———. 1980. "Ways of Seeing—Ways of Remembering: The Photography of Prewar Japan." In Japanese Photographers Association, *A Century of Japanese Photography,* 3–20. New York: Pantheon.

———. 1983. "Crests." In *Kodansha Encyclopedia of Japan,* 2:42–43.

———. 1986. *War without Mercy: Race and Power in the Pacific War.* New York: Pantheon Books.

———. 1988. "Discussion." In *The Occupation of Japan: Arts and Culture,* edited by Thomas W. Burkman, 107–23. Norfolk, Va.: General Douglas MacArthur Foundation.

———. 1993a. "Graphic Others / Graphic Selves: Cartoons in War and Peace." In John W. Dower, *Japan in War & Peace: Selected Essays,* 287–300. New York: New Press.

———. 1993b. "Japanese Cinema Goes to War." In John W. Dower, *Japan in War & Peace: Selected Essays,* 33–54. New York: New Press.

———. 1999. *Embracing Defeat: Japan in the Wake of World War II.* New York: W. W. Norton.

Earhart, David C. 1994. "Nagai Kafū's Wartime Diary: The Enormity of Nothing." *Japan Quarterly* 41 (October–December): 488–504.

———. 2008. *Certain Victory: Japanese Media Representations of World War II.* Armonk, N.Y.: M. E. Sharpe.

Earhart, H. Byron. 1965a. "Four Ritual Periods of Haguro *Shugendo* in Northeastern Japan." *History of Religions* 5, no. 1 (Summer): 93–113.

———. 1965b. "Shugendo, the Traditions of En no Gyoja, and Mikkyo Influence." In *Studies of Esoteric Buddhism and Tantrism,* 297–317. Koyasan: Koyasan University Press. Reprinted in Richard K. Payne, ed., *Tantric Buddhism in East Asia,* 191–206. Boston: Wisdom Publications, 2006.

———. 1968. "The Celebration of *Haru-yama* (Spring Mountain): An Example of Folk Religious Practices in Contemporary Japan." *Asian Folklore Studies* 27, no. 1: 1–18.

———. 1970. *A Religious Study of the Mount Haguro Sect of Shugendo: An Example of Japanese Mountain Religion.* Tokyo: Sophia University Press.

———. 1983. *The New Religions of Japan: A Bibliography of Western-Language Materials.* Michigan Papers in Japanese Studies, no. 9. Ann Arbor: Center for Japanese Studies, University of Michigan.

———. 1989. *Gedatsu-kai and Religion in Contemporary Japan: Returning to the Center.* Bloomington: Indiana University Press.

———. 1990. *Fuji: Sacred Mountain of Japan.* Video. Available online, in two parts, at http:// bit.ly/fuji-sacred-mountain-pt1 and http://bit.ly/fuji-sacred-mountain-pt2 (accessed May 16, 2011).

———. 1994. "Mechanisms and Process in Japanese Amulets." In *Nihon shūkyō e no shikaku,* edited by Okada Shigekiyo, 611–20. Osaka: Tōhō Shuppan.

———. 2004. *Japanese Religion: Unity and Diversity.* 4th ed. Belmont, Calif.: Wadsworth.

———. 2011. "Mount Fuji: Shield of War, Badge of Peace." *Asia-Pacific Journal,* vol. 9, issue 20, article no. 1, May 16, 2011, http://japanfocus.org/-H__Byron-Earhart/3528 (accessed May 16, 2011).

Eck, Diana L. 1987. "Mountains." In *The Encyclopedia of Religion,* edited by Mircea Eliade et al., 10:130–34. New York: Macmillan.

Eliade, Mircea. 1959. *The Sacred and the Profane: The Nature of Religion.* Translated by Willard R. Trask. New York: Harper & Row.

Eliade, Mircea, and Lawrence E. Sullivan. 1987. "Center of the World." In *The Encyclopedia of Religion,* edited by Mircea Eliade et al., 3:166–71. New York: Macmillan.

Ellmann, Richard. 1988. *Oscar Wilde.* New York: Knopf.

Ellwood, Robert S. 1984. "A Cargo Cult in Seventh-Century Japan." *History of Religions* 23, no. 3: 222–39.

Endo, Shusaku. 1979. *Volcano.* Translated by Richard A. Schuchert. Tokyo: Charles E. Tuttle.

Endō Hideo. 1978. "Fuji shinkō no seiritsu to murayama shugen." In *Fuji-ontake to chūbu reizan,* edited by Suzuki Shōei, 26–57. Tokyo: Meichō.

———. 1987. "Fujisan shinkō no hassei to sengen shinkō no seiritsu." In *Fuji sengen shinkō,* edited by Hirano Eiji, 3–32. Tokyo: Yūzankaku.

———. 1988. *Fujisan: Shinwa to densetsu.* Tokyo: Meichō.

Ernst, Earle. 1956. *The Kabuki Theatre.* Oxford: Oxford University Press. Reprinted, Honolulu: University of Hawaii Press, 1974.

Fagioli, Marco. 1998. *Shunga: The Erotic Art of Japan.* New York: Universe.

Faure, Bernard. 1995. "The Kyoto School and Reverse Orientalism." In *Japan in Traditional and Postmodern Perspectives,* edited by Charles Wei-hsun Fu and Steven Heine, 245–81. Albany: State University of New York Press.

Fickeler, Paul. 1962. "Fundamental Questions in the Geography of Religions." In *Readings in Cultural Geography,* edited by Philip L. Wagner and Marvin W. Mikesell, 94–117. Chicago: University of Chicago Press.

Field, Norma. 1993. *In the Realm of a Dying Emperor.* New York: Random House.

Floyd, Phyllis. 1996. "Japonisme." In *The Dictionary of Art,* edited by Jane Turner, 17:440–42. New York: Grove's Dictionaries.

Forrer, Matthi. 1991. *Hokusai: Prints and Drawings.* Munich: Prestel.

———. 2003. "Western Influences in Hokusai's Art." In *Hokusai,* edited by Gian Carlo Calza, 23–31. London: Phaidon.

French, Calvin L. 1974. *Shiba Kōkan: Artist, Innovator, and Pioneer in the Westernization of Japan.* New York: Weatherhill.

———. 1977. *Through Closed Doors: Western Influence on Japanese Art 1639–1853.* Rochester, Mich.: Meadow Brook Art Gallery, Oakland University.

———. 1983a. "Satake Shozan." In *Kodansha Encyclopedia of Japan,* 7:25.

———. 1983b. "Shiba Kōkan." In *Kodansha Encyclopedia of Japan,* 7:84.

Frodsham, J. D. 1967. "Landscape Poetry in China and Europe." *Comparative Literature* 19, no. 3: 193–215.

Fujitani, Takashi. 1996. *Splendid Monarchy: Power and Pageantry in Modern Japan.* Berkeley: University of California Press.

Funayama, Takashi. 1986. "*Three Japanese Lyrics* and Japonisme." In *Confronting Stravinsky: Man, Musician, and Modernist,* edited by Jann Pasler, 273–83. Berkeley: University of California Press.

Funke, Mark C. 1994. "Hitachi no Kuni Fudoki." *Monumenta Nipponica* 49, no. 1: 1–29.

Fyne, Robert. 1994. *The Hollywood Propaganda of World War II.* Metuchen, N.J.: Scarecrow Press.

Garon, Sheldon M. 1997. *Molding Japanese Minds: The State in Everyday Life.* Princeton, N.J.: Princeton University Press.

Gerstle, Andrew, and Anthony Milner. 1994. "Recovering the Exotic: Debating Said." In *Recovering the Orient: Artists, Scholars, Appreciation,* edited by Andrew Gerstle and Anthony Milner, 1–6. Chur, Switzerland: Harwood Academic Publishers.

Gilmore, Allison B. 1998. *You Can't Fight Tanks with Bayonets: Psychological Warfare against the Japanese Army in the Southwest Pacific.* Lincoln: University of Nebraska Press.

Gluck, Carol. 1985. *Japan's Modern Myths: Ideology in the Late Meiji Period.* Princeton, N.J.: Princeton University Press.

Gorai Shigeru. 1979. "Yama no shinkō to nihon no bunka." In *Sangaku shūkyō*, edited by Sasaki Hiromoto et al., 3–33. Gendai Shūkyō, vol. 2. Tokyo: Shunjūsha.

———. 1980. "Shugendō bunka ni tsuite (ichi)." In *Shugendō no bijutsu-geinō-bungaku*, edited by Gorai Shigeru, 1:2–14. Tokyo: Meichō.

Graeburn, Nelson H. H. 1983. *To Pray, Pay and Play: The Cultural Structure of Japanese Domestic Tourism.* Aix-en-Provence: Université de droit, d'économie et des sciences, Centre des hautes études touristiques.

Graham, Patricia J. 1983. "Nakabayashi Chikutō." In *Kodansha Encyclopedia of Japan*, 5:311.

Grapard, Allan G. 1982. "Flying Mountains and Walkers of Emptiness: Toward a Definition of Sacred Space in Japanese Religions." *History of Religions* 21, no. 3: 195–221.

———. 1984. "Japan's Ignored Revolution: The Separation of Shinto and Buddhist Divinities in Meiji (*shimbutsu bunri*) and a Case Study: Tonomine." *History of Religions* 23, no. 3: 240–65.

———. 1986. "Lotus in the Mountain, Mountain in the Lotus." *Monumenta Nipponica* 41, no. 1: 21–50.

Groner, Paul. 1984. *Saicho: The Establishment of the Japanese Tendai School.* Berkeley: Center for South and Southeast Asian Studies, University of California at Berkeley, Institute of Buddhist Studies.

Guth, Christine M. E. 1988. "The Pensive Prince of Chuguji: Maitreya Cult and Image in Seventh-Century Japan." In *Maitreya, the Future Buddha*, edited by Alan Sponberg and Helen Hardacre, 191–213. Cambridge: Cambridge University Press.

———. 2004. "Modernist Painting in Japan's Cultures of Collecting." In *Japan & Paris: Impressionism, Postimpressionism, and the Modern Era*, edited by Honolulu Academy of Arts, 12–27. Honolulu: Honolulu Academy of Arts.

Haberland, Detlef. 1996. *Engelbert Kaempfer 1651–1716: A Biography.* Translated by Peter Hogg. London: British Library.

Haga, Tōru. 1983. "Hiraga Gennai." In *Kodansha Encyclopedia of Japan*, 3:142.

Hahn, Thomas. 1988. "The Standard Taoist Mountain." *Cahiers d'Extrême-Asie* 4, no. 4: 145–56.

Hakeda, Yoshito S., trans. 1972. *Kukai: Major Works.* New York: Columbia University Press.

Hall, John W., and Toyoda Takeshi, eds. 1977. *Japan in the Muromachi Age.* Berkeley: University of California Press.

Hardacre, Helen. 1986. *Kurozumikyo and the New Religions of Japan.* Princeton, N.J.: Princeton University Press.

———. 1988. "Maitreya in Modern Japan." In *Maitrya, the Future Buddha*, edited by Alan Sponberg and Helen Hardacre, 270–84. Cambridge: Cambridge University Press.

———. 1989. *Shinto and the State 1868–1988.* Princeton, N.J.: Princeton University Press.

Harootunian, H. D. 1988. *Things Seen and Unseen: Discourse and Ideology in Tokugawa Nativism.* Chicago: University of Chicago Press.

Hawks, Francis. 1856. *Narrative of the Expedition of an American Squadron to the China Seas and Japan, Performed in the Years 1852, 1853, and 1854, under the Command of Commodore M. C. Perry, United States Navy, by Order of the Government of the United States.* 3 vols. Washington, D.C.: A. O. P. Nicholson.

Hearn, Lafcadio. 1898. *Exotics and Retrospectives.* Boston: Little, Brown and Company.

Heine, Steven, and Charles Wei-hsun Fu. 1995. *Japan in Traditional and Postmodern Perspectives.* Albany: State University of New York Press.

Heiwa Hakubutsukan o Tsukuru Kai, ed. 1990. *Kami no sensō dentan: bōryaku-senden-bira wa kataru.* Tokyo: Emīrusha.

Heldt, Gustav. 1997. "Saigyō's Traveling Tale: A Translation of *Saigyō Monogatari*." *Monumenta Nipponica* 52, no. 4: 467–521.

Hendry, Joy. 1993. *Wrapping Culture: Politeness, Presentation, and Power in Japan and Other Societies.* Oxford: Clarendon Press.

Herlin, Denis. 1999. *Nocturnes* (by Claude Debussy). In *Oeuvres Complète de Claude Debussy*, series 5, vol. 3. Paris: Durand.

Hillier, Jack. 1980. *The Art of Hokusai in Book Illustration.* Berkeley: University of California Press.

Hirano, Kyoko. 1992. *Mr. Smith Goes to Tokyo: Japanese Cinema under the American Occupation, 1945–1952.* Washington, D.C.: Smithsonian Institution.

Hirano, Takakuni. 1972. "On the Truth: A Study Considering the Religious Behavior Concerning Mt. Fuji." *Diogenes*, no. 79 (Fall): 109–27.

Hirano Eiji, ed. 1987. *Fuji sengen shinkō.* Tokyo: Yūzankaku.

Hobsbawn, Eric, and Terence Ranger, eds. 1983. *The Invention of Tradition.* Cambridge: Cambridge University Press.

Hockley, Allen. 2004. "Packaged Tours: Photo Albums and Their Implications for the Study of Early Japanese Photography." In *Reflecting Truth: Japanese Photography in the Nineteenth Century,* edited by Nicole Coolidge Rousmaniere and Mikiko Hirayama, 66–85. Amsterdam: Hotei.

Holtom, Daniel C. 1938. *The National Faith of Japan: A Study in Modern Shinto.* New York: Dutton. Reprint, New York: Paragon Book Reprint, 1965.

Hori, Ichiro. 1958. "On the Concept of *Hijiri* (Holy Man)." *Numen* 5, no. 2: 128–60; no. 3: 199–232.

———. 1961. "Self-mummified Buddhas in Japan: An Aspect of the Shugen-do (Mountain Asceticism) Sect." *History of Religions* 1, no. 2: 222–42.

———. 1966. "Mountains and Their Importance for the Idea of the Other World in Japanese Folk Religion." *History of Religions* 6, no. 1: 1–23.

———. 1968. *Folk Religion in Japan: Continuity and Change.* Edited by Joseph M. Kitagawa and Alan L. Miller. Chicago: University of Chicago Press.

Horodisch, A. 1979. "Graphic Art on Japanese Postage Stamps." In *A Sheaf of Japanese Papers,* edited by Matthi Forrer, Willem R. van Gulik, and Jack Hillier, 85–88. The Hague: Society for Japanese Arts and Crafts.

Howat, Roy. 1994. "Debussy and the Orient." In *Recovering the Orient: Artists, Scholars, Appropriations,* edited by Andrew Gerstle and Anthony Milner, 45–81. Chur, Switzerland: Harwood Academic Publishers.

———, ed. 1998. *Oeuvres Complètes de Claude Debussy.* Series 1, vol. 3. Paris: Durand-Costallat.

Ienaga, Saburo. 1973. *Painting in the Yamato Style.* Translated by John M. Shields. New York: Weatherhill/Heibonsha.

———. 1978. *The Pacific War, 1931–1945: A Critical Perspective on Japan's Role in World War II.* Translated by Frank Baldwin. New York: Pantheon Books.

Ihara, Saikaku. 1963. *The Life of an Amorous Woman.* Edited and translated by Ivan Morris. Norfolk, Conn.: New Directions.

———. 1964. *The Life of an Amorous Man.* Translated by Kengi Hamada. Rutland, Vt.: Tuttle.

Iida, Yumiko. 2002. *Rethinking Identity in Modern Japan: Nationalism as Aesthetics.* London: Routledge.

Inagaki, Hisao. 1988. *A Dictionary of Japanese Buddhist Terms.* 3rd ed. Kyoto: Nagata Bunshodo.

Inobe Shigeo. 1928a. *Fuji no rekishi.* Fuji no kenkyū, vol. 1. Tokyo: Kokon. Reprinted, Tokyo: Meichō, 1973.

———. 1928b. *Fuji no shinkō.* Fuji no kenkyū, vol. 3. Tokyo: Kokon. Reprinted, Tokyo: Meichō, 1973.

Ishiguro, Keisho. 1999. *Shimooka Renjō shashinshū* [English title provided as *Renjo Shimooka, the Pioneer Photographer in Japan*]. Tokyo: Shinchōsha.

Ito, Kimio. 1998. "The Invention of *Wa* and the Transformation of the Image of Prince Shotoku in Modern Japan." In *Mirror of Modernity: Invented Traditions of Modern Japan,* edited by Stephen Vlastos, 37–47. Berkeley: University of California Press.

Ives, Colta. 1974. *The Great Wave: the Influence of Japanese Woodcuts on French Prints.* New York: Metropolitan Museum of Art.

Iwashina, Koichirō. 1983. *Fujikō no rekishi.* Tokyo: Meichō.

Jenkins, Donald. 1983. "Ukiyo-e." In *Kodansha Encyclopedia of Japan,* 8:138–44.

Jippensha, Ikku. 1960. *Shanks' Mare: Being a Translation of the Tokaido Volumes of Hizakurige, Japan's Great Comic Novel of Travel & Ribaldry.* Translated by Thomas Satchell. Tokyo: C. E. Tuttle.

Kaempfer, Engelbert. 1929. *The History of Japan . . . Together with a Description of the Kingdom of Siam 1690–1692.* 2 vols. Translated by J. G. Scheuchzer. Kyoto: Koseikaku, 1929. Facsimile of the edition first published in London, 1727, in 2 vols.; reprinted as 2 vols. in 1 in 1929.

———. 1999. *Kaempfer's Japan: Tokugawa Culture Observed.* Edited, translated, and annotated by Beatrice M. Bodart-Bailey. Honolulu: University of Hawai'i Press.

Kageyama, Haruki. 1973. *The Arts of Shinto.* Translated by Christine Guth. New York: Weatherhill/Shibundo.

Kaneko, Ryūichi. 2003. "Realism and Propaganda: The Photographer's Eye Trained on Society." In *The History of Japanese Photography,* by Anne Wilkes Tucker et al., edited and translated by John Junkerman, 184–207. New Haven, Conn.: Yale University Press.

Kano Hiroyuki. 1994. *"Akafuji" no fuokuroa.* Tokyo: Heibonsha.

Kaputa, Catherine. 1983. "Kanō Tan'yū." In *Kodansha Encyclopedia of Japan,* 4: 150–51.

Karatani, Kōjin. 1989. "One Spirit, Two Nineteenth Centuries." In *Postmodernism and Japan,* edited by Masao Miyoshi and H. D. Harootunian, 259–72. Durham, N.C.: Duke University Press.

———. 1994. "Japan as Museum: Okakura Tenshin and Ernest Fenollosa." Translated by Sabu Kohso. In *Japanese Art after 1945: Scream against the Sky,* edited by Alexandra Munroe, 33–39. New York: Abrams.

Katsushika, Hokusai. 1966. *The Thirty-six Views of Mount Fuji.* Tokyo: Heibonsha; Honolulu: East-West Center Press.

Kawabata, Yasunari. 1999. "First Snow on Fuji." In *First Snow on Fuji,* translated by Michael Emmerich, 124–52. Washington, D.C.: Counterpoint.

Keene, Donald. 1955. *Japanese Literature. An Introduction for Western Readers.* New York: Grove Press.

———, trans. 1956. "The Tale of the Bamboo Cutter." *Monumenta Nipponica,* 21: 330–55.

Kelsey, W. Michael. 1981. "The Raging Deity in Japanese Mythology." *Asian Folklore Studies* 40, no. 2: 213–36.

Kenney, Elizabeth, and Edmund T. Gilday, eds. 2000. *Mortuary Rites in Japan.* Special issue, *Japanese Journal of Religious Studies* 27.

Kenney, James T. 1983. "Naturalism." In *Kodansha Encyclopedia of Japan,* 5:351.

Ketelaar, James Edward. 1989. *Of Heretics and Martyrs in Meiji Japan: Buddhism and Its Persecution.* Princeton, N.J.: Princeton University Press.

Kidder, J. Edward. 1966. *Japan before Buddhism.* New ed. rev. London: Thames and Hudson.

Kinoshita, Naoyuki. 2003. "The Early Years of Japanese Photography." In Anne Wilkes Tucker et al., *The History of Japanese Photography,* 14–99. New Haven, Conn.: Yale University Press.

Kishimoto, Hideo. 1960. "The Role of Mountains in the Religious Life of the Japanese People." In *Proceedings of the Ninth International Congress for the History of Religions, 1958,* 545–49. Tokyo: Maruzen.

Kitagawa, Joseph M. 1967. "Three Types of Pilgrimage in Japan." In *Studies in Mysticism and Religion,* edited by E. E. Urbach, R. J. Zwi Werblowsky, and Ch. Wirszubski, 155–64. Jerusalem: Magnes Press, Hebrew University.

———. 1987a. "'A Past of Things Present': Notes on Major Motifs of Early Japanese Religions." In *On Understanding Japanese Religion,* edited by Joseph M. Kitagawa, 43–58. Princeton, N.J.: Princeton University Press.

———. 1987b. "Prehistoric Background of Japanese Religion." In *On Understanding Japanese Religion,* edited by Joseph M. Kitagawa, 3–40. Princeton, N.J.: Princeton University Press.

Kiyota, Minoru. 1978. *Shingon Buddhism: Theory and Practice.* Los Angeles: Buddhist Books International.

Klein, Bettina. 1984. "Mount Fuji in Japanese Painting and Applied Arts." *Swissair Gazette* (October): 19–26.

Kodansha. 1993. *Japan: An Illustrated Encyclopedia.* 2 vols. Tokyo: Kodansha.

Kodera, T. James. 1983. "Ippen (139–1289)." In *Kodansha Encyclopedia of Japan,* 3:328–29.

Kokudo Chiriin. 1990. *The National Atlas of Japan / Geographical Survey Institute*. Rev. ed. Tokyo: Japan Map Center.

Kominz, Laurence R. 1995. *Avatars of Vengeance: Japanese Drama and the Soga Literary Tradition*. Ann Arbor: Center for Japanese Studies, University of Michigan.

Kondō, Nobuyuki. 1987. "Mount Fuji, Light and Shadow." *Japan Quarterly* 34, no. 2: 162–70.

Kornicki, P. F. 1994. "Public Display and Changing Values: Early Meiji Exhibitions and Their Precursors." *Monumenta Nipponica* 49, no. 2: 167–96.

Koschmann, J. Victor. 1996. *Revolution and Subjectivity in Postwar Japan*. Chicago: University of Chicago Press.

Koyama, Kosuke. 1984. *Mount Fuji and Mount Sinai: A Critique of Idols*. Maryknoll, N.Y.: Orbis Press.

Koyasu, Nobukuni. 1983. "Kokugaku." In *Kodansha Encyclopedia of Japan*, 4:257–59.

Krause, Chester L., and Clifford Mishler. 2004. *Standard Catalog of World Coins*. Iola, Wis.: Krause Publications.

Kuroda, Toshio. 1981. "Shinto in the History of Japanese Religion." Translated by James C. Dobbins and Suzanne Gay. *Journal of Japanese Studies* 7, no. 1: 1–21.

Kusano, Shinpei. 1991. *Mt Fuji: Selected Poems 1943–1986*. Translated by Leith Morton. Rochester, Mich.: Katydid Books.

La Farge, John. 1897. *An Artist's Letters from Japan*. New York: Century Co. Reprinted, New York: Hippocrene Books, 1986.

———. 1904. *The Great Masters*. New York: McClure, Phillips and Company. First published in *McClure's* (magazine), 1903; later reprinted, Freeport, N.Y.: Books for Libraries Press, 1968.

LaFleur, William. 1973. "Saigyo and the Buddhist Value of Nature, Part I." *History of Religions* 13, no. 2: 93–128; "Part II," *History of Religions* 13, no. 3: 227–48.

———, trans. 1978. *Mirror for the Moon: A Selection of Poems by Saigyo (1118–1190)*. Includes an introduction by LaFleur. New York: New Directions.

———. 2003. *Awesome Nightfall: The Life, Times and Poetry of Saigyō*. Boston: Wisdom Publications.

Lane, Richard. 1978. *Images from the Floating World: The Japanese Print, Including an Illustrated Dictionary of Ukiyo-e*. New York: Putnam.

———. 1989. *Hokusai: Life and Work*. London: Barrie & Jenkins.

Lazar, Margarete. 1982. "The Manuscript Maps of Engelbert Kaempfer." *Imago Mundi* 34: 66–71.

Lee, Sherman E., et al. 1983. *Reflections of Reality in Japanese Art*. Cleveland, Ohio: Cleveland Museum of Arts; Bloomington: Distributed by Indiana University Press.

Lehmann, Jean-Pierre. 1984. "Old and New Japonisme: The Tokugawa Legacy and Modern European Images of Japan." *Modern Asian Studies* 18, no. 4: 757–68.

Leighton, Alexander, and Morris Opler. 1977. "Psychological Warfare and the Japanese Emperor." In *Personalities and Cultures: Readings in Psychological Anthropology*, edited by Robert Hunt, 251–60. Austin: University of Texas Press.

Lesure, François. 1975. *Claude Debussy[: reproductions de photos concernant sa vie]*. Geneva: Éditions Minkoff.

Levy, Ian Hideo. 1981. *The Ten Thousand Leaves: A Translation of the Man'yōshū, Japan's Premier Anthology of Classical Poetry*. Vol. 1. Princeton, N.J.: Princeton University Press.

Lidin, Olof G. 1983. *Ogyū Sorai's Journey to Kai in 1706, with a Translation of the Kyōchūkikō*. London: Curzon.

Linebarger, Paul Myron Anthony. 1948. *Psychological Warfare*. Washington, D.C.: Infantry Journal Press.

Littlewood, Ian. 1996. *The Idea of Japan: Western Images, Western Myths*. Chicago: Ivan R. Dee.

Lyons, Phyllis I. 1985. *The Saga of Dazai Osamu: A Critical Study with Translations*. Stanford, Calif.: Stanford University Press.

Major, John S. 1987. "Yin-yang wu-hsing." In *The Encyclopedia of Religion*, edited by Mircea Eliade et al., 15:515–16. New York: Macmillan.

Mandel, Gabriele. 1983. *Shunga: Erotic Figures in Japanese Art.* Translated by Alison L'Eplattenier. New York: Crescent Books.

Manyoshu, The: One Thousand Poems. 1940. Prepared by the Japanese classics translation committee of the Nippon gakujutsu shinko-kai. Tokyo: Iwanami Shoten. Reprinted, New York: Columbia University Press, 1965.

Maruyama, Masao. 1969. *Thought and Behavior in Modern Japanese Politics.* Expanded and edited by Ivan Morris. Tokyo: Oxford University Press.

Mason, Penelope E. 1981. "The Wilderness Journey: The Soteric Value of Nature in Japanese Narrative Painting." In *Art, the Ape of Nature: Studies in Honor of H. W. Janson,* edited by Moshe Barasch and Lucy Freeman Sandler, 67–90. New York: Abrams, 1981.

Massarella, Derek. 1995. "The History of *The History*: The Purchase and Publication of Kaempfer's *History of Japan.*" In *The Furthest Goal: Engelbert Kaempfer's Encounter with Tokugawa Japan,* edited by Beatrice M. Bodart-Bailey and Derek Massarella, 96–131. Sandgate, Folkestone: Japan Library.

Matisoff, Susan. 2002. "Barred from Paradise? Mount Kōya and the Karukaya Legend." In *Engendering Faith: Women and Buddhism in Premodern Japan,* edited by Barbara Ruch, 463–500. Ann Arbor: Center for Japanese Studies, University of Michigan.

Matsuda, Matt. 2002. "East of No West: The *Posthistoire* of Postwar France and Japan." In *Confluences: Postwar Japan and France,* edited by Doug slaymaker, 15–33. Ann Arbor: Center for Japanese Studies, University of Michigan.

Mayo, Marlene J., and J. Thomas Rimer, eds. 2001. *War, Occupation, and Creativity: Japan and East Asia, 1920–1960.* With H. Eleanor Kerkham. Honolulu: University of Hawai'i Press.

McCullough, Helen Craig, trans. 1968. *Tales of Ise: Lyrical Episodes from Tenth-Century Japan.* Stanford, Calif.: Stanford University Press.

———. 1973. "Social and Psychological Aspects of Heian Ritual and Ceremony." In Japan P.E.N. Club, *Studies on Japanese Culture,* 2 vols., 2:275–79.

———, trans. 1985. *Kokin Wakashū: The First Imperial Anthology of Japanese Poetry.* Stanford, Calif.: Stanford University Press.

McKinney, Meredith, trans. 1998. *The Tale of Saigyō.* Ann Arbor: Center for Japanese Studies, University of Michigan.

McNally, Mark. 2005. *Proving the Way: Conflict and Practice in the History of Japanese Nativism.* Cambridge, Mass.: Harvard University Press.

Meech, Julia. 1988. *The Matsukata Collection of Ukiyo-e Prints: Masterpieces from the Tokyo National Museum.* With catalogue entries by Christine Guth. New Brunswick, N.J.: Jane Voorhees Zimmerli Art Museum, Rutgers University.

Meech, Julia, and Gabriel P. Weisberg. 1990. *Japonisme Comes to America: The Japanese Impact on the Graphic Arts 1876–1925.* New York: H. N. Abrams.

Meech-Pekarik, Julia. 1986. *The World of the Meiji Print: Impressions of a New Civilization.* New York: Weatherhill.

Mikesh, Robert C. 1993. *Japanese Aircraft: Code Names and Designations.* Atglen, Pa.: Schiffer Military History.

Mills, D. E. 1975. "*Soga Monogatari, Shintoshu* and the Taketori Legend." *Monumenta Nipponica* 30, no. 1: 37–68.

Mills, Douglas E. 1983. "Taketori monogatari." In *Kodansha Encyclopedia of Japan,* 7:325–26.

Miner, Earl. 1979. *Japanese Linked Poetry: An Account with Translations of Renga and Haikai Sequences.* Princeton, N.J.: Princeton University Press.

Miner, Earl, Hiroko Odagiri, and Robert E. Morrell. 1985. *The Princeton Companion to Classical Japanese Literature.* Princeton, N.J.: Princeton University Press.

Mitsui, Takaharu. 1940. "Japan Portrayed in Her Postage Stamps." *Tourist* (August): 9–11.

Miyake, Hitoshi. 1987. "The Influence of *Shugendo* on the 'New Religions.'" In *Japanese Buddhism: Its Tradition, New Religions, and Interaction with Christianity,* edited by Minoru Kiyota et al., 71–82. Tokyo: Buddhist Books International.

———. 2001. *Shugendō: Essays on the Structure of Japanese Folk Religion*. Edited by H. Byron Earhart. Ann Arbor: Center for Japanese Studies, University of Michigan.

Miyata, Noboru. 1987. "Redefining Folklore for the City." *Japan Quarterly* 34, no. 1: 30–33.

———. 1989. "Types of Maitreya Belief in Japan." In *Maitreya, the Future Buddha*, edited by Alan Sponberg and Helen Hardacre, 175–90. Cambridge: Cambridge University Press.

Miyazaki Fumiko. 1976. "'Furikawari' to 'miroku no miyo.'" *Gendai Shūkyō* 1, no. 5: 64–82.

———. 1977. "Kinseimatsu no minshū shūkyō—fujidō no shisō to kōdō." *Nihon rekishi* 344 (January): 105–22.

———. 1987. "Fujidō no rekishikan—Jikigyō Miroku to Sangyō Rokuō no kyōten o chūshin ni." In *Fuji sengen shinkō*, edited by Hirano Eiji, 255–79. Tokyo: Yūzankaku.

———. 1990. "The Formation of Emperor Worship in the New Religions—the Case of Fujidō." *Japanese Journal of Religions Studies* 17: 281–314.

———. 2005. "Female Pilgrims and Mt. Fuji: Changing Perspectives on the Exclusion of Women." *Monumenta Nipponica* 60, no. 3: 339–91.

Moeran, Brian, and Lise Skov. 1997. "Mount Fuji and the Cherry Blossoms: A View from Afar." In *Japanese Images of Nature: Cultural Perspectives*, edited by Pamela J. Asquith and Arne Kalland, 181–205. Surrey: Curzon.

Moerman, D. Max. 2005. *Localizing Paradise: Kumano Pilgrimage and the Religious Landscape of Premodern Japan*. Cambridge: Harvard.

Montanus, Arnoldus. 1670. *Atlas Japannensis: Being remarkable addresses by way of embassy from the East-India Company of the United Provinces to the Emperor of Japan*. "English'd and adorn'd . . . by John Ogilby." London: "Printed by Tho. Johnston for the author. . . ." Microfilm reproduction of original in Beinecke Library, Yale University.

Morella, Joe, Edward Z. Epstein, and John Griggs. 1973. *The Films of World War II*. Secaucus, N.J.: Citadel Press.

Morita, Toshitaka. 2001. *Fuji / Mt. Fuji and Fuji-like Mountains in Japan*. Kyoto: Suiko Shoin.

Morris, Ivan. 1964. *The World of the Shining Prince: Court Life in Ancient Japan*. New York: Knopf.

———, trans. 1971. *As I Crossed a Bridge of Dreams: Recollections of a Woman in Eleventh Century Japan*. New York: Dial.

Morse, Anne Nishimura. 2004. "Souvenirs of 'Old Japan': Meiji-Era Photography and the Meisho Tradition." In *Art & Artifice: Japanese Photographs of the Meiji Era*, edited by Anne Nishimura Morse et al., 41–50. Boston: MFA Publications.

Morton, Leith. 1985. "A Dragon Rising: Kusano Shinpei's Poetic Vision of Mt Fuji." *Oriental Society of Australia* 17, no. 1: 39–63.

Mostow, Joshua S. 1996. *Pictures of the Heart: The Hyakunin Isshu in Word and Image*. Honolulu: University of Hawaii Press.

Motonaka, Makoto. 2003. "Conservation of the Cultural Landscape in Asia and the Pacific Region: Terraced Rice Fields and Sacred Mountains." In *World Heritage Paper*, 127–33. Paris: UNESCO World Heritage Centre.

Munakata, Kiyohiko. 1991. *Sacred Mountains in Chinese Art*. Urbana: University of Illinois Press.

Murakami, Hyoe, and Donald Richie, eds. 1980. *A Hundred More Things Japanese*. Tokyo: Japan Culture Institute.

Murakami, Shigeyoshi. 1980. *Japanese Religion in the Modern Century*. Translated by H. Byron Earhart. Tokyo: Tokyo University Press.

Murakami Shigeyoshi and Yasumaru Yoshio, eds. 1971a. *Minshū shūkyō no shisō*. Tokyo: Iwanami.

———, eds. 1971b. "Ominuki." In *Minshū shūkyō no shisō*, edited by Murakami Shigeyoshi and Yasumaru Yoshio, 482–83. Tokyo: Iwanami.

Murakami Toshio. 1943. *Shugendō no hattatsu*. Tokyo: Unebi Shobō.

Murasaki, Shikibu. 2001. *Genji Monogatari*. Translated by Royall Tyler. New York: Viking.

Nagata, Mizu. 2002. "Transitions in Attitudes toward Women in the Buddhist Canon: The Three Obligations, the Five Obstructions, and the Eight Rules of Reverence." In *Engendering Faith:*

Women and Buddhism in Premodern Japan, edited by Barbara Ruch, 279–95. Ann Arbor: Center for Japanese Studies, University of Michigan.

Nagata, Seiji. 1995. *Hokusai: Genius of the Japanese Ukiyo-e.* Translated by John Bester. Tokyo: Kodansha.

Naitō Yōsuke. 2003. *Gaikoku kitte ni egakareta Nippon.* Tokyo: Kōbunsha.

Najita, Tetsuo, and J. Victor Koschmann, eds. 1982. *Conflict in Modern Japanese History: The Neglected Tradition.* Princeton, N.J.: Princeton University Press.

Nakamura, Kyoko Motomochi, trans. 1973. *Miraculous Stories from the Japanese Buddhist Tradition: The Nihon Ryoiki of Monk Kyokai.* Cambridge, Mass.: Harvard University Press.

Namihira, Emiko. 1977. "*Hare, Ke* and *Kegare*: The Structure of Japanese Folk Belief." Ph.D. diss., University of Texas, Austin.

Naruse Fujio. 1982. "Nihon kaiga ni okeru Fujizu no teikeiteki hyōgen ni tsuite." *Bijutsushi* 31, no. 2: 112.

———. 2005. *Fujisan no kaigashi.* Tokyo: Chūō Kōron Bijutsu Shuppan.

Nash, Roderick. 1982. *Wilderness and the American Mind.* 3rd ed. New Haven, Conn.: Yale University Press.

Natsume, Soseki. 1977. *Sanshiro.* Translated by Jay Rubin. Seattle: University of Washington Press.

Naumann, Nelly. 1963–64. "Yama no Kami—die japanische Berggottheit. Teil I: Grundvorstellungen." *Folklore Studies* 22 (1963): 133–336; "Yama no Kami—die japanische Berggottheit. Teil II: Zusätzliche Vorstellungen." *Folklore Studies* 23 (1964): 48–199.

Nenzi, Laura. 2008. *Excursions in Identity: Travel and the Intersection of Place, Gender and Status in Edo Japan.* Honolulu: University of Hawai'i Press.

Neuss, Margret. 1983. "Shiga Shigetaka." In *Kodansha Encyclopedia of Japan,* 7:91.

Nicolson, Marjorie. 1963. *Mountain Gloom and Mountain Glory: The Development of the Aesthetics of the Infinite.* New York: W. W. Norton. First published, Ithaca, N.Y.: Cornell University Press, 1959.

Nihon Shashinka Kyōkai (Japanese Photographers Association). 1980. *A Century of Japanese Photography.* New York: Pantheon.

———. 2000. *Nihon gendai shashinshi: 1945–95* [English title provided as *The History of Japanese Contemporary Photography: 1945–95*]. Tokyo: Heibonsha.

Nishiyama, Matsunosuke. 1997. *Edo Culture: Daily Life and Diversions in Urban Japan, 1600–1868.* Translated by Gerald Groemer. Honolulu: University of Hawai'i Press.

Nitschke, Günther. 1995. "Building the Sacred Mountain: Tsukuriyama in Shinto Tradition." In *The Sacred Mountains of Asia,* edited by John Einarsen, 110–18. Boston: Shambhala.

Noguchi, Yoné. 1936. *Hiroshige and Japanese Landscapes.* 2nd ed. Tokyo: Maruzen.

Nornes, Abé Mark, and Fukushima Yukio, eds. 1994. *The Japan/America Film Wars: World War II Propaganda and Its Cultural Contexts.* Chur, Switzerland: Harwood Academic Publishers.

Nosco, Peter. 1990. *Remembering Paradise: Nativism and Nostalgia in Eighteenth-Century Japan.* Cambridge, Mass.: Harvard University Press.

Ōba Iwao. 1948. *Nihon ni okeru sangaku shinkō no kōkogakuteki kōsatsu.* Tokyo: Jinja Shinpōsha.

O'Brien, Rodney. 1986. "Sewing Up the Earth: Yumiko Otsuka." *PHP Intersect* 2 (September): 22–23.

Ohnuki-Tierney, Emiko. 1993. *Rice as Self: Japanese Identities through Time.* Princeton, N.J.: Princeton University Press.

———. 2002. *Kamikaze, Cherry Blossoms, and Nationalisms.* Chicago: University of Chicago Press.

Ohyama, Yukio. 1987. *Mt. Fuji.* New York: E. P. Dutton.

———. 1988. *Mt. Fuji: Silhouette of the Gods.* Tokyo: Genkosha.

Okada Koyo. 1964. *Fuji* [English title provided as *Mt. Fuji*]. Tokyo: Hobundo.

———, ed. (196?). *Fugaku* [English title provided as *Photo Collection of Mt. Fuji*]. Tokyo: Yamaichi Securities.

Okakura, Tenshin. 1903. *The Ideals of the East, with Special Reference to the Art of Japan.* London: J. Murray.

Ota, Yuzo. 1998. *Basil Hall Chamberlain: Portrait of a Japanologist.* Richmond, Surrey: Japan Library.

Ouwehand, Cornelius. 1964. *Namazu-e and Their Themes: An Interpretative Approach to Some Aspects of Japanese Folk Religion.* Leiden: E. J. Brill.

———. 1984. "Fujisan—the Centre of a Nation-wide Mount Cult." *Swissair Gazette* (October): 11–16.

Palmer, Edwina. 2001. "Calming the Killing *Kami*: The Supernatural, Nature and Culture in *Fudoki.*" *Nichibunken: Japan Review* 13: 3–31.

Paul, Diana. 1985. *Women in Buddhism: Images of the Feminine in Mahayana Tradition.* 2nd ed. Berkeley: University of California Press.

Philippi, Donald L., trans. 1968. *Kojiki.* Tokyo: University of Tokyo Press.

Pick, Albert. 1994–95. *Standard Catalog of World Paper Money.* 2 vols. Edited by Neil Shafer and Collin R. Bruce II. Iola, Wis.: Krause Publications.

Plutschow, Herbert E. 1990. *Chaos and Cosmos: Ritual in Early and Medieval Japanese Literature.* Leiden: Brill.

Ponsonby-Fane, R. A. B. 1953. *Studies in Shinto and Shrines.* Rev. ed. Kamikamo, Kyoto: Ponsonby Memorial Society.

Price, Larry W. 1981. *Mountains & Man: A Study of Process and Environment.* Berkeley and Los Angeles: University of California Press.

Ray, Deborah Kogan. 2001. *Hokusai: The Man Who Painted a Mountain.* New York: Frances Foster Books.

Reader, Ian. 2005. *Making Pilgrimages: Meaning and Practice in Shikoku.* Honolulu: University of Hawai'i Press.

Reader, Ian, and Paul L. Swanson, eds. 1994. "Conflict and Religion in Japan." Special issue, *Japanese Journal of Religious Studies* 21.

———. 1997. "Pilgrimage in Japan." Special issue, *Japanese Journal of Religious Studies* 24.

Rhodes, Anthony Richard Ewart. 1976. *Propaganda: The Art of Persuasion in World War II.* Edited by Victor Margolin. New York: Chelsea House.

Richie, Donald. 1994. *The Honorable Visitors.* Rutland, Vt.: Charles E. Tuttle.

———. 1997. "The Occupied Arts." In *The Confusion Era: Art and Culture of Japan during the Allied Occupation, 1945–1952,* edited by Mark Sandler, 11–21. Washington, D.C.: Arthur M. Sackler Gallery, Smithsonian Institution.

———. 2001. *A Hundred Years of Japanese Film: A Concise History, with a Selective Guide to Videos and DVDs.* Tokyo: Kodansha.

Rilke, Rainer Maria. 1964. *New Poems.* Translated by J. B. Leishman. Norfolk, Conn.: New Directions.

———. 1987. *New Poems: The Other Part.* Translated by Edward Snow. San Francisco: North Point.

———. 1992. *Neue Gedichte: New Poems.* Translated by John Bayley. Manchester, U.K.: Carcanet.

Roberts, Laurance P. 1976. *A Dictionary of Japanese Artists: Painting, Sculpture, Ceramics, Prints, Lacquer.* Tokyo: Weatherhill.

Robinson, Basil William. 1982. *Kuniyoshi: The Warrior-Prints.* Ithaca, N.Y.: Cornell University Press.

Rodd, Laurel Rasplica. 1984. *Kokin Wakashū.* Princeton, N.J.: Princeton University Press.

Rogers, Michael. 1993. "Mount Fuji Prominent on Japanese Stamps." *Linn's Stamp News,* April 26, 36.

Rolf, Marie. 1997. *La mer.* Oeuvres Complètes de Claude Debussy, series 5, vol. 5. Paris: Durand.

Rosenfield, John M. 2001. "Nihonga and Its Resistance to 'the Scorching Drought of Modern Vulgarity.'" In *Births and Rebirths in Japanese Art: Essays Celebrating the Inauguration of the Sainsbury Institute for the Study of Japanese Arts and Cultures,* edited by Nicole Coolidge Rousmaniere, 163–97. Leiden: Hotei.

————. 2003. "Hokusai the Individualist in Two of His Painting Manuals." In *Hokusai*, edited by Gian Carlo Calza, 32–49. London: Phaidon.

Rotermund, Hartmut O. 1965. "Die Legende des Enno-Gyōja." *Oriens Extremus* 12, no. 2: 221–41.

Rotermund, Hartmut O., et al. 1988. *Religions, croyances et traditions populaires du Japon.* Paris: Maisonneuve & Larose.

Rousmaniere, Nicole Coolidge, ed. 2002. *Kazari: Decoration and Display in Japan, 15–19th Centuries.* New York: Abrams.

Ruch, Barbara. 1977. "Medieval Jongleurs and the Making of a National Culture." In *Japan in the Muromachi Age*, edited by John W. Hall and Takeshi Toyoda, 279–309. Berkeley: University of California Press.

————, ed. 2002. *Engendering Faith: Women and Buddhism in Premodern Japan.* Ann Arbor: Center for Japanese Studies, University of Michigan.

Said, Edward W. 1978. *Orientalism.* New York: Pantheon.

Saitō Nazuna. 1989. "Fuji." *Biggu komikku* 22, no. 2 (January 25): 139–42.

Sakamoto, Tarō 1991. *The Six National Histories of Japan.* Translated by John S. Brownlee. Vancouver: UBC Press.

Sakura nihon kitte katarogu [English title provided as *Sakura—Catalog of Japanese Stamps 1998*]. 1997. 33rd ed. Tokyo: Japan Philatelic Society Foundation.

Sato, Hirosaki, and Burton Watson, eds. and trans. 1981. *From the Country of Eight Islands: An Anthology of Japanese Poetry.* Garden City, N.Y.: Anchor Press / Doubleday.

Satow, Sir Ernest M. 1879. "Ancient Japanese Rituals." *Transactions of the Asiatic Society of Japan,* 1st series, 7, part 2, 95–126; 7, part 4 (1881): 393–434; 9, part 2 (1882): 183–211. Reprinted in "Reprints Vol. 2, December, 1927."

Saunders, E. Dale. 1960. *Mudrâ: A Study of Symbolic Gestures in Japanese Buddhist Sculpture.* New York: Pantheon.

Sawa, Takaaki (or Ryūken). 1972. *Art in Esoteric Buddhism.* Translated by Richard L. Gage. New York: Weatherhill/Heibonsha.

Sawada, Janine Anderson. 1993. *Confucian Values and Popular Zen: Sekimon Shingaku in Eighteenth-Century Japan.* Honolulu: University of Hawaii Press.

————. 1998. "Mind and Morality in Nineteenth-Century Japanese Religions: Misogi-kyō and Maruyama-kyō." *Philosophy East and West* 48, no. 1: 108–41.

Sawada, Janine Tasca. 2004. *Practical Pursuits: Religion, Politics, and Personal Cultivation in Nineteenth-Century Japan.* Honolulu: University of Hawai'i Press.

————. 2006. "Sexual Relations as Religious Practice in the Late Tokugawa Period: Fujidō." *Journal of Japanese Studies* 32, no. 2: 341–66.

Sawada Akira. 1928. *Fuji no bungaku.* Fujinomiya-shi: Sengen Jinja.

Schmeisser, Jörg. 1995. "Changing the Image: The Drawings and Prints of Kaempfer's *The History of Japan.*" In *The Furthest Goal: Engelbert Kaempfer's Encounter with Tokugawa Japan*, edited by Beatrice M. Bodart-Bailey and Derek Massarella, 132–51. Sandgate: Japan Library.

Schurhammer, Georg. 1922. "Die Yamabushis; nach gedruckten und ungedruckten Berichten des 16. und 17. Jahrhunderts." *Zeitschrift für Missionswissenschaft und Religionswissenschaft* 12: 206–28. Reprinted, *Mitteilungen der Deutschen Gesellschaft für Natur- und Völkerkunde Ostasiens* 46 (1965): 47–83.

————. 1923. *Shin-to: The Way of the Gods in Japan, according to the Printed and Unprinted Reports of the Japanese Jesuit Missionaries in the Sixteenth and Seventeenth Centuries.* Bonn: Kurt Schroeder. (German and English texts in double columns.)

Scott Standard Postage Stamp Catalogue, 2005. 2004. 16th ed. 6 vols. Sidney, Ohio: Scott.

Screech, Timon. 1999. *Sex and the Floating World: Erotic Images in Japan 1700–1820.* London: Reaktion Books.

Seager, Richard Hughes. 1995. *The World's Parliament of Religions: The East/West Encounter, Chicago, 1893.* Bloomington: Indiana University Press.

Sharf, Frederic A. 2004. "A Traveler's Paradise." In *Art & Artifice: Japanese Photographs of the Meiji Era*, edited by Anne Nishimura Morse et al., 7–14. Boston: MFA Publications.

Shepard, Paul. 1967. *Man in the Landscape: A Historic View of the Esthetics of Nature.* New York: Knopf.

Shiki, Masahide. 1983. "Fujisan." In *Kodansha Encyclopedia of Japan,* 2: 344–45.

Shirane, Haruo. 2000. "Introduction: Issues in Canon Formation." In *Inventing the Classics: Modernity, National Identity, and Japanese Literature,* edited by Haruo Shirane and Tomi Suzuki, 1–27. Stanford, Calif.: Stanford University Press.

Shull, Michael S., and David Edward Wilt. 1996. *Hollywood War Films, 1937–1945: An Exhaustive Filmography of American Feature-length Motion Pictures Relating to World War II.* Jefferson, N.C.: McFarland & Co.

Singer, Robert T., with John T. Carpenter et al. 1998. *Edo Art in Japan 1615–1868.* Washington, D.C.: National Gallery of Art; New Haven, Conn.: Yale University Press.

Skov, Lisa. 1996. "Fashion Trends, Japonisme and Postmodernism, or 'What Is So Japanese about Comme Des Garçons?'" In *Contemporary Japan and Popular Culture,* edited by John Whittier Treat, 137–68. Honolulu: University of Hawaii Press.

Slaymaker, Doug, ed. 2002. *Confluences: Postwar Japan and France.* Ann Arbor: Center for Japanese Studies, University of Michigan.

Smith, Henry D., II. 1978. "Tokyo as an Idea: An Exploration of Urban Thought until 1945." *Journal of Japanese Studies* 4, no. 1: 45–80.

———. 1986. "Fujizuka: The Mini-Mount Fujis of Tokyo." *Asiatic Society of Japan Bulletin,* no. 3: 2–6.

———, ed. 1988. *Hokusai: One Hundred Views of Mt. Fuji.* New York: Braziller.

———. 1997. "Hiroshige in History." In *Hiroshige: Prints and Drawings,* edited by Matthi Forrer, 33–45. London: Royal Academy of Arts.

Smith, Henry D., II, et al. 1986. *One Hundred Famous Views of Edo/Hiroshige.* New York: G. Braziller.

Snellen, J. S., trans. 1934. "*Shoku-Nihongi:* Chronicles of Japan, Continued, from 697–791 A.D." *Transactions of the Asiatic Society of Japan,* 2nd series, 11: 151–239; 14 (1937): 209–78.

Sodei, Rinjiro. 1988. "Satire under the Occupation: The Case of Political Cartoons." In *The Occupation of Japan: Arts and Culture,* 93–106. Norfolk, Va.: General Douglas MacArthur Foundation.

Soper, Alexander. 1962. *The Art and Architecture of China.* Harmondsworth, U.K.: Penguin Books.

Soviak, Eugene. 1983. "Freedom and People's Right Movement, Interpretations of the Movement." In *Kodansha Encyclopedia of Japan,* 6:336–37.

Starr, Frederick. 1924. *Fujiyama, the Sacred Mountain of Japan.* Chicago: Covici-McGee.

Steichen, Edward, ed. 1980. *U.S. Navy War Photographs: Pearl Harbor to Tokyo Bay.* Rev. and aug. ed. New York: Crown. First edition published, 1946.

Stein, Rolf A. 1990. *The World in Miniature: Container Gardens and Dwellings in Far Eastern Religious Thought.* Translated by Phyllis Brooks. Stanford, Calif.: Stanford University Press.

Steinhoff, Patricia G. 1983. "Tenkō." In *Kodansha Encyclopedia of Japan,* 8:6–7.

———. 1991. *Tenkō: Ideology and Societal Integration in Prewar Japan.* New York: Garland.

Stewart, Basil. 1979. *A Guide to Japanese Prints and Their Subject Matter.* New York: Dover.

Sullivan, Michael. 1962. *The Birth of Landscape Painting in China.* Berkeley: University of California Press.

Suzuki, Daisetz Teitaro. 1936. "Zen Buddhism and the Japanese Love of Nature." *Eastern Buddhist* 7: 65–113.

———. 1973. *Zen and Japanese Culture.* Princeton, N.J.: Princeton University Press.

Suzuki Akira and Yamamoto Akira, eds. 1977. *Hiroku bōryaku senden bira: Taiheyō Sensō no "kami no bakudan"* [English title given as *Propaganda Leaflets of the Pacific War*]. Tokyo: Kōdansha.

Suzuki Shōei. 1978. "Fuji-Ontake to chūbu reizan." In *Fuji-Ontake to chūbu reizan,* edited by Shōei Suzuki, 2–24. Tokyo: Meichō.

Swanson, Paul L., ed. 1987. *Tendai Buddhism in Japan.* Special issue, *Japanese Journal of Religious Studies* 14.

————. 1989. *Foundations of T'ien-T'ai Philosophy: The Flowering of the Two Truths Theory in Chinese Buddhism*. Berkeley, Calif.: Asian Humanities.

Tahara, Mildred M., trans. 1980. *Tales of Yamato: A Tenth-Century Poem-Tale*. Honolulu: University of Hawaii Press.

Takai, Fuyuji, et al. 1963. *Geology of Japan*. Tokyo: University of Tokyo Press.

Takayanagi Mitsutoshi. 1928. *Fuji no bungaku*. Fuji no kenkyū, vol. 4. Edited by Sengen Jinja. Tokyo: Kokon.

Takemi, Momoko. 1983. "'Menstruation Sutra' Belief in Japan." *Japanese Journal of Religious Studies* 10, no. 2/3: 229–46.

Takeuchi, Melinda. 1983. "Ike Taiga: A Biographical Study." *Harvard Journal of Asian Studies* 43, no. 1: 141–86.

————. 1984. "Tradition, Innovation, and 'Realism' in a Pair of Eighteenth-Century Japanese Landscape Screens." *Register of the Spencer Museum of Art* 6, no. 1: 34–66.

————. 1986. "City, Country, Travel, and Vision in Edo Cultural Landscapes." In *Edo Art in Japan 1615–1868*, edited by Robert T. Singer, 261–81. New Haven, Conn.: Yale University Press.

————. 1992. *Taiga's True Views: The Language of Landscape Painting in Eighteenth-Century Japan*. Stanford, Calif.: Stanford University Press.

————. 2002. "Making Mountains: Mini-Fujis, Edo Popular Religion and Hiroshige's *One Hundred Famous Views of Edo*." *Impressions* 24: 25–47.

Takeya Yukie. 2002. "Kindai nihon no kyōkasho to fujisan." In *Fujisan to nihonjin*, edited by Seikyūsha Henshūbu, 58–86. Tokyo: Seikyūsha.

Tamai, Kensuke. 1983. "Censorship." In *Kodansha Encyclopedia of Japan*, 1:251–55.

Tamai Tetsuo, ed. 1992. *Yomigaeru Meiji no Tōkyō*. Tokyo: Kadokawa Shoten.

Tanabe, George J., Jr., and Ian Reader. 1998. *Practically Religious: Worldly Benefits and the Common Religion of Japan*. Honolulu: University of Hawai'i Press.

Tanaka, Stefan. 1993. *Japan's Orient: Rendering Pasts into History*. Berkeley: University of California Press.

Teikoku-Shoin, ed. 1989. *Teikoku's Complete Atlas of Japan*. 10th ed. Tokyo: Teikoku-Shoin.

ten Grotenhuis, Elizabeth. 1999. *Japanese Mandalas: Representations of Sacred Geography*. Honolulu: University of Hawai'i Press.

Thal, Sarah. 2005. *Rearranging the Landscape of the Gods: The Politics of a Pilgrimage Site in Japan, 1573–1912*. Chicago: University of Chicago Press.

Toby, Ronald P. 1986. "Carnival of the Aliens: Korean Embassies in Edo-Period Art and Popular Culture." *Monumenta Nipponica* 41, no. 4: 415–56.

————. 2001. "Three Realms / Myriad Countries: An 'Ethnography' of Other and the Rebounding of Japan, 1550–1750." In *Constructing Nationhood in Modern East Asia*, edited by Kai-wing Chow, Kevin M. Doak, and Poshek Fu, 15–45. Ann Arbor: University of Michigan Press.

Torrance, Robert M., ed. 1999. *Encompassing Nature: A Sourcebook*. Washington, D.C.: Counterpoint.

Traganou, Jilly. 2004. *The Tōkaidō Road: Traveling and Representation in Edo and Meiji Japan*. New York: RoutledgeCurzon.

Trezise, Simon. 1994. *Debussy: "La mer."* Cambridge: Cambridge University Press.

————, ed. 2003. *The Cambridge Companion to Debussy*. Cambridge: Cambridge University Press.

Tsuji, Nobuo. 1994. "Hokusai Studio Works and Problems of Attribution." In *Hokusai: Selected Essays*, edited by Gian Carlo Calza, 31–41. Venice: International Hokusai Research Centre, University of Venice.

Tsuya, Hiromichi. 1968. *Geology of Volcano Mt. Fuji*. Special Geological Maps, and Explanatory Texts, 12. [Japan:] Geological Survey of Japan.

Tucker, Anne Wilkes, et al. 2003. *The History of Japanese Photography*. New Haven, Conn.: Yale University Press.

Tucker, John A., trans. 2006. *Ogyū Sorai's Philosophical Masterworks: The* Bendō *and* Benmei. Honolulu: University of Hawai'i Press.

Turner, Victor W., and Edith Turner. 1995. *Image and Pilgrimage in Christian Culture: Anthropological Perspectives.* New York: Columbia University Press.

Tyler, Royall. 1981. "A Glimpse of Mt. Fuji in Legend and Cult." *Journal of the Association of Teachers of Japanese* 16, no. 2: 140–65.

————. 1984. "The Tokugawa Peace and Popular Religion: Suzuki Shosan, Kakugyo Tobutsu, and Jikigyo Miroku." In *Confucianism and Tokugawa Culture,* edited by Peter Nosco, 92–119. Princeton, N.J.: Princeton University Press.

————. 1993. "'The Book of the Great Practice': The Life of the Mt Fuji Ascetic Kakugyō Tōbutsu Kū." *Asian Folklore Studies* 52, no. 2: 251–331.

Uhlenbeck, Chris, and Merel Molenaar. 2000. *Mount Fuji: Sacred Mountain of Japan.* Leiden: Hotei.

Umeda Yoshihiko. 1968. "Myōjin." In *Shintō Jiten,* edited by Anzu Motohiko and Umeda Yoshihiko, 572–73. Osaka: Hori Shoten.

van der Velde, Paul. 1995. "The Interpreter Interpreted: Kaempfer's Japanese Collaborator Imamura Genemon Eisei." In *The Furthest Goal: Engelbert Kaempfer's Encounter with Tokugawa Japan,* edited by Beatrice M. Bodart-Bailey and Derek Massarella, 44–58. Sandgate, Folkestone: Japan Library.

Vaporis, Constantine Nomikos. 1994. *Breaking Barriers: Travel and the State in Early Modern Japan.* Cambridge, Mass.: Harvard University Press.

Virgin, Louise E., cataloger. 2001. *Japan at the Dawn of the Modern Age: Woodblock Prints from the Meiji Era, 1868–1912.* Boston: MFA Publications.

Vlastos, Stephen. 1986. *Peasant Protests and Uprisings in Tokugawa Japan.* Berkeley: University of California Press.

————, ed. 1998a. *Mirror of Modernity: Invented Traditions of Modern Japan.* Berkeley: University of California Press.

————. 1998b. "Tradition: Past/Present Culture and Modern Japanese History." In *Mirror of Modernity: Invented Traditions of Modern Japan,* edited by Stephen Vlastos, 1–16. Berkeley: University of California Press.

Walthal, Anne. 1986. *Social Protest and Popular Culture in Eighteenth-Century Japan.* Tucson: University of Arizona Press.

Walther, Ingo F., and Rainer Metzger. 1993. *Vincent van Gogh: The Complete Paintings.* 2 vols. Translated by Michael Hulse. Cologne: Benedikt Taschen.

Warner, Dennis, and Peggy Warner, "with Commander Sadao no Seno, JMSDF, Ret." 1982. *The Sacred Warriors: Japan's Suicide Legions.* New York: Van Nostrand Reinhold.

Watanabe, Manabe. 1987. "Religious Symbolism in Saigyō's Verses: A Contribution to Discussions of His Views on Nature and Religion." *History of Religions* 26, no. 4: 382–400.

Watanabe, Toshio. 1984. "The Western Image of Japanese Art in the Late Edo Period." *Edo Culture and Its Modern Legacy.* Special issue, *Modern Asian Studies* 18, no. 4: 667–84.

Waterhouse, David. 1996. "Notes on the kuji." In *Religion in Japan: Arrows to Heaven and Earth,* edited by P. F. Kornicki and I. J. McMullen, 514–27. New York: Cambridge University Press.

Watson, Burton, trans. 1991. *Saigyō: Poems of a Mountain Home.* New York: Columbia University Press.

Watson, William, ed. 1981. *The Great Japan Exhibition: Art of the Edo Period 1600–1868.* London: Weidenfeld and Nicolson.

Watsuji, Tetsurō. 1988. *A Climate and Culture: A Philosophical Study.* Translated by Geoffrey Bownas. New York: Greenwood Press.

We Love Fuji / Furusato no Fujisan. 1988. Fuji: Fuji Shōkō Kaigisho.

Weisberg, Gabriel P. 1986. *Art Nouveau Bing: Paris Style 1900.* New York: Abrams.

————. 1993. *The Independent Critic: Philippe Burty and the Visual Arts of Mid-Nineteenth-Century France.* Bern: Peter Lang.

————. 1996. "Burty, Philippe." In *The Dictionary of Art,* edited by Jane Turner, 5:284. New York: Grove's Dictionaries.

Weisberg, Gabriel P., et al. 1975. *Japonisme: Japanese Influence on French Art, 1854–1910.* Exhibition catalog. Cleveland, Ohio: Cleveland Museum of Art.

Weisberg, Gabriel P., and Yvonne M. L. Weisberg. 1990. *Japonisme: An Annotated Bibliography.* New Brunswick, N.J.: International Center for Japonisme, Rutgers University; New York: Garland.

Weisenfeld, Gennifer. 2000. "Touring Japan-as-Museum: *NIPPON* and Other Japanese Imperialist Travelogues." *Positions* 8, no. 3: 747–93.

Wentworth, Michael. 1984. *James Tissot.* New York: Oxford.

White, James W. 1995. *Ikki: Social Conflict and Political Protest in Early Modern Japan.* Ithaca, N.Y.: Cornell University Press.

White, Julia M. 1998. "Hokusai and Hiroshige through the Collector's Eyes." In *Hokusai and Hiroshige: Great Japanese Prints from the James A. Michener Collection, Honolulu Academy of Arts,* 11–17. Asian Art Museum of San Francisco. Seattle: University of Washington Press.

Wichmann, Siegfried. 1999. *Japonisme: The Japanese Influence on Western Art since 1858.* London: Thames & Hudson.

Winkler, Allan M. 1978. *The Politics of Propaganda: The Office of War Information, 1942–1945.* New Haven, Conn.: Yale University Press.

Wood, Christopher. 1986. *The Life and Work of Jacques Joseph Tissot 1836–1902.* London: Weidenfeld and Nicolson.

Woodson, Yoko. 1998. "Hokusai and Hiroshige: Landscape Prints of the Ukiyo-e School." In *Hokusai and Hiroshige: Great Japanese Prints from the James A. Michener Collection, Honolulu Academy of Arts,* 31–43. Asian Art Museum of San Francisco. Seattle: University of Washington Press.

Worswick, Clark, ed. 1979. *Japan, Photographs, 1854–1905.* New York: Knopf.

————. 1983. "Photography." In *Kodansha Encyclopedia of Japan,* 6:185.

Yamamoto, Yokichi. 1962. *Japanese Postage Stamps.* 3rd ed. Tokyo: Japan Travel Bureau.

Yamanouchi, Yasushi, J. Victor Koschmann, and Ryūichi Narita, eds. 1999. *Total War and "Modernization."* Ithaca, N.Y.: East Asia Program, Cornell University.

Yanagita, Kunio. 1947. *Yamamiya kō.* Tokyo: Koyama.

Yasumaru Yasuo. 1971. "Fujikō." In *Minshū shūkyō no shisō,* edited by Shigeyoshi Murakami and Yasuo Yasumaru, 634–45. Nihon shisō taikei, vol. 67. Tokyo: Iwanami.

Yokohama Kaikō Shiryōkan, ed. 1987. *F. Beato bakumatsu Nihon shashinshū.* Yokohama: Yokohama Kaikō Shiryōkan.

Yonemura, Ann. 1990. *Yokohama: Prints from Nineteenth-Century Japan.* Washington, D.C.: Smithsonian Institution.

Zelazny, Roger. 1991. "24 Views of Mount Fuji, by Hokusai." In *The New Hugo Winners, Volume II,* 7–64. "Presented by Isaac Asimov." Riverdale, N.Y.: Baen Books.

INDEX

ABOUT THE AUTHOR

For more than four decades H. BYRON EARHART has taught and published in the areas of comparative religion and Japanese religion. An emeritus professor of comparative religion at Western Michigan University, he is the author *Japanese Religion: Unity and Diversity*, *Religions of Japan: Many Traditions within One Sacred Way*, and other books. Earhart lives in San Diego, where he continues to teach online courses on world religions and Japanese religion, and to research the history of religions and human religiosity.